ORIGINAL NARRATIVES
OF EARLY AMERICAN HISTORY

REPRODUCED UNDER THE AUSPICES OF THE
AMERICAN HISTORICAL ASSOCIATION

GENERAL EDITOR, J. FRANKLIN JAMESON, PH.D., LL.D.

DIRECTOR OF THE DEPARTMENT OF HISTORICAL RESEARCH IN THE
CARNEGIE INSTITUTION OF WASHINGTON

NARRATIVES OF
NEW NETHERLAND

1609 — 1664

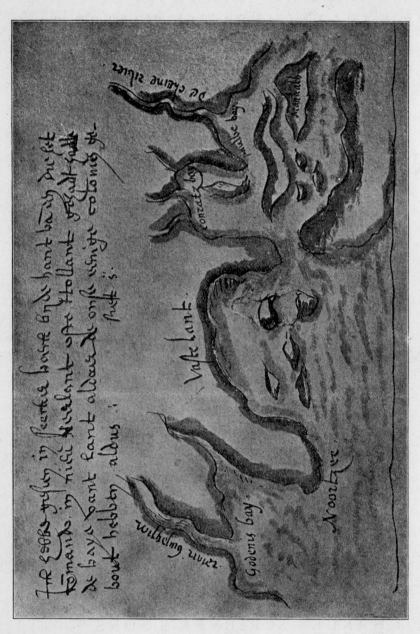

MAP OF NEW NETHERLAND

"By a Former Governor" (Peter Minuit?).

ORIGINAL NARRATIVES
OF EARLY AMERICAN HISTORY

NARRATIVES OF
NEW NETHERLAND

1609—1664

EDITED BY

J. FRANKLIN JAMESON, Ph.D., LL.D.

DIRECTOR OF THE DEPARTMENT OF HISTORICAL RESEARCH IN THE CARNEGIE INSTITUTION
OF WASHINGTON

WITH THREE MAPS AND A FACSIMILE

CHARLES SCRIBNER'S SONS
NEW YORK - - - - - - 1909

PREFACE

THERE is no one classical narrative of the history of New Netherland—nothing corresponding in position to Bradford's *History of Plymouth Plantation* or Governor Winthrop's *Journal*. A volume intended to convey the best contemporary representation of New Netherland history must perforce be composed of several pieces, most of them not of high literary merit, but having the advantage of showing New Netherland and its events from various angles. The limits of the volume have not permitted the inclusion of every interesting or important contemporary narrative of the colony, but it is believed that all the best are here. One piece, the "Description of the Towne of Mannadens as it was in September, 1661," has not been printed before.

Most of the early narratives of New Netherland are written in Dutch. Hence the first difficulty with such a volume, next after that of selection, is that of securing good translations of seventeenth-century Dutch pieces, some of them distinctly crabbed and rough in style. The old translations, published fifty or sixty years ago in the *Collections of the New York Historical Society*, the *Documentary History of the State of New York*, and similar volumes, are in some cases very bad, and in nearly all cases susceptible of considerable improvement. For the purposes of the present book they have been carefully revised or remade, by comparison with the originals. The introductions to several of the pieces express the editor's obligations to friends who have aided him in this revision. In the case of certain of the pieces, of which the originals are manuscripts at the Hague, this work of revision was performed by Professor William I. Hull, of Swarthmore College, and Dr. Johannes de Hullu, of the Rijksarchief (Dutch National Archives); others, of which the John Carter Brown Library contained printed copies, were revised by Professor A. Clinton Crowell, of Brown University; one, from a manuscript in New York, by Mr. S. G. Nissenson. In other instances the editor himself did this part of the work. If, however, the volume, as is believed, substitutes unusually correct translations for the imperfect

v

versions hitherto current, the credit is largely due to the scholarship
and patience of Mr. A. J. F. van Laer, archivist of the State of New
York, who has, with great care, gone over all the translations of which
the Dutch originals were accessible to him in Albany, and, the editor
will freely admit with regard to his own portion of the work, has
greatly improved it.

It may be well to mention that, the provinces of Holland and
Zeeland having adopted the reformed calendar in 1582, dates in
Dutch narratives of the seventeenth century will usually be found
expressed in New Style, while the English used Old Style; that the
Dutch were accustomed to use a man's patronymic after his Christian
name, in such a manner that names of the form Jacobsz, Jacobsen,
Jacobzoon (meaning the son of Jacob) are sometimes employed as
middle names, and often with entire omission of the surname, *e. g.*,
Cornelis Jacobsz for Cornelis May or Cornelis Jacobsz May; and
that the first volume of John Romeyn Brodhead's *History of the
State of New York* (New York, 1853) still remains the best history
of New Netherland.

Of the illustrations in the volume, the most curious is certainly
the map by "a former commander in New Netherland" (Minuit?),
which appears as the frontispiece. A correspondent of the editor,
Dr. Johannes de Hullu, of the Dutch National Archives at the Hague,
while examining a bound volume of manuscripts which had once belonged to a Dutch antiquary of the seventeenth century, found this
map, hitherto unknown. The antiquary was Arend van Buchell
(Arnoldus Buchellius), who died in 1641. He had been a director
of the East India Company, and from 1621 to 1630 a shareholder in
the West India Company, of which his brother-in-law was one of the
first directors. Portions of his interesting diaries have lately been
published in Holland,[1] but contain nothing relating to New Netherland.
The map bears the inscription: "Ick hebbe gesien in seecker boeck
byde hand van een die het commando in nieu Neerlant ofte Hollant
gehadt hadde de baye vant lant aldaer de onse eenige colonien gebout
hebben, aldus": or, in translation, "I have seen in a certain book
from the hand of one who had had the command in New Netherland
or [New] Holland the bay of the country where our people have
planted some colonies, thus." Then follows what is apparently a
reference: "siet s," *i. e.*, "look (or looks) south," meaning, perhaps,

---

[1] *Diarium van Arend van Buchell*, ed. Brom and Langeraad, published as
Vol. XXI. of the third series of the *Werken* of the Utrecht Historical Society.

to inform the reader that the bay, the chief object of the map, extends southward from the town.   Upon the map itself the editor sought the counsel of Mr. J. H. Innes, author of *New Amsterdam and Its People* (New York, 1902), whose authority in such matters is of the highest.   Mr. Innes has kindly prepared a statement, printed after the present preface, as to the historical aspects of this newly discovered map.

The second of the illustrations, which, like the third, we owe to the kindness of Mr. Wilberforce Eames, of the Lenox Library, is a fac-simile of the title-page of the pamphlet of 1630 in which the company first printed its Privileges and Exemptions of 1629.   That pamphlet is the first separate publication relating to New Netherland. Its text is to be found translated on pp. 90–96 of the present volume. The title-page would be translated: "Privileges granted by the Meeting of the Nineteen of the Chartered West India Company to all those who shall plant any Colonies in New Netherland, published in order to make known what Profits and Advantages are to be obtained in New Netherland for [or by] the Colonists, their Patroons and Masters, and also the Shareholders who plant Colonies there," with the motto:

> "West India can bring Netherland great gain,
> Lessen the might, divert the wealth, of Spain.'

The title-page is embellished with an interesting picture of contemporary ships, flying the Dutch tricolor, and coming to land on the American coast.

Later in the volume is presented a reproduction, in the original size, of the map of New Netherland which appeared in the second edition (1656) of Adriaen van der Donck's *Beschryvinge van Nieuw-Nederlant*.   The map was reduced from a larger one published shortly before (1655) by Nicholas Visscher.   At the foot of the map appears a view of New Amsterdam, showing the fort, the windmill, the church, the flag-staff, the gibbet, the tavern, and perhaps eighty houses—such a town as might, perhaps, have a population of a little less than a thousand inhabitants.   It has been supposed that we owe this view to Augustin Herrman, a skilful draughtsman (see p. 289, *post*).   In a letter of Governor Stuyvesant to the directors of the West India Company, dated October 6, 1660, he says:[1] "After the closing of our letter the burgomasters [of New Amsterdam] have shown us the

[1] *N. Y. Col. Docs.*, xiv. 486.

plan of the city, which we did not think would be ready before the sailing of this ship. In case you should be inclined to have it engraved and publish it, we thought it advisable to send you also a small sketch of the city, drawn in perspective by Sieur Augustin Heermans, three or four years ago, or perhaps you will hang it up in some place or other there." Nevertheless, the view on the Van der Donck map may be that of Herrman, published soon after it was drawn, without Stuyvesant's knowing the fact.

It does not appear that the plan of New Amsterdam, alluded to above, and drawn in the summer of 1660 by the surveyor Jacques Cortelyou, was ever engraved or is now extant. But there is preserved in the British Museum ("King's MSS., Maps, K. cxxi. 35"), but without note of its origin, a very interesting plan entitled "A Description of the Towne of Mannados or New Amsterdam as it was in September, 1661." This map has, by kind permission of the authorities of the British Museum, been photographed for reproduction in this volume, and the reproduction appears as the fourth and last of our illustrations. One cannot but be struck by the close resemblance between the original title written on the map, and that of the description printed on pp. 417–424, *post*, both documents being in English; but the explanation is lacking, as we know nothing of the origin of either. Upon the map the date 1664 has been inserted below the original title and date, and British ships and flags have been added. This led the late Dr. George H. Moore, who claimed its discovery, to give it, without warrant, the name of "The Duke's Plan," as if it had been demonstrably made for the benefit of James, Duke of York. Dr. Moore wrote this name upon it in the colored lithographic fac-simile in which it was first published, in Valentine's *Manual of the Common Council of New York* for 1859. All subsequent reproductions, except the present and that in Janvier's *Founding of New York*, have been made from Moore's lithograph or his manuscript, and have repeated the unwarranted designation. It will be observed that the plan has the gates of the fort, correctly, in the middle of its north and south sides, not, as stated in the "Description" in the text, on the east and west. The palisade so strongly marked on the plan, at the upper end of the town, follows from its east end the present line of Wall Street, which takes its name therefrom.

J. FRANKLIN JAMESON.

NOTE ON THE BUCHELLIUS CHART

(Map of New Netherland "by a Former Governor")

THE early chart, found among the papers of Arnoldus Buchellius, of a portion of the New Netherland coast is of great historical interest. Though very crude, either in its original form or in the copy made for Buchellius, it shows a fairly correct conception of the geographical features of the land, with one or two notable exceptions; from the latter some important deductions arise, which will be considered hereafter. It will be desirable to discuss in some detail the geographical features of the chart in order if possible to draw some information from them which will aid in determining its approximate date.

At the left-hand side of the chart we have what is probably the earliest delineation of a fairly distinct character now extant of the modern Delaware Bay. It appears here as Godenis (or Godeins) Bay, named from Samuel Godyn, president of the Chamber of Amsterdam of the West India Company. The main affluent of the bay, the modern Delaware River, appears on the chart under the otherwise unknown appellation of *Wilhelmus rivier*. The unnamed affluent of the bay is undoubtedly what is known at present as the Mauritius River, a small stream flowing through the southern part of New Jersey. It appears to be greatly exaggerated in size, but hardly more so than on the famous Herrman map of Virginia and Maryland of 1670, or on Roggeveen's map of 1676. It is to be remembered, too, that the old cartographers were in the habit of including in their delineations of streams the marshes near their mouths ordinarily overflowed by the tides; and these are quite extensive in the case of the New Jersey stream.[1]

---

[1] The name Mauritius River was applied at a very early date to the Hudson, in honor, as is well known, of Prince Maurice, son of William the Silent, Prince of Orange, and it was for a score of years the ordinary appellation of that river; see pp. 67, 75, 188, 259. Upon the discovery of the great river of the south, however, convenience seems to have led to the designation of the two chief waterways of New Netherland as the Noort Rivier and the Zuydt Rivier. These terms were in official use as early as 1629 (see Privileges and Exemptions,

The land-locked lagoons and marshes of the New Jersey coast
next appear, separated from the ocean by the five large islands or
sand-hills which are conspicuous on the early maps, as on those of
Van der Donck and Herrman.   Then follows, in a much distorted
form, the passage into the outer bay of New York, between Sandy
Hook and Coney Island.   Above this lies the modern Raritan Bay,
called Sand Bay by the Paskaert of about 1621, as also on the Carte
Figurative of about 1614, but here designated as Conratz bay, undoubtedly in honor of Albert Coenraets Burgh, one of the first patroons
under the charter of Privileges and Exemptions.   It was, in fact,
spoken of as Conraet's Bay in the Letter of De Rasieres in 1627, and
it appears under that name upon the map of "Nova Anglia, Novum
Belgium," etc., by Johannes Jansonius, in Mercator's *Atlas* (English
edition of 1636).[1]   Three affluents of this bay are shown: the first of
these, coming from the southwest, is evidently the Middletown Point
Creek, with its estuary of three-quarters of a mile in width; the next,
flowing from the south of west, appears to be the Cheesequake
Creek, a stream of no great size at present, but flowing through a
marshy basin a mile in width and extending three miles into the land.
The last of these affluents is the Raritan River, coming from the northwest; its broad estuary is shown to the northward of what the cartographer seems to have been inclined to regard as an island of considerable size, but was not sure of it.   As a matter of fact, it is probably the
tract of land known at present as Sayreville and South Amboy; it
is really a peninsula, but it is so surrounded by water and by extensive salt meadows that to any observer coasting the shore of the bay
it would appear as an island.

Staten and Manhattan islands come next in order, but they are
so distorted that some special attention will be paid to them hereafter.
Newark Bay, with its "kill" emptying into the North River, follows;
the inscription upon the chart seems plainly to be *pauwe bay*,
that name having been given to honor Michiel Pauw, proprietor of
the colony of Pavonia.   Into this last-named bay a stream is shown
flowing from the northwest; it is called upon the chart *de cleine rivier*,
and is doubtless the modern Passaic River, but upon the Paskaert it

p. 92). Doubtless in order to avoid an apparent disregard of the memory of
Prince Maurice, his name was soon applied to the river in New Jersey, and so
appears on the Herrman map.

[1] This map seems to have been constructed about 1628 or 1629, and is apparently the same as the one upon page 89 of De Laet's *Beschrijvinghe van West
Indien* (second edit., 1630).

is called *R. Achter Kol.* A faintly drawn semi-circular mark near the shore, shown upon the chart at this place, resembles at first sight a water stain, but it is believed by the writer to have been intended to designate the limits of Pauw's recently established colony.

The fact that the names of the three patroons appear upon the chart, and that they are not found collectively upon any other map known to be in existence, fixes the date of the chart within narrow limits. It was in December, 1628, according to the statement of the patroon Kiliaen van Rensselaer, in the *Van Rensselaer Bowier Manuscripts,* that Samuel Godyn sent over Giles Houset and Jacob Jansz to examine the lands upon the bay of the South River, and to purchase the same from the natives. On June 19, 1629, in conformity with the then recently ratified charter of Privileges and Exemptions, he registered himself in Amsterdam as the patroon of a colony to be established on the bay of the South River (west side). Godyn was followed by Albert Coenraets, who on November 1, 1629, registered as patroon of a colony to be established on the east side of the South Bay extending from the mouth of the bay to the narrows of the South River. As by the fifth article of the Privileges and Exemptions the patroons were allowed to extend their colonies as far inland as occasion required, *Conratz bay* of the chart really lay at the rear of his colony. Finally, on January 10, 1630, Michiel Pauw registered himself as patroon of the colony of Pavonia on the North River. All of these enterprises were unfortunate and short-lived. The settlement established by Godyn in 1631 was destroyed by the Indians, probably in the same year; Coenraets made no attempt to settle his colony; and Pauw, after the experience of two or three unprofitable years with his own, joined the others in surrendering their rights to the West India Company before the spring of 1634.[1] It is quite evident, therefore, that the chart is not likely to have been prepared before the year 1630, nor any considerable length of time after 1634.

If we turn our attention again to the chart we shall notice the remarkable fact that the main channel seaward from Manhattan Island and from the North River is placed to the right or west of Staten Island; that the west side of Manhattan Island, instead of running in a straight direction, as it really does, is thrown into a great obtuse angle, while on the contrary the east side is represented as

[1] See the *Van Rensselaer Bowier Manuscripts,* pp. 138, 154, 155, 164, 175, 314, 316.

nearly straight, with no indications of the great projection of Cor-
laers Hoek. Now it is quite impossible to conceive how a person
with a sufficient ability to draw the chart itself, however crude it may
be, could have made such a mistake as this if he constructed his chart
at the Manhattans or its vicinity, where one glance seaward would
show him the general contours of the harbor. The writer, therefore,
is led to the conclusion that the chart was not prepared in New
Netherland at all, but in Holland, from the most convenient materials
at hand for the cartographer. Now let us see if there was any material then extant which can furnish a clew to the origin of the error, it
being borne in mind that to construct anything like an accurate delineation of a complicated coast line from mere memory is next to
impossible.

About the close of 1627, or in the first two or three months of
1628, there was a view of the fort and of the recently commenced
village of New Amsterdam taken from the heights of Long Island.
The person taking it is not known, but is believed by the writer to
have been Kryn Frederickz, a skilful engineer and surveyor, who
was in charge of the construction of Fort Amsterdam at this time.
This view is remarkable as having been taken with the *camera ob-
scura*, then recently brought into use. This instrument, when used
in its primitive form without reflecting mirror or compound lens, takes,
as is well known, an accurate but reversed picture. The object of the
draughtsman was undoubtedly to present a view of the fort then in
process of construction as it should appear when constructed according to certain plans then proposed but not ultimately carried out.
The rest of the picture he evidently regarded as mere accessories of
little importance. It is likely that he was aware that the view was
reversed, but the process of restoring it to its proper form was a
difficult one, and the lines of the fort in its position on the point of the
island between two rivers were sufficiently well shown for his purposes,
no doubt; at any rate the view in this condition found its way to
Holland. In 1651, when Joost Hartgers was about to publish his
Beschrijvinghe van Virginia, he came upon this view (probably
among the records of the West India Company), and inserted it in
his work, still in its reversed condition, as did Adriaen van der Donck
in 1655 in the first edition of his *Beschrijvinge van Niew Nederlant*.
It was reproduced from time to time, exciting no special comments
except as to its supposed clumsy and uncouth drawing, until, in 1901,
when the writer was engaged in the preparation of his work on *New*

Amsterdam and Its People, he discovered that the view was a reverse, and restored it for the first time to its proper state, when its great historical importance became at once manifest.[1] As all the erroneous contours of the New York harbor which have been set forth above in relation to the chart under discussion appear at a glance in the reversed view of 1627–1628, there can be no reasonable doubt that the view was used in drawing up the Buchellius chart.

There remains a further word to be said as to the probable author of the chart. By the words used in the inscription, "one who had had the command in New Netherland," nothing else can reasonably be inferred except that an ex-director-general is referred to. Arnoldus Buchellius died in 1641, and prior to that time three of the directors-general contemporaneous with the patroons had returned to the Netherlands; these were Pieter Minuit, director-general from 1626 to 1632 (died *cir.* 1638), Sebastiaen Jansz Krol, from 1632 to 1633, and Wouter van Twiller, from 1633 to 1638. Van Twiller, however, had so little to do with the patroons, who had become only a memory long before his term of office expired, that he may be safely left out of the account. As between Minuit and Krol, there is one thing which seems to be of controlling importance. Minuit was a German, who had been long resident in the Netherlands, but who never lost his national characteristics. His writings exist, says Mr. A. J. F. van Laer, editor of the *Van Rensselaer Bowier Manuscripts,* "in good Dutch, though with distinctly German spelling." In the light of these remarks, when we find upon the Buchellius chart the German forms: *bay,* for the Dutch *baai*; *cleine,* for *kleyn*; and *Conrat,* for *Coenrad,* the writer is led to the conclusion that the Buchellius chart was prepared in Holland by Pieter Minuit. His further conclusions are that it represents the period of 1631–1632; and he is also led to suspect that it may have been so prepared by Minuit upon his application for a command upon the South or "Wilhelmus Rivier" in the service of the crown of Sweden, the "Wilhelmus" being, perhaps, Willem Usselinx, projector of the Swedish West India Company.

J. H. INNES.

[1] The view is discussed at some length in a note on page 2 of *New Amsterdam and Its People.*

CONTENTS

NARRATIVES OF NEW NETHERLAND

Edited by J. Franklin Jameson

CONTENTS

CONTENTS

CONTENTS

MAPS AND FACSIMILE REPRODUCTION

ON HUDSON'S VOYAGE,
BY EMANUEL VAN METEREN, 1610

INTRODUCTION

In 1609 the federal republic of the United Netherlands was approaching the height of its greatness. After forty years of warfare under William of Orange and his son Count Maurice of Nassau, it had brought its revolt against Spain to such a pitch of success that on June 17 of the year named a truce of twelve years was concluded. Art and literature and science were being cultivated to so high a point that presently the Netherlands became their best abode in all Europe. When the Pilgrim Fathers fled from England to Holland they were passing to a country more advanced in civilization than their own, and teeming with the results of industrial activity and commercial enterprise. The city of Amsterdam was superior to London; the university of Leyden, near which they settled down in 1609, was much superior to that of Oxford. Dutch commerce surpassed that of any other country. The Dutch East India Company, incorporated in 1602, was paying annual dividends of from twenty to fifty per cent., and Willem Usselinx had already, when the truce brought a temporary interruption to his endeavors, been agitating for several years the formation of a Dutch West India Company. Somewhat by accident, the former of these two companies became responsible for an expedition which, under the conduct of an Englishman, led to the foundation of the chief Dutch colony in America and of a city whose commercial greatness has in the end surpassed even that of Amsterdam.

Henry Hudson was probably the grandson of a London alderman who had had a part in the foundation of the Muscovy Company. The younger Hudson first comes to our knowledge as the commander of a vessel sent out by that company in 1607 to sail across the pole to the "islands of spicery." In this expedition he reached the northern point of Spitzbergen. In the next year he sailed to Nova Zembla, still for the Muscovy Company, in a vain endeavor to find the northeast passage to Cathay. During the following winter he entered into negotiations with the Dutch East India Company. A committee of the Amsterdam Chamber or division of that company made a contract with him in January, 1609, for a voyage of exploration in which, sailing around the north side of Nova Zembla, he should attempt to discover the northeast passage. It was in the course of this third voyage that Hudson explored the river that bears his name. In 1610 he sailed upon that fatal voyage to Hudson's Bay from which he never returned.

Three accounts of his third voyage, the only three original accounts of any importance, are given in this volume. The first is contained in a general history of the Netherlands by Emanuel van Meteren, entitled, in the two editions here concerned, *Belgische ofte Nederlantsche Oorlogen ende Geschiedenissen* ("Belgian or Dutch Wars and Events"), and *Historie der Neder-landscher ende haerder Naburen Oorlogen ende Geschiedenissen* ("History of the Wars and Events of the Netherlands and Their Neighbors").

Emanuel van Meteren was born in Antwerp in 1535, but his Protestant parents took him in 1550 to London, where he associated himself with his cousin Abraham Ortelius, the celebrated geographer, and where for twenty-nine years, from 1583 to his death in 1612, he was Dutch consul. His position and his tastes led him to collect information on the wonderful struggle which his countrymen had been carrying on through most of the years of his manhood. In 1599 he published at Delft the first (authorized) edition of his Dutch history, which at once took rank as a classical authority, for it was the first excellent general history of these wars that had appeared; it was accurate and carefully composed, from good sources of information, and it was well, though dryly, written—so well written, indeed, that the average reader of Motley would be surprised to see how much of what interests him in the brilliant narrative is already present in the sober black-letter pages of Meteren.

A fresh edition of the *History of the Netherlanders* was issued at Delft in 1605. Others, continued down into later years, were printed at Utrecht in 1609, and again in 1611. It is in the thirty-first book of this last edition that Meteren first tells the story of Hudson's third voyage. His narrative was written in London, soon after the voyager's return to England, apparently in the early part of 1610, and probably from the journal of Hudson's Dutch mate. Though briefer than the account by Robert Juet, which follows, it contains some facts which Juet does not give, especially as to the dubious days from May 5 to May 19, and as to the influence of Captain John Smith's representations upon Hudson's resolves, and it has throughout an independent value.

The passage was first directly translated into English, from the edition of 1611, in Henry C. Murphy's *Henry Hudson in Holland* (Hague, 1859), pp. 62–65, and, less correctly, from the Hague edition of 1614, in G. M. Asher's *Henry Hudson the Navigator* (Hakluyt Society, 1860), pp. 147–153. These two Dutch editions differ in no essential respect. The present version is based on Asher's, carefully corrected by means of the original text of 1614.

ON HUDSON'S VOYAGE, BY EMANUEL VAN METEREN, 1610

WE have observed in our last book that the Directors of the East India Company in Holland had sent out in March last,[1] on purpose to seek a passage to China by northeast or northwest, a skilful English pilot, named Herry Hutson, in a Vlie boat,[2] having a crew of eighteen or twenty men, partly English, partly Dutch, well provided.

This Henry Hutson left the Texel on the 6th of April, 1609,[3] doubled the Cape of Norway the 5th of May, and directed his course along the northern coasts towards Nova Zembla; but he there found the sea as full of ice as he had found it in the preceding year, so that they lost the hope of effecting anything during the season. This circumstance, and the cold, which some of his men, who had been in the East Indies, could not bear, caused quarrels among the crew, they being partly English, partly Dutch, upon which Captain Hutson laid before them two propositions. The first of these was to go to the coast of America, to the latitude of 40°, moved thereto mostly by letters and maps which a certain Captain Smith had sent him from Virginia, and by which he indicated to him a sea leading into the western ocean, by the north of the southern English colony. Had this information been true (experience goes as yet to the contrary), it would have been of great ad-

---

[1] This means March, 1609. This part of Van Meteren's work must have been written early in 1610. The "last book," as printed, does not, in fact, mention the matter. The contract, mentioned in our introduction, says nothing of a northwest passage.

[2] The *Half Moon* (its name is known with certainty from contemporary memoranda of the East India Company) was not a Vlie boat but a yacht, for she had a topsail. A Vlie boat was a broad, flat-bottomed vessel intended to navigate the shoals at the Vlie; it had two masts, as the yacht had, but no topmast. The *Half Moon* was of eighty tons.

[3] New style. "Cape of Norway" means the North Cape.

vantage, as indicating a short way to India. The other proposition was to direct their search through Davis's Straits. This meeting with general approval, they sailed thitherward on the 14th of May, and arrived on the last day of May with a good wind at the Faroe Islands, where they stopped but twenty-four hours, to supply themselves with fresh water. After leaving these islands, they sailed on, till on the 18th of July they reached the coast of Nova Francia, under 44°, where they were obliged to run in, in order to get a new foremast, having lost theirs. They found one, and set it up. They found this a good place for cod-fishing, as also for traffic in good skins and furs, which were to be got there at a very low price. But the crew behaved badly towards the people of the country, taking their property by force, out of which there arose quarrels among themselves. The English, fearing that between the two they would be outnumbered and worsted, were therefore afraid to pursue the matter further. So they left that place on the 26th of July, and kept out at sea till the 3d of August, when they came near the coast, in 42° of latitude. Thence they sailed on, till on the 12th of August they again reached the shore, under 37° 45′. Thence they sailed along the shore until they reached 40° 45′, where they found a good entrance, between two headlands, and entered on the 12th of September into as fine a river as can be found,[1] wide and deep, with good anchoring ground on both sides.

Their ship finally sailed up the river as far as 42° 40′. But their boat went higher up. In the lower part of the river they found strong and warlike people; but in the upper part they found friendly and polite people, who had an abundance of provisions, skins, and furs, of martens and foxes, and many other commodities, as birds and fruit, even white and red grapes, and they traded amicably with the people. And of all the above-mentioned commodities they brought some home. When they had thus been about fifty leagues[2] up the river, they returned on the 4th of October, and went again to sea. More could have been done if there had been good-will among the crew and if the want of some necessary provisions had not

[1] Hudson River.

[2] The Dutch *mijl*, equivalent to three English miles and a fraction, is in this volume uniformly translated "league."

prevented it. While at sea, they held counsel together, but were of different opinions.[1] The mate, a Dutchman, advised to winter in Newfoundland, and to search the northwestern passage of Davis throughout. This was opposed by Skipper Hutson. He was afraid of his mutinous crew, who had sometimes savagely threatened him; and he feared that during the cold season they would entirely consume their provisions, and would then be obliged to return, [with] many of the crew ill and sickly. Nobody, however, spoke of returning home to Holland, which circumstance made the captain still more suspicious. He proposed therefore to sail to Ireland, and winter there, which they all agreed to. At last they arrived at Dartmouth, in England, the 7th of November, whence they informed their employers, the Directors in Holland, of their voyage. They proposed to them to go out again for a search in the northwest, and that, besides the pay, and what they already had in the ship, fifteen hundred florins should be laid out for an additional supply of provisions. He [Hudson] also wanted six or seven of his crew exchanged for others, and their number raised to twenty. He would then sail from Dartmouth about the 1st of March, so as to be in the northwest towards the end of that month, and there to spend the whole of April and the first half of May in killing whales and other animals in the neighborhood of Panar Island,[2] then to sail to the northwest, and there to pass the time till the middle of September, and then to return to Holland around the northeastern coast of Scotland. Thus this voyage ended.

A long time elapsed, through contrary winds, before the Company could be informed of the arrival of the ship in England. Then they ordered the ship and crew to return as soon as possible. But, when this was about to be done, Skipper Herry Hutson and the other Englishmen of the ship were commanded by the government there not to leave [England], but to serve their own country. Many persons thought it strange that captains should thus be prevented from laying their accounts and reports before their employers, having been sent out for

[1] It will be observed that Juet's narrative, which follows this, does not mention these dissensions. They cast light on the mutiny that brought Hudson's next voyage to so tragic a close; but we know of them only from Meteren.

[2] Unknown; perhaps in the neighborhood of Newfoundland.

the benefit of navigation in general. This took place in January, [1610]; and it was thought probable that the English themselves would send ships to Virginia, to explore further the aforesaid river.

FROM "THE THIRD VOYAGE OF MASTER
HENRY HUDSON," BY ROBERT JUET, 1610

INTRODUCTION

Robert Juet, of Limehouse, to whom we owe the fullest original account of Hudson's third voyage and of his exploration of the North River, was an officer of the *Half Moon*—not, however, its first mate. We know nothing of his previous life. His subsequent history is an ampler but unhappy one. Accompanying Hudson on his fourth voyage, through Hudson's Strait and into Hudson's Bay, he was one of the leaders of those who mutinied against the intrepid explorer in that bay, and aided in setting him adrift to perish in its inhospitable waters. Juet himself, however, did not survive the voyage, dying on board ship shortly before those who returned reached the shores of England. His account of the third voyage must therefore in all probability have been composed before the sailing upon the fourth in the spring of 1610. Indeed, its character is nearly that of a log-book kept from day to day during the expedition. For the history of the third voyage this minute narrative has very great value, although it has some significant omissions, particularly at points where Meteren's account shows us the ship's company as disaffected or insubordinate to the captain.

Juet's journal was preserved by the Reverend Richard Hakluyt, the celebrated cosmographer and author of "the great prose epic of the English nation." After the publication of his *Principall Navigations* in 1600, Hakluyt continued to accumulate further materials of the same sort. When he died, in 1616, he left them to another geographer, less excellent but well-deserving, who for a year or more had been assisting him in his work of collection and editing. This was the Reverend

Samuel Purchas (1577–1626), chaplain to the Archbishop of Canterbury and rector of St. Martin's, Ludgate, who in 1625 brought out Juet's journal as a part of the third volume of his great folio collection, *Hakluytus Posthumus, or Purchas his Pilgrimes.*

The passage which is quoted in the following pages is to be found on pages 591–595 of Purchas's third volume. The preceding pages describe the voyage to Nova Zembla, the return thence to the Faroe Islands and across the Atlantic and the banks of Newfoundland, and the landing on the coast of Maine. Thence Hudson sailed southwestward to Cape Cod and to the mouth of Chesapeake Bay. Passing northward along the coast, he on August 28 entered a "great bay with rivers," Delaware Bay, and anchored there. Presently he stood out to sea again, and ran northward along the low sandy coast of what is now New Jersey. Our extract begins with the approach to Sandy Hook, September 1, new style. It may help to keep in mind the chronological setting of the events if we remember that on July 30, 1609, Samuel de Champlain was engaged in the great fight with the Iroquois, on Lake Champlain near Ticonderoga, and that the period of Hudson's voyaging along the Maryland and Jersey coasts and up and down the North River, August 18 to October 4, was contemporary with the last seven weeks of the administration of his friend Captain John Smith as president of Virginia.

Juet's narrative was reprinted in 1811 in the first volume of the *Collections of the New York Historical Society,* pp. 102–146. The society also reprinted the part beginning August 28 in the first volume of the second series of *Collections,* pp. 320–332. Asher printed the whole in his *Henry Hudson the Navigator* (London, Hakluyt Society, 1860), pp. 45–93, and it is also to be found in the new edition of Purchas, XIII. 333–374 (London, 1906); while the portions which follow, beginning September 1, have been printed in *Old South Leaflets,* No. 94.

Hudson's voyage had two important results. On the one hand it called the attention of the Dutch to the desirableness of the North River region and its value for the fur-trade. On the other hand, Hudson gave nearly the finishing blow to the notion, discredited for many years but revived in the years just before his voyage, that there was a strait in the forties of north latitude which led through to the western sea. Bold and energetic, he tried all the main paths that had been suggested from the north Atlantic to the lands of spice—first, that to the north; secondly, that to the northeast; thirdly, that to the westward in 42°. In a fourth attempt, made by the northwest, he lost his life.

FROM "THE THIRD VOYAGE OF MASTER HENRY HUDSON," BY ROBERT JUET, 1610

The Third Voyage of Master Henry Hudson, toward Nova Zembla, and at his Returne, his Passing from Farre Islands to New-found Land, and along to Fortie-foure Degrees and Ten Minutes, and thence to Cape Cod, and so to Thirtie-three Degrees; and along the Coast to the Northward, to Fortie-two Degrees and an Halfe, and up the River Neere to Fortie-three Degrees.
Written by Robert Juet of Lime-house.

. . . THE first of September, faire weather, the wind variable betweene East and South; we steered away North Northwest. At noone we found our height [1] to bee 39 degrees 3 minutes. Wee had soundings thirtie, twentie seven, twentie foure, and twentie two fathomes, as wee went to the Northward. At sixe of the clocke wee had one and twentie fathomes. And all the third watch [2] till twelve of the clocke at mid-night, we had soundings one and twentie, two and twentie, eighteene, two and twentie, one and twentie, eighteene, and two and twentie fathoms, and went sixe leagues neere hand North North-west.

The second, in the morning, close weather, the winde at South in the morning; from twelve untill two of the clocke we steered North North-west, and had sounding one and twentie fathoms; and in running one Glasse [3] we had but sixteene fathoms, then seventeene, and so shoalder and shoalder untill it came to twelve fathoms. We saw a great Fire, but could not see the Land; then we came to ten fathoms, whereupon we brought our tackes aboord,[4] and stood to the Eastward East

---

[1] Latitude.   [2] From 8.00 to 12.00 p. m.
[3] Half an hour, measured by the sand-glass.
[4] *I. e.*, hauled in the weather clews of the (square) sails, so as to sail on the starboard tack.

South-east, foure Glasses. Then the Sunne arose, and wee steered away North againe, and saw the Land from the West by North to the North-west by North, all like broken Ilands,[1] and our soundings were eleven and ten fathoms. Then wee looft [2] in for the shoare, and faire by the shoare we had seven fathoms. The course along the Land we found to be North-east and by North. From the Land which we had first sight of, untill we came to a great Lake of water, as wee could judge it to bee, being drowned Land, which made it to rise like Ilands, which was in length ten leagues. The mouth of that Lake hath many shoalds, and the Sea breaketh on them as it is cast out of the mouth of it. And from that Lake or Bay the Land lyeth North by East, and wee had a great streame out of the Bay; and from thence our sounding was ten fathoms two leagues from the Land. At five of the clocke we Anchored, being little winde, and rode in eight fathoms water; the night was faire. This night I found the Land to hall the Compasse 8 degrees.[3] For to the Northward off us we saw high Hils. For the day before we found not above 2 degrees of Variation. This is a very good Land to fall with, and a pleasant Land to see.

The third, the morning mystie, untill ten of the clocke; then it cleered, and the wind came to the South South-east, so wee weighed and stood to the Northward. The Land is very pleasant and high, and bold to fall withall. At three of the clock in the after-noone, wee came to three great Rivers. So we stood along to the Northermost, thinking to have gone into it, but we found it to have a very shoald barre before it, for we had but ten foot water. Then wee cast about to the Southward, and found two fathoms, three fathoms, and three and a quarter, till we came to the Souther side of them, then we had five and sixe fathoms, and Anchored. So wee sent in our Boate to sound, and they found no lesse water then foure, five, sixe, and seven fathoms, and returned in an houre and a halfe. So wee weighed and went in, and rode in five fathoms Ozie ground, and saw many Salmons, and Mullets, and Rayes, very great. The height is 40 degrees, 30 minutes.

---

[1] Sandy Hook.   [2] Luffed, sailed nearer to the wind.

[3] *I. e.*, found that the variation of the needle from the true north was eight degrees to the westward.

The fourth, in the morning, as soone as the day was light, wee saw that it was good riding farther up. So we sent our Boate to sound, and found that it was a very good Harbour, and foure and five fathomes, two Cables length from the shoare.[1] Then we weighed and went in with our ship. Then our Boate went on Land with our Net to Fish, and caught ten great Mullets, of a foot and a halfe long a peece, and a Ray as great as foure men could hale into the ship. So wee trimmed our Boate and rode still all day. At night the wind blew hard at the North-west, and our Anchor came home, and wee drove on shoare, but tooke no hurt, thanked bee God, for the ground is soft sand and Oze. This day the people of the Countrey came aboord of us, seeming very glad of our comming, and brought greene Tabacco, and gave us of it for Knives and Beads. They goe in Deere skins loose, well dressed. They have yellow Copper. They desire Cloathes, and are very civill. They have great store of Maiz, or Indian Wheate, whereof they make good Bread. The Countrey is full of great and tall Oakes.

The fifth, in the morning, as soone as the day was light, the wind ceased and the Flood came. So we heaved off our ship againe into five fathoms water, and sent our Boate to sound the Bay, and we found that there was three fathoms hard by the Souther shoare. Our men went on Land there, and saw great store of Men, Women and Children, who gave them Tabacco at their comming on Land. So they went up into the Woods, and saw great store of very goodly Oakes and some Currants. For one of them came aboord and brought some dryed, and gave me some, which were sweet and good. This day many of the people came aboord, some in Mantles of Feathers, and some in Skinnes of divers sorts of good Furres. Some women also came to us with Hempe. They had red Copper Tabacco pipes, and other things of Copper they did weare about their neckes. At night they went on Land againe, so wee rode very quiet, but durst not trust them.

The sixth, in the morning, was faire weather, and our Master sent John Colman, with foure other men in our Boate, over to the North-side to sound the other River,[2] being foure leagues from us. They found by the way shoald water, two

---

[1] Sandy Hook Harbor.   [2] The Narrows, probably.

fathoms; but at the North of the River eighteen, and twentie fathoms, and very good riding for Ships; and a narrow River [1] to the Westward, betweene two Ilands. The Lands they told us were as pleasant with Grasse and Flowers, and goodly Trees, as ever they had seene, and very sweet smells came from them. So they went in two leagues and saw an open Sea,[2] and returned; and as they came backe, they were set upon by two Canoes, the one having twelve, the other fourteene men. The night came on, and it began to rayne, so that their Match went out; and they had one man slaine in the fight, which was an English-man, named John Colman, with an Arrow shot into his throat, and two more hurt. It grew so darke that they could not find the ship that night, but labored to and fro on their Oares. They had so great a streame, that their grapnell would not hold them.

The seventh, was faire, and by ten of the clocke they returned aboord the ship, and brought our dead man with them, whom we carryed on Land and buryed, and named the point after his name, Colmans Point.[3] Then we hoysed in our Boate, and raised her side with waste boords for defence of our men. So we rode still all night, having good regard to our Watch.

The eight, was very faire weather, wee rode still very quietly. The people came aboord us, and brought Tabacco and Indian Wheat, to exchange for Knives and Beades, and offered us no violence. So we fitting up our Boate did marke them, to see if they would make any shew of the Death of our man; which they did not.

The ninth, faire weather. In the morning, two great Canoes came aboord full of men; the one with their Bowes and Arrowes, and the other in shew of buying of Knives to betray us; but we perceived their intent. Wee tooke two of them to have kept them, and put red Coates on them, and would not suffer the other to come neere us. So they went on Land, and two other came aboord in a Canoe: we tooke the one and let the other goe; but hee which wee had taken, got up and leapt over-boord. Then we weighed and went off into the channell of the River, and Anchored there all night.

[1] The Kill van Kull.　　　　　　　　　　[2] Upper New York Bay.
[3] Apparently Sandy Hook.

The tenth, faire weather, we rode still till twelve of the clocke. Then we weighed and went over, and found it shoald all the middle of the River, for wee could finde but two fathoms and a halfe, and three fathomes for the space of a league; then wee came to three fathomes, and foure fathomes, and so to seven fathomes, and Anchored, and rode all night in soft Ozie ground. The banke is Sand.

The eleventh, was faire and very hot weather. At one of the clocke in the after-noone, wee weighed and went into the River, the wind at South South-west, little winde. Our soundings were seven, sixe, five, sixe, seven, eight, nine, ten, twelve, thirteene, and fourteene fathomes. Then it shoalded againe, and came to five fathomes. Then wee Anchored, and saw that it was a very good Harbour for all windes, and rode all night. The people of the Countrey came aboord of us, making shew of love, and gave us Tabacco and Indian Wheat, and departed for that night; but we durst not trust them.

The twelfth, very faire and hot. In the after-noone at two of the clocke wee weighed, the winde being variable, betweene the North and the North-west. So we turned into the River [1] two leagues and Anchored. This morning at our first rode in the River, there came eight and twentie Canoes full of men, women and children to betray us: but we saw their intent, and suffered none of them to come aboord of us. At twelve of the clocke they departed. They brought with them Oysters and Beanes, whereof wee bought some. They have great Tabacco pipes of yellow Copper, and Pots of Earth to dresse their meate in. It floweth South-east by South within.

The thirteenth, faire weather, the wind Northerly. At seven of the clocke in the morning, as the floud came we weighed, and turned foure miles into the River. The tide being done wee anchored. Then there came foure Canoes aboord: but we suffered none of them to come into our ship. They brought great store of very good Oysters aboord, which we bought for trifles. In the night I set the variation of the Compasse, and found it to be 13 degrees. In the after-noone we weighed, and turned in with the floud, two leagues and a halfe further, and anchored all night, and had five fathoms

---

[1] The North or Hudson River.

soft Ozie ground; and had an high point of Land, which
shewed out to us, bearing North by East five leagues off us.

The fourteenth, in the morning being very faire weather, the
wind South-east, we sayled up the River twelve leagues, and
had five fathoms, and five fathoms and a quarter lesse; and
came to a Streight betweene two Points,[1] and had eight, nine,
and ten fathoms: and it trended North-east by North, one
league: and wee had twelve, thirteene, and fourteene fathomes.
The River is a mile broad: there is very high Land on both
sides. Then wee went up North-west, a league and an halfe
deepe water. Then North-east by North five miles; then
North-west by North two leagues, and anchored. The Land
grew very high and Mountainous. The River is full of fish.

The fifteenth, in the morning was misty, untill the Sunne
arose: then it cleered. So wee weighed with the wind at
South, and ran up into the River twentie leagues, passing by
high Mountaines.[2] Wee had a very good depth, as sixe, seven,
eight, nine, ten, twelve, and thirteene fathoms, and great store
of Salmons in the River. This morning our two Savages got
out of a Port and swam away. After we were under sayle,
they called to us in scorne. At night we came to other Mountaines, which lie from the Rivers side.[3] There wee found very
loving peeple, and very old men: where wee were well used.
Our Boat went to fish, and caught great store of very good
fish.

The sixteenth, faire and very hot weather. In the morning
our Boat went againe to fishing, but could catch but few, by
reason their Canoes had beene there all night. This morning
the people came aboord, and brought us eares of Indian Corne,
and Pompions, and Tabacco: which wee bought for trifles.
Wee rode still all day, and filled fresh water; at night wee
weighed and went two leagues higher, and had shoald water:[4]
so wee anchored till day.

The seventeenth, faire Sun-shining weather, and very hot.
In the morning, as soone as the Sun was up, we set sayle, and
ran up sixe leagues higher, and found shoalds in the middle of
the channell, and small Ilands, but seven fathoms water on

<hr />

[1] Stony Point and Verplanck's Point. Apparently Hudson anchored this
night near West Point.   [2] The upper Highlands.
    [3] The Catskills.   [4] Probably near Hudson and Athens.

both sides. Toward night we borrowed so neere the shoare, that we grounded: so we layed out our small anchor, and heaved off againe. Then we borrowed on the banke in the channell, and came aground againe; while the floud ran we heaved off againe, and anchored all night.

The eighteenth, in the morning was faire weather, and we rode still. In the after-noone our Masters Mate went on land with an old Savage, a Governour of the Countrey; who carried him to his house, and made him good cheere. The nineteenth, was faire and hot weather: at the floud, being neere eleven of the clocke, wee weighed, and ran higher up two leagues above the shoalds, and had no lesse water then five fathoms; wee anchored, and rode in eight fathomes. The people of the Countrie came flocking aboord, and brought us Grapes and Pompions, which wee bought for trifles. And many brought us Bevers skinnes, and Otters skinnes, which wee bought for Beades, Knives, and Hatchets. So we rode there all night.[1]

The twentieth, in the morning was faire weather. Our Masters Mate with foure men more went up with our Boat to sound the River, and found two leagues above us but two fathomes water, and the channell very narrow; and above that place, seven or eight fathomes. Toward night they returned: and we rode still all night. The one and twentieth, was faire weather, and the wind all Southerly: we determined yet once more to goe farther up into the River, to trie what depth and breadth it did beare; but much people resorted aboord, so wee went not this day. Our Carpenter went on land, and made a fore-yard. And our Master and his Mate determined to trie some of the chiefe men of the Countrey, whether they had any treacherie in them. So they tooke them downe into the Cabbin, and gave them so much Wine and *Aqua vitæ*, that they were all merrie: and one of them had his wife with him, which sate so modestly, as any of our countrey women would doe in a strange place. In the end one of them was drunke, which had beene aboord of our ship all the time that we had beene there: and that was strange to them; for they could not tell how to take it. The Canoes and folke went all on shoare: but some of them came againe, and brought stropes of Beades:

<hr>

[1] Near the present site of Albany. Meteren, it will have been observed, mentions 42° 40′ north, which is almost exactly the latitude of Albany.

some had sixe, seven, eight, nine, ten; and gave him. So he slept all night quietly.

The two and twentieth, was faire weather: in the morning our Masters Mate and foure more of the companie went up with our Boat to sound the River higher up. The people of the Countrey came not aboord till noone: but when they came, and saw the Savages well, they were glad. So at three of the clocke in the after-noone they came aboord, and brought Tabacco, and more Beades, and gave them to our Master, and made an Oration, and shewed him all the Countrey round about. Then they sent one of their companie on land, who presently returned, and brought a great Platter full of Venison dressed by themselves; and they caused him to eate with them: then they made him reverence, and departed all save the old man that lay aboord. This night at ten of the clocke, our Boat returned in a showre of raine from sounding of the River; and found it to bee at an end for shipping to goe in. For they had beene up eight or nine leagues,[1] and found but seven foot water, and unconstant soundings.

The three and twentieth, faire weather. At twelve of the clocke wee weighed, and went downe two leagues to a shoald that had two channels, one on the one side, and another on the other, and had little wind, whereby the tide layed us upon it. So, there wee sate on ground the space of an houre till the floud came. Then we had a little gale of wind at the West. So wee got our ship into deepe water, and rode all night very well.

The foure and twentieth was faire weather: the winde at the North-west, wee weighed, and went downe the River seven or eight leagues; and at halfe ebbe wee came on ground on a banke of Oze in the middle of the river, and sate there till the floud. Then wee went on Land, and gathered good store of Chest-nuts. At ten of the clocke wee came off into deepe water, and anchored.

The five and twentieth was faire weather, and the wind at South a stiffe gale. We rode still, and went on Land [2] to walke on the West side of the River, and found good ground for Corne and other Garden herbs, with great store of goodly

---

[1] Perhaps above the mouth of the Mohawk.
[2] Near Athens, apparently.

Oakes, and Wal-nut trees, and Chest-nut trees, Ewe trees, and trees of sweet wood in great abundance, and great store of Slate for houses, and other good stones.

The sixe and twentieth was faire weather, and the wind at South a stiffe gale, wee rode still. In the morning our Carpenter went on Land, with our Masters Mate, and foure more of our companie, to cut wood. This morning, two Canoes came up the River from the place where we first found loving people, and in one of them was the old man that had lyen aboord of us at the other place. He brought another old man with him, which brought more stropes of Beades, and gave them to our Master, and shewed him all the Countrey there about, as though it were at his command. So he made the two old men dine with him, and the old mans wife: for they brought two old women, and two young maidens of the age of sixteene or seventeene yeeres with them, who behaved themselves very modestly. Our Master gave one of the old men a Knife, and they gave him and us Tabacco. And at one of the clocke they departed downe the River, making signes that wee should come downe to them; for wee were within two leagues of the place where they dwelt.

The seven and twentieth, in the morning was faire weather, but much wind at the north, we weighed and set our fore top-sayle, and our ship would not flat, but ran on the Ozie banke at halfe ebbe. Wee layed out anchor to heave her off, but could not. So wee sate from halfe ebbe to halfe floud: then wee set our fore-sayle and mayne top-sayl, and got downe sixe leagues. The old man came aboord, and would have had us anchor, and goe on Land to eate with him: but the wind being faire, we would not yeeld to his request; So hee left us, being very sorrowfull for our departure. At five of the clocke in the after-noone, the wind came to the South South-west. So wee made a boord or two, and anchored in fourteene fathomes water. Then our Boat went on shoare to fish right against the ship. Our Masters Mate and Boat-swaine, and three more of the companie went on land to fish, but could not finde a good place. They tooke foure or five and twentie Mullets, Breames, Bases, and Barbils; and returned in an houre. We rode still all night.

The eight and twentieth, being faire weather, as soone as the day was light, wee weighed at halfe ebbe, and turned downe two leagues belowe water; for, the streame doth runne the last quarter ebbe: then we anchored till high water. At three of the clocke in the after-noone we weighed, and turned downe three leagues, untill it was darke: then wee anchored.

The nine and twentieth was drie close weather: the wind at South, and South and by West, we weighed early in the morning, and turned downe three leagues by a lowe water, and anchored at the lower end of the long Reach;[1] for it is sixe leagues long. Then there came certaine Indians in a Canoe to us, but would not come aboord. After dinner there came the Canoe with other men, whereof three came aboord us. They brought Indian Wheat, which wee bought for trifles. At three of the clocke in the after-noone wee weighed, as soone as the ebbe came, and turned downe to the edge of the Mountaines, or the Northermost of the Mountaines, and anchored: because the high Land hath many Points, and a narrow channell, and hath many eddie winds. So we rode quietly all night in seven fathoms water.

The thirtieth was faire weather, and the wind at Southeast a stiffe gale betwene the Mountaynes. We rode still the after-noone.[2] The people of the Countrey came aboord us, and brought some small skinnes with them, which we bought for Knives and Trifles. This a very pleasant place to build a towne on. The Road is very neere, and very good for all winds, save an East North-east wind. The Mountaynes looke as if some Metall or Minerall were in them. For the Trees that grow on them were all blasted, and some of them barren with few or no Trees on them. The people brought a stone aboord like to Emery (a stone used by Glasiers to cut Glasse) it would cut Iron or Steele: yet being bruised small, and water put to it, it made a colour like blacke Lead glistering; It is also good for Painters Colours. At three of the clocke they departed, and we rode still all night.

The first of October, faire weather, the wind variable betweene the West and the North. In the morning we weighed at seven of the clocke with the ebbe, and got downe below the Mountaynes, which was seven leagues. Then it fell calme and

---

[1] Below Poughkeepsie.   [2] Near Newburgh.

the floud was come, and wee anchored at twelve of the clocke.[1]
The people of the Mountaynes came aboord us, wondering at
our ship and weapons. We bought some small skinnes of
them for Trifles. This after-noone, one Canoe kept hanging
under our sterne with one man in it, which we could not keepe
from thence, who got up by our Rudder to the Cabin window,
and stole out my Pillow, and two Shirts, and two Bandeleeres.
Our Masters Mate shot at him, and strooke him on the brest,
and killed him. Whereupon all the rest fled away, some in
their Canoes, and so leapt out of them into the water. We
manned our Boat, and got our things againe. Then one of
them that swamme got hold of our Boat, thinking to overthrow
it. But our Cooke tooke a Sword, and cut off one of his hands,
and he was drowned. By this time the ebbe was come, and
we weighed and got downe two leagues, by that time it was
darke. So we anchored in foure fathomes water, and rode
well.

The second, faire weather. At breake of day wee weighed,
the wind being at North-west, and got downe seven leagues;
then the floud was come strong, so we anchored. Then came
one of the Savages that swamme away from us at our going up
the River with many other, thinking to betray us. But wee
perceived their intent, and suffered none of them to enter our
ship. Whereupon two Canoes full of men, with their Bowes
and Arrowes shot at us after our sterne: in recompence whereof
we discharged sixe Muskets, and killed two or three of them.
Then above an hundred of them came to a point of Land to
shoot at us. There I shot a Falcon [2] at them, and killed
two of them: whereupon the rest fled into the Woods. Yet
they manned off another Canoe with nine or ten men, which
came to meet us. So I shot at it also a Falcon, and shot it
through, and killed one of them. Then our men with their
Muskets killed three or foure more of them. So they went
their way, within a while after, wee got downe two leagues
beyond that place, and anchored in a Bay, cleere from all danger of them on the other side of the River, where we saw a very
good piece of ground: and hard by it there was a Cliffe, that
looked of the colour of a white greene, as though it were either

---

[1] Near Stony Point.   [2] A small piece of ordnance.

Copper, or Silver myne: and I thinke it to be one of them, by the Trees that grow upon it. For they be all burned, and the other places are greene as grasse, it is on that side of the River that is called *Manna-hata*. There we saw no people to trouble us: and rode quietly all night; but had much wind and raine.[1]

The third, was very stormie; the wind at East North-east. In the morning, in a gust of wind and raine, our Anchor came home, and we drove on ground, but it was Ozie. Then as we were about to have out an Anchor, the wind came to the North North-west, and drove us off againe. Then we shot an Anchor, and let it fall in foure fathomes water, and weighed the other. Wee had much wind and raine, with thicke weather: so we roade still all night.

The fourth, was faire weather, and the wind at North North-west, wee weighed and came out of the River, into which we had runne so farre. Within a while after, wee came out also of the great mouth of the great River, that runneth up to the North-west, borrowing upon the Norther side of the same, thinking to have deepe water: for wee had sounded a great way with our Boat at our first going in, and found seven, six, and five fathomes. So we came out that way, but we were deceived, for we had but eight foot and an halfe water: and so to three, five, three, and two fathomes and an halfe. And then three, foure, five, sixe, seven, eight, nine and ten fathomes. And by twelve of the clocke we were cleere of all the Inlet. Then we tooke in our Boat, and set our mayne-sayle and sprit-sayle, and our top-sayles, and steered away East South-east, and South-east by East off into the mayne sea: and the Land on the Souther side of the Bay or Inlet, did beare at noone West and by South foure leagues from us.

The fift, was faire weather, and the wind variable betweene the North and the East. Wee held on our course South-east by

---

[1] It is plain that these events of October 2 took place near the upper part of Manhattan Island, but to distribute them between east and west shore is not easy. It would appear from what precedes that the attack was by the west-shore savages, and that the anchorage which was chosen for safety from them was on the east side; and the application of the name Manna-hata in the early writers seems nowise to vary. But if so, how should an E.N.E. wind blow the *Half Moon* ashore, and a N.N.W. wind drive her off, as related in the next paragraph? And the cliff answering the description seems to be in Hoboken.

East. At noone I observed and found our height to bee 39 degrees, 30 minutes. Our Compasse varied sixe degrees to the West.

We continued our course toward England, without seeing any Land by the way, all the rest of this moneth of October:[1] And on the seventh day of November, *stilo novo*, being Saturday: by the Grace of God we safely arrived in the Range of Dartmouth in Dovenshire, in the yeere 1609.

[1] Juet says nothing of those mutinous dissensions which Meteren mentions and which brought the expedition to a close. Juet himself may have had a discreditable part in them. His part in the mutiny of 1610 has been mentioned in the introduction. The *Half Moon* returned to Amsterdam in July, 1610, and the next spring sailed with other vessels of the company to the East Indies. In 1616 she was at the island of Sumatra, but her subsequent history is unknown.

FROM THE "NEW WORLD,"
BY JOHAN DE LAET, 1625, 1630, 1633, 1640

INTRODUCTION

In 1625, Johan or Johannes de Laet, of Leyden, a director
of the Dutch West India Company and a man of note for
various learning, published through the famous house of
Elzevier in that city a large folio volume in Dutch, entitled
Nieuwe Wereldt, ofte Beschrijvinghe van West-Indien (" New
World, or Description of West-India," *i. e.*, America), which at
once took high rank among such publications. The author,
born in Antwerp in 1582,[1] migrated to Leyden, like so many
other Belgian Protestants, and in 1597 was matriculated at
the Leyden university. There we find him the friend of
Joseph Scaliger, the greatest of scholars, who writes to him
as to a dear young friend, and of Salmasius and Daniel Hein-
sius, eminent scholars more nearly his contemporaries. He
sat in the Synod of Dort, 1618–1619, as an elder of the church
in Leyden. He was a director in the Amsterdam Chamber of
the West India Company, apparently from its first organization until his death. He corresponded with the Pilgrims at
Plymouth and with the British ambassador. Eagerly interested in the acquiring of geographical knowledge, he was one
of the chief workers for the firm of Elzevier in the composition
of their popular series of manuals sometimes called *Respublicae
Elzevirianae*, writing some eight or nine little volumes on the
geography and government of as many different countries.

[1] M. Pierre Kickx, in an article on De Laet as a man of science, in the
Bulletin de l'Académie Royale de Belgique (1852), XIX., iii., 582–601, cites a record
in Antwerp, showing the birth of Johan de Laet, son of Johan, in that city in
1593. But that must have been another, for I am informed by Dr. Johannes de
Hullu of the Dutch National Archives that De Laet's engraved portrait is lettered
"Ætatis 60," and dated 1642, and that at matriculation at Leyden in 1597 he was
stated to be fifteen years old.

De Laet's most direct interest in New Netherland arose some years after he had published the first edition of the *New World*. In 1630, soon after the institution of the system of patroonships, he became a partner in the abortive Dutch settlements on either side of Delaware Bay, and in the more permanent patroonship of Rensselaerswyck. Six letters of Kiliaen van Rensselaer to him and three of De Laet's own letters regarding this colony are printed in the recently published volume of *Van Rensselaer Bowier Manuscripts*. Friction arose between the partners because of questions as to their respective legal rights, and ended in a law-suit. Van Rensselaer writes to a friend that De Laet never exerted himself for the colony in the counsels of the Company nor before the States General, and "seldom or never called on me except to inquire about rarities or to ask me for some copy or document." Yet his letters are very clear-headed, and at all events the States General decided the suit in his favor. Unfortunately for us, too, he was too good a man of business to disclose in any of the editions of his book much of that information regarding Rensselaerswyck which he must have possessed in abundance. The island opposite Fort Orange was for a time called De Laet's Island.

When, in 1642, Hugo Grotius published his dissertation on the origin of the American Indians, attempting to demonstrate that they were of comparatively recent European descent, De Laet combated his views in two small controversial books maintaining that the Americans were a distinct race. In 1644 he published a larger work reviewing the history of the West India Company, *Historie ofte Jaerlijck Verhael*, etc. It is an able work, but contains substantially nothing on New Netherland. De Laet died at Leyden on December 15, 1649.[1] He

[1] A reference in *New York Colonial Documents*, I. 521, might be thought to indicate that he was alive in 1653. But Dr. de Hullu tells me that the register of deaths in Leyden, under December 15, 1649, mentions "de Heer de Laet," dwelling on the Rapenburggracht, and that this was our author is made clear by

seems never to have visited America, but his daughter Johanna is recorded as living in New Netherland from 1653 to 1673 at least, as the wife successively of Johan de Hulter and of Jeronimus Ebbingh.

The *Nieuwe Wereldt* is chiefly a work of geographical description. Now that the States General have at last chartered the West India Company, the preface addressed to them declares, it is a patriotic duty to provide all useful information respecting the American regions embraced in its patent. The work, in the first two editions, is divided into fifteen books. The first treats of the West India Islands, the second of New France, the third of "Virginia," the fourth of Florida, the fifth of New Spain, the others of countries lying farther to the southward. In Book III., from which our extracts are taken, the first chapter deals with Verrazano, chapters 2–6 with New England (chapter 6 being devoted to New Plymouth), chapters 7–11 with New Netherland, chapters 12–21 with Virginia and its history to 1621, chapters 22–25 with the Raleigh colonies. There are maps, very well executed, but the first edition contains none relating to New Netherland. We may presume that actual composition of the book was begun after the chartering of the Company in June, 1621. Since the vote of copyright by the States General is dated July 17, 1624, it may be assumed that the book was then nearly or quite ready. The preface is dated November 15, 1624.

The full title of the book is, *New World, or Description of West-India, collected out of Various Writings and Notes from Various Nations by Joannes de Laet, and provided with needful Maps and Tables.* This declaration as to sources of information is amplified in various passages of the prefatory matter. For many years, the author tells us, he had eagerly collected

a letter in the British Museum, *Add. MSS.* 6395, which his oldest son wrote on December 7 to Sir William Boswell. De Laet's library was offered for sale at auction in April, 1650 (*Huth Catalogue*, II. 414).

whatever was printed in various countries respecting America. His list of books chiefly used embraces the principal books then existing for Virginia and New England, but none for New Netherland. But he adds that he used "also divers manuscript journals of divers captains and navigators, whose names we have printed here and there in our *Description*." Thus it is that we have in his text invaluable extracts from the lost journal of Henry Hudson, which perhaps the Amsterdam directors of the East India Company lent to the compiler, and which so light up the voyage of the *Half Moon;* and he seems also to have had the use of the journals of Adriæn Block, Hendrick Christiaensz and Cornelis May. Two folio manuscript volumes of his notes are still in existence, and show us something of his methods, though they do not relate to New Netherland. He heightens our interest in the question of his sources and our appreciation of the value of his work, by telling us in one of his prefaces that he has been always scrupulous to give credit to those from whom he has drawn, thinking any other course to be sheer dishonesty. He begs that no one will expect to find in his book a fine Dutch style, since in its composition he has used Italian, French, Spanish and English writings, and in borrowing from them has erred on the side of literalness.

A young friend of Scaliger was not likely to lack knowledge of proper principles in historical work. De Laet's work is composed with system, precision and accuracy, and covers in excellent fashion the geography of the various portions of America, their natural productions, the manners and customs of their natives, and the history and status of the European settlements.

A new edition of the book was published in Dutch in 1630. It contains some additional matter in the chapters devoted to New Netherland, and an interesting map of "Nova Anglia, Novum Belgium et Virginia," the middle part of which is reproduced in Winsor's *Narrative and Critical History of America*, IV. 436. In 1633 a Latin version, *Novus Orbis*, was published in eighteen books (the additional books relate to South America), and in 1640 a French, *Histoire du Nouveau Monde*. The text of the former is more carefully prepared than that of the latter. In both, the map above mentioned appears unchanged; nor are additional authorities cited in the preface. But both these later editions show signs of that increasing interest in natural history which marked De Laet's later years. They contain many excellent plates of American animals and plants. There are similar additions to the text, so that chapters 10 and 11 of Book III. are mostly new matter;[1] on the other hand, many passages of the Dutch are much abridged in these later versions.

In the following pages the attempt is made to give the reader all that is historically valuable in any of these editions. Chapters 7–11 of Book III. are first given from the Dutch edition of 1625, but the reader will also find, inserted in square brackets, the longer of the additions which are interpolated in the edition of 1630, and, in the foot-notes, the minor variations in that edition and in those parts of the Latin and French versions which correspond to these three chapters. Then follow chapters 10 and 11 of the Latin and French, these two chapters being almost entirely new matter.

A translation of all these chapters appeared in 1841 and 1849 in the *Collections of the New York Historical Society*, second series, I. 282–316, II. 373; a part is translated in Asher's *Henry Hudson the Navigator*, pp. 154–163. After careful revision, and comparison of all the editions, these versions have been used in the following pages.

---

[1] Chapters 7 and 8 of Book III. of the Latin and French versions correspond with the same chapters of the Dutch; chapter 9 of the former with chapters 9 and 10 of the latter; chapter 12 of the former with chapter 11 of the latter.

FROM THE "NEW WORLD," BY JOHAN DE LAET, 1625, 1630, 1633, 1640

Nieuwe Wereldt, 1625, 1630, Book III., "Virginia," Sect. "Nieuw-Nederlandt"

CHAPTER 7

The First Discovery and General Description of that Part of the Country called by our Countrymen New-Netherland.

In the foregoing chapters we have spoken of that portion of the West Indies lying to the north, which the French, as related in the last book, for some years more fully discovered and explored, and to which the English a few years ago began to give the name of New England.[1] And thus we have come to Cape Cod, as the English call it, and in the foregoing book, to Cape Malebarre and Port Fortuné, according to the discoveries of the French. From this point the main land makes a great inward bend, which extends nearly east and west to a great river, from which the coast again stretches to the southwest, or nearly so, to the extremity of Florida. This part of the coast, situated as we have described, including several islands, and two very large rivers, the most southerly in latitude 38° and fifty minutes, and the most northerly in latitude 40° 30', which flows from the north, a great distance inland—this portion of the West Indies, I say, our countrymen call New Netherland, because it was at first more fully discovered at the charge of our Netherlanders, and for some years in succession was visited, and provided with a fort and habitations, by the Netherlanders, acting with a special charter

---

[1] The Latin version of 1633 and the French version of 1640 say "New Scotland and New England."

from, and under the authority of, their High Mightinesses the
States General of these United Provinces.[1]

As to the first discovery, the Directors of the Chartered
East India Company, in 1609, dispatched the yacht *Half Moon*,
under the command of Hendrick Hudson, captain and supercargo, to seek a passage to China by the northeast. But they
changed their course and stood over towards New France; and,
having passed the banks of Newfoundland in latitude 43° 23′,
made the land in latitude 44° 15′, with a west-northwest
and northwest course, and went on shore at a place where
there were certain natives with whom, as they understood,
the French come every year to trade. Sailing hence, they bent
their course to the south until, running south-southwest and
southwest by south, they again made land in latitude 41° 43′,
which they supposed to be an island, and gave it the name of
New Holland, but afterwards discovered that it was Cape
Cod, and that, according to their observation, it lay fully
seventy-five leagues to the west of its place on all the charts.
From here they fell down to 37° 15′, where they again saw
land. The coast was low, running north and south; and along
it stretched a bank or shoal, inside of which there was a depth
of eight, nine, ten, eleven, seven, and six and a half fathoms,
with a sandy bottom. They called this place Dry Cape.[2]

Running thence to the northward, they again discovered
land in latitude 38° 9′, where there was a white sandy shore,
and within it an abundance of green trees. The direction of the
coast was north-northeast and south-southwest for about
eight leagues, then north and south for seven leagues, and
afterwards southeast and northwest for five leagues. They
continued to run along the coast to the north, until they
reached a point from which the land stretched to the west-
northwest, and there was a bay into which several rivers discharged. From this point land was seen to the east-northeast, which they took to be an island; but it proved to be the

---

[1] The versions of 1633 and 1640 describe New Netherland as extending from
the great river in 38° 30′ (Delaware Bay) to 44°, mention that the settlement was
made "with the consent of the savages," and declare that, though this coast had
been seen by navigators of other nations, none had penetrated well into the bay
or explored the chief river till the Dutch did so in 1609.

[2] Probably Cape Charles.

main land, and the second point of the bay, in latitude 38° 54'.
Standing upon a course northwest by north, they found themselves embayed, and, encountering many breakers, stood out
again to the south-southeast. They suspected that a large
river discharged into the bay, from the strength of the current
that set out, and caused these sands and shoals.[1]

Continuing their course along the shore, they observed a
white sandy beach and drowned land within, beyond which
the land was full of trees, the coast running northeast by
north and southwest by south. Afterwards the direction of
the coast changed to north by east, and was higher land than
they had yet seen, along to a lofty promontory, behind which
was situated a bay, where they ran up into a roadstead behind a
low sandy point, in latitude 40° 18'. There they were visited
by two savages clothed in elk-skins, who showed them every
sign of friendship. On the land they found an abundance of
blue plums and the finest oaks for height and thickness that one
could ever see; together with poplars, *Lonen*,[2] and various
other kinds of wood useful in ship-building. Sailing hence in
a north-by-east direction, they ascended the river to about 43°
north latitude, where it became so narrow and of so little depth
that they turned back.

From all that they could judge and learn, there had never
been any ships or Christians in that quarter before; so that they
were the first to discover this river and ascend it so far. Hendrick
Hudson having returned to Amsterdam with this report, in
the year 1610 some merchants [3] again sent a ship thither—that
is to say, to the second river discovered, which was called Manhattes from the savage nation that dwells at its mouth. And
in the subsequent years their High Mightinesses the States
General granted to these merchants the exclusive privilege of
navigating this river and trading there.[4] Whereupon, in the
year 1615, a redoubt or small fort was erected, up the said river,

[1] Delaware Bay and River.

[2] I cannot find *Lonen* in any Dutch dictionary, old or modern. Chagrin in
leaving the word unexplained is lessened by the course which De Laet himself
has pursued regarding it in his Latin and French versions of 1633 and 1640; he
leaves it out altogether. Mr. van Laer suggests that the word may be the Frisian
word *loonen*, woods, and so "poplar woods."

[3] "Merchants of Amsterdam," say the versions of 1633 and 1640.

[4] "And our people wintered there," say the later versions.

and occupied by a small garrison, of which we shall hereafter speak. Our countrymen have continued to make voyages thither each year, and continuously some of our people remain there for the purpose of trafficking with the natives; and on this account the country has justly received the name of New Netherland.

CHAPTER 8

Situation of the Coast of New Netherland from Pye Bay to the Great River of Mountains.

To understand somewhat better the situation of the coast and the shape of these countries,[1] we shall begin somewhat farther to the north than their limits actually extend, namely at Pye Bay,[2] as it is called by some of our navigators, in latitude 42° 30'. The distance from thence to the longitude of the Lizard, according to the observations and reckoning of Captain Adriaen Block, is 690 leagues, or thereabout. Around the cape of this bay the ground is muddy sand; a numerous people inhabit there, who are extremely well-looking, but timid and shy of Christians, so that it requires some address to approach them. From this place to a point called by the aforenamed Captain Block Cape Bevechier, (from its great resemblance to Bevechier, the land being clifflike, and not very elevated,) across Wyck Bay, (another bay so called by our people, extending to the southeast,) the distance is twelve leagues, and the course to the northwest by west and southeast by east. The coast trends from this cape, in the first place, northwest and southeast, for five leagues, and then north by east and south by west for six leagues, to another sandy point. From the latter to Cape Malebarre, the distance is nine leagues, and the direction of the coast northeast by north and southwest by south. This cape was also called by our countrymen Flat Hook; the surf breaks very much upon the point at its extremity, although there is three fathoms' water at low tide,

---

[1] These two paragraphs following are not reproduced in the Latin or French versions.

[2] Pye Bay is perhaps that of Marblehead, Massachusetts.

so that there are treacherous currents, rendering the navigation dangerous to those who are not acquainted with them.

Our Netherland ship-masters do not quite agree about the shoals in this quarter, although according to some accounts there are sand banks or a reef extending out to sea in a southerly direction for the distance of thirty leagues. Not that it is very shallow for so great a distance, but only that the bottom can be reached with the lead; and there is the least depth of water eight or nine leagues off from the shore and out of sight of land. The soundings are very unequal, so that one will sometimes have thirty fathoms, at one cast, and at the next only seven or eight. But on the other hand it is said by others, that no such shoals or reefs lie so far out to sea to the south of this cape, but only to the eastward of the bay or port of Malebarre. We shall leave this matter to be settled among the skippers by the more complete discoveries hereafter.[1]

Three leagues to the west of Cape Malebarre lies an island about two leagues from the shore, and one league in extent, or thereabout; but at a distance one might suppose that it was part of the main land; it was called by some, as I conjecture, Petockenock.[2] In respect to the bearing of the coast in this quarter, I do not find it laid down in any statements of our countrymen that have come to my hands. But a number of islands lie off this coast, as, for instance, one that is commonly called by our Dutch captains, Texel,[3] and by others Cape Ack. It is a large island, and appears white and clifflike, according to the description of Captain Cornelis Jacobsz. May. About a league and a half from the southwest extremity of

---

[1] The reference is to George's Banks.

[2] Petockenock is probably Nantucket.

[3] "On account of a certain resemblance," say the later versions, meaning some resemblance to the island of the Texel, at the mouth of the Zuyder Zee. Cape Ack is a perversion of Capawak, the Indian name. The island meant is that now called Martha's Vineyard. That which De Laet mentions below as "Marten vingers Island" is the islet now called No Man's Land. The Dutch edition of 1630 and the Latin and French versions give the name more correctly, "Marthaes Vyneard," "Vineam Marthae," "Vigne de Marthe," saying that the English so call it; and all three state the latitude properly as 41° 15'. All three, however, then proceed to describe the lesser island in terms fitting the larger. All three give to Gay Head Gosnold's name of Dover Cliff, and all three mention Gosnold's islet and fort in the fresh-water pond on Cuttyhunk.

this island, Texel, lies another small island, which was named
by our countrymen Hendrick Christiaens. Island, and by
others Marten vingers Island. In this vicinity are likewise
several small islands, called Elizabeth's Islands, which are upon
the starboard side in coming from the river or bay of Nassau;
and in order to run on the outside of Hendrick Christiaensz.
Island, it is necessary to steer a southeast course. Beyond
these lies also an island to which our countrymen have given
the name of Block's Island, from Captain Adriaen Block.
This island and the Texel above mentioned are situated east
by north and west by south from one another, and the distance
is such that you can see both from the quarter deck when you
are half way between.

To the north of these islands and within the main land, is
situated first the river or bay of Nassau,[1] which extends from the
above named Block's Island northeast by east and southwest
by west. This bay or river of Nassau is very large and wide,
and according to the description of Captain Block is full two
leagues in width; it has in the midst of it a number of islands,
which one may pass on either side. It extends inward east-
northeast about eight leagues, but in the rear it is not more than
two petard shots wide, and has generally seven, eight, nine,
five, and four fathoms of water, except in a shallow in the
uppermost part of the bay, at a petard shot's distance from an
island in that direction, where there is but nine feet water.
Beyond this shallow we have again three and a half fathoms of
water; the land in this vicinity appears very fine, and the
inhabitants seem sturdy and fairly tall. They are somewhat
shy, however, since they are not accustomed to trade with
strangers, otherwise there are beaver and fox skins, etc., to be
had, as in other places in that quarter.

From the westerly passage into this bay of Nassau to the
most southeastern entrance of Anchor Bay,[2] the distance is
seven leagues, according to the reckoning of our skippers,
and the course is east by south and west by north. Our
countrymen have given two names to this bay, as it has an
island in the centre and discharges into the sea by two mouths,
the most easterly of which they call Anchor Bay, and the most

---

[1] Buzzard's Bay.   [2] Narragansett Bay.

westerly Sloop Bay. The southeast shore of this bay runs northeast by north and north-northeast. In the lower part of the bay dwell the Wapenocks, a nation of savages like the rest. Captain Adriaen Block calls the people who inhabit the west side of this bay Nahicans,[1] and their sagamore Nathattou; another chief was named Cachaquant. Towards the northwest side there is a sandy point with a small island, bearing north by west, and bending so as to form a handsome bay with a sandy bottom. On the end of the sandy point there is but two fathoms water, and farther on three and three and a half fathoms, with a sharp bottom, where lies a small rocky island. From Sloop Bay, or the most westerly passage of this inlet, it is eight leagues to the Great Bay,[2] which is situated between the main land and some broken land or several islands, that extend into the bay which lies at the mouth of the Great River.[3] In this great bay are many islands both large and small, that have no particular names, so far as is known to us, except that on a chart of this quarter made some years since, several small islands at the entrance to this great bay, near Fisher's Hook,[4] of which we shall speak presently, are named Gesellen (the Companions). And another, called Long Island, lies over across the bay, to avoid which, when rounding Fisher's Hook and running for the small Frisian River, one must steer to the northwest.

On the main land within the bay lies a curved promontory, behind which there is a small stream or inlet, which is called by our people East River, since it extends towards the east.[5] To this succeeds, on the same coast, farther towards the west, another small river, which our countrymen call the river of Siccanamos after the name of the Sagimos or Sacmos;[6] here is a good roadstead behind a sand-point about half a league from the western shore in two and a half fathoms water. The river comes for the most part from the north-by-east, and is in some places very shallow, having but nine feet of water, and there but little current, and in other places only six feet. But there are holes with full five fathoms water, but naviga-

---

[1] Nanhigansetts or Narragansetts.   [2] Long Island Sound.
[3] Hudson. On the early Dutch maps, Long Island is laid down as a group of islands into which it was supposed to be divided by the various inlets.
[4] Montauk Point.   [5] Pawcatuck River.   [6] Sagamore.

tion for ships extends only five or six leagues. Salmon are
found there. The people who dwell on this river, according
to the statements of our people, are called Pequatoos,[1] and are
the enemies of the Wapanoos.

A small island lies to the southwest by south from this
river, as the coast runs; near the west end of it a northwest
by west moon causes low water. We next find on the main a
small stream to which our people gave the name of the Frisian
River,[2] where some trade is carried on with the natives, who
are called Morhicans.

Next, on the same south coast, succeeds a river named by
our countrymen Fresh River,[3] which is shallow at its mouth, and
lies between two courses, north by east and west by north; but
according to conjecture, its general direction is from the north-
northwest. In some places it is very shallow, so that at
about fifteen leagues up the river there is not much more
than five feet of water. There are few inhabitants near the
mouth of the river, but at the distance of fifteen leagues
above they become numerous; their nation is called Sequins.
From this place the river stretches ten leagues, mostly in a
northerly direction, but is very crooked; the reaches extend
from northeast to southwest by south, and it is impossible to sail
through them all with a head wind. The depth of water varies
from eight to twelve feet, is sometimes four and five fathoms,
but mostly eight and nine feet. The natives there plant
maize, and in the year 1614 they had a village resembling a fort
for protection against the attacks of their enemies. They are
called Nawaas, and their sagamore was then named Morahieck.
They term the bread made of maize, in their language, *leganick*.
This place is situated in latitude 41° 48'. The river is not
navigable with yachts for more than two leagues farther, as it is
very shallow and has a rocky bottom. Within the land dwells
another nation of savages, who are called Horikans; they
descend the river in canoes made of bark. This river has always a downward current, so that no assistance is derived from
it in going up, but a favorable wind is necessary.

From Fresh River to another called the river of Royen-
berch,[4] it is eight leagues, west by north and east by south;

---

[1] Pequods. The river is the Thames. [2] Four Mile River.
[3] The Connecticut. [4] Quinipiac River, near New Haven.

this stream stretches east-northeast, and is about a bow-shot wide, with a depth of three and a half fathoms at high water. It rises and falls about six feet; a southeast by south moon causes high water at its mouth. The natives who dwell here are called Quiripeys. They take many beavers, but it is necessary for them to get into the habit of trade, otherwise they are too indolent to hunt the beaver.

Four leagues further to the west there lies a small island, where good water is to be found; and four leagues beyond there are a number of islands, so that Captain Adriaen Block gave the name of Archipelagus to the group. The great bay is there about four leagues wide. There is a small stream on the main that does not extend more than half a league in from the shore, when it becomes perfectly dry. The natives here are called Siwanois, and dwell along the coast for eight leagues, to the neighborhood of Hellegat. At the entrance of this bay, as we have already mentioned, are situated several islands, or broken land, on which a nation of savages have their abode, who are called Matouwax; they obtain a livelihood by fishing within the bay; whence the most easterly point of the land received from our people the name of Fisher's Hook and also Cape de Baye.[1] This cape and Block Island are situated about four leagues apart, in a course east by north and west by south.

Hellegat, as named by our people, is another river,[2] according to the description of Captain Adriaen Block, that flows from the great bay into the great river; and the current according to his statement, comes a distance of about thirty-seven leagues east of the great river. The two currents of the great river and the Hellegat meet one another near Noten Island.[3] In coming from the great river to the bay, the reaches extend east by north, and east-northeast and east-southeast, formed almost entirely by islands. The natives here bring on board the ships oysters, squirrels, and wild ducks. We have now come to the great river, of which we shall next speak.

---

[1] Montauk Point.

[2] Hellegat means Hell Gut or Strait; the Latin version has *inferni os*. The name is applied here to the whole East River. The thirty-seven leagues of current are reckoned from the eastern entrance of Long Island Sound.

[3] Isle of Nuts, now Governor's Island.

CHAPTER 9

Of the Great North River of New-Netherland, and its Situation.

The great North River of New-Netherland is called by some the Manhattes River, from the people who dwell near its mouth; by others, also, Rio de Montaigne; but by our countrymen it is generally called the Great River.[1] There is a large bay at its entrance, which has now for some time[2] been named by our captains Port May, and has at its mouth a sandy point; and off the eastern point of the river extends a reef, that is very bold, since while we have twelve fathoms water at one cast, there will be only five or six at the next, and again but one and a half, or the bottom. About a league and a half within the hook of the river, near the eastern shore, lies an island not more than half a league in extent, to which our people give the name of Noten Island, because excellent nut trees grow there. On the east side, upon the main land, dwell the Manatthans, a bad race of savages, who have always been very obstinate and unfriendly towards our countrymen.[3] On the west side are the Sanhikans, who are the deadly enemies of the Manathans, and a much better people; they[4] dwell within the sandy hook, and along the bay, as well as in the interior of the country.

The entrance to this river lies in latitude 40° 28' or 30'. Over against Noten Island, close to the western shore, there are four other small islands.[5] The river is fourteen or fifteen fath-

[1] The versions of 1633 and 1640 mention also the name Nassau River, but say that Great River and North River (the latter by distinction from the South River, our Delaware) are the most usual. Port May, they say, is named from Captain Cornelis May. They name a tribe of Aquamachuques inhabiting its borders.

[2] The edition of 1630 says, "was formerly called," and after "sandy point" adds, "now known by the name of Godijn's Point."

[3] The Latin version of 1633 adds, "Yet our people have bought from them the island separated from the rest of the land by the Hellgate, and have there laid the foundations of a fort, and of a town called New Amsterdam." So also the French. Both versions mention a tribe of Machkentiwomi as dwelling "over against" the Manhattans.

[4] The edition of 1630 here adds, "as well as the Aquamachuques."

[5] Three or four, say the later versions. Bedloe's Island, Ellis Island and Black Tom, we may assume. 40° 28' is the latitude of Sandy Hook.

oms deep at its mouth, and continues of that depth in a straight channel; it is for the most part a musket shot wide, but varies somewhat in its width. Its course is between northeast and north-northwest, according as the reaches extend. Within the first reach, on the western bank of the river, where the land is low, there dwells a nation of savages, named Tappaans. The river here is quite shallow in the middle, but deep on both sides. The stream flows north and south out of the northern channel, and a southeast and northwest moon causes the highest tides. About a league inland there is a bay sheltered from all winds, about six leagues and a half in circuit; there flows here a strong flood and ebb, but the ebb is not more than four feet, on account of the great quantity of water that comes from above, overflowing the low lands in the spring.

The second reach of the river extends upward to a narrow part, named by our people Haverstroo;[1] then comes the Sailmaker's Reach, as our people call it; and next a curved reach, in the form of a crescent, called by our people the Cook's Reach. Next is High Reach, and then follows Foxes' Reach, which extends to Klinckersberch; this is succeeded by Fisher's Reach, where, on the east bank of the river, dwells a nation of savages called Pachami. This reach extends to another narrow pass, where, on the west side of the river, there is a sharp point of land that juts out, with some shoals, and opposite a bend in the river, on which another nation of savages, the Waoranecks, have their abode, at a place called Esopus. A little beyond on the west side, where there is a creek, and the river becomes more shallow, the Waranawankougs reside; here are several small islands.[2] Next comes another reach called Kleverack [Clover Reach], where the water is deeper on the west side, while on the eastern side are shoals. Then follow Baker's Reach, Jan Playsier's Reach, and Vasterack, as far as Hinnenhoeck. All these reaches are dotted with sands and shallow, both on the east side, and in the middle of the river.

Finally, the Hart's Reach succeeds as far as the Kinderhoeck; at this place and beyond, the river at its greatest depth has but five fathoms of water, and generally only two or three.

---

[1] Oat-straw.

[2] The margin adds, "At latitude 41° 58' [latitude of Kingston and Rhinebeck] Hudson found the variation of the compass nine degrees N. W."

Beyond the Kinderhoeck there are several small islands in the river, one of which is called Beeren Island.[1] After this we come to a sheltered retreat named Ouwe Ree,[2] and farther on are Sturgeon's Hook and Fisher's Hook, over against which, on the east side of the river, dwell the Mohicans. On the east lies a long broken island, through which several creeks find a passage, forming several islands, extending nearly to the island on which the fort was erected, in latitude 43°. The tide flows to this place, and the river is navigable for ships. Higher up it becomes so shallow that small skiffs can with difficulty sail there; and one sees in the distance a high range of mountains, from which most of the water in the river flows. Judging from appearances, this river extends to the great river of St. Lawrence, or Canada, since our skippers assure us that the natives come to the fort from that river, and from Quebecq and Tadoussac.

The fort was built here in the year 1614,[3] upon an island on the west side of the river, where a nation of savages dwells called the Mackwaes,[4] the enemies of the Mohicans. Almost all those who live on the west side, are enemies of those on the east, and cultivate more intercourse and friendship with our countrymen than the latter. The fort was built in the form of a redoubt, surrounded by a moat eighteen feet wide; it was mounted with two pieces of cannon and eleven pedereros, and the garrison consisted of ten or twelve men. Henderick Christiaensz. first commanded here, and in his absence Jaques Elckens, on behalf of the company which in 1614 received authority from their High Mightinesses, the States General.[5]

---

[1] Bears' Island.   [2] Old Anchorage.

[3] Fort Orange, the versions of 1633 and 1640 call it; which also mention that additional population has come to the settlement by reason of the chartering and the efforts of the West India Company.   [4] Mohawks.

[5] In March, 1614, the States General of the United Netherlands promised by a general ordinance that discoverers of new lands should, if they reported their discoveries promptly, have for the period of four voyages a monopoly of trade to the new-found regions. On October 11 a group of merchants of Amsterdam and North Holland, who for three years had been sending trading-ships to the region about the North River, and under whose auspices Block, Christiaenzen and May had made their explorations, asked and obtained from the States General, under the ordinance named, a monopoly of trade in the region from 40° to 45° N. latitude, to continue during four voyages, or three years. The charter gives to the

This fort was constantly occupied for three years, after which it partly went to decay.   On this river there is a great traffick in the skins of beavers, otters, foxes, bears, minks, wild cats, and the like.   The land is excellent and agreeable, full of noble forest trees and grape vines, and nothing is wanting but the labor and industry of man to render it one of the finest and most fruitful lands in that part of the world; for the savages who inhabit there are indolent, and some of them are evil thieves and wicked people.

CHAPTER 10

Of the Nature of the Land and Manners of the Folk on the Great River of Mountains.

Hendrick Hudson, who first discovered this river, and all that have since visited it, express their admiration of the noble trees growing there.   He himself describes to us the manners and appearance of the people that he found dwelling immediately within this bay, in the following terms:

When I came on shore, the swarthy natives all stood and sang in their fashion.   Their clothing consists of the skins of foxes and other animals, which they dress and make the garments from skins of various sorts.   Their food is Turkish wheat,[1] which they cook by baking, and it is excellent eating.   They soon came on board, one after another, in their canoes, which are made of a single piece of wood.   Their weapons are bows and arrows, pointed with sharp stones, which they fasten with hard resin.   They had no houses, but slept under the blue heavens, some on mats of bulrushes interwoven, and some on the leaves of trees.   They always carry with them all their goods, as well as their food and green tobacco, which is strong and good for use.   They appear to be a friendly people, but are much inclined to steal, and are adroit in carrying away whatever they take a fancy to.

In latitude 40° 48′, where the savages brought very fine

region the name of New Netherland.   A facsimile and translation of the charter may be seen in General James Grant Wilson's *Memorial History of the City of New York*, I. 128–130.
   [1] Maize or Indian corn.

oysters to his ship, the aforesaid Hudson describes the country in the following manner:

It is as pleasant a land as one can tread upon, very abundant in all kinds of timber suitable for ship-building, and for making large casks. The people had copper tobacco pipes, from which I inferred that copper must exist there; and iron likewise according to the testimony of the natives, who, however, do not understand preparing it for use.

He also states that they caught in the river all kinds of fresh-water fish with seines, and young salmon and sturgeon. In latitude 42° 18' the said Hudson landed. He says:

I sailed to the shore in one of their canoes, with an old man, who was the chief of a tribe, consisting of forty men and seventeen women; these I saw there in a house well constructed of oak bark, and circular in shape, with the appearance of having a vaulted ceiling. It contained a great quantity of maize, and beans of the last year's growth, and there lay near the house for the purpose of drying enough to load three ships, besides what was growing in the fields. On our coming near the house, two mats were spread out to sit upon, and immediately some food was served in well made red wooden bowls; two men were also despatched at once with bows and arrows in quest of game, who soon after brought in a pair of pigeons which they had just shot. They likewise killed at once a fat dog, and skinned it in great haste, with shells which they get out of the water. They supposed that I would remain with them for the night, but I returned after a short time on board the ship. The land is the finest for cultivation that I ever in my life set foot upon, and it also abounds in trees of every description. The natives are a very good people; for, when they saw that I would not remain, they supposed that I was afraid of their bows, and taking the arrows, they broke them in pieces, and threw them into the fire, etc.

They found there also vines and grapes, pumpkins, and other fruits. From all these things there is sufficient reason to conclude that it is a pleasant and fruitful country, and that the natives are well disposed, if they are only well treated; although they are very changeable, and of the same general character as all the savages in the north. They have no religion whatever, nor any divine worship, [but serve the Devil; yet not with such ceremonies as the Africans. They call him Menutto; and every thing that is wonderful and strange or that surpasses human understanding, that they also call Menutto].[1]   Much less have they any political government, except that they have their chiefs, whom they call Sackmos, or Sagimos.   On different occasions some of our people have been surprised by them and slain; for they are revengeful and very suspicious, and because often engaged in wars among themselves, they are very fearful and timid.   But with mild and proper treatment, and especially by intercourse with Christians, this people might be civilized and brought under better regulation; particularly if a sober and discreet population were brought over and good order preserved.   They are, besides, very serviceable, and allow themselves to be employed in many things for a small compensation; even to performing a long day's journey, in which they discover greater fidelity than could be expected of such a people.

As to the climate and seasons of the year, they nearly agree with ours, for it is a good deal colder there than it ought to be according to the latitude; it freezes and snows severely in winter, so that often there is a strong drift of ice in the river. But this occurs some years more than others, as with us.   There is also the same variety of winds in that country, and in summer thunder and lightning with violent showers.   In short, it is a country well adapted for our people to inhabit, on account of the similarity of the climate and the weather to our own; especially since it seems to lack nothing that is needful for the subsistence of man, except domestic cattle, which it would be easy to carry there; and besides producing many things of which our own country is destitute.   Wine can be made there with industry, since vines are already found that require nothing but cultivation.   We have before stated how the country there abounds in timber suitable for ship-building; it is sought by our people for that purpose, who have built there several sloops and tolerable yachts.   And particularly Captain Adriaen Block, when his ship was accidentally burnt in the year 1614, constructed there a yacht with a keel thirty-eight feet long, forty-four and a half feet from stem to stern, and eleven and a half feet wide.   In this vessel he sailed through Hellegat into the great bay, and explored all the places thereabout; and continued therewith

---

[1] Addition in the edition of 1630.

as far as Cape Cod, whence he came home in the ship of Hendrick Christiansz, leaving the yacht on that coast for further trading.

CHAPTER 11

Further Description of the Coast to the Second Great River, and from thence to Latitude 38°, [and what the free Netherlanders have done there].[1]

In coming out of the bay that lies at the mouth of the great River of the Mountains, we have a tolerably deep channel by keeping the river or its mouth to the north-by-east, and the outer cape of the high land of the bay to the south-by-east. From the sandy hook of the bay or Port May to Fishers' Hook, or the eastern extremity of the broken land where the Matouwacks dwell, the land stretches to the east and north-by-east and the distance is about twenty-seven or twenty-eight leagues, according to the report of some navigators, but according to Cornelis Jacopsz. May only twenty-five. When one is outside of the above mentioned hook of Port May, and bound to the south, the coast runs south-southwest and north-northeast, and a double shore-line is visible. Beyond, the coast runs southwest by south, and northeast by north, and presents a fine, bold shore, with tolerably high sand hills, and the interior land is continuous with the shore lands. But farther south the coast is somewhat lower, and is but a strip of shore, beyond which water is visible within, and here and there a low sandhill. Continuing our course we meet with a gut or inlet, and farther on another gut, in about latitude 39° 15', which is called by our people Eyerhaven,[2] and also Baye Haven. This is a small river or kill, within which all is broken land, and in the bay are several small islands. A little beyond, in the same direction, a fine tall forest is seen upon a low strand, and then succeeds a flat sandy shore with very small and low dunes; and then towards the south a lofty hilly woodland, and here and there slight elevations.

---

[1] This addition to the title appears in the edition of 1630, and refers to the last paragraph of the chapter in that edition, a paragraph the translation of which is printed below in square brackets.   [2] *I. e.*, Egg Harbor.

From thence to Cape May the coast runs mostly east-northeast and west-southwest, and the guts or inlets are so numerous that there appears to be one for every short league. But one should be cautious not to approach too near the coast, since there are *polders*,[1] on which the sea breaks with great violence; and the water rapidly grows more shallow, so that at one cast of the lead there may be seven fathoms, at another but five, and a third only three or less. As we approach Cape May, the coast runs west-southwest and east-northeast, and three or four leagues out to sea lies a bank of sand, where there is but four and a half fathoms water, while nearer to the land we have seven fathoms or more.

The second river lies also within a great bay, called by our people New Port May: it has two capes or headlands, of which the northern is named Cape May, and the southern Cape Cornelius,[2] and these two capes lie east-northeast, well to the north, and west-southwest, well to the south, of one another, so far distant that one is scarcely able to see across with the eye. To the southwest of Cape May, over towards Cape Cornelius and full half-way to the south-southeast, there are sandbanks; the bay also within is full of sand bars and shoals, so that numerous channels are formed, and one should not come in unless he is familiar with the bay, for it is highly dangerous. Within this bay is the other large river, called the South River, of which we have spoken in the seventh chapter; and several smaller streams, [running into the large river][3] which I shall

[1] Low places enclosed within banks.

[2] Both capes, say the Latin and French versions, were named after their discoverer, Cornelius May. They are now called May and Henlopen, though the Dutch applied the name Henlopen to a "false cape" some twelve miles farther south. See the next paragraph, which is found in both the editions of 1625 and 1630. Yet, regardless of this, the edition of 1630 adds at this present point, after "Cornelius," the words "or also Hinlopen." It also adds 38° 55′ as the latitude of Cape May.

[3] Ed. 1630, which, at the passage below, relating to Indian tribes, reads: "On this South River dwell divers nations of savages, namely, the Sauwanoos, Naraticons, Ermomex, Sankicans. The Minquaas, Capitanasses, Gacheos, Sennecaas, Canomakers, Konekotays, Matanackouses, Armeomecks, etc., dwell further inland and upon another river. It is not yet certain whether this also flows into the South River or whether it falls into the great bay of Chesepeack, for the South River, after running some distance northwest, in the same direction as its bay, makes a bend to the northeast, and comes very near to the estuary of

omit to describe, as their true bearing and situation have not reached me, although some of our navigators are well acquainted with these rivers, which they discovered and have visited for several years. Several nations of savages inhabit the banks of these rivers, namely, the Sauwanoos, Sanhicans, Minquaas, Capitanasses, Gacheos, Sennecaas, Canomakers, Naratekons, Konekotays, Matanackouses, Armeomecks, etc., nearly all of whom are of the same character and condition as those we have already described. They plant the land and have much maize, beans, and whatever else the other natives possess.

The most southerly cape, called by us Cape Cornelius, has a white shining appearance, and a reef runs off from it to the south-southeast, into the sea; it is situated in latitude 38° 54'. Four leagues from this cape lies another, which our countrymen call Cape Hinloopen, and the course is northeast by east and southwest by south. From here the coast stretches first mostly north and south, and then southwest and north-northeast, and also south by west and north by east. Along the shore there is six and seven fathoms water, and the bottom is excellent; then again in two or three tacks we have only three fathoms. From hence to latitude 38° 18' the land trends to the southwest, well to the south, and northeast, well to the north, with a very narrow strip of beach, and within there is a spacious body of water together with low broken land; this continues for about eight leagues. To the south of the aforesaid beach the land runs mostly northeast by east and southwest by west, and is a very uneven bottom, varying from six or seven to five fathoms water.

[Into New Netherland, and upon both these rivers described by us in the foregoing chapters, several colonies have been sent by the Directors of the Chartered West India Company,[1] from the very commencement of that company, to

the North River, in the region where dwell the Sankikans and Matovancons." See the map in that edition, reproduced in part in Winsor, IV. 436. The Latin and French versions attempt to list with more precision the tribes on Delaware Bay and River, naming eight or nine tribes not named in the previous editions.

[1] The Dutch West India Company was chartered by the States General on June 3, 1621; see the introduction to the next division of this volume (Wassenaer). Its charter may be found, in Dutch text, and also correctly translated into English for the first time, in the *Van Rensselaer Bowier Manuscripts*, edited by A. J. F. van Laer (Albany, 1908), pp. 86–115.

wit, from the year 1623, in order to continue the possession of those quarters, and to maintain the trade in peltries. They have there, at the uppermost part of the North River, in the latitude of 43 degrees or thereabouts, a small fort, which our people call Fort Orange, round about which several colonizers have settled themselves under the patronage of the aforesaid company. And again another fort of greater importance at the mouth of the same North River, upon an island which they call Manhattes or Manhatans Island, because this nation of Indians happened to possess the same, and by them it has been sold to the company. Here our people have made, as it were, their headquarters or principal colony, which they call New Amsterdam. The ships which are yearly sent thither harbor there, and prosecute their trade with boats and sloops higher up the North River, in the South River, and in all the other rivers and bays hereinbefore described by us.]

Novus Orbis, 1633; Histoire du Nouveau Monde, 1640; Book III., "Virginia," sect. "Novum Belgium," "Nouvelle Belgique"

CHAPTER 10

The Nature of the Climate and Soil, the Fruits, Plants, etc., of New Netherland.

Our countrymen who first explored this river, and those who subsequently made frequent voyages thither, describe the wonderful size of the trees, (a good proof of the luxuriance of the soil,) suitable for edifices and vessels of the largest class. Wild grape vines are abundant, and walnut trees, the fruit of which differs from ours, being smaller and the shell harder and smoother.[1] This is also the case with other trees, shrubs, and plants that grow spontaneously; but when cultivated with the labor and industry of man, maize or Indian corn, for example,

---

[1] Lat. *leviora*, which might be either "lighter" or "smoother." The Fr. has *plus legere*, but the sense seems to require "smoother," since the reference is to hickory nuts as compared with "English" walnuts.

yields a prolific return. So with various kinds of pulse, especially beans, which have an admirable variety of colors; pumpkins of the finest species, melons, and similar fruits of a useful character; so that nothing is wanting but human industry. Our people have begun in different places to sow wheat and several other kinds of grain, and also flax, hemp, and other European seeds, to which the soil is extremely well adapted. There is a great variety of herbaceous plants, some of which bear splendid flowers, and others are considered valuable for their medicinal properties. I cannot avoid describing here two of this class, although their use is not yet known.

Two plants were sent to me from New Netherland that grew finely last year in the medical garden of this city,[1] one of which I have caused to be figured below, but the other was destroyed by the inclemency of the winter before it could be drawn. They were congeners, though differing somewhat in shape and the size of the leaves and stalks. They agreed in having their leaves of the form of the iron head, with which the East Indians and Africans point their darts; both likewise had tender and very flexible stalks, either four or five angled, rough with small prickles, and nodose or jointed; the leaves growing from the joints, and other footstalks springing from the axils of the leaves. They differed in these respects:—the leaves of the one that perished, were broader and smooth on both sides; of the other, beside being narrower, the under side was rough and of a paler green; in the second place, the leaves of the former were supported by long petioles, while those of the latter had very short ones; thirdly, the stems of the former were of a greenish red color, of the latter wholly green; and finally, while the first seemed to bear no flowers, on the latter, both from the joints and the summit of the principal stalk sprang minute flowers of a reddish white color, resembling in form and general appearance the flowers of the water pepper

[1] The already famous Hortus Academicus of the University of Leyden. De Laet himself had a very large herbarium. He devoted a vast amount of time to preparing for publication, at the instance of Count John Maurice of Nassau, the *Historia Rerum Naturalium Brasileae* which George Marcgraf, the count's naturalist during his governorship of Brazil, had left unfinished. The botanical species *Laetia* was named after de Laet by Linnaeus himself.

except that they are somewhat handsomer, and grow in clusters of a more globular form.   Some one has remarked, perhaps not without good reason, that one of these plants might be the male and the other the female.   Both perished last winter, on which account I was unable to make farther observations.   I here add a figure of the flowering plant.[1]

The forests everywhere contain a great variety of wild animals, especially of the deer kind, and other quadrupeds that are indigenous to this part of North America.   Innumerable birds are also found here, both large and small, those that frequent the rivers and lakes, as well as the forests, and possess plumage of great elegance and variety of colors.   In winter superior turkey cocks are taken, very fat, and with flesh of the best quality.   The rivers produce excellent fish, such as the salmon, sturgeon, and many others.

The temperature of the climate differs little from our own; for although the country is many degrees nearer to the equator than the Netherlands, yet it is not less cold in winter; the frost is very intense; deep and frequent snows fall and cover the ground for a long time, with the same variety of years as with us.   The winds are equally changeable; and in summer there is much thunder and lightning with violent showers.   I am therefore of the opinion that scarcely any part of America is better adapted for the settlement of colonies from our country, especially since nothing is wanting that is necessary to sustain life, and the soil can be rendered still more productive by labor and industry; only cattle and beasts of burden are wanted, which can be easily transported there and kept with the utmost convenience on account of the abundance of fodder found almost everywhere.   The grape-vines also, if properly attended to, seem to promise a rich supply of wine.

---

[1] A drawing of the plant appears in both the Latin and the French editions, from which, in connection with the above description, it appears that the one which perished first was *polygonum arifolium*, or halberd-leaved tear-thumb, and the one that survived longer *polygonum sagittatum*, or arrow-leaved tear-thumb, common weeds of no value.

CHAPTER 11

The Manners and Customs of the Natives of New-Netherland, and the Language of the Sankikans.

The barbarians being divided into many nations and people, differ much from one another in language though very little in manners; they possess the same constitution of body as those that inhabit a great part of New France. Their clothing is composed of the skins of wild animals, especially beavers, foxes, and the like, sewed together in the manner of savages, with which they cover themselves entirely in winter, and slightly in summer. Their food principally consists of maize or Indian corn, from which they bake cakes resembling loaves of bread; fish, birds, and wild game. Their weapons are bows and arrows, the latter pointed with sharp flint stones or the bones of fishes. Their boats are one piece of wood, hollowed out by fire from the solid trunks of trees. Some of them lead a wandering life in the open air with no settled habitations; lying stretched upon the ground or on mats made of bulrushes, they take both their sleep and food, especially in summer, when they go nearer to the sea for the sake of fishing. Others have fixed places of abode, and dwellings built with beams in the form of an oven, covered above with the bark of trees, so large that they are sufficient for several families. Their household furniture is slight and scanty, consisting of mats and wooden dishes, hatchets made of hard flint stone by dint of savage labor, and tubes for smoking tobacco formed likewise of flint stone ingeniously perforated, so that it is surprising how, in so great a want of iron implements, they are able to carve the stone. They neither desire nor know riches.

They have no sense of religion, no worship of God; they indeed pay homage to the Devil, but not so solemnly nor with such precise ceremonies as the Africans do. They call him in their language *Menutto* or *Menetto*, and whatever is wonderful and seems to exceed human capacity, they also call *Menetto*; evidently in the same manner in which, as we have mentioned above, the Canadians use the word *Oqui*.

They have no form of political government, except that they

have their chiefs, whom they call *sackmos* and *sagamos*, who are not much more than heads of families, for they rarely exceed the limits of one family connexion. They are like most barbarians suspicious and fearful, although greedy of revenge; they are fickle, but if humanely treated, hospitable and ready to perform a service; they ask only a small remuneration for what they do, and will make very long journeys in a short time with greater fidelity than could be justly expected from such a barbarous people. Nor is it to be doubted that by associating with Christians they could be imbued with civilized manners and with religion, especially if there should be planted among them colonies of well ordered people, who would employ their services without violence or abuse, and in return accustom them to the worship of the true God and the habits of civilized life.

I cannot omit giving some idea of the language of these barbarians, (as I have done with others), and especially of the Sankikans,[1] who dwell on the upper part of the South River, as we shall presently relate.[2]

Their names of numerals are the following:—

1	Cotté	8	Gechas	60	Cottegynagh
2	Nyssé	9	Pescon	70	Nyssastigen
3	Nacha	10	Terren	80	Gahashynagh
4	Wywe	20	Myssynach	90	Pescongynach
5	Parenagh	30	Nachynagh	100	Cottapach.
6	Cottach	40	Weywynagh		
7	Nyssas	50	Parathgynah		

The parts of the human body are thus named:

Head	Wyer.
Eye	Schinquoy.
Mouth	Toonne.

[1] Sankikans or Sanhikans, it appears from early Dutch maps and descriptions, means the Indians of northern New Jersey. The words given below are pure Delaware, some Munsi some Unami, the forms being in many cases almost identical with those noted down by Zeisberger and Heckewelder a hundred and fifty years later.

[2] *I. e.*, in chapter 12 of the Latin and French versions, corresponding to chapter 11 of the Dutch, already presented in this volume, pp. 52, 53 *supra*.

Tongue	Wyeranou.
Shoulder	Duchke.
Arms	Nachk.
Nails	Hyckaes.
Stomach	These.
Feet	Syt.
Hair	Mytrach.
Nose	Akywan.
Lip	Chettoen.
Chin	Hochquoy.
Breast	Toorsay.
Fingers	Rinskan.
Nerve	Cheet.
Belly	Nathey.
Forehead	Nachkaronck.
Ear	Hyttrwack.
Tooth	Wypyt.
Neck	Nequoykangan.
Breasts	Noenackan.
Thumb	Rideren.
Blood	Mohocht.
Thigh	Promine.

The names of the sexes are: male, Renoes; female, Orquoywe.

The elements and what is composed of them:

Fire	Tinteywe.
Rain	Soukeree.
Hail	Tasseckii.
Water	Empye.
Frost	Kepatten.
Tree	Hitteocke.
Snow	Wynoywee.

The names of animals:

Deer	Atto.
Bear	Machquoyvo.
Beaver	Temaquoy.
Wolf	Metumnu.

Lion . . . . Synquoy Mackyrggh.
Otter . . . . Counamoch.
Dog . . . . Aram.
Fox . . . . Woucous.

Of birds:

Swan . . . . Wynkyckso.
Duck . . . . Comconcke.
Turkey . . . . Sickenum.
Partridge . . . . Ourikinck.
Crane . . . . Tarecka.
Turtle dove . . . . . . Mymy.
Goose . . . . Ciahack.

Of fishes:

Pike . . . . Caopyte.
Trout . . . . Cackykane.
Eel . . . . Syackameck.
Perch . . . . Cawycakanesse.

Qualities:

Good . . . . Ouret.
Bad . . . . Matet.

FROM THE "HISTORISCH VERHAEL,"
BY NICOLAES VAN WASSENAER, 1624–1630

INTRODUCTION

IN the early part of the seventeenth century newspapers were but just beginning to exist. News-pamphlets, not periodical, were more numerous. Annual or semi-annual volumes detailing the events or news of the year, after the manner of the *Annual Register* of our time, began, so far as the present writer knows, with the *Mercure François* in 1605. But one of the very earliest of such compilations was the *Historisch Verhael alder ghedenck-weerdichste Geschiedenissen die hier en daer in Europa*, etc., *voorgevallen syn* ("Historical Account of all the most Remarkable Events which have happened in Europe," etc.), which began to be published at Amsterdam in 1622 by Nicolaes van Wassenaer, the first volume covering the months from January to June, 1621, and the preface being dated August 30, 1621.

Nicolaes Janszoon van Wassenaer was the son of a minister of the Reformed Church in Amsterdam. He studied at Geneva at the expense of the Amsterdam magistrates. In their records, under date of September 11, 1586, we read their resolve that "when the student who was sent to Geneva at the city's expense has returned, [it was the famous Jacobus Arminius, and he returned in 1587], another shall be sent thither, and that the preference shall be given to the son of the late preacher Jan Claaszoon" [Wassenaer]. A learned scholar, Wassenaer published first (1605) a Greek poem on the siege of Haarlem, where in 1621 he was "conrector" in the school. Then he removed to Amsterdam, and practised as a physician. Though he wrote a history of the Turks (1624) and a medical work of some repute, his importance to us is solely that of the compiler of the *Historisch Verhael*, which appeared in twenty-one semi-annual parts, covering the years 1621–1631. We are not to expect too much from such compilations of news, nor to attribute too much accuracy to their statements respecting remote happenings, when the means of information were so imperfect and so casual. Yet Amsterdam was doubtless the best place in which to gather news of New Netherland, and we may perhaps take it as a sign of special interest that Wassenaer dedicates his second issue to the West India Company (the first bears no dedication), while the third is dedicated to Prince Maurice, the fourth to the States General, and the fifth to Count Frederick Henry. At all events, these journalistic jottings concerning the New Netherland of 1623–1630 have for us a considerable value because we have so little other testimony concerning those years, especially the earlier of them, and because of their periodical issue, which enables us to follow the progress of the colony in narratives almost contemporary. All that bears on New Netherland is included in the following pages. A translation of nearly all was printed in 1850 in Dr. E. B. O'Callaghan's *Documentary History of the State of New York*, III. 27–48, but it is believed that the present translation is considerably more correct.

The chief event of New Netherland history, in the period between the voyages of Block and the publication of Wassenaer's first narrative, was the incorporation by the States General of the Dutch West India Company, June 3, 1621, under whose control New Netherland remained from that time to the English conquest in 1664. Willem Usselinx, the founder of that company, an Antwerp merchant whose biography by the present writer is printed in the second volume of the *Papers of the American Historical Association*, had been for thirty years agitating the formation of a West India Company which might repeat in the western world the achievements and prosperity of the Dutch East India Company, and might also play a more warlike part by attacking the King of Spain in his own colonial dominions. Party dissensions in the Dutch republic had hindered the promotion of the project, and the Twelve Years' Truce had stopped it for a time; but with the overthrow of Oldenbarneveld and the resumption of war with Spain it was revived, and the company was chartered.

The "Chartered West India Company" was given a monopoly of trade between Dutch ports and the west coast of Africa and all the coasts of America. Within these ample limits it could form alliances with native princes and tribes, appoint and discharge governors and other officers, administer justice and promote trade and colonization. Under the superior control of the States General, its government was vested in five federated chambers or boards of managers, the chief one at Amsterdam, others representing the investors of Zeeland, of the towns on the Maas, of North Holland and of the northern provinces of Friesland and Groningen. General executive powers were vested in the College of the Nineteen; and the government promised aid and protection. New Netherland was not specifically mentioned, and in all colonies the position and rights of colonists were left to be defined by a corporation formed for war and commerce. Throughout all the earlier part of the company's history, its interest in New Netherland was far less than in the conquest of Brazil from Spain, the maintenance of Brazil as a Dutch colony, and the war against the Portuguese for its retention, ending with its loss in 1654.

It was two years from the granting of the charter (June, 1621–June, 1623) before the West India Company had perfected its internal organization and become ready to prosecute with energy the objects of its incorporation. Meanwhile voyages of private adventurers had continued, the Pilgrims had made their settlement permanent at Plymouth, and the English government had begun the long series of diplomatic attacks upon the Dutch title to New Netherland which ended in the English conquest in 1664.

This may be the most appropriate point at which to give for reference a list of the governors or directors general of New Netherland: Cornelis Jacobsen May, 1624–1625; Willem Verhulst, 1625–1626; Peter Minuit, 1626–1632; Sebastiaen Jansen Krol, 1632–1633; Wouter van Twiller, 1633–1638; Willem Kieft, 1638–1647; Petrus Stuyvesant, 1647–1664.

FROM THE "HISTORISCH VERHAEL,"
BY NICOLAES VAN WASSENAER, 1624-1630

[*Under February*, 1624.][1]

NUMEROUS voyages realize so much profit for adventurers: that they discover other countries, which are afterwards settled and planted with people. Virginia, a country lying in 42½ degrees, is one of these. It was first peopled by the French, afterwards by the English and is to-day a flourishing colony. The Lords States General observing the great abundance of their people as well as their desire to occupy other lands, have allowed the West India Company to settle that same country. Many from the United Provinces did formerly and do still trade there; yea, for the greater security of the traders, a castle—Fort Nassau—has been built on an island in 42 degrees, on the north side of the River Montagne, now called Mauritius. But as the nation there was somewhat discontented, and not easy to live with, the builders let it fall into decay,[2] intending now to plant a colony among the Maikans, a nation lying 25 leagues on both sides of the river.

This river, or the bay, lies in 40 degrees; is easy to enter, being as broad or wide as the Thames, and navigable full fifty leagues up, through divers nations, who sometimes manifest themselves with arrows, like enemies, sometimes like friends; but when they have seen the ships once or twice, or traded with our people, they become altogether friendly.

Below the Maikans are situate these tribes: Mechkentowoon, Tapants, on the west side; Wiekagjock, Wyeck, on the east side. Two nations lie there lower down at Klinckersberg.

---

[1] This passage is on pp. 144 recto–147 recto of part VI. of Wassenaer, the section for February, 1624, of which the preface is dated June 1, 1624.

[2] Fort Nassau, built in 1614 or 1615, on Castle Island, near where Albany now stands, was abandoned in 1617 on account of injury by freshets.

At the Fisher's hook are Pachany, Warenecker, Warrawan-nankonckx. Near one place, Esopes, are two or three tribes. The Manhates are situate at the mouth. In the interior are also many, as the Maquas. Full fifty leagues higher are found likewise many villages, all which come to this river to trade from the interior which is very swampy, great quantities of water running to the river, overflowing the adjoining country, which was the cause that Fort Nassau frequently lay under water and was abandoned.

This country now called New Netherland [1] is usually reached in seven or eight weeks from here. The course lies towards the Canary Islands; thence to the savage islands, then towards the mainland of Virginia, steering across, in fourteen days, leaving the Bahamas on the left, and the Bermudas on the right hand, between which the winds are variable with which the land is made.

Respecting religion we as yet cannot learn that they have any knowledge of God, but there is something that is in repute among them. What they have is transmitted to them by tradition, from ancestor to ancestor. They say that mention was made to their forefathers many thousand moons ago, of good and evil spirits, to whose honor, it is supposed, they burn fires or sacrifices. They wish to stand well with the good spirits; they like exhortations about them. The ministry of their spiritual affairs is attended to by one they call *Kitzinacka*, which, I suppose, is priest. When any one among them is sick, he visits him; sits by him and bawls, roars and cries like one possessed. If a man die, he is laid in the earth without a coffin, with all his finest garments of skins. This priest has no house-keeping of his own. He lodges where he pleases, or where he last officiated; must not eat any food prepared by a married woman. It must be cooked by a maiden or old woman. He never cohabits with them, living like a capuchin. When a child arrives at the age of twelve, then they can determine whether he shall be a *Kitsinacka* or not. If he says so, then he is brought up to such office. Becoming of age, he undertakes the exercise of it.

All the natives pay particular attention to the sun, the

[1] Apparently the first mention of the name New Netherland in print; it had been formally bestowed by the charter of October 11, 1614.

moon, and the stars, as they are of as great interest to them, as to us, having like summer and winter. But geographers are aware that the length and shortness of the days differ, on account of situation. The first moon following that at the end of February is greatly honored by them. They watch it with great devotion, and when it comes, they compliment it with a festival; then they collect together from all quarters, and revel in their way, with wild game or fish, and drink clear river water to their fill. They have nothing with which they can become intoxicated. It appears that the year commences then, this moon being a harbinger of the summer. Shortly afterwards the women, who in that land provide the food, as respects both planting and gathering, begin to make preparations, and carry their seed into the field. They allow the succeeding moons to appear without any feasting; but they celebrate the new August moon by another festival, as their harvest then approaches, which is very abundant in consequence of the great mildness of the climate. The summers are frequently very hot, and the land moist, which produces abundance of fruits and grain. Turkish wheat [1] is abundant there, and is pounded by the women, made into meal, and baked into cakes in the ashes, after the olden fashion, and used for food.

As they care nothing for the spiritual, they direct their study to the physical, closely observing the seasons. The women there are the most skilful star-gazers; there is scarcely one of them but can name all the stars; their rising, setting; the position of the *Arctos*, that is the Wain, is as well known to them as to us, and they name them by other names. But Him who dwells above they know not; affording all us Christians an argument to thank Him, that He hath so beneficently granted us knowledge of Him, leaving these in darkness; so that what the apostle says is found to be true. It is not of him that willeth, nor of him that runneth, but of God that sheweth mercy.[2]

There is little authority known among these nations. They live almost all equally free. In each village, indeed, is found a person who is somewhat above the others and commands abso-

---

[1] Indian corn.   [2] Rom. IX. 16.

lutely when there is war and when they are gathered from all the villages to go to war.   But the fight once ended, his authority ceases.   They are very much afraid of death; but when they perceive that they must die, they are very brave and more ferocious than beasts.   When a lad desires a wife, he buys her generally in a neighboring village, and she, being a maiden, is then delivered to him by two or three other women, carrying on the head meal, roots, corn or other articles, to the young man's hut, and he receives her.   The dwellings are commonly circular, with a vent hole above to let out the smoke, closed with four doors, and made mostly of the bark of trees which are very abundant there.   They sleep on the ground covered with leaves and skins.   At their meals they sit on the ground. Each highly esteems his own children, bringing them up very much spoiled.   The women sew skins into clothing, prepare bread, cook the meat which the men hunt and kill with arrows, especially in the winter when all is bare in the fields and but scanty forage is to be picked off the snow; then the animals approach the villages and are shot.

It is very common among them for one man to buy and to have many wives, but not in one place; when he journeys five or six leagues he finds another wife who also takes care of him; five or ten leagues further, he again finds another wife who keeps house and so on to several, constantly buying up peltries through the country.   But as those inland find that furs sold too cheap among them, they come down themselves to the rivers and trade with the nations as best they can. Also those who will trade with them must furnish them food at an inhabitant's in the village—let them cook their meat and fish there, as much as they like, and then they thank the trader. In other respects, they are extremely hospitable; the one lodges with the other without thought of compensation. Those who come far from the interior, yea thirty days' journey, declare there is considerable water everywhere and that the upper country is marshy; those that dwell still higher make mention of great waves that water their lands; so that what many think may be true, that Hudson's Strait runs through to the South Sea, and is navigable, unless obstructed by the ice, since it extends to the northward.   It were desirable that it were once more tested.   Those who made the last voyage are of the same opinion, as they found all open sea, a rapid current and whales.

They live in summer mostly on fish. The men repair to the river and catch a great quantity in a short time, as it is full and furnishes various sorts. The arrows they use are pointed with little bones, iron or copper, with which they, being good marksmen, shoot deer, fawns, hares, and foxes and all such. The country is full of game: hogs, bears, leopards, yea lions, as appears by the skins which were brought on board. Oxen and horses there are none.

In the woods are found all sorts of fruits: plums, wild cherries, peaches; yea, fruits in great profusion. Tobacco is planted in abundance, but much better grows in the wild parts of Brazil; it is called Virginian. Vines grow wild there; were there wine-growers who understood the pressing, good wine could be brought hither in great quantity, and even as must, the voyage thence being often made in thirty days.

Their trade consists mostly in peltries, which they measure by the hand or by the finger. It happened that a woman who had seen a skipper's lace shirt, fell sick; finding she should die she gave her husband three fine peltry skins to present to the skipper for the shirt, which he willingly gave her, for she wished to be buried in it; imitating the Christians in the sumptuousness of their burials. In exchange for peltries they receive beads, with which they decorate their persons; knives, adzes, axes, chopping-knives, kettles and all sorts of iron work which they require for house-keeping.

In their waters are all sorts of fowls, such as cranes, bitterns, swans, geese, ducks, widgeons, wild geese, as in this country. Birds fill also the woods so that men can scarcely go through them for the whistling, the noise, and the chattering. Whoever is not lazy can catch them with little difficulty. Turkey beans [1] is a very common crop. Pigeons fly wild; they are chased by the foxes like fowls. Tortoises are very small, and are not eaten, because there is plenty of other food. The most wonderful are the dreadful frogs, in size about a span, which croak with a ringing noise in the evening, as in this country. 'Tis surprising that storks have not been found there,

---

[1] French beans.

since it is a marshy country. Spoon-bills, ravens, eagles, sparrow-hawks, vultures are numerous and are quickly shot or knocked down by the natives.

'Tis worthy of remark that, with so many tribes, there is so great a diversity of language. They vary frequently not over five or six leagues; forthwith comes another language; if they meet they can hardly understand one another. There are some who come sixty leagues from the interior, and can not at all understand those on the river. All are very cunning in trade; yea, frequently, after having sold everything, they will retract the bargain, and that forcibly, in order to get something more; and then they return upwards, thirty and forty strong, all clothed in skins, with the fur outside.

It appears by the statements of the highlanders, there are larger animals in the interior. On seeing the head of the Bull, one of the signs of the heavens, the women know how to explain that it is a horned head of a big, wild animal which inhabits the distant country, but not theirs, and when it rises in a certain part of the heavens, at a time known to them, then is the season for planting; then they begin to break up the soil with mattocks and to throw in the seed; like the boors in Italy who appear by Virgil in the *Bucolics* to take their time from the signs.

The science of foretelling or interpreting of events is altogether undeveloped and unknown to them; delivering no oracles or revelations of the one or the other sort, as they have very little knowledge of future or past things.

It is somewhat strange that among these most barbarous people, there are few or none cross-eyed, blind, crippled, lame, hunch-backed or limping men; all are well fashioned people, strong and sound of body, well fed, without blemish.

In some places they have abundant means, with herbs and leaves or roots, to cure their ailments. There is not an ailment they have not a remedy for; but in other localities they are altogether devoid of succor, leaving the people to perish like cattle.

Chastity appears to be of some repute among them, for the women are not all equally loose. There are some who would not cohabit with ours for any compensation. Others hold it in small esteem; especially as they are free, living without law.

In the rearing of their offspring, they exhibit great laxity; nevertheless when the children in great numbers follow after this nation, they forbid it as not beseeming; yea, command them to return back.

They are not, by nature, the most gentle. Were there no weapons, especially muskets, near, they would frequently kill the traders for sake of the plunder; but whole troops run before five or six muskets. At the first coming [of the whites] they were accustomed to fall prostrate on the report of the gun; but now they stand still from habit, so that the first colonists will stand in need of protection.

In the South Bay,[1] some miles nearer Florida, is a more temperate country. There is no winter there save in January, and then but for a few days.

Their numerals run no higher than ours; twenty being twice ten. When they desire twenty of anything, they stick the ten fingers up and point with them to the feet on which are ten toes. They count, *Honslat, Tegeni, Hasse, Kajeri, Wisk, Iajack, Satach, Siattege, Tiochte, Ojeri.* The names of their months are these: *Cuerano,* the first with them, February; 2. *Weer-hemska*; 3. *Heemskan*; 4. *Oneratacka*; 5. *Oneratack*, then men begin to sow and to plant: 6. *Hagarert*; 7. *Iakou-varatta*; 8. *Hatterhonagat*; 9. *Genhendasta*; then the grain and every thing is ripe. 10. *Digojenjattha*, then is the seed housed. Of January and December they take no note, being of no use to them.[2]

A ship was fitted out under a commission from the West India Company, and freighted with families, to plant a colony among this people. But to go forward safely, it is first of all necessary that they be placed in a good defensive position and well provided with forts and arms, since the Spaniard, who claims all the country, will never allow any one to gain a possession there; and as the Spaniards have made many incursions as well above as below, in Florida, Virginia and thereabouts, I deem it not uncalled-for to tell something thereof, being a mirror in which every one can see and defend himself, and how the Spaniards always aim as well in general

[1] Delaware Bay.

[2] Nearly all the numerals and some of the names of months can be identified as Mohawk words.

as in particular at monarchy. Such description shall be presented in the commencement of Part the Seventh, as this Book cannot contain it.

[*Under April*, 1624.] [1]

Homo est animal sociabile, is in some sense a definition, in some sense a description, of man. Men's sociability led them to congregate and to live peaceably together, from which arose hamlets, villages and cities, and afterwards chiefs were chosen among them; these, observing that the collected mass frequently so increased that they could with difficulty support themselves, separated a number of their people, who took up and settled the neighboring places. The patriarchs of the Old Testament, finding themselves altogether too many in their countries, sent some of theirs into the uninhabited valleys, and cultivated these. The Assyrians wishing to enlarge their monarchy caused their subjects to inhabit the invaded countries in great numbers. Those of the Persian monarchy did the same. But the Greeks extended their limits very far; for they by navigation peopled entire islands, as appears by the highly learned Petrus Cluverius, who furnishes us correct information on all points in his published *Italy*. [2] The Romans domineering over the western world, spread colonies all over it, as is proved by the carved stones found everywhere; but what order they observed herein is well known to us. Those sent thither, must acknowledge the senders as their lords, pay them homage, and remain under their sovereignty; they were also protected by these by suitable weapons furnished also to them. And whereas, God be praised, it hath come about that the Honorable Messrs. Directors of the West India Company have, with the consent of the Noble High and Mighty Lords States General, undertaken to plant some colonies, I shall give the particulars of them, as follows:—

We treated in our preceding discourse of the discovery of some rivers in Virginia; the studious reader will learn how affairs proceeded. The West India Company being char-

---

[1] This passage is from part VII. of Wassenaer, pp. 10 verso–11 verso. The preface to this part is dated December 1, 1624.

[2] The allusion is to the *Italia Antiqua* of *Philip* Cluverius (Leyden, 1624).

tered to navigate these rivers, did not neglect so to do, but equipped in the spring [1] a vessel of 130 lasts, called the *Nieu Nederlandt*, whereof Cornelis Jacobsz May of Hoorn was skipper, with a company of 30 families, mostly Walloons, to plant a colony there.[2] They sailed in the beginning of March, and directing their course by the Canary Islands, steered towards the Wild Coast,[3] and gained the west wind which luckily [took] them in the beginning of May into the river called, first *Rio de Montagnes*, now the River *Mauritius*,[4] lying in 40½ degrees. He found a Frenchman lying in the mouth of the river, who would erect the arms of the King of France there; but the Hollanders would not permit it, forbidding it by commission from the Lords States General and the Directors of the West India Company; and in order not to be frustrated therein, with the assistance of those of the yacht *Maeckereel* which had lain above, they caused a yacht of two guns to be manned, and convoyed the Frenchman out of the river, who would do the same thing in the South River, but he was also prevented by the settlers there.

This being done, the ship sailed up to the Maykans,[5] 44 leagues, and they built and completed a fort named "Orange" with four bastions, on an island, by them called Castle Island. They forthwith put the spade in the ground and began to

---

[1] Of 1623.

[2] This group of Walloons (*i. e.*, French-speaking Belgians) had in the spring of 1622 applied to the States of the Province of Holland for transportation to New Netherland as colonists, and the matter had been referred to the Amsterdam Chamber of the West India Company. In the *Documentary History of New York*, III. 49–51, are two depositions made in 1685 and 1688 by Catelina Trico, one of the company who came out in this first voyage. She gives interesting details respecting the distribution of the immigrants to the Connecticut River, Delaware River and Manhattan, and respecting her voyage with the remainder, "about 18 families," up to Albany, where she lived three years, "all which time the said Indians were all as quiet as Lambs." But in details where she differs from this contemporary account by Wassenaer, we are not to place much reliance on recollections stated sixty years later. Skipper May was the same who had been exploring these coasts since 1613, and for whom Cape May is named; 130 lasts=260 tons.

[3] The seventeenth-century Dutch name for Guiana.

[4] North River, called sometimes by the name of Prince Maurice of Orange.

[5] Mohicans. Fort Orange was not built on the island, but on the present site of Albany.

plant, and before the yacht *Maeckereel* sailed, the grain was nearly as high as a man, so that they are bravely advanced. They also placed a fort which they named "Wilhelmus" on Prince's Island, heretofore called Murderer's Island;[1] it is open in front, and has a curtain in the rear and is garrisoned by sixteen men for the defence of the river below. On leaving there, the course lies for the west wind, and having got it, to the Bermudas and so to the Channel and in a short time to the Fatherland. The yacht *Maeckereel* sailed out last year on the 16th of June and arrived yonder on the 12th of December. That was indeed somewhat late, but it wasted time in the savage islands, to catch a fish,[2] and did not catch it, so ran the luck. The worthy Daniel van Krieckebeeck, for brevity called Beeck, was supercargo on it, and so did his duty that he was thanked.

Respecting this colony, it has already a prosperous beginning; and the hope is that it will not fall through provided it be zealously sustained, not only in that place but in the South River. For their increase and prosperous advancement, it is highly necessary that those sent out be first of all well provided with means both of support and defence, and that being freemen, they be settled there on a free tenure; that all they work for and gain be theirs to dispose of and to transfer it according to their pleasure; that whoever is placed over them as commander act as their father not as their executioner, leading them with a gentle hand; for whoever rules them as a friend and associate will be beloved by them, while he who will order them as a superior will subvert everything and bring it to naught; yea, they will excite against him the neighboring provinces to which they will fly. 'Tis better to rule by love and friendship than by force.

[*Under December*, 1624.][3]

At the same time that the fleet arrived from Archangel, a large quantity of otter skins was received here in Amsterdam from France, finer than had ever been seen in this country,

---

[1] Site not certain.   [2] Jocose expression, meaning a Spanish prize.

[3] This passage is from part VIII. of Wassenaer, pp. 84 verso–85 recto. The preface of part VIII. is dated May 20, 1625.

sold by those of Canada and the circumjacent places. The
natives are in the habit of clothing themselves with them; the
fur or hair inside, the smooth side without, which, however,
they paint so beautifully that, at a distance, it resembles lace.
They are so clever that they make use of the best for that purpose; what is poor of substance they deem unsuitable for their
clothing. When they bring their commodities to the traders,
and find they are desirous to buy them, they make so very little
matter of it, that they at once rip up the skins they are clothed
with and sell them as being the best. They use the beaver skins
mostly for the sleeves, as they are not so expensive; and they
frequently come several days' journey from the interior, to exchange their goods with the tribes.

The same course is followed in New Netherland. It is
very pleasant, all products being in abundance, though wild.
Grapes are of very good flavor, but will be henceforward better
cultivated by our people. Cherries are not found there.
There are all sorts of fowls, both in the water and in the air.
Swans, geese, ducks, bitterns, abound. The men never labor,
except to provide some game, either fowl or other wild sort,
for cooking, and then they have provided everything. The
women must attend to the remainder, tilling the soil, etc. As
soon as our people arrived there, they proceeded to clear and
plant. Before this vessel had left, the harvest was far advanced. It excites little attention if any one [of the Indians]
abandon his wife; in case she have children, they usually follow
her. Their summers are fine, but the days there are shorter
than with us here. The winters are severe, but there is plenty
of fuel, as the country is well wooded and it is at the service of
whoever wants it.

There is some respect paid to those in authority amongst
them; but these are no wise richer than others. There is
always so much in it, that the chief is feared and obeyed as long
as he is near; but he must shift for himself like others. There
is nothing seen in his house more than in those of the rest.
But our people must pay their respects to him with a kettle or
an axe, and he comes forward to beg a draught of brandy along
with the rest.

As regards the prosperity of New Netherland, we learn by
the arrival of the ship whereof Jan May of Hoorn was skipper,

that everything there was in good condition. The colony began to advance bravely and to live in friendship with the natives. The fur or other trade remains in the West India Company, others being forbidden to trade there. Rich beavers, otters, martins and foxes are found there. This voyage five hundred otter skins, and fifteen hundred beavers, and a few other skins were brought hither, which were sold in four parcels for twenty-eight thousand, some hundred guilders.[1]

This country, or the River Montagne, called by ours Mauritius, was first sailed to by the worthy Hendrick Christiaensz of Cleves. When he had been on a voyage to the West Indies, he happened near there. But his vessel being laden, and a ship belonging to Monickendam having been wrecked in that neighborhood, he durst not approach that land; this he postponed, being desirous to do so another time. It so happened that he and the worthy Adriaen Block chartered a ship with the skipper Ryser, and accomplished his voyage thither, bringing back with him two sons of the principal sachem there. Though very dull men, they were expert enough in knavery. Hudson, the famous English pilot, had been there also, to reach the South Sea, but found no passage; as one may read in the *Netherlands History*, in the year 1612.[2]

This aforesaid Hendrick Christiaensz, after Adriaen Block had dissolved partnership with him, made ten voyages thither, under a grant from the Lords States, who granted him that privilege for the first opening up of the place. On the expiration of that privilege, this country was granted to the West India Company, to draw their profits thence; as has already been done, and shall still further increase from the products which are manifest there, whereof further detail will be given in the next, as much depends on the success.

---

[1] Wassenaer, VIII. 105, notes the sale of cargo under date of December 20, 1624. But de Laet, who was probably more exact, notes for this year 4,000 beavers and 700 otters, brought in by two ships, and selling for 25,000 to 27,000 guilders; *Jaerlyck Verhael*, app., pp. 26, 29. "Jan May" above is apparently a mistake for Cornelis Jacobsz May.

[2] The reference is probably to Meteren.

[*Under April*, 1625.] [1]

Though good care was taken by the directors of the West India Company in the spring to provide everything for the colony in Virginia, by us called New Netherland, on the river Mauritius, near the Maykans, an extraordinary shipment was sent thither this month,[2] to strengthen it with what was needful, as follows:

As the country is well adapted for agriculture and the raising of everything that is produced here, the aforesaid gentlemen resolved to take advantage of the circumstance, and to provide the place with many necessaries, through the worthy Pieter Evertsen Hulft, who undertook to ship thither, at his risk, whatever was asked of him, to wit; one hundred and three head of live stock—stallions, mares, bulls and cows—for breeding and multiplying, besides all the hogs and sheep that they thought expedient to send thither; and to distribute these in two ships of one hundred and forty lasts, in such a manner that they should be well foddered and attended to. Each animal has its own stall, with a floor of three feet of sand, arranged as comfortably as any stall here. Each animal has its respective servant who attends to it and knows what he is to get if he delivers it there alive. All suitable forage is there, such as oats, hay and straw, and what else is useful. Country people have also joined the expedition, who take with them all furniture proper for the dairy; all sorts of seed, ploughs and agricultural implements are also present, so that nothing is wanting. What is most remarkable is, that nobody in the two ships can discover where the water is stowed for these cattle. In order to use the same plan another time if needful, I shall here add it:—the above-named manager caused a deck to be constructed in the ship. Beneath this were stowed in each ship three hundred tuns of fresh water, which was pumped up and thus distributed among the cattle. On this deck lay the ballast and thereupon stood the horses and bulls, and thus there was nothing wanting. He added the third ship as an

---

[1] This passage is from part IX. of Wassenaer, pp. 40, 44; the preface is dated December 1, 1625.   [2] April, 1625.

extra, so that, should the voyage, which is ordinarily made in six weeks, continue longer, nothing should be wanting and he should be able to fulfill his contract.   So, in the eyes of the far-seeing, this colony, which lies right beside the Spanish passage from the West Indies, has great prospects.

In company with these, goes a fast sailing yacht at the risk of the Directors.   In these aforesaid vessels also go six completely equipped families, with some single persons, so that forty-five new comers or inhabitants are taken out, to remain there.   The natives of New Netherland are found to be very well disposed so long as no injury is done them.   But if any wrong be committed against them they remember it long, and should any one against whom they have a grudge be peaceably walking in the woods or hunting, even after a long lapse of time, they will slay him, though they are sure it will cost them their lives on the spot, so highly prized is vengeance among them. . . .

In our previous discourses, mention is made of New Netherland.   Here is additional information: On further enquiry it is found, that they have a chief in time of war, named a *Sacjama*,[1] but above him is a greater *Sacjama* (pointing to Heaven) who rules the sun and moon.   When they wage war against each other, they fortify their tribe or nation with palisades, serving them for a fort, and sally out the one against the other.   They have a tree in the centre, on which they place sentinels to observe the enemy and discharge arrows.   None are exempt in war, but the popes or priests, and the women, who carry their husbands' arrows and food.   The meat they eat consists of game and fish; but the bread is cakes baked forefather's fashion, in the ashes; they almost all eat that, even in war.   They are a wicked, bad people, very fierce in arms.   Their dogs are small.   When the worthy Lambrecht van Twenhuyzen[2] had once given the skipper a big dog, and it was brought to them on ship-board, they were very much afraid of it; calling it, also, a sachem of dogs, as being one of the biggest.   The dog, tied with a rope on board, was very furious against them, they being clad like beasts with skins, for he thought they were wild animals; but when they gave him some

---

[1] Sachem.

[2] Lambrecht van Tweenhuyzen was one of the patentees of 1614.

of their bread made of Indian corn, which grows there, he learned to distinguish them, that they were men.

There are oaks of very close grain; yea, harder than any in this country, as thick as three or four men. There is a red wood which, being burned, smells very agreeably; when men sit by the fire on benches made from it, the whole house is perfumed by it. When they keep watch by night against their enemies, then they place it [the fire] in the centre of their huts, to warm their feet by it; they do not sit, then, up in the tree, but make a hole in the roof, and keep watch there, to prevent attacks.

Poisonous plants have been found there, which those who cultivate the land should look out for. Hendrick Christiaensen carried thither, by order of his employers, bucks and goats, also rabbits, but they were found to be poisoned by the herbs. The Directors intended to send thither this spring voyage [1625] a quantity of hogs which will be of great service to the colony; and cows, with young calves, as shall follow.

Very large oysters, sea fish and river fish are in such great abundance there, that they cannot be sold; and in rivers so deep, as to be navigated upwards with large ships.

The two lads brought hither by Adriaen Block were named Orson and Valentine.[1] This Orson was a thoroughly wicked fellow, and after his return to his own country was the cause of Hendrick Christiaensen's death. But he was paid in like coin; he got a bullet as his recompense.

Chastity appears, on further enquiry, to hold a place among them, they being unwilling to cohabit with ours, through fear of their husbands. But those who are single, evince only too friendly a disposition. The common people fish everywhere. Whatever else is of value in the country, such as mines and other ores, shall by time and further exploration be made known to us. Much profit is to be expected from good management.

---

[1] After two characters in a famous old romance, twin sons of the Emperor of Constantinople, of whom Orson was carried off by a bear and reared in the forest as a savage.

[*Under July*, 1625.] [1]

At the same time arrived a small ship from New Netherland, mostly with furs. As far as good order is concerned, all goes well there. The vessels with the cattle had not yet got there; the crops which our colonists had planted, looked well, but there was no certain information thereof. The next will bring their owners good news.

[*Under November*, 1625.] [2]

A ship came, at the same time, for the aforesaid Company from New Germany,[3] laden mostly with peltries, and had had a favorable voyage. The cattle carried thither were removed upwards to a convenient place abounding with grass and pasture. Only two animals died on the passage. This gave great satisfaction to the freighter, who had managed the transportation so neatly.

[*Under November*, 1626.] [4]

In our preceding discourse mention was made of New Netherland and its colony planted by the West India Company, situate in Virginia on the river called by the French Montaigne, and by us Mauritius, and that some families were sent thither out of Holland, now increased to two hundred souls; and afterwards some ships, one with horses, the other with cows, and the third with hay; two months afterwards a fly-boat was equipped carrying sheep, hogs, wagons, ploughs and all other implements of husbandry.

[1] From part IX. of Wassenaer, p. 123 verso; preface dated December 1, 1625.

[2] From part x., pp. 82 verso–83 recto (misnumbered 81 and 84 respectively); preface dated June 1, 1626. De Laet, *Jaerlyck Verhael*, app., p. 29, notes for 1625, 5,295 beavers and 463 otters from New Netherland, sold for 35,825 guilders; for 1626, 7,258 beavers and 857 otters, etc., yielding 45,050 guilders; and still more in 1627, 1628, 1629 and 1630.

[3] The margin has the reading " Nieu Nederlant."

[4] This passage is from part XII., pages erroneously numbered 39 verso, 38 recto, 40 verso, 39 recto, 37 verso; preface dated June 14, 1627.

These cattle were, on their arrival, first landed on Nut Island, three miles up the river, where they remained a day or two. There being no means of pasturing them there, they were shipped in sloops and boats to the Manhates, right opposite the said island. Being put out to pasture here, they throve well, but afterwards full twenty in all died. The opinion is, that they had eaten something bad from an uncultivated soil. But they went in the middle of September [1625] to meadow grass, as good and as long as could be desired.

The colony is now established on the Manhates, where a fort has been staked out by Master Kryn Frederycks, an engineer. It is planned to be of large dimensions. The ship which has returned home this month [November][1] brings samples of all sorts of produce growing there, the cargo being 7246 beaver skins, 675 otter skins, 48 mink, 36 wild cat, and various other sorts; many pieces of oak timber and hickory.

The counting-house there is kept in a stone building, thatched with reed; the other houses are of the bark of trees. Each has his own house. The Director and *Koopman*[2] live together; there are thirty ordinary houses on the east side of the river, which runs nearly north and south. The Honorable Pieter Minuit is Director there at present; Jan Lempou *schout*; Sebastiaen Jansz. Crol and Jan Huych, comforters of the sick, who, whilst awaiting a clergyman, read to the commonalty there, on Sundays, texts of Scripture and the commentaries. François Molemaecker is busy building a horse-mill, over which shall be constructed a spacious room sufficient to accommo-

---

[1] Peter Minuit of Wesel, sent out by the company as Director General of New Netherland, had arrived in the *Meeuwken* (Seamew) May 4, 1626, and presently bought Manhattan Island from the Indians for sixty guilders ($24). On July 27 arrived the *Wapen van Amsterdam* (Arms of Amsterdam), bringing the secretary, Isaac de Rasieres. This is the vessel mentioned above, for it sailed from Manhattan September 23 and arrived at Amsterdam November 4. A facsimile and a translation of a contemporary letter reporting the voyage to the States General may be seen in General Wilson's *Memorial History of New York*, I. 159, 160.

[2] Chief commercial agent of the company, acting also as secretary of the province. A *schout* or *schout-fiscael*, in a Dutch municipality of that time, was an officer whose functions combined those of an English sheriff and a public prosecutor. The comforters or visitors of the sick were recognized officers of the Reformed Church in Holland. Huych is probably to be identified with Jan Huygen, Minuit's brother-in-law, mentioned by Michaëlius.

date a large congregation, and then a tower is to be erected where the bells brought from Porto Rico will be hung.[1]

The council there administers justice in criminal matters as far as imposing fines, but not as far as corporal punishment. Should it happen that any one deserves that, he must be sent to Holland with his sentence. Cornelis May of Hoorn was the first Director there, in the year 1624; Willem van Hulst[2] was the second, in the year 1625. He returns now. Everyone there who fills no public office is busy about his own affairs. Men work there as in Holland; one trades, upwards, southwards and northwards; another builds houses, the third farms. Each farmer has his farmstead on the land purchased by the Company, which also owns the cows; but the milk remains to the profit of the farmer; he sells it to those of the people who receive their wages for work every week. The houses of the Hollanders now stand outside the fort, but when that is completed, they will all repair within, so as to garrison it and be secure from sudden attack.

Those of the South River will abandon their fort,[3] and come hither. At Fort Orange, the most northerly point at which the Hollanders traded, no more than fifteen or sixteen men will remain; the remainder will come down [to the Manhates]. Right opposite is the fort of the Maykans which they built against their enemies, the Maquaes,[4] a powerful people.

It happened this year, that the Maykans, going to war with the Maquaes, requested to be assisted by the commander of Fort Orange and six others. Commander Krieckebeeck went up with them; a league from the fort they met the Maquaes who fell so boldly upon them with a discharge of arrows, that they were forced to fly, and many were killed, among whom were the commander and three of his men. Among the latter was Tymen Bouwensz., whom they devoured, after having well

---

[1] This bark-mill, the first house of Christian worship on Manhattan Island, stood where now stand 32 and 34 South William Street. See "The Old Bark Mill," by J. H. Innes, in *Federation*, vol. III., no. 5. The bells alluded to were some of the nine captured at the sack of San Juan de Porto Rico, in October, 1625, by the Dutch West India Company's fleet under Admiral Boudewyn Hendricksz.

[2] Verhulst.

[3] Fort Nassau, near the present site of Gloucester, New Jersey. A post at Trenton was also abandoned.

[4] Mohawks.

roasted him. The rest they burnt. The commander was buried with the other two by his side. Three escaped; two Portuguese and a Hollander from Hoorn. One of the Portuguese was wounded by an arrow in the back whilst swimming. The Indians carried a leg and an arm home to be divided among their families, as a sign that they had conquered their enemies.

Some days after the worthy Pieter Barentsz, who usually was sent upwards and along the coast with the sloops, visited them; they wished to excuse their act, on the plea that they had never set themselves against the whites, and asked the reason why the latter had meddled with them; otherwise, they would not have shot them.

There being no commander, Pieter Barentsen assumed the command of Fort Orange by order of Director Minuit. There were eight families there, and ten or twelve seamen in the Company's service. The families were to leave there this year —the fort to remain garrisoned by sixteen men, without women —in order to strengthen with people the colony near the Manhates, who are becoming more and more accustomed to the strangers.

The natives are always seeking some advantage by thieving. The crime is seldom punished among them. If any one commit that offence too often he is stript bare of his goods, and must seek fresh means. The husband who abandons his wife without cause must leave all her goods; in like manner the wife the husband's. But as they love the children ardently, these are frequently the cause of their coming again together. The girls allow their hair to be shaved all around, like the priests, when they are unwell for the first time. They are set apart from all in a separate house, where food is furnished them on a stick. They remain therein until they are sick a second time. Then they make their appearance among their relatives again, and are caused to marry. They then again dress their hair, which before they may not touch. The married women let their hair grow to the waist and smear it with oil. When they are unwell they do not eat with their husbands, and they sup their drink out of the hand. The men let the hair grow on one side of the head into a braid; the rest is cut off. If one kill the other, it is not punished; whoever it concerns sets vengeance on foot; if not, nothing is done. In the month of August a universal torment seizes them, so that they run like men possessed, regarding neither hedges nor ditches, and like mad dogs resting not till exhausted. They have in such men a singular sight. The birds most common are wild pigeons; these are so numerous that they shut out the sunshine.

When the fort, staked out at the Manhates, will be completed, it is to be named Amsterdam. The fort at the South River is already vacated, in order to strengthen the colony. Trading there is carried on only in yachts, in order to avoid expense.

The Sickenanes [1] dwell toward the North, between the Brownists and the Dutch. The chief of this nation has lately made an agreement with Pieter Barentsz. not to trade with any other than him. Jaques Elekes imprisoned him in the year 1622 in his yacht and obliged him to pay a heavy ransom, or else he would cut off his head. He paid one hundred and forty fathoms of *Zeewan,* which consists of small beads they manufacture themselves, and which they prize as jewels. On this account he has no confidence in any one but this one [Barentsen] now.

The Brownists, who live beyond them, are Englishmen, who removed thither by consent of the King.[2] They call themselves Puritans, because they seek after purity in the Orthodox religion. They wished not to live in England; desiring not wealth, but merely necessaries and a moderate condition.

The nations that come the longest distance from the north known to the traders, are the Indians from French Canada. Thereabout are the Orankokx, the Achkokx and others,[3] both men and women. On entering the river, if they bring women with them, it is a sign they come as friends; if they visit the yachts without these, every one must be on his guard.

The belief of the Maikans regarding the departure of the soul is, that it goes up westward on leaving the body. There it meets with great rejoicing the others who have died previously; there they all wear black otter or bear skins, which among them are signs of gladness. They have no desire to be with them. The Mahieu, captain of the Maykans, who is named Cat, is of the opinion that death comes from the Devil, who is

[1] Or Sequins, dwelling on the Connecticut River.
[2] The Pilgrims of New Plymouth.   [3] I cannot identify these names.

evil. A skipper denying this, said, God had control over death.
Thereupon he asked, if He being good had the power to give,
or take away, life? And he was answered, Yea; which he
could not understand, how this good God should inflict evil,
that is death. But there was no one who gave him proper
instruction; he therefore remained in his darkness. When
they have a corpse, they place it, before it becomes rigid, squat
on the heels, as children sit in this country before the fire; and
so they place it in the grave, sitting; its face to the east.

It appears that the Sickanamers before mentioned, make a
sort of sacrifice. They have a hole in a hill in which they place
a kettle full of all sorts of articles that they either have by them,
or can procure, as a part of their treasures. Then a snake
comes in, then they all depart, and the *Manittou*, that is the
Devil, comes in the night and takes the kettle away, according
to the statement of the *Koutsinacka*, or devil-hunter, who
presides over the ceremony.

This Pieter Barentz., already spoken of, can understand all
the tribes thereabout; he trades with the Sickenames, to whom
the whole north coast is tributary; with the Zinnekox, Wap-
penox,[1] Maquaes and Maikans, so that he visits all the tribes
with sloops and trades in a friendly manner with them, only for
peltries. And he brought back this year a valuable cargo in
the ship the *Arms of Amsterdam*, whereof Adriaen Joris is skipper, who went out there on the 19th of December of the year
1625 with the ship the *Sea-mew* and conveyed Pieter Minuit
aforesaid, who now sends for his wife thither. The *Sea-mew*
arrived there 4th May, 1626.

[*Under October*, 1628.][2]

Two ships came from New Netherland for the benefit of the
said [West India] Company, with ten thousand peltries, or
skins, together with a large quantity of timber, fit for the
building of the vessels which are shortly to be launched.
Those ships were despatched by the commander there, called

---

[1] The Shinnecocks lived in the east part of Long Island; the Wappingers
(Wapanachki) in the highlands on the east side of Hudson River.

[2] From part XVI. of Wassenaer, p. 13; preface dated June 1, 1629.

Minuict; one ship was the *Three Kings*, Skipper Jan Jacobsz. of Wieringhen; the other was the *Arms of Amsterdam*.

The government over the people of New Netherland continued on the 19th of August of this year in the aforesaid Minuict, successor to Verhulst. He went thither from Holland on January 9, Anno 1626, and took up his residence in the midst of a nation called Manates, building a fort there, to be called Amsterdam, having four bastions and faced outside entirely with stone, as the ramparts crumbled away like sand, and are now to be more substantial. The population consists of two hundred and seventy souls, including men, women and children. They remained as yet without the fort, in no fear, as the natives live peaceably with them. They are situate three leagues from the sea, on the river by us called Mauritius, by others, Rio de Montagne.

These strangers for the most part occupy their farms. Whatever they require is supplied by the Directors. The winter grain has turned out well there, but the summer grain which ripened before it was half grown in consequence of the excessive heat, was very light. The cattle sent thither have thriven well, and everything promises increase, as soon as the land is improved, which is full of weeds and poor.

There are now no families at Fort Orange, situated higher up the river among the Maikans. They have all been brought down. Five or six and twenty persons, traders, remain there. Bastiaen Jansz Crol is vice-director there; who has remained there since the year 1626, when the others came down.

Those of the West India Company have also removed all those who were at the South River. They retain only one vessel trading there. Traders who come from a great distance have lion skins which they will not barter, because being clothed in them they find them much warmer than others.

Beyond the South River, in 37 degrees,[1] Englishmen are settled, freemen, but planted there by merchants on condition that they deliver as much tobacco to their masters as is agreed on; the remainder is their own. Considerable trade is carried on with them, and many ships come thither from England.

On the north side are the English Brownists who maintain

---

[1] *I. e.*, in Virginia.

themselves very well and are much resorted to, supporting their reputation bravely with the natives, whom they do not fear, having acted strictly with these from the first, and so continuing.

In the beginning of this year, war broke out between the Maikans near Fort Orange and the Makuaes, but these beat and captured the Maikans and drove off the remainder who have settled towards the north by the Fresh River, so called;[1] where they begin again to cultivate the soil; and thus the war has come to an end.

[*Under March*, 1630.][2]

After the Right Honorable Directors of the Chartered West India Company in the United Netherlands had provided everything for the defence of New Netherland and put everything there in good order, they taking into consideration the advantages of said place, the favorable nature of the air and soil, and that considerable trade and goods and many commodities may be obtained from thence, sent some free emigrants thither with all sorts of cattle and implements necessary for agriculture, so that in the year 1628 there already resided on the island of the Manhattes two hundred and seventy souls, men, women and children, under Governor Minut, Verhulst's successor, and lived there in peace with the natives. But as the land, being extensive and in many places full of weeds and wild growth, could not be properly cultivated in consequence of the scantiness of the population, the said Directors of the West India Company, the better to people their lands, and to bring the country to produce more abundantly, resolved to grant divers Privileges, Freedoms and Exemptions to all patroons, masters or individuals who should plant any colonies and cattle in New Netherland, and they accordingly have constituted and published in print these following exemptions, to afford better encouragement and infuse greater zeal into whosoever should be inclined to reside and plant his colony in New Netherland.

---

[1] Connecticut.   [2] From part XVIII., p. 94.

*Privileges and Exemptions for Patroons, Masters and Private
Individuals, who will Settle any Colonies and Cattle in
New Netherland, resolved upon for the Service of the General
West India Company in New Netherland, and for the
Benefit of the Patroons, Masters and Individuals.*[1]

I. Such participants in the said Company as may be inclined to
settle any colonies in New Netherland, shall be permitted to send in
the ships of this Company going thither, three or four persons to
inspect the situation of the country, provided that they, with the
officers and ship's company, swear to the articles, so far as they relate
to them, and pay for provisions and for passage, going and coming,
six stivers [2] per diem (and such as desire to eat in the cabin, twelve
stivers); and undertake to be subordinate and give assistance like
others, in cases offensive and defensive; and if any ships be taken
from the enemy, they shall receive, *pro rata*, their proportions with the
ship's company, each according to his quality; that is to say, the
colonists eating out of the cabin shall be rated with the sailors, and
those who eat in the cabin with those of the Company's people who
eat at table and receive the lowest wages.

II. Nevertheless in this respect shall be preferred such persons as
have first appeared and desired the same from the Company.

III. All such shall be acknowledged patroons of New Netherland
who shall undertake, within the space of four years next after they
have given notice to any of the chambers of the Company here, or to
the commander or council there, to plant a colony there of fifty souls,
upwards of fifteen years old; one-fourth part within one year, and
within three years after the sending of the first, making together four
years, the remainder, to the full number of fifty persons, to be shipped
from hence, on pain, in case of manifest neglect, of being deprived
of the privileges obtained; but it is to be observed that the Company
reserve the island of the Manhattes to themselves.

---

[1] This document, so important in New Netherland history as the foundation
of the system of patroonships, was printed in 1630 by the West India Company as
a pamphlet; a fac-simile of the title-page is given on the opposite page of this
volume. The document was also printed by Wassenaer, part XVIII., pp. 94 recto–
98 verso. Mr. van Laer prints the Dutch text and an excellent English translation
in *Van Rensselaer Bowier Manuscripts*, pp. 136–153. The present translation had
been made by correcting, with the aid of the original Dutch, the version printed
in *N. Y. Col. Doc.*, II. 553–557. Mr. van Laer's translation then arriving a few
improvements were borrowed from it.

[2] The stiver was a twentieth part of a guilder, or two cents.

VR.YHEDEN

By de Vergaderinghe van de Negenthiene vande Geoctroyeerde West-Indische Compagnie vergunt aen allen den ghenen / die eenighe Colonien in Nieu-Nederlandt sullen planten.

In het licht ghegheven

Om bekent te maken wat Profijten ende Voordeelen aldaer in Nieu-Nederlandt, voor de Coloniers ende der selver Patroonen ende Meesters, midtsgaders de Participanten, die de Colonien aldaer planten, zijn becomen.

Westindjen Kan sijn Nederlands groot gewin.
Verkleynt seyands Macht brengt silver-platen in.

T'AMSTELREDAM,

By Marten Iansz Brandt Boeckvercooper / woonende by de nieuwe Kerck / in de Gereformeerde Catechismus, Anno 1630.

TITLE PAGE OF THE "PRIVILEGES AND EXEMPTIONS"

IV. They shall, from the time they make known the situation of the places where they propose to settle colonies, have the preference over all others of the absolute property of such lands as they have there chosen; but in case the situation should not afterwards please them, or they should have been deceived in the selecting of the land, they may, after remonstrating concerning the same to the commander and council there, be at liberty to choose another place.

V. The patroons, by their agents, shall and may be permitted, at such places as they shall settle their colonies, to extend their limits four leagues along the shore, or on one side of a navigable river, or two leagues on each side of a river, and so far into the country as the situation of the occupiers shall permit; it being understood that the Company keep to themselves the lands lying and remaining between the limits of colonies, to dispose thereof, when and at such time as they shall think proper, in such manner, however, that no person shall be allowed to come within seven or eight leagues of them without their consent, unless the situation of the land thereabout be such that the commander and council, for good reasons, should order otherwise; always observing that the first occupiers are not to be prejudiced in the right they have obtained, except in case the service of the Company should require it, for the building of fortifications, or something of that sort; the command of each bay, river or island (apart from such exceptions), belonging to the first settled colony, under the supreme jurisdiction of their High Mightinesses the States General and the Company: but that the colonies subsequently settled on the same river or island may appoint one or more deputies to join with the first in considering what may be necessary for the prosperity of the colonies on the said river and island.

VI. They shall forever possess and enjoy all the lands lying within the aforesaid limits, together with the fruits, crops, minerals, rivers and fountains thereof; as also the high, middle and low jurisdictions, fisheries, fowling and grinding, to the exclusion of all others, to be holden from the Company as a perpetual inheritance, without its ever devolving again to the Company, and in case it should devolve, to be redeemed and repossessed with twenty guilders per colony, to be paid to this Company, at the chamber here or to their commander there, within a year and six weeks after the same occurs, each at the chamber where he originally sailed from; provided further, that no person or persons whatsoever shall be privileged to fish and hunt but the patroons and such as they shall permit. And in case any one should in time prosper so much as to found one or more towns, he shall have power and authority to establish officers and magistrates there, and to make use of the title of his colony, according to his pleasure and to the quality of the persons.

VII. There shall likewise be granted to all patroons who shall desire the same, *venia testandi*, or liberty to dispose of their aforesaid heritage by testament.

VIII. The patroons may make use of all lands, rivers and woods lying contiguous to their property, until this Company, or other patroons or private persons, shall take possession of them.

IX. Those who shall send persons over to settle colonies shall furnish them with proper instructions in order that they may be ruled and governed conformably to the rule of government made, or to be made, by the Board of the Nineteen,[1] as well in the political as in the judicial government; which instructions they shall be obliged first to lay before the directors of the respective chambers.

X. The patroons and colonists shall be privileged to send all their people and effects thither in ships belonging to the Company, provided they take the oath, and pay the Company for bringing over the people, as mentioned in the first article; and for freight of the goods, five per cent. ready money, to be reckoned on the prime cost of the goods here, in which are, however, not to be included such cattle and implements as are necessary for the cultivation and improvement of the lands, which the Company are to carry over for nothing, if there is room in their ships. But the patroons shall, at their own expense, provide and make places for them, together with everything necessary for the support of the cattle.

XI. But in case it should not suit the Company to send any ships, or there should be no room in those sailing thither, then in such case the said patroons, after having communicated their intentions, and after having obtained consent from the Company in writing, may send their own ships or vessels thither; provided that, in going or coming, they go not out of their ordinary course, giving security to the Company for the same and taking on board an assistant,[2] to be victualled by the patroons, and paid his monthly wages by the Company, on pain, for doing the contrary, of forfeiting all the right and property they have obtained to the colony.

XII. And inasmuch as it is the intention of the Company to people the island of the Manhattes first, all fruits and wares that are produced on the North River and lands lying thereabout shall, for the present, be brought there before being sent elsewhere, excepting such as are, from their nature, unnecessary there, or such as cannot, without great loss to the owners thereof, be brought there; in which case the owners thereof shall be obliged to give timely notice in writing of the difficulty attending the same to the Company here, or the commander and

---

[1] The governing board of the Dutch West India Company.
[2] Supercargo.

council there, that provision may be made in respect to them as the necessity thereof shall be found to require.

XIII. All patroons of the colonies in New Netherland, and also colonies on the island of the Manhattes shall be at liberty to sail and traffic all along the coast, from Florida to Newfoundland, provided that they do again return with all such goods as they shall get in trade to the island of the Manhattes, and pay five per cent. duty to the Company, in order that, if possible, after the necessary inventory of the goods shipped be taken, the same may be sent hither.   And if it should so happen that they could not return, by reason of contrary currents or otherwise, in such case such goods shall not be brought to any other place but to these dominions, in order that, under the inspection of the directors, at the place where they may arrive, they may be unladen, an inventory made, and the aforesaid duty of five per cent. paid to the Company here, on pain, if they do the contrary, of the forfeiture of their goods so trafficked for, or the true value thereof.

XIV. In case the ships of the patroons, in going to, or coming from, or sailing on the coast from Florida to Newfoundland, and no further, within the bounds of our grant, should overpower any prizes of the enemy, they shall be obliged to bring, or cause to be brought, such prize to the chamber of the place from whence they sailed out, in order that that chamber may obtain its profits from it; the Company shall keep the one-third part thereof, and the remaining two-thirds shall belong to them, in consideration of the cost and risk they have been at, all according to the orders of the Company.

XV. It shall be also free for the aforesaid patroons to traffic and trade all along the coast of New Netherland and places circumjacent, with such goods as they have acquired there, and receive in return for them all sorts of merchandise that may be had there, except beavers, otters, minks, and all sorts of peltry, which trade the Company reserve to themselves.   But the same shall be permitted at such places where the Company have no factories, on condition that such traders shall be obliged to bring all the peltry they may obtain to the island of the Manhattes, if it is at all practicable, and there deliver to the Director, to be by him shipped hither with the ships and goods; or, if they should come here without going there, then to unload them with notice to the Company, and the making of a proper inventory, in order that they may pay to the Company one guilder for each merchantable beaver and otter skin; the retailing, risk and all other charges remaining on the account of the patroons or owners.

XVI. All coarse wares that the colonists of the patroons there shall produce, such as pitch, tar, potash, wood, grain, fish, salt, limestone and such like things, shall be conveyed in the Company's ships, at the rate of eighteen guilders per last, four thousand weight to be accounted a last; and the Company's ship's crews shall be obliged to wheel and bring the salt on board, whereof ten lasts make a hundred. And, in case of the lack of ships, or of room in the ships, they may order it over, at their own cost, in ships of their own, and enjoy in these dominions such liberties and benefits as have been granted to the Company; but in either case they shall be obliged to pay, over and above the duty of five per cent., eighteen guilders for each hundred of salt that is carried over in the Company's ships.

XVII. For all wares which are not mentioned in the foregoing article, and which are not carried by the last, there shall be paid one dollar for each hundred pounds weight; and for wines, brandies, verjuice and vinegar, there shall be paid eighteen guilders per cask.

XVIII. The Company promises the colonists of the patroons that they shall be free from customs, tolls, excise, imposts or any other contributions for the space of ten years; and after the expiration of the said ten years, at the highest, such customs as the goods pay here at the present time.

XIX. That they will not take from the service of the patroons any of their colonists, either man or woman, son or daughter, man-servant or maid-servant; and, though any of these should desire the same, they will not receive them, much less permit them to leave their patroons, and enter into the service of another, unless on consent obtained from their patroons in writing, and this for and during so many years as they are bound to their patroons; after the expiration whereof, it shall be in the power of the patroons to send hither all such colonists as will not continue in their service, and not to set them at liberty until then. And any colonist who shall enter into the service of another patroon, or shall, contrary to his contract, betake himself to freedom, we promise to do everything in our power to deliver the same into the hands of his patroon or attorney, that he may be proceeded against according to the customs of this country, as occasion may require.

XX. From all judgments given by the courts of the patroons for upwards of fifty guilders, there may be an appeal to the Company's commander and council in New Netherland.

XXI. In regard to such private persons as on their own account, or others in the service of their masters here in less numbers than in case of patroons, shall be inclined to go thither and settle, they shall, with the approbation of the Director and Council there, be at liberty to take up and take possession of as much land as they shall be able properly to improve, and shall enjoy the same in full property either for themselves or masters.

XXII. They shall have free liberty of hunting and fowling, as well by water as by land, generally, in public and private woods and rivers about their colonies, according to the orders of the Director and Council.

XXIII. Whosoever, whether colonists of patroons for their patroons, or free persons for themselves, or others for their masters, shall discover any shores, bays or other fit places for erecting fisheries, or the making of salt ponds, they may take possession thereof, and begin to work on them as their own absolute property, to the exclusion of all others. And it is permitted that the patroons of colonists may send ships along the coast of New Netherland, on the cod fishery, and with the fish they catch may trade direct to Italy or other neutral countries, paying in such cases to the Company a duty of six guilders per last; and if they should come with their lading hither, they shall be at liberty, though they shall not, under pretext of this consent, or leave from the Company, carry any other goods to Italy on pain of punishment, at discretion, the Company being furthermore at liberty to put a supercargo on board each ship, as in the eleventh article.

XXIV. In case any of the colonists shall, by his industry and diligence, discover any minerals, precious stones, crystals, marbles or such like, or any pearl fisheries, the same shall be and remain the property of the patroon or patroons of such colony, the discoverer being assigned such premium as the patroon shall beforehand have stipulated with his colonists by contract. And the patroons shall be exempt from the payment of duty to the Company for the term of eight years, and pay only for freight, to bring them over, two per cent., and after the expiration of the aforesaid eight years, for duty and freight, the one-eighth part of what the same may be worth here.

XXV. The Company shall take all the colonists, as well free as those that are in service, under their protection, and them defend against all foreign and domestic wars and violence, with the forces they have there, as much as lies in their power.

XXVI. Whosoever shall settle any colony out of the limits of the Manhattes island, shall be obliged to satisfy the Indians for the land they shall settle upon, and they may extend or enlarge the limits of their colonies if they settle a proportionate number of colonists thereon.

XXVII. The patroons and colonists shall in particular, and in the speediest manner, endeavor to find out ways and means whereby they may support a minister and schoolmaster, that the service of God and zeal for religion may not be neglected among them, and they shall, at the first, provide a comforter of the sick there.

XXVIII. The colonies that shall happen to lie on the respective rivers or islands (that is to say, each river or island for itself), shall be at liberty to appoint a deputy, who shall give information to the commander and council of that region, and further the interests of his colony, of which deputies there shall be one changed in every two years; and all colonies shall be obliged, at least once in every twelve months, to make exact report of their condition and of the lands thereabout to the commander and council there.

XXIX. The colonists shall not be permitted to make any woollen, linen or cotton cloth, nor weave any other stuffs there, on pain of being banished, and as perjurers, to be punished, at discretion.

XXX. The Company shall use their endeavors to supply the colonists with as many blacks as they can, on conditions hereafter to be made, in such manner, however, that they shall not be bound or held to do it for a longer time than they shall think proper.

XXXI. The Company promise to finish the fort on the island of the Manhattes as soon as possible, and to put it in a posture of defence; and to cause these Privileges and Exemptions to be approved and confirmed by their High Mightinesses the Lords States General.[1]

By these means many persons have become inclined to repair thither and to plant their colonies there, so that it is hoped—since the land itself is fruitful, and adapted if well cultivated to bring forth rye, wheat and other grains, as has now been demonstrated on various voyages, and since also good traffic can be carried on there in all sorts of peltries, which are plentiful there and fine—that good profits may be expected thence for the Company and the colonists.

[1] This was done on June 7, 1629. Although the issue of these Privileges and Exemptions made better provision than had hitherto existed for local government and for agricultural occupation of the province by small independent proprietors, it also, in its provision for large manorial grants, transferred to the New World some undesirable features of the (modified) feudalism of the Netherlands; and by opening very profitable opportunities to directors and other rich members of the Company, tempted them to assume interests opposed to those of the Company and paved the way for much dissension between patroons and directors general. Forthwith Samuel Godyn and Samuel Blommaert secured a patroonship on the west side of Delaware Bay, other associates another on the east side, Michiel Pauw one which he called Pavonia, extending along the west side of the North River from the Narrows to Hoboken and including Staten Island. All these proved temporary. Kiliaen van Rensselaer established a great and more permanent patroonship, Rensselaerswyck, by securing broad lands on the west side, later extended to both sides of the Hudson, above and below Fort Orange.

LETTER OF ISAACK DE RASIERES
TO SAMUEL BLOMMAERT, 1628 (?)

INTRODUCTION

In 1841 the state of New York commissioned John Romeyn Brodhead as agent to search the archives of Europe for materials illustrating the colonial history of the state. Never did an American state send out a better record-agent. After four years of diligent search and labor he returned with eighty volumes of manuscript copies of documents procured in the Netherlands, France and England (sixteen of them from the Netherlands), which were subsequently published as the series entitled *Documents relating to the Colonial History of the State of New York* (commonly abbreviated, as in this book, *N. Y. Col. Doc.*). Little escaped his search, and little New Netherland material not catalogued by him has since come into the archives of the kingdom of the Netherlands. But about 1847 a deputy-librarian in the Royal Library at the Hague found, in a parcel of manuscripts recently bought, the original of the following letter, which contains what is, in one sense at least, the earliest description we have of New Netherland and its neighborhood from the pen of an eye-witness. The deputy-librarian at once sent a copy of the letter to Mr. Brodhead, who translated it, and the translation was printed (1849) in the second volume of the second series of the *Collections of the New York Historical Society*, pp. 339–354. The translation here presented is a revision of this, made by Professor William I. Hull from the original, now preserved in the National Archives at the Hague. Unfortunately, of the sixteen pages of which the letter seems originally to have been composed, pp. 7–10 were missing from the manuscript when it was acquired, and are still missing. The letter has no date, but it was evidently written from memory after the writer's return to Holland. It may have been written in 1628, 1629 or 1630. In this uncertainty, we may properly place it before the letter of Domine Michaëlius, because it relates to New Netherland at an earlier time than that of the latter's arrival.

Most of what we know of Isaack de Rasieres, apart from his connection with New Netherland, is derived from a short communication by Mr. Rammelman Elsevier in the *Navorscher*, the Dutch "Notes and Queries,' vol. XX. (1870). Rasieres was born in Middelburg in 1595. He had a brother who was a commercial agent in the service of the East India Company. In 1626, two or three months after Director Minuit, he came out to New Netherland as chief commercial agent for the company and secretary of the province. Governor Bradford of Plymouth, to whom he made a visit described in the ensuing letter and in Bradford's letter-book and *History*, describes him as "their upper commis or chief merchant, and second to the Governor, a man of a fair and genteel behavior; but soon after fell into disgrace amongst them, by reason of their factions." This must have happened at some time between November, 1627, and September, 1630, when we find his successor officiating as secretary.

In 1633 Rasieres married at Amsterdam the niece of one of the directors of the West India Company, and presently a certain group in that body attempted to make him governor of New Netherland in place of Wouter van Twiller.[1] Failing of this, Rasieres soon went to Brazil, where one of his sons was born in 1637, and another, who became a sea-captain in the company's service, in 1641. There he was in 1651; but in 1669, when the second son was married in Amsterdam, the record reads, "parents departed to Barbados." There was a family legend that Isaack de Rasieres became governor of Tobago.

[1] *Van Rensselaer Bowier Manuscripts*, p. 270.

Samuel Blommaert (1583–1654), to whom the letter was written, probably soon after the writer's return from New Netherland, was a prominent merchant who, after early experiences in the East Indies, had settled down in Amsterdam in 1612, and was a director of the West India Company from 1622 to 1629 and again from 1636 to 1642. In this latter period he was a salaried commissioner of Sweden in the Netherlands, and he had a prominent part in the Swedish colonizing of Delaware and in Minuit's expedition. His letters to the Swedish chancellor Oxenstjerna were published in 1908 by the Historical Society of Utrecht, but contain nothing as to Rasieres.

LETTER OF ISAACK DE RASIERES
TO SAMUEL BLOMMAERT, 1628 (?)

Mr. Blommaert:

As I feel myself much bound to your service, and in return know not how otherwise to recompense you than by this slight memoir, (wherein I have in part comprised as much as was in my power concerning the situation of New Netherland and its neighbors, and should in many things have been able to treat of or write the same more in detail, and better than I have now done, but that my things and notes, which would have been of service to me herein, have been taken away from me),[1] I will beg you to be pleased to receive this, on account of my bounden service, etc.

On the 27th of July, Anno 1626, by the help of God, I arrived with the ship *The Arms of Amsterdam*, before the bay of the great Mauritse River, sailing into it about a musket shot from Godyn's Point,[2] into Coenraet's Bay;[3] (because there the greatest depth is, since from the east point there stretches out a sand bank on which there is only from 9 to 14 feet of water), then sailed on, northeast and north-northeast, to about half way from the low sand bank called Godyn's Point to the Hamels-Hoofden,[4] the mouth of the river, where we found at half ebb 16, 17, 18 feet water, and which is a sandy reef a musket shot broad, stretching for the most part northeast and south-west, quite across, and, according to my opinion, having been formed there by the stream, inasmuch as the flood runs into the bay from the sea, east-southeast; the depth at Godyn's Point is caused by the tide flowing out along there with such rapidity.

Between the Hamels-Hoofden the width is about a cannon's

---

[1] It is not known how or why. [2] Sandy Hook. [3] Sandy Hook Bay.
[4] Narrows. The two islands mentioned next are Staten Island and Long Island. Fisher's Hook is Montauk Point.

shot of 2,000 [yards]; the depth 10, 11, 12 fathoms. They are tolerably high points, and well wooded. The west point is an island, inhabited by from 80 to 90 savages, who support themselves by planting maize. The east point is a very large island, full 24 leagues long, stretching east by south and east-southeast along the sea-coast, from the river to the east end of the Fisher's Hook. In some places it is from three to four leagues broad, and it has several creeks and bays, where many savages dwell, who support themselves by planting maize and making *sewan*, and who are called Souwenos and Sinnecox.[1] It is also full of oaks, elms, walnut and fir trees, also wild cedar and chestnut trees. The tribes are held in subjection by, and are tributary to, the Pyquans, hereafter named.[2] The land is in many places good, and fit for ploughing and sowing. It has many fine valleys, where there is good grass. Their form of government is like that of their neighbors, which is described hereafter.

The Hamels-Hoofden being passed, there is about a league width in the river, and also on the west side there is an inlet, where another river runs up about twenty leagues,[3] to the north-northeast, emptying into the Mauritse River in the highlands, thus making the northwest land opposite to the Manhatas an island eighteen leagues long. It is inhabited by the old Manhatans [*Manhatesen*]; they are about 200 to 300 strong, women and men, under different chiefs, whom they call *Sackimas*. This island is more mountainous than the other land on the southeast side of the river, which opposite to the Manhatas is about a league and a half in breadth. At the side of the before-mentioned little river, which we call "Achter Col," there is a great deal of waste reedy land; the rest is full of trees, and in some places there is good soil, where the savages plant their maize, upon which they live, as well as by hunting. The other side of the same small river, according to conjecture, is about 20 to 23 leagues broad to the South River,[4] in the neighborhood of the Sancicans, in so far as I have been able

[1] The Siwanoys lived near Pelham; the Shinnecocks at the east end of Long Island.

[2] No doubt in the missing portion; the Pequots are apparently meant.

[3] The Kill von Kull and Hackensack or Passaic River, whose upper waters come near to the Hudson, though without emptying into it.   [4] Delaware.

to make it out from the mouths of the savages; but as they live in a state of constant enmity with those tribes, the paths across are but little used, wherefore I have not been able to learn the exact distance; so that when we wish to send letters overland, they (the natives) take their way across the bay, and have the letters carried forward by others, unless one amongst them may happen to be on friendly terms, and who might venture to go there.

The island of the Manhatas extends two leagues in length [1] along the Mauritse River, from the point where the Fort "New Amsterdam" is building. It is about seven leagues in circumference, full of trees, and in the middle rocky to the extent of about two leagues in circuit. The north side has good land in two places, where two farmers, each with four horses, would have enough to do without much clearing at first. The grass is good in the forest and valleys, but when made into hay is not so nutritious for the cattle as here,[2] in consequence of its wild state, but it yearly improves by cultivation. On the east side there rises a large level field, of from 70 to 80 morgens of land,[3] through which runs a very fine fresh stream; so that that land can be ploughed without much clearing. It appears to be good. The six farms, four of which lie along the River Hellgate,[4] stretching to the south side of the island, have at least 60 morgens of land ready to be sown with winter seed, which at the most will have been ploughed eight times. But as the greater part must have some manure, inasmuch as it is so exhausted by the wild herbage, I am afraid that all will not be sown; and the more so, as the managers of the farms are hired men. The two hindermost farms, Nos. 1 and 2, are the best; the other farms have also good land, but not so much, and more sandy; so that they are best suited for rye and buckwheat.

The small fort, New Amsterdam, commenced to be built, is situated on a point opposite to Noten Island; [the channel between] is a gun-shot wide, and is full six or seven fathoms

---

[1] In fact, nearly four leagues.   [2] In Holland.

[3] A morgen is about two acres.

[4] I. e., East River. The West India Company's six farms lay east of the present Bowery, and extended from a fresh-water swamp occupying the site of the present Roosevelt and James Streets northward to Eighteenth or Twentieth Street.

deep in the middle. This point might, with little trouble, be made a small island, by cutting a canal through Blommaert's valley, so as to afford a haven winter and summer, for sloops and ships; and the whole of this little island ought, from its nature, to be made a superb fort, to be approached by land only on one side (since it is a triangle), thus protecting them both.[1] The river marks out, naturally, three angles; the most northern faces and commands, within the range of a cannon shot, the great Mauritse River and the land; the southernmost commands, on the water level, the channel between Noten Island and the fort, together with the Hellegat; the third point, opposite to Blommaert's valley, commands the lowland; the middle part, which ought to be left as a market-place, is a hillock, higher than the surrounding land, and should always serve as a battery, which might command the three points, if the streets should be arranged accordingly.

Up the river the east side is high, full of trees, and in some places there is a little good land, where formerly many people have dwelt, but who for the most part have died or have been driven away by the Wappenos.

These tribes of savages all have a government. The men in general are rather tall, well proportioned in their limbs, and of an orange color, like the Brazilians; very inveterate against those whom they hate; cruel by nature, and so inclined to freedom that they cannot by any means be brought to work; they support themselves by hunting, and when the spring comes, by fishing. In April, May, and June, they follow the course of these [the fish], which they catch with a drag-net they themselves knit very neatly, of the wild hemp, from which the women and old men spin the thread. The kinds of fish which they principally take at this time are shad, but smaller than those in this country ordinarily are, though quite as fat, and very bony; the largest fish is a sort of white salmon, which is of very good flavor, and quite as large; it has white scales; the heads are so full of fat that in some there are two or three spoonfuls, so that there is good eating for one who is fond of

---

[1] *I. e.*, both Fort Amsterdam and the little island itself. Blommaert's Vly was a low, damp depression running northeast and southwest about on the line of the present Broad Street. A ditch to drain it was constructed before 1643, and widened into a canal about 1657.

picking heads. It seems that this fish makes them lascivious, for it is often observed that those who have caught any when they have gone fishing, have given them, on their return, to the women, who look for them anxiously. Our people also confirm this. . . .

As an employment in winter they make *sewan*, which is an oblong bead that they make from cockle-shells, which they find on the sea-shore, and they consider it as valuable as we do money here, since one can buy with it everything they have; they string it, and wear it around the neck and hands; they also make bands of it, which the women wear on the forehead under the hair, and the men around the body; and they are as particular about the stringing and sorting as we can be here about pearls. They are very fond of a game they call *Senneca*, played with some round rushes, similar to the Spanish feather-grass, which they understand how to shuffle and deal as though they were playing with cards; and they win from each other all that they possess, even to the lappet with which they cover their private parts, and so they separate from each other quite naked. They are very much addicted to promiscuous intercourse. Their clothing is [so simple as to leave the body] almost naked. In the winter time they usually wear a dressed deer skin; some have a bear's skin about the body; some a coat of scales; some a covering made of turkey feathers which they understand how to knit together very oddly, with small strings. They also use a good deal of duffel cloth, which they buy from us, and which serves for their blanket by night, and their dress by day.

The women are fine looking, of middle stature, well proportioned, and with finely cut features; with long and black hair, and black eyes set off with fine eyebrows; they are of the same color as the men. They smear their bodies and hair with grease, which makes them smell very rankly; they are very much given to promiscuous intercourse.

They have a marriage custom amongst them, namely: when there is one who resolves to take a particular person for his wife, he collects a fathom or two of sewan, and comes to the nearest friends of the person whom he desires, to whom he declares his object in her presence, and if they are satisfied with him, he agrees with them how much sewan he shall give

her for a bridal present; that being done, he then gives her
all the Dutch beads he has, which they call *Machampe,* and
also all sorts of trinkets. If she be a young virgin, he must
wait six weeks more before he can sleep with her, during
which time she bewails or laments over her virginity, which
they call *Collatismarrenitten;* all this time she sits with a
blanket over her head, without wishing to look at any one, or
any one being permitted to look at her. This period being
elapsed, her bridegroom comes to her; he in the mean time has
been supporting himself by hunting, and what he has taken he
brings there with him; they then eat together with the friends,
and sing and dance together, which they call *Kintikaen.* That
being done, the wife must provide the food for herself and her
husband, as far as breadstuffs are concerned, and [should
they fall short] she must buy what is wanting with her sewan.

For this reason they are obliged to watch the season for
sowing. At the end of March they begin to break up the earth
with mattocks, which they buy from us for the skins of beavers
or otters, or for sewan. They make heaps like molehills, each
about two and a half feet from the others, which they sow or
plant in April with maize, in each heap five or six grains; in
the middle of May, when the maize is the height of a finger or
more, they plant in each heap three or four Turkish beans,
which then grow up with and against the maize, which serves
for props, for the maize grows on stalks similar to the sugar-
cane. It is a grain to which much labor must be given, with
weeding and earthing-up, or it does not thrive; and to this
the women must attend very closely. The men would not
once look to it, for it would compromise their dignity too much,
unless they are very old and cannot follow the chase. Those
stalks which are low and bear no ears, they pluck up in August,
and suck out the sap, which is as sweet as if it were sugar-cane.
When they wish to make use of the grain for bread or porridge,
which they call *Sappaen,* they first boil it and then beat it
flat upon a stone; then they put it into a wooden mortar,
which they know how to hollow out by fire, and then they have
a stone pestle, which they know how to make themselves, with
which they pound it small, and sift it through a small basket,
which they understand how to weave of the rushes before
mentioned. The finest meal they mix with lukewarm water,

and knead it into dough, then they make round flat little cakes
of it, of the thickness of an inch or a little more, which they
bury in hot ashes, and so bake into bread; and when these are
baked they have some clean fresh water by them in which they
wash them while hot, one after another, and it is good bread,
but heavy. The coarsest meal they boil into a porridge, as is
before mentioned, and it is good eating when there is butter
over it, but a food which is very soon digested. The grain
being dried, they put it into baskets woven of rushes or wild
hemp, and bury it in the earth, where they let it lie, and go
with their husbands and children in October to hunt deer,
leaving at home with their maize the old people who cannot
follow; in December they return home, and the flesh which
they have not been able to eat while fresh, they smoke on the
way, and bring it back with them. They come home as fat
as moles.

When a woman here addicts herself to fornication, and the
husband comes to know it, he thrashes her soundly, and if he
wishes to get rid of her, he summons the Sackima with her
friends, before whom he accuses her; and if she be found guilty
the Sackima commands one to cut off her hair in order that she
may be held up before the world as a whore, which they call
poerochque; and then the husband takes from her everything
that she has, and drives her out of the house; if there be
children, they remain with her, for they are fond of them beyond measure. They reckon consanguinity to the eighth
degree, and revenge an injury from generation to generation
unless it be atoned for; and even then there is mischief enough,
for they are very revengeful.

And when a man is unfaithful, the wife accuses him before
the Sackima, which most frequently happens when the wife
has a preference for another man. The husband being found
guilty, the wife is permitted to draw off his right shoe and left
stocking (which they make of deer or elk skins, which they
know how to prepare very broad and soft, and wear in the
winter time); she then tears off the lappet that covers his
private parts, gives him a kick behind, and so drives him out
of the house; and then "Adam" scampers off.

It would seem that they are very libidinous—in this respect very unfaithful to each other; whence it results that they

breed but few children, so that it is a wonder when a woman
has three or four children, particularly by any one man whose
name can be certainly known. They must not have intercourse with those of their own family within the third degree,
or it would be considered an abominable thing.

Their political government is democratic. They have a
chief Sackima whom they choose by election, who generally
is he who is richest in sewan, though of less consideration in
other respects. When any stranger comes, they bring him to
the Sackima. On first meeting they do not speak—they
smoke a pipe of tobacco; that being done, the Sackima asks:
"Whence do you come?" the stranger then states that, and
further what he has to say, before all who are present or choose
to come. That being done, the Sackima announces his opinion
to the people, and if they agree thereto, they give all together a
sigh—"*He!*"—and if they do not approve, they keep silence,
and all come close to the Sackima, and each sets forth his
opinion till they agree; that being done, they come all together again to the stranger, to whom the Sackima then announces what they have determined, with the reasons moving
them thereto.

All travellers who stop over night come to the Sackima,
if they have no acquaintances there, and are entertained by
the expenditure of as much sewan as is allowed for that purpose; therefore the Sackimas generally have three or four
wives, each of whom has to furnish her own seed-corn.

The Sackima has his fixed fine of sewan for fighting and
causing blood to flow. When any are—[*here four pages, at
least, are missing in the original manuscript*].

Coming out of the river Nassau,[1] you sail east-and-by-north
about fourteen leagues, along the coast, a half mile from the
shore, and you then come to "Frenchman's Point" at a small
river where those of Patucxet have a house made of hewn oak
planks, called Aptucxet,[2] where they keep two men, winter and

[1] Though De Laet gives the name "river or bay of Nassau" to Buzzard's Bay,
and the same is plainly intended by the map in the *Westindische Paskaert* of 1621,
De Rasieres apparently means Sakonnet River.

[2] Or Manomet, now improperly called Monument, at the north end of Buzzard's Bay, where the Plymouth settlers had lately established a trading-post.
See Bradford's *History of Plymouth Plantation*, in this series, p. 222.

summer, in order to maintain the trade and possession. Here also they have built a shallop, in order to go and look after the trade in sewan, in Sloup's Bay and thereabouts, because they are afraid to pass Cape Mallabaer, and in order to avoid the length of the way; which I have prevented for this year by selling them fifty fathoms of sewan, because the seeking after sewan by them is prejudicial to us, inasmuch as they would, by so doing, discover the trade in furs; which if they were to find out, it would be a great trouble for us to maintain, for they already dare to threaten that if we will not leave off dealing with that people, they will be obliged to use other means; if they do that now, while they are yet ignorant how the case stands, what will they do when they do get a notion of it? [1]

From Aptucxet the English can come in six hours, through the woods, passing several little rivulets of fresh water, to New Plymouth, the principal place in the district Patucxet, so called in their patent from His Majesty in England.[2]

New Plymouth lies in a large bay to the north of Cape Cod, or Mallabaer, east and west from the said [north] point of the cape, which can be easily seen in clear weather. Directly before the commenced town lies a sand-bank,[3] about twenty paces broad, whereon the sea breaks violently with an easterly and

---

[1] These remarks, and the interesting description of New Plymouth which follows, are due to a visit which Rasieres paid to the colony in October, 1627. Friendly correspondence between the two colonies had begun in the preceding March, with a letter from Rasieres as secretary which Bradford translates in his *History*, pp. 223–225, and Bradford's reply, which is given there, and, with other letters, in the *Collections of the Massachusetts Historical Society*, III. 51–57. Among these is one which Rasieres wrote, on arriving at Frenchman's Point, "from aboard the bark *Nassau*, the 4th of October."

[2] "They came up with their barke to Manamete, to their house ther, in which came their Secretarie Rasier; who was accompanied with a noyse of trumpeters, and some other attendants; and desired that they would send a boat for him, for he could not travill so farr over land. So they sent a boat to Manonscussett, and brought him to the plantation, with the cheefe of his company. And after some few days entertainmente, he returned to his barke, and some of them wente with him, and bought sundry of his goods. . . . But that which turned most to their profite, in time, was an entrance into the trade of Wampampeake. . . . Neither did the English of this plantation, or any other in the land, till now that they had knowledge of it from the Dutch, so much as know what it was, much less that it was a commoditie of that worth and valew." Bradford, pp. 234, 235 of the edition in this series.   [3] Plymouth Beach.

east-northeasterly wind. On the north side there lies a small island [1] where one must run close along, in order to come before the town; then the ships run behind that bank and lie in a very good roadstead. The bay is very full of fish, [chiefly] of cod, so that the governor before named has told me that when the people have a desire for fish they send out two or three persons in a sloop, whom they remunerate for their trouble, and who bring them in three or four hours' time as much fish as the whole community require for a whole day—and they muster about fifty families.

At the south side of the town there flows down a small river of fresh water, very rapid, but shallow, which takes its rise from several lakes in the land above, and there empties into the sea; where in April and the beginning of May, there come so many shad from the sea which want to ascend that river, that it is quite surprising. This river the English have shut in with planks, and in the middle with a little door, which slides up and down, and at the sides with trellice work, through which the water has its course, but which they can also close with slides.

At the mouth they have constructed it with planks, like an eel-pot, with wings, where in the middle is also a sliding door, and with trellice work at the sides, so that between the two [dams] there is a square pool, into which the fish aforesaid come swimming in such shoals, in order to get up above, where they deposit their spawn, that at one tide there are 10,000 to 12,000 fish in it, which they shut off in the rear at the ebb, and close up the trellices above, so that no more water comes in; then the water runs out through the lower trellices, and they draw out the fish with baskets, each according to the land he cultivates, and carry them to it, depositing in each hill three or four fishes, and in these they plant their maize, which grows as luxuriantly therein as though it were the best manure in the world. And if they do not lay this fish therein, the maize will not grow, so that such is the nature of the soil.

New Plymouth lies on the slope of a hill stretching east towards the sea-coast, with a broad street about a cannon shot of 800 feet long, leading down the hill; with a [street] crossing

[1] Saquish.

in the middle, northwards to the rivulet and southwards to the land.[1]   The houses are constructed of hewn planks, with gardens also enclosed behind and at the sides with hewn planks, so that their houses and court-yards are arranged in very good order, with a stockade against a sudden attack; and at the ends of the streets there are three wooden gates.   In the centre, on the cross street, stands the governor's house, before which is a square stockade upon which four patereros are mounted, so as to enfilade the streets.   Upon the hill they have a large square house, with a flat roof, made of thick sawn plank, stayed with oak beams, upon the top of which they have six cannon, which shoot iron balls of four and five pounds, and command the surrounding country.   The lower part they use for their church, where they preach on Sundays and the usual holidays. They assemble by beat of drum, each with his musket or firelock, in front of the captain's door; they have their cloaks on, and place themselves in order, three abreast, and are led by a sergeant without beat of drum.   Behind comes the governor, in a long robe; beside him, on the right hand, comes the preacher with his cloak on, and on the left hand the captain with his side-arms, and cloak on, and with a small cane in his hand; and so they march in good order, and each sets his arms down near him.   Thus they are constantly on their guard night and day.

Their government is after the English form.   The governor has his council, which is chosen every year by the entire community, by election or prolongation of term.   In inheritances they place all the children in one degree, only the eldest son has an acknowledgment [2] for his seniority of birth.   They have made stringent laws and ordinances upon the subject of fornication and adultery, which laws they maintain and enforce very strictly indeed, even among the tribes which live amongst them.   They speak very angrily when they hear from the savages that we live so barbarously in these respects, and without punishment.   Their farms are not so good as ours, because they are more stony, and consequently not so suitable for the plough.   They apportion their land according as each has means to contribute to the eighteen thousand guilders which

---

[1] He reverses the actual bearings; and the street first mentioned was longer, 1,150 feet.   [2] A double share.

they have promised to those who had sent them out;· whereby
they have their freedom without rendering an account to any
one; only if the King should choose to send a governor-general
they would be obliged to acknowledge him as sovereign over-
lord.   The maize seed which they do not require for their own
use is delivered over to the governor, at three guilders the
bushel, who in his turn sends it in sloops to the north [2] for the
trade in skins among the savages; they reckon one bushel
of maize against one pound of beaver's skins; the profits are
divided according to what each has contributed, and they are
credited for the amount in the account of what each has to
contribute yearly towards the reduction of his obligation.
Then with the remainder they purchase what next they require,
and which the governor takes care to provide every year.
They have better sustenance than ourselves, because they have
the fish so abundant before their doors.   There are also many
birds, such as geese, herons and cranes, and other small-legged
birds, which are in great abundance there in the winter.

The tribes in their neighborhood have all the same customs
as already above described, only they are better conducted
than ours, because the English give them the example of better
ordinances and a better life; and who also, to a certain degree,
give them laws, in consequence of the respect they from the
very first have established amongst them.

The savages [there] utilize their youth in labor better than
the savages round about us: the young girls in sowing maize,
the young men in hunting. They teach them to endure
privation in the field in a singular manner, to wit:

When there is a youth who begins to approach manhood, he
is taken by his father, uncle, or nearest friend, and is conducted
blindfolded into a wilderness, in order that he may not know
the way, and is left there by night or otherwise, with a bow
and arrows, and a hatchet and a knife. He must support
himself there a whole winter with what the scanty earth furnishes at this season, and by hunting. Towards the spring
they come again, and fetch him out of it, take him home and

---

[1] By the agreement of November 15, 1626, with the merchant adventurers,
for which see Bradford, pp. 214–215. Rasieres roughly translates £1,800 into
18,000 g.

[2] To the Kennebec region, where the Plymouth people had a trading-post.

feed him up again until May. He must then go out again
every morning with the person who is ordered to take him in
hand; he must go into the forest to seek wild herbs and roots,
which they know to be the most poisonous and bitter; these
they bruise in water and press the juice out of them, which he
must drink, and immediately have ready such herbs as will
preserve him from death or vomiting; and if he cannot retain
it, he must repeat the dose until he can support it, and until
his constitution becomes .accustomed to it so that he can
retain it.

Then he comes home, and is brought by the men and
women, all singing and dancing, before the Sackima; and if he
has been able to stand it all well, and if he is fat and sleek, a
wife is given to him.

In that district there are no lions or bears, but there are
the same kinds of other game, such as deers, hinds, beavers,
otters, foxes, lynxes, seals and fish, as in our district of country.
The savages say that far in the interior there are certain beasts
of the size of oxen, having but one horn, which are very fierce.
The English have used great diligence in order to see them, but
cannot succeed therein, although they have seen the flesh and
hides of them which were brought to them by the savages.
There are also very large elks there, which the English have
indeed seen.

The lion skins which we sometimes see our savages wear
are not large, so that the animal itself must be small; they are
of a mouse-gray color, short in the hair and long in the claws.

The bears are some of them large and some small; but the
largest are not so large as the middle-sized ones which come
from Greenland. Their fur is long and black and their claws
large. The savages esteem the flesh and grease as a great
dainty.

Of the birds, there is a kind like starlings, which we call
maize thieves, because they do so much damage to the maize.
They fly in large flocks, so that they flatten the corn in any place
where they alight, just as if cattle had lain there. Sometimes
we take them by surprise and fire amongst them with hail-
shot, immediately that we have made them rise, so that sixty,
seventy, and eighty fall all at once, which is very pleasant
to see.

There are also very large turkeys living wild; they have very long legs, and can run extraordinarily fast, so that we generally take savages with us when we go to hunt them; for even when one has deprived them of the power of flying, they yet run so fast that we cannot catch them unless their legs are hit also.

In the autumn and in the spring there come a great many geese, which are very good, and easy to shoot, inasmuch as they congregate together in such large flocks. There are two kinds of partridges; the one sort are quite as small as quails and the other like the ordinary kind here. There are also hares, but few in number, and not larger than a middle-sized rabbit; and they principally frequent where the land is rocky.

This, sir, is what I have been able to communicate to you from memory, respecting New Netherland and its neighborhood, in discharge of my bounden duty; I beg that the same may so be favorably received by you, and I beg to recommend myself for such further service as you may be pleased to command me in, wherever you may find me.

In everything your faithful servant,

ISAACK DE RASIERES.

LETTER OF REVEREND JONAS MICHAËLIUS,
1628

INTRODUCTION

THE established church in the United Netherlands was the Reformed Church. Its polity was that of Geneva or of Presbyterianism. The minister and ruling or lay elders of the local church formed its consistory, corresponding to the Scottish or American kirk session. The next higher power, administrative or judicial, resided in the classis, consisting of all the ministers in a given district and one elder from each parish therein, and corresponding to the presbytery. It had power to license and ordain, install and remove ministers. Above this body stood the provincial synod, and above that the (occasional) national synods. In 1624 the synod of North Holland decreed that supervision over the churches in the East Indies should belong to the churches and classes within whose bounds were located the various "chambers" of the East India Company. The same rule was applied in the case of the West India Company's settlements. Under this rule the first minister sent out to New Netherland was placed under the jurisdiction of the Classis of Amsterdam, since the colony was under the charge of the Amsterdam Chamber. Many extracts from the minutes of that classis, and what remains of its correspondence with the ministers in New Netherland, are printed in the volumes published by the State of New York under the title *Ecclesiastical Records, State of New York* (six volumes, Albany, 1901–1905). From 1639, if not earlier, a committee of the classis, called "Deputati ad Res Exteras," was given charge of most of the details of correspondence with the Dutch Reformed churches in America, Africa, the East and foreign European countries.

As mentioned by Wassenaer (p. 83 above), "comforters of

the sick," who were ecclesiastical officers but not ministers, were first sent out to New Netherland. The first minister was Reverend Jonas Jansen Michielse, or, to employ the Latinized form of his name which he, according to clerical habit, was accustomed to use, Jonas Johannis Michaëlius. Michaëlius was born in North Holland in 1577, entered the University of Leyden as a student of divinity in 1600, became minister at Nieuwbokswoude in 1612 and at Hem, near Enkhuizen, in 1614. At some time between April, 1624, and August, 1625, he went out to San Salvador (Bahia, Brazil), recently conquered by the West India Company's fleet, and after brief service there to one of their posts on the West African coast. Returning thence, he was, early in 1628, sent out to Manhattan, where he arrived April 7. It is not known just when he returned to Holland, but he appears to have been under engagement for three years. In 1637–1638 we find the classis vainly endeavoring to send him again to New Netherland, but prevented by the Company, which had a veto upon all such appointments in its dominions.

About half a century ago the following precious letter of Michaëlius, describing New Netherland as it appeared in its earliest days to the eyes of an educated clergyman of the Dutch Church, was discovered in Amsterdam, and printed by Mr. J. J. Bodel Nijenhuis in the *Kerk-historisch Archief*, part i. An English translation of it, with an introduction, was then privately printed in a pamphlet by Mr. Henry C. Murphy, an excellent scholar in New Netherland history, who was at that time minister of the United States to the Netherlands. This pamphlet, entitled *The First Minister of the Dutch Reformed Church in the United States* (The Hague, 1858), was reprinted in 1858 in *Documents relative to the Colonial History of the State of New York*, II. 757–770, in 1881 in the *Collections of the New York Historical Society*, XIII, and in 1883, at Amsterdam, by Frederik Muller and Co., who added a photographic fac-simile of full size and a transcript of the Dutch text. In 1896 a reduced fac-simile of the original letter, with an amended translation by Reverend John G. Fagg, appeared in the *Year Book* of the (Collegiate) Reformed Protestant Dutch Church of New York City, and also separately for private circulation, and in 1901 the Dutch text with Reverend Mr. Fagg's translation was printed in *Ecclesiastical Records*, I. 49–68, which also contains (p. 336) a photographic fac-simile of the concluding portion of the manuscript. Another is in *Memorial History*, I. 166. The original is in the New York Public Library (Lenox Building). Reverend Adrianus Smoutius, to whom the letter was addressed, was an ultra-Calvinist clergyman, who led a stormy life, but from 1620 to 1630 was a minister of the collegiate churches of Amsterdam, and as such a member of the classis under whose charge Michaëlius served.

For many years this letter of August 11, 1628, was supposed to be the earliest extant letter or paper written at Manhattan. But a letter of three days earlier was recently discovered, which Michaëlius wrote on August 8 to Jan Foreest, a magistrate of Hoorn and secretary to the Executive Council (*Gecommitteerde Raden*) of the States of the Province of Holland. This letter mentions epistles also sent to two clergymen in Holland and to the writer's brother. It was printed by Mr. Dingman Versteeg in *Manhattan in* 1628 (New York, 1904). All these letters were presumably prepared to be sent home on the same ship. The two which are extant parallel each other to a large extent. That which follows, though second in order of time, is intrinsically a little more interesting than the other. Mr. Fagg's translation has in the main been followed.

LETTER OF REVEREND JONAS MICHAËLIUS,
1628

The Reverend, Learned and Pious Mr. Adrianus Smoutius, Faithful Minister of the Holy Gospel of Christ in his Church, dwelling upon the Heerengracht, not far from the West India House at Amsterdam. By a friend, whom God preserve.
The Peace of Christ to You.

Reverend Sir, Well Beloved Brother in Christ, Kind Friend!

THE favorable opportunity which now presents itself of writing to your Reverence I cannot let pass, without embracing it, according to my promise. And, first to unburden myself in this communication of a sorrowful circumstance, it pleased the Lord, seven weeks after we arrived in this country, to take from me my good partner, who had been to me, for more than sixteen years, a virtuous, faithful, and altogether amiable yoke-fellow; and I now find myself alone with three children,[1] very much discommoded, without her society and assistance. But what have I to say? The Lord himself has done this, against whom no one can oppose himself. And why should I even wish to, knowing that all things must work together for good to them that love God? I hope therefore to bear my cross patiently, and by the grace and help of the Lord, not to let the courage fail me which in my duties here I so especially need.

The voyage was long, namely, from the 24th of January till the 7th of April, when we first set foot upon land here. Of storm and tempest which fell hard upon the good wife and children, though they bore it better as regards sea-sickness and

[1] Two daughters and a son, Jan, whom he had placed in the house and custody of skipper Jan Jansen Brouwer.

fear than I had expected, we had no lack, particularly in the vicinity of the Bermudas and the rough coasts of this country. Our fare in the ship was very poor and scanty, so that my blessed wife and children, not eating with us in the cabin, on account of the little room in it, had a worse lot than the sailors themselves; and that by reason of a wicked cook who annoyed them in every way; but especially by reason of the captain himself,[1] who, although I frequently complained of it in the most courteous manner, did not concern himself in the least about correcting the rascal; nor did he, even when they were all sick, give them anything which could do them any good, although there was enough in the ship: as he himself knew very well where to find it in order, out of meal times, to fill his own stomach. All the relief which he gave us, consisted merely in liberal promises, with a drunken head; upon which nothing followed when he was sober but a sour face; and he raged at the officers and kept himself constantly to the wine, both at sea and especially here while lying in the river; so that he daily walked the deck drunk and with an empty head, seldom coming ashore to the Council and never to Divine service. We bore all with silence on board the ship; but it grieves me, when I think of it, on account of my wife; the more, because she was so situated as she was—believing that she was with child—and the time so short which she had yet to live. On my first voyage I roamed about with him a great deal, even lodged in the same hut, but never knew that he was such a brute and drunkard. But he was then under the direction of Mr. Lam,[2] and now he had the chief command himself. I have also written to Mr. Godyn [3] about it, considering it necessary that it should be known.

Our coming here was agreeable to all, and I hope, by the grace of the Lord, that my service will not be unfruitful. The people, for the most part, are rather rough and unrestrained, but I find in almost all of them both love and respect towards me; two things with which hitherto the Lord has everywhere

---

[1] "Evert Croeger, with whom, prior to this, I had made long voyages, but never before did I know him well."—Letter of August 8 to Jan Foreest.

[2] Admiral Jan Dirckszoon Lam, who in 1625 and 1626 was in command of a Dutch squadron on the west coast of Africa.

[3] Probably Samuel Godyn, a prominent director of the company.

graciously blessed my labors, and which in our calling, as your Reverence well knows and finds, are especially desirable, in order to make our ministry fruitful.

From the beginning we established the form of a church; and as Brother Bastiaen Crol [1] very seldom comes down from Fort Orange, because the directorship of that fort and the trade there is committed to him, it has been thought best to choose two elders for my assistance and for the proper consideration of all such ecclesiastical matters as might occur, intending the coming year, if the Lord permit, to let one of them retire, and to choose another in his place from a double number first lawfully proposed to the congregation. One of those whom we have now chosen is the Honorable Director [2] himself, and the other is the storekeeper of the Company, Jan Huygen, [3] his brother-in-law, persons of very good character, as far as I have been able to learn, having both been formerly in office in the Church, the one as deacon, and the other as elder in the Dutch and French churches, respectively, at Wesel. [4]

At the first administration of the Lord's Supper which was observed, not without great joy and comfort to many, we had fully fifty communicants—Walloons and Dutch; of whom, a portion made their first confession of faith before us, and others exhibited their church certificates. Others had forgotten to bring their certificates with them, not thinking that a church would be formed and established here; and some who brought

---

[1] Sebastian Janszoon Krol came out to New Netherland in 1626 as a "comforter of the sick" at Manhattan, but before long went up to Fort Orange, where he was chief agent for the company most of the time to March, 1632. Then, on Minuit's recall, he was director-general till Wouter van Twiller's arrival in April, 1633.

[2] Peter Minuit, born of Huguenot parentage in 1580 in Wesel, west Germany, was made director general of New Netherland in December, 1625, arrived in May, 1626, bought Manhattan Island of the Indians that summer, and remained in office till recalled early in 1632. In 1636–1637 he made arrangements with Blommaert and the Swedish government, in consequence of which he conducted the first Swedish colony to Delaware Bay, landing there in the spring of 1638, and establishing New Sweden on territory claimed by the Dutch. During the ensuing summer he perished in a hurricane at St. Christopher, in the West Indies.

[3] Probably the same as Jan Huych, comforter of the sick, mentioned on p. 83.

[4] Jan Huyghens was deacon of the Dutch Reformed church at Wesel in 1612; and probably Minuit was elder in the French church there.

them, had lost them unfortunately in a general conflagration, but they were admitted upon the satisfactory testimony of others to whom they were known, and also upon their daily good deportment, since one cannot observe strictly all the usual formalities in making a beginning under such circumstances.

We administer the Holy Supper of the Lord once in four months, provisionally, until a larger number of people shall otherwise require. The Walloons and French have no service on Sundays, otherwise than in the Dutch language, for those who understand no Dutch are very few. A portion of the Walloons are going back to the Fatherland, either because their years here are expired, or else because some are not very serviceable to the Company. Some of them live far away and could not well come in time of heavy rain and storm, so that they themselves cannot think it advisable to appoint any special service in French for so small a number, and that upon an uncertainty. Nevertheless, the Lord's Supper is administered to them in the French language, and according to the French mode, with a sermon preceding, which I have before me in writing, so long as I can not trust myself extemporaneously.[1] If in this and in other matters your Reverence and the Reverend Brethren of the Consistory, who have special superintendence over us here, deem it necessary to administer to us any correction, instruction or good advice, it will be agreeable to us and we shall thank your Reverence therefor; since we must all have no other object than the glory of God in the building up of his kingdom and the salvation of many souls. I keep myself as far as practicable within the pale of my calling, wherein I find myself sufficiently occupied. And although our small consistory embraces at the most—when Brother Crol is down here—not more than four persons, all of whom, myself alone excepted, have also public business to attend to, I still hope to separate carefully the ecclesiastical from the civil matters which occur, so that each one will be occupied with his own subject.

And though many things are *mixti generis*, and political and ecclesiastical persons can greatly assist each other, nevertheless

---

[1] That is, to preach extempore in French.

the matters and officers proceeding together must not be mixed but kept separate, in order to prevent all confusion and disorder. As the Council of this place consists of good people, who are, however, for the most part simple and have little experience in public affairs, I should have little objection to serve them in any difficult or dubious affair with good advice, provided I considered myself capable and my advice should be asked; in which case I suppose that I should not do amiss nor be suspected by any one of being a πολυπράγμων or ἀλλοτριοεπίσκοπος.[1]

In my opinion it would be well that the Honorable Directors should furnish this place with plainer and more precise instructions to the rulers, that they may distinctly know how to conduct themselves in all possible public difficulties and events; and also that I should some time have here all such *Acta Synodalia*, as have been adopted in the synods of Holland; both the special ones of our quarter,[2] and those which are provincial and national, in relation to ecclesiastical difficulties; or at least such of them as in the judgment of the Honorable Brethren at Amsterdam would be most likely to be of service to us here. In the meantime, I hope matters will go well here, if only on our part we do our best in all sincerity and honest zeal; whereunto I have from the first entirely devoted myself, and wherein I have also hitherto, by the grace of God, had no just cause to complain of any one. And if any dubious matters of importance come before me, and especially if they will admit of any delay, I shall refer myself to the good and prudent advice of the Honorable Brethren, to whom I have already wholly commended myself.

As to the natives of this country, I find them entirely savage and wild, strangers to all decency, yea, uncivil and stupid as garden poles, proficient in all wickedness and godlessness; devilish men, who serve nobody but the Devil, that is, the spirit which in their language they call Menetto; under which title they comprehend everything that is subtle and crafty and

---

[1] I Peter iv. 15; a meddler or "busy-body in other men's matters."

[2] *I. e.*, acts of the synod of North Holland. North Holland was not at this time a province, but merely a part of the province of Holland, the chief of the seven United Provinces. The national *Acta* would probably be those of the six fundamental synodical conventions of 1568–1586 and the Synod of Dort.

beyond human skill and power. They have so much witch-craft, divination, sorcery and wicked arts, that they can hardly be held in by any bands or locks. They are as thievish and treacherous as they are tall; and in cruelty they are altogether inhuman, more than barbarous, far exceeding the Africans.[1]

I have written concerning this matter to several persons elsewhere, not doubting that Brother Crol will have written sufficient to your Reverence, or to the Honorable Directors; as also of the base treachery and the murders which the Mohicans, at the upper part of this river, had planned against Fort Orange, but which failed through the gracious interposi-tion of the Lord, for our good—who, when it pleases Him, knows how to pour, unexpectedly, natural impulses into these unnatural men, in order to prevent them. How these people can best be led to the true knowledge of God and of the Media-tor Christ, is hard to say. I cannot myself wonder enough who it is that has imposed so much upon your Reverence and many others in the Fatherland, concerning the docility of these people and their good nature, the proper *principia religionis* and *vestigia legis naturae* which are said to be among them; in whom I have as yet been able to discover hardly a single good point, except that they do not speak so jeeringly and so scoffingly of the godlike and glorious majesty of their Creator as the Africans dare to do. But it may be because they have no certain knowledge of Him, or scarcely any. If we speak to them of God, it appears to them like a dream; and we are com-pelled to speak of him, not under the name of Menetto, whom they know and serve—for that would be blasphemy—but of one great, yea, most high, *Sackiema*, by which name they—living without a king—call him who has the command over several hundred among them, and who by our people are called *Sackemakers;* and as the people listen, some will begin to mutter and shake their heads as if it were a silly fable; and others, in order to express regard and friendship for such a proposition, will say *Orith* (That is good). Now, by what means are we to lead this people to salvation, or to make a salutary breach among them? I take the liberty on this point of en-larging somewhat to your Reverence.

---

[1] He had served on the west coast of Africa; see the introduction.

Their language, which is the first thing to be employed with them, methinks is entirely peculiar. Many of our common people call it an easy language, which is soon learned, but I am of a contrary opinion. For those who can understand their words to some extent and repeat them, fail greatly in the pronunciation, and speak a broken language, like the language of Ashdod.[1] For these people have difficult aspirates and many guttural letters, which are formed more in the throat than by the mouth, teeth and lips, to which our people not being accustomed, make a bold stroke at the thing and imagine that they have accomplished something wonderful. It is true one can easily learn as much as is sufficient for the purposes of trading, but this is done almost as much by signs with the thumb and fingers as by speaking; and this cannot be done in religious matters. It also seems to us that they rather design to conceal their language from us than to properly communicate it, except in things which happen in daily trade; saying that it is sufficient for us to understand them in that; and then they speak only half sentences, shortened words, and frequently call out a dozen things and even more; and all things which have only a rude resemblance to each other, they frequently call by the same name. In truth it is a made-up, childish language; so that even those who can best of all speak with the savages, and get along well in trade, are nevertheless wholly in the dark and bewildered when they hear the savages talking among themselves.

It would be well then to leave the parents as they are, and begin with the children who are still young. So be it. But they ought in youth to be separated from their parents; yea, from their whole nation. For, without this, they would forthwith be as much accustomed as their parents to the heathenish tricks and deviltries, which are kneaded naturally in their hearts by themselves through a just judgment of God; so that having once, by habit, obtained deep root, they would with great difficulty be emancipated therefrom. But this separation is hard to effect. For the parents have a strong affection for their children, and are very loth to part with them; and when they are separated from them, as we have already had

---

[1] An allusion to Nehemiah xiii. 24

proof, the parents are never contented, but take them away stealthily, or induce them to run away. Nevertheless, although it would be attended with some expense, we ought, by means of presents and promises, to obtain the children, with the gratitude and consent of the parents, in order to place them under the instruction of some experienced and godly schoolmaster, where they may be instructed not only to speak, read, and write in our language, but also especially in the fundamentals of our Christian religion; and where, besides, they will see nothing but good examples of virtuous living; but they must sometimes speak their native tongue among themselves in order not to forget it, as being evidently a principal means of spreading the knowledge of religion through the whole nation. In the meantime we should not forget to beseech the Lord, with ardent and continual prayers, for His blessing; who can make things which are unseen suddenly and opportunely to appear; who gives life to the dead; calls that which is not as though it were; and being rich in mercy has pity on whom He will; as He has compassionated us to be His people; and has washed us clean, sanctified us and justified us, when we were covered with all manner of corruption, calling us to the blessed knowledge of His Son, and out of the power of darkness to His marvellous light. And this I regard so much the more necessary, as the wrath and curse of God, resting upon this miserable people, is found to be the heavier. Perchance God may at last have mercy upon them, that the fulness of the heathen may be gradually brought in and the salvation of our God may be here also seen among these wild savage men. I hope to keep a watchful eye over these people, and to learn as much as possible of their language, and to seek better opportunities for their instruction than hitherto it has been possible to find.

As to what concerns myself and my household affairs: I find myself by the loss of my good and helpful partner very much hindered and distressed—for my two little daughters are yet small; maid servants are not here to be had, at least none whom they can advise me to take; and the Angola slave women [1] are thievish, lazy, and useless trash. The young man

---

[1] Slavery was introduced into New Netherland two or three years before this, a number of negroes, some of them from Angola, having been imported in 1625 or 1626.

whom I took with me, I discharged after Whitsuntide, for the reason that I could not employ him out-of-doors at any working of the land, and in-doors he was a burden to me instead of an assistance.   He is now elsewhere at service among the farmers.

The promise which the Honorable Directors of the Company had made me of some morgens or acres of land for me to sustain myself, instead of a free table which otherwise belonged to me, is void and useless.   For their Honors well knew that there are no horses, cows, or laborers to be obtained here for money. Every one is short in these particulars and wants more.   I should not mind the expense if the opportunity only offered, for the sake of our own comfort, although there were no profit in it (the Honorable Directors nevertheless remaining indebted to me for as much as the value of a free table), for refreshment of butter, milk, etc., cannot be here obtained; though some is indeed sold at a very high price, for those who bring it in or be-speak it are jealous of each other.   So I shall be compelled to pass through the winter without butter and other necessities, which the ships do not bring with them to be sold here.   The rations, which are given out here, and charged for high enough, are all hard stale food, such as men are used to on board ship, and frequently not very good, and even so one cannot obtain as much as he desires.   I began to get considerable strength, by the grace of the Lord, but in consequence of this hard fare of beans and gray peas, which are hard enough, barley, stockfish, etc., without much change, I cannot fully recuperate as I otherwise would.   The summer yields something, but what is that for any one who does not feel well?   The savages also bring some things, but one who has no wares, such as knives, beads, and the like, or *seewan*, cannot come to any terms with them.   Though the people trade such things for proper wares, I know not whether it is permitted by the laws of the Company.   I have now ordered from Holland almost all necessaries; and I hope to pass through the winter, with hard and scanty food.

The country yields many good things for the support of life, but they are all too unfit and wild to be gathered.   Better regulations should be established, and people brought here who have the knowledge and implements for seeking out all kinds of things in their season and for securing and gathering them.

No doubt this will gradually be done. In the meanwhile, I wish the Honorable Directors to be courteously enquired of, how I can best have the opportunity to possess a portion of land, and (even at my own expense) to support myself upon it. For as long as there is no more accommodation to be obtained here from the country people, and I shall be compelled to order everything from the Fatherland at great expense and with much risk and trouble, or else live here upon these poor and hard rations alone, it will badly suit me and my children. We want ten or twelve more farmers with horses, cows and laborers in proportion, to furnish us with bread, milk products, and suitable fruits. For there are convenient places which can be easily protected and are very suitable, which can be bought from the savages for trifling toys, or could be occupied without risk, because we have more than enough shares which have never been abandoned but have been always reserved for that purpose.

The business of furs is dull on account of the new war of the Maechibaeys [1] against the Mohicans at the upper end of this river. There have occurred cruel murders on both sides. The Mohicans have fled and their lands are unoccupied and are very fertile and pleasant. It grieves us that there are no people, and that there is no order from the Honorable Directors to occupy the same. Much timber is cut here to carry to the Fatherland, but the vessels are too few to take much of it. They are making a windmill to saw lumber and we also have a gristmill. They bake brick here, but it is very poor. There is good material for burning lime, namely, oyster shells, in large quantities. The burning of potash has not succeeded; the master and his laborers are all greatly disappointed.

We are busy now in building a fort of good quarry stone, which is to be found not far from here in abundance. May the Lord only build and watch over our walls. There is good opportunity for making salt, for there are convenient places, the water is salt enough, and there is no want of heat in summer. Besides, what the waters yield, both of the sea and rivers, in all kinds of fish; and what the land possesses in all kinds of birds, game, and woods, with vegetables, fruits, roots, herbs and plants, both for eating and medicinal purposes, and with which wonderful cures can be effected, it would take too long

[1] Mohawks.

to tell, nor could I yet tell accurately. Your Reverence has already obtained some knowledge thereof and will be able to obtain from others further information. The country is good and pleasant, the climate is healthy, notwithstanding the sudden changes of cold and heat. The sun is very warm, the winter is fierce and severe and continues fully as long as in our country. The best remedy is not to spare the wood, of which there is enough, and to cover one's self with rough skins, which can also easily be obtained.

The harvest, God be praised, is in the barns, and is larger than ever before. There has been more work put on it than before. The ground is fertile enough to reward labor, but they must clear it well, and till it, just as our lands require. Until now there has been distress because many people were not very industrious, and also did not obtain proper sustenance for want of bread and other necessaries. But affairs are beginning to go better and to put on a different appearance, if only the Directors will send out good laborers and exercise all care that they be maintained as well as possible with what this country produces.

I had intended and promised [to write] to the Honorable Brethren, Rudolphus Petri, Joannes Sylvius and Domine Cloppenburg, who, with your Reverence, were charged with the superintendence of these regions;[1] but as this would take long and the time is short, and my occupations at the present time many, your Reverence will please to give my friendly and kind regards to their Reverences, and to excuse me, on condition that I remain their debtor to fulfill my promise—God willing— the next time. Be pleased also to give my sincere respects to the Reverend Domine Triglandius, and to all the Brethren of the Consistory [2] besides, to all of whom I have not thought it necessary to write particularly at this time, as they are made by me participants in these tidings, and are content to be fed from the hand of your Reverence. If it shall be convenient for your Reverence or any of the Reverend Brethren to write to me a letter concerning matters which might be important in

---

[1] This duty had been committed to them by the synod of North Holland. The preachers named in the text were all at this time active in Amsterdam; Sylvius and Triglandius since 1610, Petri since 1612, and Johannes Cloppenburg since 1621.   [2] Of Amsterdam.

any degree to me, it would be very interesting to me, living here in a wild country without any society of our order, and would be a spur to write more assiduously to the Reverend Brethren concerning what may happen here. And especially do not forget my hearty salutations to the beloved wife and brother-in-law of your Reverence, who have shown me nothing but friendship and kindness above my deserts. If there were anything in which I could in return serve or gratify your Reverence, I should be glad to do so, and should not be delinquent in anything.

Concluding then herewith, and commending myself to your Reverence's favor and to your holy prayers to the Lord,

Reverend and Learned Sir, Beloved Brother in Christ, and Kind Friend:

Heartily commending your Reverence and all of you to Almighty God, to continued health and prosperity, and to eternal salvation, by His Grace.

From the island of Manhatas in New Netherland, this 11th of August, Anno 1628, by me, your Reverence's very obedient servant in Christ,

JONAS MICHAËLIUS.

NARRATIVE OF A JOURNEY INTO THE MOHAWK AND ONEIDA COUNTRY, 1634-1635

INTRODUCTION

THE manuscript of the narrative which follows was found in Amsterdam in the summer of 1895 by General James Grant Wilson. "It consists," he says, "of 32 pages of well-preserved foolscap, which had been buried in a Dutch garret of Amsterdam for two hundred and sixty years." It is apparently identical with a journal which Mr. Nicolaas de Roever, late archivist of the city of Amsterdam, in his articles in *Oud Holland* on Kiliaen van Rensselaer and his colony of Rensselaerswyck (articles lately translated in the *Van Rensselaer Bowier Manuscripts*), mentioned in 1890 as then existing among the papers of the original patroon. General Wilson published a translation of the journal in the *Independent*, XLVII. 1317, and again, with an introduction and notes, in the *Annual Report of the American Historical Association* for 1895, pp. 81–104.

The journal acquired by General Wilson was represented to have been written by Arent van Curler, afterwards a man of much distinction in the colony, especially in relations with the Indians, and it was printed as Van Curler's. But it has now been shown in the *Van Rensselaer Bowier Manuscripts*, pp. 78, 390, that Van Curler first came out in 1637, a youth of eighteen. Upon the supposition that the second sentence read "came to our commissioners (or factors) Marten Gerritsen and me," and that therefore the author must be sought among the *commis* of the Dutch West India Company at Fort Orange, Mr. A. J. F. van Laer, the learned editor of that volume, has conjectured that the journal was written by Dirck Cornelisz Duyster, who was *commis* at the fort at about this epoch. But, as will be seen from the text below, the proper reading puts that word in the singular number, "came to our factor Marten Gerritsen and (to) me"; phrases in the letters of Kiliaen van Rensselaer, moreover, seem to imply that Duyster was in Holland at the time of the journey. Yet the use of the word "our" indicates that the writer was in the employ of the Company, as Marten Gerritsen was, and not of the patroon. It is also evident that he was a man of education and some importance. In view of these circumstances Mr. van Laer is now inclined to believe that Harmen Meyndertsz van den Bogaert, the surgeon of the fort, was the author.

Whoever the author may have been, the narrative has a high importance as presenting the first description of the life of the Iroquois by any man who had travelled among them. The writer and his companions made their way in the depth of winter through the country of the Mohawks and the Oneidas (though he calls them Senecas), and saw some of the Onondagas. As will be seen from the attempts made in the foot-notes to trace his route, he penetrated up the valley of the Mohawk River as far as the old castle of the Oneidas, or to a point midway between Utica and Syracuse. His "leagues" (Dutch *mylen*) are, it should be mentioned, short leagues, nearer two English miles than three, as would be natural to one making his way for the first time through the wilderness.

Marten Gerritsen the factor had been one of Director van Twiller's council, and an early settler of Rensselaerswyck. Jeronimus de Lacroix is several times referred to in letters of the patroon Kiliaen van Rensselaer, 1634–1643, but not in such a way as to define his position. Of Willem Tomassen nothing seems to be known.

The version which follows is a revision of the previous translation, made by Mr. S. G. Nissensen from the original manuscript, of which we were permitted to make use through the kindness of its present owner, Mr. W. A. White.

NARRATIVE OF A JOURNEY INTO THE
MOHAWK AND ONEIDA COUNTRY, 1634–1635

Praise the Lord above all—Fort Orange, 1634.

December 11. JOURNAL kept of the principal events that happened during the journey to the Maquas and Sinnekens [1] Indians. First, the reasons why we went on this journey were these, that the Maquas and Sinnekens very often came to our factor [*commis*] Marten Gerritsen and me stating that there were French Indians in their land, and that they had made a truce with them so that they, namely, the Maquas, wished to trade for their skins, because the Maquas Indians wanted to receive just as much for their skins as the French Indians did. So I proposed to Mr. Marten Gerritsen to go and see if it was true, so soon to run counter to their High Mightinesses; and, besides, trade was doing very badly, therefore I went as above with Jero[ni]mus [de] la Croex and Willem Tomassen. May the Lord bless my voyage! We went between nine and ten o'clock with five Maquas Indians, mostly northwest above eight leagues, and arrived at half-past twelve in the evening at a hunter's cabin, where we slept for the night, near the stream that runs into their land and is named Oyoge.[2] The Indians here gave us venison to eat. The land is mostly full of fir trees, and the flat land is abundant. The stream runs through their land

[1] Mohawks and Senecas (Oneidas).

[2] The Jesuit Father Jacques Bruyas, missionary to the Iroquois from 1667 to 1700, gives *Ohioge* as meaning to or at the river, in his *Radices Verborum Iroquæorum* (New York, 1863), or Iroquois dictionary; and this is probably the word intended above. The identification of the places mentioned by the narrator is in some cases insecure, partly because the Indians not infrequently moved their villages. The best aids are the Reverend Dr. William M. Beauchamp's *Aboriginal Occupation of New York*, Bulletin No. 32 of the New York State Museum (Albany, 1900), and the same author's *Aboriginal Place Names of New York*, Bulletin No. 108 (Albany, 1907).

near their (Maquas) castle, but we could not ascend it on account of the heavy freshet.

December 12. At three hours before daylight, we proceeded again, and the savages that went with us would have left us there if I had not noticed it; and when we thought of taking our meal we perceived that their dogs had eaten our meat and cheese. So we had then only dry bread and had to travel on that; and, after going for an hour, we came to the branch [1] that runs into our river and past the Maquas villages, where the ice drifted very fast. Jeronimus crossed first, with one savage in a canoe made of the bark of trees, because there was only room for two; after that Willem and I went over; and it was so dark that we could not see each other if we did not come close together. It was not without danger. When all of us had crossed, we went another league and a half and came to a hunter's cabin, which we entered to eat some venison, and hastened farther, and after another half league we saw some Indians approaching; and as soon as they saw us they ran off and threw their sacks and bags away, and fled down a valley behind the underwood, so that we could not see them. We looked at their goods and bags, and took therefrom a small [loaf of] bread. It was baked with beans, and we ate it. We went farther, and mostly along the aforesaid kill that ran very swiftly because of the freshet. In this kill there are a good many islands, and on the sides upward of 500 or 600 morgen [2] of flat land; yes, I think even more. And after we had been marching about eleven leagues, we arrived at one o'clock in the evening half a league from the first castle [3] at a little house. We found only Indian women inside. We should have gone farther, but I could hardly move my feet because of the rough road, so we slept there. It was very cold, with northerly wind.

December 13. In the morning we went together to the castle over the ice that during the night had frozen on the kill, and, after going half a league, we arrived in their first castle, which is built on a high hill. There stood but 36 houses, in

---

[1] The Mohawk River, which they now ascend.

[2] A thousand or 1,200 acres.

[3] Apparently this first castle of the Mohawks, Onekagoncka, stood near Auriesville, west of the mouth of Schoharie Creek.

rows like streets, so that we could pass nicely. The houses are made and covered with bark of trees, and mostly are flat at the top. Some are 100, 90, or 80 paces long and 22 and 23 feet high.[1] There were some inside doors of hewn boards, furnished with iron hinges. In some houses we saw different kinds of iron work, iron chains, harrow irons, iron hoops, nails—which they steal when they go forth from here. Most of the people were out hunting deer and bear. The houses were full of corn that they call *onersti*,[2] and we saw maize; yes, in some of the houses more than 300 bushels. They make canoes and barrels of the bark of trees, and sew with bark as well.[3] We had a good many pumpkins cooked and baked that they called *anansira*.[4] None of the chiefs were at home, but the principal chief is named Adriochten, who lived a quarter of a mile from the fort in a small house, because a good many savages here in the castle died of smallpox. I sent him a message to come and see us, which he did; he came and bade me welcome, and said that he wanted us very much to come with him. We should have done so, but when already on the way another chief called us, and so we went to the castle again. This one had a big fire lighted, and a fat haunch of venison cooked, of which we ate. He gave us two bearskins to sleep upon, and presented me with three beaver skins. In the evening Willem Tomassen, whose legs were swollen from the march, had a few cuts made with a knife therein, and after that had them rubbed with bear grease. We slept in this house, ate heartily of pumpkins, beans and venison, so that we were not hungry, but were treated as well as is possible in their land. We hope that all will succeed.

December 14. Jeronimus wrote a letter to our *commis* (factor), Marten Gerritsen, and asked for paper, salt, and *atsochwat*[5]—that means tobacco for the savages. We went out to shoot turkeys with the chief, but could not get any. In the evening I bought a very fat one for two hands of seewan.

---

[1] This is one of the celebrated "long houses" of the Iroquois, described more fully by Lafitau and Bartram. The best discussion of the subject, quoting their descriptions, is to be found in Mr. H. M. Lloyd's edition of Morgan's *League of the Iroquois* (New York, 1904), II. 287–302.

[2] *Onnenste*=corn (Bruyas).   [3] With the inner bark of the elm.

[4] *Onnoñsira*=pumpkin (Bruyas).   [5] *Atsogwan*=to smoke (Bruyas).

The chief cooked it for us, and the grease he mixed with our beans and maize. This chief showed me his idol; it was a male cat's head, with the teeth sticking out; it was dressed in duffel cloth. Others have a snake, a turtle, a swan, a crane, a pigeon, or the like for their idols, to tell the fortune; they think they will always have good luck in doing so. From here two savages went with their skins to Fort Orange.

December 15. I went again with the chief to hunt turkeys, but could not get any; and in the evening the chief again showed us his idol, and we resolved to stay here for another two or three days till there should be an opportunity to proceed, because all the footpaths had disappeared under the heavy snowfalls.

December 16. After midday a famous hunter came here named Sickarus, who wanted very much that we should go with him to his castle. He offered to carry our goods and to let us sleep and remain in his house as long as we liked; and because he was offering us so much I gave him a knife and two awls as a present, and to the chief in whose house we had been I presented a knife and a pair of scissors; and then we took our departure from this castle, named Onekagoncka, and after going for half a league over the ice we saw a village with only six houses, of the name Canowarode; but we did not enter it, because he said it was not worth while, and after another half league we passed again a village where twelve houses stood. It was named Schatsyerosy. These were like the others, he saying they likewise were not worth while entering; and after passing by great stretches of flat land, for another league or league and a half, we came into this castle, at two good hours after dark. I did not see much besides a good many graves. This castle is named Canagere.[1] It is built on a hill, without any palisades or any defense. We found only seven men at home, besides a party of old women and children. The chiefs of this castle, named Tonnosatton and Tonewerot, were hunting; so we slept in the house of Sickarus, as he had promised us; and we counted in his house 120 pieces of salable

[1] The second castle, Kanagiro (Banagiro) of Megapolensis, Canagero of Van der Donck's map. According to Megapolensis it was the castle of the Bear clan; "*Ganniagwari*, a she-bear, it is the name of the Mohawks" (Bruyas). At this time it was on the south side of the Mohawk River.

beaver skins that he captured with his own dogs. Every day we ate beaver meat here. In this castle are sixteen houses, 50, 60, 70, or 80 paces long, and one of sixteen paces, and one of five paces, containing a bear to be fattened. It had been in there upward of three years, and was so tame that it took everything that was given to it to eat.

December 17. Sunday we looked over our goods, and found a paper filled with sulphur, and Jeronimus took some of it and threw it in the fire. They saw the blue flame and smelled the smoke, and told us they had the same stuff; and when Sickarus came they asked us to let them take a look at it, and it was the same; and we asked him where he obtained it. He told us they obtained it from the stranger savages, and that they believed it to be good against many maladies, but principally for their legs when they were sore from long marching and were very tired.

December 18. Three women of the Sinnekens came here with dried and fresh salmon; the latter smelled very bad. They sold each salmon for one florin or two hands of seawan. They brought, also, a good quantity of green tobacco to sell; and had been six days on the march. They could not sell all their salmon here, but went farther on to the first castle; and when they returned we were to go with them, and in the evening Jeronimus told me that a savage tried to kill him with a knife.

December 19. We received a letter from Marten Gerritsen dated December 18, and with it we received paper, salt, tobacco for the savages, and a bottle of brandy, and secured an Indian that was willing to be our guide to the Sinnekens. We gave him half a yard of cloth, two axes, two knives, and two awls. If it had been summer, many Indians would have gone with us, but as it was winter they would not leave their land, because it snowed very often up to the height of a man. To-day we had a great rainfall, and I gave the guide a pair of shoes. His name was Sqorhea.

December 20. We took our departure from the second castle, and, after marching a league, our savage, Sqorhea, came to a stream that we had to pass. This stream ran very fast; besides, big cakes of ice came drifting along, for the heavy rainfall during yesterday had set the ice drifting. We were in great danger, for if one of us had lost his footing it had cost us our lives; but God the Lord preserved us, and we came

through safely.   We were wet up to above the waist, and after
going for another half league we came thus wet, with our
clothes, shoes and stockings frozen to us, to a very high hill on
which stood 32 houses, like the other ones.   Some were 100, 90,
or 80 paces long; in every house we saw four, five, or six fire-
places where cooking went on.   A good many savages were at
home, so we were much looked at by both the old and the
young; indeed, we could hardly pass through.   They pushed
each other in the fire to see us, and it was more than mid-
night before they took their departure.   We could not absent
ourselves to go to stool; even then they crawled around us
without any feeling of shame.   This is the third castle and is
named Schanidisse.[1] The chief's name is Tewowary.   They
lent me this evening a lion skin [2] to cover myself; but in the
morning I had more than a hundred lice.   We ate much
venison here.   Near this castle there is plenty of flat land, and
the wood is full of oaks and nut trees.   We exchanged here one
beaver skin for one awl.

December 21.   We started very early in the morning, and
thought of going to the fourth castle, but after a half league's
marching we came to a village with only nine houses, of the
name of Osquage;[3] the chief's name was Oquoho—that is,
wolf.   And here we saw a big stream that our guide did not
dare to cross, as the water was over one's head because of the
heavy rainfall; so we were obliged to postpone it till the next
day.   The chief treated us very kindly; he did us much good
and gave us plenty to eat, for everything to be found in his
houses was at our service.   He said often to me that I was his
brother and good friend; yes, he told me even how he had been
travelling overland for thirty days, and how he met there an
Englishman, to learn the language of the Minquase [4] and to
buy the skins.   I asked him whether there were any French
savages there with the Sinnekens.   He said yes; and I felt
gratified and had a good hope to reach my aim.   They called
me here to cure a man that was very sick.

December 22.   When the sun rose, we waded together
through the stream; the water was over the knee, and so cold

[1] Schanatissa appears on Van der Donck's map.   [2] Panther's.
[3] "Place of hulled-corn soup."
[4] Conestogas, on the lower course of the Susquehanna River.

that our shoes and stockings in a very short time were frozen as hard as armor. The savages dared not go through, but went two by two, with a stick and hand in hand; and after going half a league we came to a village named Cawaoge. There stood fourteen houses, and a bear to fatten. We went in and smoked a pipe of tobacco, because the old man who was our guide was very tired. Another old man approached us, who shouted, "Welcome, welcome! you must stop here for the night"; but we wanted to be on the march and went forward. I tried to buy the bear, but they would not let it go. Along these roads we saw many trees much like the savin, with a very thick bark. This village likewise stood on a very high hill, and after going for another league we came into the fourth castle by land whereon we saw only a few trees. The name is Te notoge.[1] There are 55 houses, some one hundred, others more or fewer paces long. The kill we spoke about before runs past here, and the course is mostly north by west and south by east. On the other bank of the kill there are also houses; but we did not go in, because they were most of them filled with corn and the houses in this castle are filled with corn and beans. The savages here looked much surprised to see us, and they crowded so much around us that we could hardly pass through, for nearly all of them were at home. After awhile one of the savages came to us and invited us to go with him to his house, and we entered. This castle had been surrounded by three rows of palisades, but now there were none save six or seven pieces so thick that it was quite a wonder that savages should be able to do that. They crowded each other in the fire to see us.

December 23. A man came calling and shouting through some of the houses, but we did not know what it meant, and after awhile Jeronimus de la Croix came and told us what this was—that the savages are preparing and arming. I asked them what all this was about, and they said to me: "Nothing, we shall play with one another," and there were four men with clubs and a party with axes and sticks. There were twenty people armed, nine on one side and eleven on the other; and

---

[1] Megapolensis calls it Thenondiogo and the castle of the Wolf clan. It appears on Van der Donck's map as t'Iounontego. It seems to have been near the site of the present village of Sprakers, in Montgomery County.

they went off against each other, and they fought and threw each other. Some of them wore armor and helmets that they themselves make of thin reeds and strings braided upon each other so that no arrow or axe can pass through to wound them severely; and after they had been playing thus a good while the parties closed and dragged each other by the hair, just as they would have done to their enemies after defeating them and before cutting off their scalps. They wanted us to fire our pistols, but we went off and left them alone. This day we were invited to buy bear meat, and we also got half a bushel of beans and a quantity of dried strawberries, and we bought some bread, that we wanted to take on our march. Some of the loaves were baked with nuts and cherries and dry blueberries and the grains of the sunflower.

December 24. It was Sunday. I saw in one of the houses a sick man. He had invited two of their doctors that could cure him—they call them *simachkoes*; and as soon as they came they began to sing and to light a big fire. They closed the house most carefully everywhere, so that the breeze could not come in, and after that each of them wrapped a snake-skin around his head. They washed their hands and faces, lifted the sick man from his place, and laid him alongside the big fire. Then they took a bucket of water, put some medicine in it, and washed in this water a stick about half a yard long, and kept sticking it in their throats so that no end of it was to be seen; and then they spat on the patient's head, and over all his body; and after that they made all sorts of farces, as shouting and raving, slapping of the hands; so are their manners; with many demonstrations upon one thing and another till they perspired so freely that their perspiration ran down on all sides.

December 25—being Christmas. We rose early in the morning and wanted to go to the Sinnekens; but, as it was snowing steadily, we could not go, because nobody wanted to go with us to carry our goods. I asked them how many chiefs there were in all, and they told me thirty.

December 26. In the morning I was offered two pieces of bear's bacon to take with us on the march; and we took our departure, escorted by many of them that walked before and after us. They kept up shouting: *"Allesa rondade!"* that is, to fire our pistols; but we did not want to do so, and at last they went back. This day we passed over many a stretch of flat land, and crossed a kill where the water was knee-deep; and I think we kept this day mostly the direction west and northwest. The woods that we traversed consisted in the beginning mostly of oaks, but after three or four hours' marching it was mostly birch trees. It snowed the whole day, so it was very heavy marching over the hills; and after seven leagues, by guess, we arrived at a little house made of bark in the forest, where we lighted a fire and stopped for the night to sleep. It went on snowing, with a sharp, northerly wind. It was very cold.

December 27. Early in the morning again on our difficult march, while the snow lay 2½ feet in some places. We went over hills and through underwood. We saw traces of two bears, and elks, but no savages. There are beech trees; and after marching another seven or eight leagues, at sunset we found another little cabin in the forest, with hardly any bark, but covered with the branches of trees. We made a big fire and cooked our dinner. It was so very cold during this night that I did not sleep more than two hours in all.

December 28. We went as before, and after marching one or two leagues we arrived at a kill that, as the savages told me, ran into the land of the Minquaass, and after another mile we met another kill that runs into the South River,[1] as the savages told me, and here a good many otter and beaver are caught. This day we went over many high hills. The wood was full of great trees, mostly birches; and after seven or eight leagues' marching we did the same as mentioned above. It was very cold.

December 29. We went again, proceeding on our voyage; and after marching a while we came on a very high hill, and as we nearly had mounted it I fell down so hard that I thought I had broken my ribs, but it was only the handle of my cutlass that was broken. We went through a good deal of flat land, with many oaks and handles for axes, and after another seven leagues we found another hut, where we rested ourselves. We

---

[1] Probably the upper waters of the Unadilla, an affluent of the Susquehanna, which rises but a few miles from the Mohawk. The party crossed no affluents of the Delaware.

made a fire and ate all the food we had, because the savages told us that we were still about four leagues distant from the castle. The sun was near setting as still another of the savages went on to the castle to tell them we were coming. We would have gone with him, but because we felt so very hungry the savages would not take us along with them. The course northwest.

December 30. Without anything to eat we went to the Sinnekens' castle,[1] and after marching awhile the savages showed me the branch of the river that passes by Fort Orange and past the land of the Maquas. A woman came to meet us, bringing us baked pumpkins to eat. This road was mostly full of birches and beautiful flat land for sowing. Before we reached the castle we saw three graves, just like our graves in length and height; usually their graves are round. These graves were surrounded with palisades that they had split from trees, and they were closed up so nicely that it was a wonder to see. They were painted with red and white and black paint; but the chief's grave had an entrance, and at the top of that was a big wooden bird, and all around were painted dogs, and deer, and snakes, and other beasts. After four or five leagues' marching the savages still prayed us to fire our guns, and so we did, but loaded them again directly and went on to the castle. And we saw to the northwest of us, a large river, and on the other side thereof tremendously high land that seemed to lie in the clouds. Upon inquiring closely into this, the savages told me that in this river the Frenchmen came to trade. And then we marched confidently to the castle, where the savages divided into two rows, and so let us pass through them by the gate, which was—the one we went through —3½ feet wide, and at the top were standing three big wooden images, carved like men, and with them I saw three scalps fluttering in the wind, that they had taken from their foes as a token of the truth of their victory. This castle has two gates, one on the east and one on the west side. On the east side a scalp was also hanging; but this gate was 1½ feet smaller than the other one. When at last we arrived in the chief's house, I saw there a good many people that I knew; and we were re-

[1] The old town of the Oneidas, near Munnsville, Madison County, and on Oriskany Creek.

quested to sit down in the chief's place where he was accustomed
to sit, because at the time he was not at home, and we felt cold
and were wet and tired. They at once gave us to eat, and they
made a good fire. This castle likewise is situated on a very
high hill, and was surrounded with two rows of palisades. It
was 767 paces in circumference. There are 66 houses, but
much better, higher, and more finished than all the others we
saw. A good many houses had wooden fronts that are painted
with all sorts of beasts. There they sleep mostly on elevated
boards, more than any other savages. In the afternoon one of
the council came to me, asking the reason of our coming into
his land, and what we brought for him as a present. I told
him that we did not bring any present, but that we only paid
him a visit. He told us that we were not worth anything,
because we did not bring him a present. Then he told us how
the Frenchmen had come thither to trade with six men, and
had given them good gifts, because they had been trading in
this river with six men in the month of August of this year.
We saw very good axes to cut the underwood, and French
shirts and coats and razors; and this member of the council
said we were scoundrels, and were not worth anything because
we paid not enough for their beaver skins. They told us that
the Frenchmen gave six hands of seawan for one beaver, and all
sorts of things more. The savages were pressing closely upon
us, so that there was hardly room for us to sit. If they had
desired to molest us, we could hardly have been able to defend
ourselves; but there was no danger. In this river here spoken
of, often six, seven, or eight hundred salmon are caught in a
single day. I saw houses where 60, 70, and more dried salmon
were hanging.

December 31. On Sunday the chief of this castle came back
(his name is Arenias), and one more man. They told us that
they returned from the French savages, and some of the
savages shouted *"Jawe Arenias!"* which meant that they
thanked him for having come back. And I told him that in
the night we should fire three shots; and he said it was all
right; and they seemed very well contented. We questioned
them concerning the situation [of the places] in their castle
and their names, and how far they were away from each other.
They showed us with stones and maize grains, and Jeronimus

then made a chart of it.   And we counted all in leagues how far each place was away from the next.   The savages told us that on the high land which we had seen by that lake there lived men with horns on their heads; and they told us that a good many beavers were caught there, too, but they dared not go so far because of the French savages; therefore they thought best to make peace.   We fired three shots in the night in honor of the year of our Lord and Redeemer, Jesus Christ.

Praise the Lord above all!   In the castle Onneyuttehage,[1] or Sinnekens, January 1, 1635.

January 1, 1635.   Another savage scolded at us.   We were scoundrels, as told before; and he looked angry.   Willem Tomassen got so excited that the tears were running along his cheeks, and the savages, seeing that we were not at all contented, asked us what was the matter, and why we looked so disgusted at him.   There were in all 46 persons seated near us; if they had intended to do mischief, they could easily have caught us with their hands and killed us without much trouble; when I had listened long enough to the Indian's chatter I told him that he was a scoundrel himself and he began to laugh, said he was not angry and said: "You must not grow so furious, for we are very glad that you came here."   And after that Jeronimus gave the chief two knives, two pairs of scissors, and a few awls and needles that we had with us.   And in the evening the savages suspended a band of seawan, and some other stringed seawan that the chief had brought with him from the French savages as a sign of peace and that the French savages were to come in confidence to them, and he sang: "*Ho schene jo ho ho schene I atsiehoewe atsihoewe,*" after which all the savages shouted three times: "*Netho, netho, netho!*" and after that another band of seawan was suspended and he sang then: "*Katon, katon, katon, katon!*" and all the savages shouted as hard as they could: "*Hy, hy, hy!*"   After long deliberation they made peace for four years, and soon after everyone returned to his home.

January 2.   The savages came to us and told us that we had better stop another four or five days.   They would provide for all our needs and have us treated nicely; but I told them we could not wait so long as that.   They replied that they had

[1] Oneida town.

sent a message to the Onondagas—that is, the castle next to theirs—but I told them they nearly starved us. Then they said that in future they would look better after us, and twice during this day we were invited to be their guests, and treated to salmon and bear's bacon.

January 3. Some old men came to us and told us they wanted to be our friends, and they said we need not be afraid. And I replied we were not afraid, and in the afternoon the council sat here—in all, 24 men—and after consulting for a long while an old man approached me and laid his hand upon my heart to feel it beat; and then he shouted we really were not afraid at all. After that six more members of the council came, and after that they presented me a coat made of beaver skin, and told me they gave it to me because I came here and ought to be very tired, and he pointed to his and my legs; and besides, it is because you have been marching through the snow. And when I took the coat they shouted three times: *"Netho, netho, netho!"* which means, "This is very well." And directly after that they laid five pieces of beaver skins on my feet, at the same time requesting me that in the future they should receive four hands of seawan and four handbreadths of cloth for every big beaver skin, because we have to go so far with our skins; and very often when we come to your places we do not find any cloth or seawan or axes or kettles, or not enough for all of us, and then we have had much trouble for nothing, and have to go back over a great distance, carrying our goods back again. After we sat for a considerable time, an old man came to us, and translated it to us in the other language, and told us that we did not answer yet whether they were to have four hands of seawan or not for their skins. I told him that we had not the power to promise that, but that we should report about it to the chief at the Manhatans, who was our commander, and that I would give him a definite answer in the spring, and come myself to their land. Then they said to me *"Welsmach-koo,"* you must not lie, and surely come to us in the spring, and report to us about all. And if you will give us four hands of seawan we will not sell our skins to anyone but you; and after that they gave me the five beaver skins, and shouted as hard as they could: *"Netho, netho, netho!"* And then, that everything should be firmly binding, they called or sang:

"Ha assironi atsimach koo kent oya kayuig wee Onneyatte Onaondaga Koyocke hoo hanoto wany agweganne hoo schene ha caton scahten franosoni yndicho." That means that I could go in all these places—they said the names of all the castles— freely and everywhere. I should be provided with a house and a fire and wood and everything I needed; and if I wanted to go to the Frenchmen they would guide me there and back; and after that they shouted again: *"Netho, netho, netho!"* and they made a present of another beaver skin to me, and we ate to-day bear meat that we were invited to. In this house, belonging to the chief, there were three or four meals a day, and they did not cook in it, as everything was brought in from the other houses in large kettles; for it was the council that took their meals here every day. And whoever then happens to be in the house receives a bowlful of food; for it is the rule here that everyone that comes here has his bowl filled; and if they are short of bowls they bring them and their spoons with them. They go thus and seat themselves side by side; the bowls are then fetched and brought back filled, for a guest that is invited does not rise before he has eaten. Sometimes they sing, and sometimes they do not, thanking the host before they return home.

January 4. Two savages came, inviting us to come and see how they used to drive away the devil. I told them that I had seen it before; but they did not move off, and I had to go; and because I did not choose to go alone I took Jeronimus along. I saw a dozen men together who were going to drive him off. After we arrived the floor of the house was thickly covered with the bark of trees for the hunters of the devil to walk upon. They were mostly old men, and they had their faces all painted with red paint—which they always do when they are going to do anything unusual. Three men among them had a wreath on their heads, on which stuck five white crosses. These wreaths are made of deer hair that they had braided with the roots of a sort of green herb. In the middle of the house they then put a man who was very sick, and who was treated without success during a considerable time. Close by sat an old woman with a turtle shell in her hands. In the turtle shell were a good many beads. She kept clinking all the while, and all of them sang to the measure; then they would proceed to catch the devil and trample him to death; they trampled the bark to atoms so that none of it remained whole, and wherever they saw but a little cloud of dust upon the maize, they beat at it in great amazement and then they blew that dust at one another and were so afraid that they ran as if they really saw the devil; and after long stamping and running one of them went to the sick man and took away an otter that he had in his hands; and he sucked the sick man for awhile in his neck and on the back, and after that he spat in the otter's mouth and threw it down; at the same time he ran off like mad through fear. Other men then went to the otter, and then there took place such foolery that it was quite a wonder to see. Yes; they commenced to throw fire and eat fire, and kept scattering hot ashes and red-hot coal in such a way that I ran out of the house. To-day another beaver skin was presented to me.

January 5. I bought four dried salmon and two pieces of bear bacon that was about nine inches thick; and we saw thicker, even. They gave us beans cooked with bear bacon to eat to-day, and further nothing particular happened.

January 6. Nothing particular than that I was shown a parcel of flint stones wherewith they make fire when they are in the forest. Those stones would do very well for firelock guns.

January 7.—We received a letter from Marten Gerritsen, dated from the last of December; it was brought by a Sinneken that arrived from our fort. He told us that our people grew very uneasy about our not coming home, and that they thought we had been killed. We ate fresh salmon only two days caught, and we were robbed to-day of six and a half hands of seawan that we never saw again.

January 8. Arenias came to me to say that he wanted to go with me to the fort and take all his skins to trade. Jeronimus tried to sell his coat here, but he could not get rid of it.

January 9. During the evening the Onondagas came. There were six old men and four women. They were very tired from the march, and brought with them some bear skins. I came to meet them, and thanked them that they came to visit us; and they welcomed me, and because it was very late I went home.

January 10. Jeronimus burned the greater part of his pantaloons, that dropped in the fire during the night, and the chief's mother gave him cloth to repair it, and Willem Tomassen repaired it.

January 11.   At ten o'clock in the morning the savages came to me and invited me to come to the house where the Onondagans sat in council.   "They will give you presents"; and I went there with Jeronimus; took our pistols with us and sat alongside of them, near an old man of the name of Canastogeera, about 55 years of age; and he said: "Friends, I have come here to see you and to talk to you;" wherefore we thanked him, and after they had sat in council for a long time an interpreter came to me and gave me five pieces of beaver skin because we had come into their council.   I took the beaver skins and thanked them, and they shouted three times *"Netho!"*   And after that another five beaver skins that they laid upon my feet, and they gave them to me because I had come into their council-house.   We should have been given a good many skins as presents if we had come into his land; and they earnestly requested me to visit their land in the summer, and after that gave me another four beaver skins and asked at the same time to be better paid for their skins.   They would bring us a great quantity if we did; and if I came back in the summer to their land we should have three or four savages along with us to look all around that lake and show us where the Frenchmen came trading with their shallops.   And when we gathered our fourteen beavers they again shouted as hard as they could, *"Zinae netho!"* and we fired away with our pistols and gave the chief two pairs of knives, some awls, and needles; and then we were informed we might take our departure.   We had at the time five pieces of salmon and two pieces of bear bacon that we were to take on the march, and here they gave a good many loaves and even flour to take with us.

January 12.   We took our departure; and when we thought everything was ready the savages did not want to carry our goods—twenty-eight beaver skins, five salmon, and some loaves of bread—because they all had already quite enough to carry; but after a good deal of grumbling and nice words they at last consented and carried our goods.   Many savages walked along with us and they shouted, *"Alle sarondade!"* that is, to fire the pistols; and when we came near the chief's grave we fired three shots, and they went back.   It was about nine o'clock when we left this place and walked only about five leagues through 2½ feet of snow. It was a very difficult road, so that some of the savages had to stop in the forest and sleep in the snow. We went on, however, and reached a little cabin, where we slept.

January 13. Early in the morning we were on our journey again, and after going seven or eight leagues we arrived at another hut, where we rested awhile, cooked our dinner, and slept. Arenias pointed out to me a place on a high mountain, and said that after ten days' marching we could reach a big river there where plenty of people are living, and where plenty of cows and horses are; but we had to cross the river for a whole day and then to proceed for six days more in order to reach it. This was the place which we passed on the 29th of December. He did us a great deal of good.

January 14. On Sunday we made ready to proceed, but the chief wished to go bear hunting and wanted to stop here but, because it was fine weather, I went alone with two or three savages. Here two Maquas Indians joined us, as they wanted to go and trade elk skins and *satteeu*.

January 15. In the morning, two hours before daylight, after taking breakfast with the savages, I proceeded on the voyage, and when it was nearly dark again the savages made a fire in the wood, as they did not want to go farther, and I came about three hours after dark to a hut where I had slept on the 26th of December. It was very cold. I could not make a fire, and was obliged to walk the whole night to keep warm.

January 16. In the morning, three hours before dawn, as the moon rose, I searched for the path, which I found at last; and because I marched so quickly I arrived about nine o'clock on very extensive flat land. After having passed over a high hill I came to a very even footpath that had been made through the snow by the savages who had passed this way with much venison, because they had come home to their castle after hunting; and about ten o'clock I saw the castle and arrived there about twelve o'clock. Upward of one hundred people came out to welcome me, and showed me a house where I could go. They gave me a white hare to eat that they caught two days ago. They cooked it with walnuts, and they gave me a

piece of wheaten bread a savage that had arrived here from
Fort Orange on the fifteenth of this month had brought with
him. In the evening more than forty fathoms of seawan were
divided among them as the last will of the savages that died of
the smallpox. It was divided in the presence of the chief and
the nearest friends. It is their custom to divide among the
chief and nearest friends. And in the evening the savages gave
me two bear skins to cover me, and they brought rushes to
lay under my head, and they told us that our kinsmen wanted
us very much to come back.

January 17. Jeronimus and Tomassen, with some savages,
joined us in this castle, Tenotogehage, and they still were all
right; and in the evening I saw another hundred fathoms of
seawan divided among the chief and the friends of the nearest
blood.

January 18. We went again to this castle, I should say
from this castle on our route, in order to hasten home. In
some of the houses we saw more than forty or fifty deer cut
in quarters and dried; but they gave us very little of it to eat.
After marching half a league we passed through the village of
Kawaoge, and after another half league we came to the village
of Osquage. The chief, Ohquahoo, received us well, and we
waited here for the chief, Arenias, whom we had left in the
castle Te Notooge.

January 19. We went as fast as we could in the morning,
proceeding on the march; and after going half a league we
arrived at the third castle, named Schanadisse, and I looked
around in some of the houses to see whether there were any
skins. I met nine Onondagas there with skins, that I told to
go with me to the second castle, where the chief, Taturot, I
should say Tonewerot, was at home, who welcomed us at once,
and gave us a very fat piece of venison, which we cooked; and
when we were sitting at dinner we received a letter from Marten
Gerritsen, brought us by a savage that came in search of us, and
was dated January 18. We resolved to proceed at once to the
first castle, and to depart on the morrow for Fort Orange, and
a good three hours before sunset we arrived at the first castle.
We had bread baked for us again, and packed the three beavers
we had received from the chief when we had first come here.
We slept here this night and ate here.

January 20. In the morning, before daylight, Jeronimus sold his coat for four beaver skins to an old man. We set forth at one hour before daylight, and after marching by guess two leagues the savages pointed to a high mountain where their castle stood nine years before.[1] They had been driven out by the Mahicans, and after that time they did not want to live there. After marching seven or eight leagues we found that the hunters' cabins had been burned, so we were obliged to sleep under the blue sky.

January 21. We proceeded early in the morning, and after a long march we took a wrong path that was the most walked upon; but as the savages knew the paths better than we did they returned with us, and after eleven leagues' marching we arrived, the Lord be praised and thanked, at Fort Orange, January 21, anno 1635.

[*Vocabulary of the Maquas.*]

Assire or oggaha . . .	Cloth.
Atoga	Axes.
Atsochta	Adze.
Assere	Knives.
Assaghe	Rapier.
Attochwat	Spoons.
Ondach	Kettles.
Endat hatste	Looking-glass.
Sasaskarisat	Scissors.
Kamewari (Garonare?) .	Awls.
Onekoera	Seawan, their money.
Tiggeretait	Combs.
Catse (Garistats?) . . .	Bell.
Dedaia witha	Shirts or coats.
Nonnewarory	Fur caps.
Eÿtroghe	Beads.
Canagosat	Scraper.
Caris	Stockings.
Achta	Shoes.

---

[1] The abandoned castle pointed out by the Mohawks seems to have marked their farthest eastern extension.

Names of animals that occur there:

Aque (Gario?)	Deer.
Aquesados	Horse.
Adiron	Cat.
Aquidagon	Ox.
Senoto wanne	Elk.
Ochquari	Bear.
Sinite	Beaver.
Tawÿne	Otter.
Eyo	Mink.
Senadondo	Fox.
Ochquoha	Wolf.
Seranda	Male cat.
Ichar or sateeni	Dog.
Tali	Crane.
Kragequa	Swans.
Kahanckt	Geese.
Schawariwane	Turkeys.
Schascari wanasi . . .	Eagles.
Tantanege	Hares.
Onckwe	Men.
Etsi (Eightjen?) . . .	A man.
Coenhechti (Gahetien?) .	A woman.
Ocstaha	An old man.
Odasqueta	An old woman.
Sine gechtera	A wooer.
Exhechta	A lass.
Ragina	Father.
Distan	Mother.
Cian	Child.
Rocksongwa (Ronwaye?)	Boy.
Canna warori	Prostitute.
Onentar	Woman in labor.
Ragenonou	Uncle.
Rackesie	Cousin.
Anochquis	Hair.
Anonsi	Head.
Ohochta	Ears.
Ohonikwa	Throat.
Oneyatsa	Nose.

Owanisse . . . . Tongue.
Onawÿ . . . . Teeth.
Onenta . . . . Arm.
Osnotsa . . . . Hands.
Onatassa . . . . Fingers.
Otich kera . . . . . Thumb.
Otsira . . . . Nails.
Onvare . . . . . . Shoulder blade.
Orochquine . . . . . Spine.
Ossidan . . . . . . Feet.
Onera . . . . Pudenda.
Oeuda . . . . Excrements.
Onsaha . . . . . . Vesicle.
Canderes . . . . . . Phallus.
Awahta . . . . . . Testicles.
Casoya . . . . Ship, canoe.
Conossade . . . . . House or hut.
Onega . . . . Water.
Oetseira . . . . . . Fire.
Oyente . . . . . . Wood (firewood).
Oscante . . . . . . Bark.
Canadera . . . . . . Bread.
Ceheda (Osaheta?) . . . Beans.
Oneste . . . . Maize.
Cinsie . . . . Fish.
Ghekeront . . . . . Salmon.
Oware . . . . Meat.
Athesera . . . . . . Flour.
Satsori . . . . To eat.
Onighira . . . . . . To drink.
Katten kerreyager . . . Very hungry.
Augustuske . . . . . Very cold.
Oyendere . . . . . . Very good.
Rockste . . . . Friends.
Iachte yendere . . . . 'Tis no good.
Quane (Kewanea?) . . Great.
Canyewa . . . . . . Small.
Wotstaha . . . . . . Broad.
Cates . . . . Thick.
Satewa . . . . Alone.

Sagat	Doubly.
Awaheya	Death.
Aghihi	Sick.
Sasnoron	Hurry up.
Archoo	At once.
Owaetsei	At present.
The derri	Yesterday.
Jorhani	To-morrow.
Careyago	The sky.
Karackwero	The sun.
Asistock	The stars.
Sintho	To sow.
Deserentekar.	Meadow.
Sorsar	To raise.
Cana	The seed.
Onea	Stone.
Canadack or cany . . .	Sack or basket.
Canadaghi	A castle.
Oyoghi.	A kill [small river].
Canaderage	A river.
Johati	A path or road.
Onstara	To weep.
Aquayesse	To laugh.
Ohonte	Grass, vegetables.
Oneggeri	Weeds or reeds or straw.
Christittye	Iron, copper, or lead.
Onegonsera	Red paint.
Cahonsÿe	Black.
Crage	White.
Ossivenda	Blue.
Endatcondere	To paint.
Joddireyo	To fight.
Aquinachoo	Angry.
Jaghac teroeni	Frightened.
Dadeneye	To gamble.
Asserie	Very strong.
Carente	Artful, crooked.
Odossera	The bacon.
Keye	The fat.
Wistotcera	The grease.

Ostie	The bone.
Aghidawe	To sleep.
Sinekaty	Carnal copulation.
Jankurangue	Very tired.
Atsochwat	Tobacco.
Canonou	Pipe.
Esteronde	The rain.
Waghideria	To sweat.
Kayontochke	Flat arable land.
Ononda	Mountains.
Cayanoghe	Islands.
Schasohadee	The overside.
Caroo	Close by.
Cadadiene	To trade.
Daweyate	To sit in council.
Agetsioga	A string of beads.
Aquayanderen	A chief.
Seronquatse	A scoundrel.
Sari wacksi	A chatterer.
Onewachten	A liar.
Tenon commenyon . . .	What do you want?
Sinachkoo	To drive the devil away.
Adenocquat	To give medicine.
Coenhasaren	To cure.
Sategat	To light the fire, make fire.
Judicha	The fire.
Catteges issewe	When will you come again?
Tosenochte	I don't know.
Tegenhondi	In the spring.
Otteyage	In the summer.
Augustuske	In the winter.
Katkaste	To cook dinner.
Jori	It is ready.
Dequoguoha	To go hunting.
Osqucha	I'll fetch it.
Seÿendere ü	I know him well.
Kristoni asseroni . . .	Netherlanders, Germans.
Aderondackx	Frenchmen or Englishmen.
Anesagghena	Mahicans, or Mohigans.
Torsas	To the north.

Kanon newage	Manhattan.
Onscat	One.
Tiggeni	Two.
Asse	Three.
Cayere	Four.
Wisch	Five.
Jayack	Six.
Tsadack	Seven.
Sategon	Eight.
Tÿochte	Nine.
Oyere	Ten.
Tawasse	Forty.
Onscat teneyawe . . .	Hundred.

A SHORT ACCOUNT OF THE MOHAWK IN-
DIANS, BY REVEREND JOHANNES
MEGAPOLENSIS, JR., 1644

INTRODUCTION

An Amsterdam jeweller, Kiliaen van Rensselaer, a director of the West India Company from 1623 on, was the chief founder and promoter of agricultural colonization in New Netherland. Under the Privileges and Exemptions he bought from the Indians lands near Fort Orange, extending four leagues along the west bank of the river, from Beeren Island to the Mohawk. This was in 1630 and 1631. He was patroon of this domain, and owner of two-fifths, later three-fifths of it. Patroons were required by the Privileges (Art. xxvii.) to provide for the ministry of the Gospel in their domains. Van Rensselaer selected the writer of the following piece and sent him out to Rensselaerswyck under a contract for six years; the contract, dated April 6, 1642, may be seen translated in the *Van Rensselaer Bowier Manuscripts*, pp. 606–608.

Born in 1603 or 1604, Johannes Megapolensis was the nephew of a minister of the same name at Coedyck, in North Holland. The name is apparently a Graeco-Latinization of Van Grootstede. Of his youth we know only what he himself says, "I relinquished Popery and was thrust out at once from my inherited estate." He had preached thirteen years in North Holland, at Wieringerweert and then at Schoorl and Bergen, when he sailed for New Netherland, under the contract mentioned and with the approval of his classis and the Company. Accompanied by his wife and four children, he arrived at Fort Orange August 13, 1642. His service was to continue for six years from that date, with a salary of a thousand florins the first three years and twelve hundred the last three. A man of scholarship, piety, energy and good sense, he was trusted by

165

the patroon, perhaps more than any one else in the colony, in
important matters. He lived on the east side of the river, in
what is now Greenbush, opposite Albany. A church was
to have been built for him there in 1643, but apparently was
never constructed. He began preaching to the Indians in
that year, three years before John Eliot began his ministrations to the Indians of Massachusetts. His kindness to Father
Jogues appears in the latter's narrative of his stay at Rensselaerswyck.

Of the tract which follows, and which gives us important
knowledge of the Mohawks at the time of first contact of white
men with them, the more important because set forth by a well-
educated observer, Adriaen van der Donck in his *Beschrijvinge
van Niew Nederlant* ascribes the origin to "certain letters
which he has written to his friends, which were printed (as he
has told me) without his consent, but may be fully credited,
he being a man of truth and of great learning, who writes in a
vigorous style."   (David Pietersen de Vries thought so well of
the tract that he borrowed whole pages from it, covering the
borrowings by somewhat clumsy devices.)   Whatever the
truth about the author's consent, there was in fact published
at Alkmaar in 1644 a pamphlet entitled *Een kort Ontwerp vande
Mahakvase Indiaenen, haer Landt, Tale, Statuere, Dracht,
Godes-Dienst ende Magistrature, aldus beschreven ende nu
kortelijck den* 26 *Augusti* 1644 *opgesonden uyt Nieuwe Neder-
Lant, door Johannem Megapolensem juniorem, Predikant aldaer*
("A Short Account of the Mohawk Indians, their Country,
Language, Stature, Dress, Religion and Government, thus described and recently, August 26, 1644, sent out of New Netherland, by Johannes Megapolensis the younger, Preacher there").
Of this tract only one copy appears to exist, a copy preserved
in the library of the University of Ghent. The tract is chiefly
known through having been reprinted by Joost Hartgers in a
book called *Beschrijvinghe van Virginia, Nieuw Nederlandt,*

Nieuw Engelandt, etc. (Amsterdam, 1651), a book also rare, but of which there are several copies in this country. Ebenezer Hazard printed a translation in 1792 in his *Historical Collections,* I. 517–526. A revised version, by J. R. Brodhead, appeared in 1857 in the *Collections of the New York Historical Society,* second series, III. 137–160. After further revision, from the text of Hartgers, by Professor A. Clinton Crowell of Brown University, this translation appears in the following pages.

When his period of service at Rensselaerswyck had expired, Megapolensis with some difficulty secured his dismission. He was at Manhattan in August, 1649, on his way home, when the Director and Council urged him to remain and supply the pulpit there, Domine Backerus having resigned. He allowed himself to be persuaded by their appeals, not to leave the settlement without all pastoral care. The classis of Amsterdam and the West India Company approved, and the result was that Domine Megapolensis remained in New Amsterdam the rest of his life. Though narrow in opposing the Lutherans and Quakers, he was useful in affairs both of church and state. He survived the surrender to the English in 1664, having indeed a large part in persuading Stuyvesant to submit, and died late in 1669.

A SHORT ACCOUNT OF THE MOHAWK IN-
DIANS, BY REVEREND JOHANNES
MEGAPOLENSIS, JR., 1644

*A Short Account of the Mohawk Indians, their Country, Lan-
guage, Stature, Dress, Religion and Government, thus
described and recently, August 26, 1644, sent out of New
Netherland, by Johannes Megapolensis the younger, Preacher
there.*

THE country here is in general like that in Germany. The
land is good, and fruitful in everything which supplies human
needs, except clothes, linen, woollen, stockings, shoes, etc.,
which are all dear here. The country is very mountainous,
partly soil, partly rocks, and with elevations so exceeding high
that they appear to almost touch the clouds. Thereon grow
the finest fir trees the eye ever saw. There are also in this
country oaks, alders, beeches, elms, willows, etc. In the
forests, and here and there along the water side, and on the
islands, there grows an abundance of chestnuts, plums, hazel
nuts, large walnuts of several sorts, and of as good a taste as in
the Netherlands, but they have a somewhat harder shell.
The ground on the hills is covered with bushes of bilberries or
blueberries; the ground in the flat land near the rivers is
covered with strawberries, which grow here so plentifully in
the fields, that one can lie down and eat them. Grapevines
also grow here naturally in great abundance along the roads,
paths, and creeks, and wherever you may turn you find them.
I have seen whole pieces of land where vine stood by vine and
grew very luxuriantly, climbing to the top of the largest and
loftiest trees, and although they are not cultivated, some of the
grapes are found to be as good and sweet as in Holland. Here is
also a sort of grapes which grow very large, each grape as big
as the end of one's finger, or an ordinary plum, and because

they are somewhat fleshy and have a thick skin we call them
Speck Druyven.[1] If people would cultivate the vines they
might have as good wine here as they have in Germany or
France. I had myself last harvest a boat-load of grapes and
pressed them. As long as the wine was new it tasted better
than any French or Rhenish Must, and the color of the grape
juice here is so high and red that with one wine-glass full you
can color a whole pot of white wine. In the forests is great
plenty of deer, which in autumn and early winter are as fat
as any Holland cow can be. I have had them with fat more
than two fingers thick on the ribs, so that they were nothing
else than almost clear fat, and could hardly be eaten. There
are also many turkies, as large as in Holland, but in some years
less than in others. The year before I came here,[2] there were
so many turkies and deer that they came to feed by the houses
and hog pens, and were taken by the Indians in such numbers
that a deer was sold to the Dutch for a loaf of bread, or a knife,
or even for a tobacco pipe; but now one commonly has to give
for a good deer six or seven guilders. In the forests here there
are also many partridges, heath-hens and pigeons that fly
together in thousands, and sometimes ten, twenty, thirty and
even forty and fifty are killed at one shot. We have here, too,
a great number of all kinds of fowl, swans, geese, ducks, widgeons, teal, brant, which sport upon the river in thousands in
the spring of the year, and again in the autumn fly away in
flocks, so that in the morning and evening any one may stand
ready with his gun before his house and shoot them as they
fly past. I have also eaten here several times of elks, which
were very fat and tasted much like venison; and besides these
profitable beasts we have also in this country lions,[3] bears,
wolves, foxes, and particularly very many snakes, which are
large and as long as eight, ten, and twelve feet. Among others,
there is a sort of snake, which we call rattlesnake, from a
certain object which it has back upon its tail, two or three
fingers' breadth long, and has ten or twelve joints, and with
this it makes a noise like the crickets. Its color is variegated
much like our large brindled bulls. These snakes have very
sharp teeth in their mouth, and dare to bite at dogs; they

[1] What we now call hog-grapes.   [2] *I. e.*, in 1641.
[3] Panthers.

make way for neither man nor beast, but fall on and bite them, and their bite is very poisonous, and commonly even deadly too.

As to the soil of this country, that on the mountains is a reddish sand or rock, but in the low flat lands, and along the rivers, and even in the jutting sides of the mountains for an hundred or two hundred paces up, there is often clay. I have been on hills here, as high as a church, to examine the soil, and have found it to be clay. In this ground there appears to be a singular strength and capacity for bearing crops, for a farmer here [1] told me that he had raised fine wheat on one and the same piece of land eleven years successively without ever breaking it up or letting it lie fallow. The butter here is clean and yellow as in Holland. Through this land runs an excellent river, about 500 or 600 paces wide. This river comes out of the Mahakas Country, about four leagues north of us. There it flows between two high rocky banks, and falls from a height equal to that of a church, with such a noise that we can sometimes hear it here with us.[2] In the beginning of June twelve of us took a ride to see it. When we came there we saw not only the river falling with such a noise that we could hardly hear one another, but the water boiling and dashing with such force in still weather, that it seemed all the time as if it were raining; and the trees on the hills near by (which are as high as Schoorler Duyn [3]) had their leaves all the time wet exactly as if it rained. The water is as clear as crystal, and as fresh as milk. I and another with me saw there, in clear sunshine, when there was not a cloud in the sky, especially when we stood above upon the rocks, directly opposite where the river falls, in the great abyss, the half of a rainbow, or a quarter of a circle, of the same color with the rainbow in the sky. And when we had gone about ten or twelve rods farther downwards from the fall, along the river, we saw a complete rainbow, like a half circle, appearing clearly in the water just as if it had been in the clouds, and this is always so according to the report of

[1] Brant Peelen, of Nykerck in Gelderland, who lived on "Brant Peelen's" or Castle Island, a little below Fort Orange. See De Vries, p. 206, *post*.

[2] The Cohoes Falls.

[3] A dune or sand hill on the coast of North Holland, near the village of Schoorl, where Domine Megapolensis had lived.

all who have ever been there.   In this river is a great plenty of
all kinds of fish—pike, eels, perch, lampreys, suckers, cat fish,
sun fish, shad, bass, etc.   In the spring, in May, the perch are
so plenty, that one man with a hook and line will catch in one
hour as many as ten or twelve can eat.   My boys have caught
in an hour fifty, each a foot long.   They have three hooks on
the instrument with which they fish, and draw up frequently
two or three perch at once.   There is also in the river a great
plenty of sturgeon, which we Christians do not like, but the
Indians eat them greedily.   In this river, too, are very beautiful islands, containing ten, twenty, thirty, fifty and seventy
morgens of land.   The soil is very good, but the worst of it is,
that by the melting of the snow, or heavy rains, the river readily
overflows and covers that low land.   This river ebbs and flows
at ordinary low water as far as this place, although it is thirty-
six leagues inland from the sea.

As for the temperature in this country, and the seasons of
the year, the summers are pretty hot, so that for the most of
the time we are obliged to go in just our shirts, and the winters
are very cold.   The summer continues long, even until All
Saints' Day; but when the winter does begin, just as it commonly does in December, it freezes so hard in one night that
the ice will bear a man.   Even the rivers, in still weather when
there is no strong current running, are frozen over in one night,
so that on the second day people walk over it.   And this
freezing continues commonly three months; for although we
are situated here in 42 degrees of latitude, it always freezes so.
And although there come warm and pleasant days, the thaw
does not continue, but it freezes again until March.   Then,
commonly, the rivers first begin to open, and seldom in February.   We have the greatest cold from the northwest, as in
Holland from the northeast.   The wind here is very seldom
east, but almost always south, southwest, northwest, and north;
so also the rain.

Our shortest winter days have nine hours sun; in the summer, our longest days are about fifteen hours.   We lie so far
west of Holland that I judge you are about four hours in advance of us, so that when it is six o'clock in the morning with
us it is ten in the forenoon with you, and when it is noon with
us, it is four o'clock in the afternoon with you.

The inhabitants of this country are of two kinds: first, Christians—at least so called; second, Indians. Of the Christians I shall say nothing; my design is to speak of the Indians only. These among us are again of two kinds: first, the Mahakinbas, or, as they call themselves, *Kajingahaga*; second, the Mahakans, otherwise called *Agotzagena*.[1] These two nations have different languages, which have no affinity with each other, like Dutch and Latin. These people formerly carried on a great war against each other, but since the Mahakanders were subdued by the Mahakobaas, peace has subsisted between them, and the conquered are obliged to bring a yearly contribution to the others. We live among both these kinds of Indians; and when they come to us from their country, or we go to them, they do us every act of friendship. The principal nation of all the savages and Indians hereabouts with which we have the most intercourse, is the Mahakuaas,[2] who have laid all the other Indians near us under contribution. This nation has a very difficult language, and it costs me great pains to learn it, so as to be able to speak and preach in it fluently. There is no Christian here who understands the language thoroughly; those who have lived here long can use a kind of jargon just sufficient to carry on trade with it, but they do not understand the fundamentals of the language. I am making a vocabulary of the Mahakuaas' language, and when I am among them I ask them how things are called; but as they are very stupid, I sometimes cannot make them understand what I want. Moreover when they tell me, one tells me the word in the infinitive mood, another in the indicative; one in the first, another in the second person; one in the present, another in the preterit. So I stand oftentimes and look, but do not know how to put it down. And as they have declensions and conjugations also, and have their augments like the Greeks, I am like one distracted, and frequently cannot tell what to do, and there is no one to set me right. I shall have to speculate in this alone, in order to become in time an Indian grammarian. When I first observed that they pronounced their words so differently, I asked the commissary of the company[3] what it

---

[1] Mohawks and Mohicans.   [2] Mohawks.

[3] Presumably Bastiaen Jansen Krol, who had been at Fort Orange most of the time from 1626.

meant. He answered me that he did not know, but imagined they changed their language every two or three years; I argued against this that it could never be that a whole nation should change its language with one consent;—and, although he has been connected with them here these twenty years, he can afford me no assistance.

The people and Indians here in this country are like us Dutchmen in body and stature; some of them have well formed features, bodies and limbs; they all have black hair and eyes, but their skin is yellow. In summer they go naked, having only their private parts covered with a patch. The children and young folks to ten, twelve and fourteen years of age go stark naked. In winter, they hang about them simply an undressed deer or bear or panther skin; or they take some beaver and otter skins, wild cat, raccoon, martin, otter, mink, squirrel or such like skins, which are plenty in this country, and sew some of them to others, until it is a square piece, and that is then a garment for them; or they buy of us Dutchmen two and a half ells of duffel, and that they hang simply about them, just as it was torn off, without sewing it, and walk away with it. They look at themselves constantly, and think they are very fine. They make themselves stockings and also shoes of deer skin, or they take leaves of their corn, and plait them together and use them for shoes. The women, as well as the men, go with their heads bare. The women let their hair grow very long, and tie it together a little, and let it hang down their backs. The men have a long lock of hair hanging down, some on one side of the head, and some on both sides. On the top of their heads they have a streak of hair from the forehead to the neck, about the breadth of three fingers, and this they shorten until it is about two or three fingers long, and it stands right on end like a cock's comb or hog's bristles; on both sides of this cock's comb they cut all the hair short, except the aforesaid locks, and they also leave on the bare places here and there small locks, such as are in sweeping-brushes, and then they are in fine array.

They likewise paint their faces red, blue, etc., and then they look like the Devil himself. They smear their heads with bear's-grease, which they all carry with them for this purpose in a small basket; they say they do it to make their hair grow better and to prevent their having lice. When they travel, they take with them some of their maize, a kettle, a wooden bowl, and a spoon; these they pack up and hang on their backs. Whenever they are hungry, they forthwith make a fire and cook; they can get fire by rubbing pieces of wood against one another, and that very quickly.

They generally live without marriage; and if any of them have wives, the marriage continues no longer than seems good to one of the parties, and then they separate, and each takes another partner. I have seen those who had parted, and afterwards lived a long time with others, leave these again, seek their former partners, and again be one pair. And, though they have wives, yet they will not leave off whoring; and if they can sleep with another man's wife, they think it a brave thing. The women are exceedingly addicted to whoring; they will lie with a man for the value of one, two, or three *schillings*,[1] and our Dutchmen run after them very much.

The women, when they have been delivered, go about immediately afterwards, and be it ever so cold, they wash themselves and the young child in the river or the snow. They will not lie down (for they say that if they did they would soon die), but keep going about. They are obliged to cut wood, to travel three or four leagues with the child; in short, they walk, they stand, they work, as if they had not lain in, and we cannot see that they suffer any injury by it; and we sometimes try to persuade our wives to lie-in so, and that the way of lying-in in Holland is a mere fiddle-faddle. The men have great authority over their concubines, so that if they do anything which does not please and raises their passion, they take an axe and knock them in the head, and there is an end of it. The women are obliged to prepare the land, to mow, to plant, and do everything; the men do nothing, but hunt, fish, and make war upon their enemies. They are very cruel towards their enemies in time of war; for they first bite off the nails of the fingers of their captives, and cut off some joints, and sometimes even whole fingers; after that, the captives are forced to sing and dance before them stark naked; and finally, they roast their prisoners dead before a slow fire for some days, and then eat

[1] The Dutch schilling was equivalent to twelve cents.

them up. The common people eat the arms, buttocks and trunk, but the chiefs eat the head and the heart.

Our Mahakas carry on great wars against the Indians of Canada, on the River Saint Lawrence, and take many captives, and sometimes there are French Christians among them. Last year, our Indians got a great booty from the French on the River Saint Lawrence, and took three Frenchmen, one of whom was a Jesuit.[1] They killed one, but the Jesuit (whose left thumb was cut off, and all the nails and parts of his fingers were bitten,) we released, and sent him to France by a yacht which was going to our country. They spare all the children from ten to twelve years old, and all the women whom they take in war, unless the women are very old, and then they kill them too. Though they are so very cruel to their enemies, they are very friendly to us, and we have no dread of them. We go with them into the woods, we meet with each other, sometimes at an hour or two's walk from any houses, and think no more about it than as if we met with a Christian. They sleep by us, too, in our chambers before our beds. I have had eight at once lying and sleeping upon the floor near my bed, for it is their custom to sleep simply on the bare ground, and to have only a stone or a bit of wood under their heads. In the evening, they go to bed very soon after they have supped; but early in the morning, before day begins to break, they are up again. They are very slovenly and dirty; they wash neither their face nor hands, but let all remain upon their yellow skin, and look like hogs. Their bread is Indian corn beaten to pieces between two stones, of which they make a cake, and bake it in the ashes: their other victuals are venison, turkies, hares, bears, wild cats, their own dogs, etc. The fish they cook just as they get them out of the water without cleansing; also the entrails of deer with all their contents, which they cook a little; and if the intestines are then too tough, they take one end in their mouth, and the other in their hand, and between hand and mouth they separate and eat them. So they do commonly with the flesh,

[1] This happened on August 2, 1642. The Jesuit whose life was spared was the celebrated Father Isaac Jogues, of whom a fuller account appears later, in the introduction to portions of his writings included in this volume. His captivity lasted till August, 1643. The relation of Megapolensis to his release is set forth in the pieces alluded to, pp. 248, 252, *post*.

for they carve a little piece and lay it on the fire, as long as one would need to walk from his house to church, and then it is done; and then they bite into it so that the blood runs along their mouths. They can also take a piece of bear's-fat as large as two fists, and eat it clear without bread or anything else. It is natural to them to have no beards; not one in an hundred has any hair about his mouth.

They have also naturally a very high opinion of themselves; they say, *Ihy Othkon*, ("I am the Devil") by which they mean that they are superior folks. In order to praise themselves and their people, whenever we tell them they are very expert at catching deer, or doing this and that, they say, *Tkoschs ko, aguweechon Kajingahaga kouaane Jountuckcha Othkon;* that is, "Really all the Mohawks are very cunning devils." They make their houses of the bark of trees, very close and warm, and kindle their fire in the middle of them. They also make of the peeling and bark of trees, canoes or small boats, which will carry four, five and six persons. In like manner they hollow out trees, and use them for boats, some of which are very large. I have several times sat and sailed with ten, twelve and fourteen persons in one of these hollowed logs. We have in our colony[1] a wooden canoe obtained from the Indians, which will easily carry two hundred *schepels*[2] of wheat. Their weapons in war were formerly a bow and arrow, with a stone axe and mallet; but now they get from our people guns, swords, iron axes and mallets. Their money consists of certain little bones, made of shells or cockles, which are found on the sea-beach; a hole is drilled through the middle of the little bones, and these they string upon thread, or they make of them belts as broad as a hand, or broader, and hang them on their necks, or around their bodies. They have also several holes in their ears, and there they likewise hang some. They value these little bones as highly as many Christians do gold, silver and pearls; but they do not like our money, and esteem it no better than iron. I once showed one of their chiefs a rix-dollar; he asked how much it was worth among the Christians; and when I told him, he laughed exceedingly at us, saying we were fools to value a piece of iron so highly; and if he had such money, he would throw it into the river. They place their dead upright in holes,

---

[1] Rensselaerswyck.   [2] The *schepel* was about three pecks.

and do not lay them down, and then they throw some trees and wood on the grave, or enclose it with palisades. They have their set times for going to catch fish, bears, panthers, beavers and eels. In the spring, they catch vast quantities of shad and lampreys, which are exceedingly large here; they lay them on the bark of trees in the sun, and dry them thoroughly hard, and then put them in *notasten*, or bags, which they plait from hemp which grows wild here, and keep the fish till winter. When their corn is ripe, they take it from the ears, open deep pits, and preserve it in these the whole winter. They can also make nets and seines in their fashion; and when they want to fish with seines, ten or twelve men will go together and help each other, all of whom own the seine in common.

They are entire strangers to all religion, but they have a *Tharonhijouaagon*, (whom they also otherwise call *Athzoock-kuatoriaho*,) that is, a Genius, whom they esteem in the place of God; but they do not serve him or make offerings to him. They worship and present offerings to the Devil, whom they call *Otskon*, or *Aireskuoni*. If they have any bad luck in war, they catch a bear, which they cut in pieces, and roast, and that they offer up to their *Aireskuoni*, saying in substance, the following words: "Oh! great and mighty Aireskuoni, we confess that we have offended against thee, inasmuch as we have not killed and eaten our captive enemies;—forgive us this. We promise that we will kill and eat all the captives we shall hereafter take as certainly as we have killed, and now eat this bear." Also when the weather is very hot, and there comes a cooling breeze, they cry out directly, *Asoronusi, asoronusi, Otskon aworouhsi reinnuha;* that is, "I thank thee, I thank thee, devil, I thank thee, little uncle!" If they are sick, or have a pain or soreness anywhere in their limbs, and I ask them what ails them they say that the Devil sits in their body, or in the sore places, and bites them there; so that they attribute to the Devil at once the accidents which befall them; they have otherwise no religion. When we pray they laugh at us. Some of them despise it entirely; and some, when we tell them what we do when we pray, stand astonished. When we deliver a sermon, sometimes ten or twelve of them, more or less, will attend, each having a long tobacco pipe, made by himself, in his mouth, and will stand awhile and look, and after-

wards ask me what I am doing and what I want, that I stand
there alone and make so many words, while none of the rest
may speak.   I tell them that I am admonishing the Christians,
that they must not steal, nor commit lewdness, nor get drunk,
nor commit murder, and that they too ought not to do these
things; and that I intend in process of time to preach the
same to them and come to them in their own country and
castles (about three days' journey from here, further inland),
when I am acquainted with their language.   Then they say
I do well to teach the Christians; but immediately add,
Diatennon jawij Assirioni, hagiouisk, that is, "Why do so
many Christians do these things?"   They call us *Assirioni,*
that is, cloth-makers, or *Charistooni,* that is, iron-workers,
because our people first brought cloth and iron among them.

They will not come into a house where there is a men-
struous woman, nor eat with her.   No woman may touch
their snares with which they catch deer, for they say the deer
can scent it.

The other day an old woman came to our house, and told
my people that her forefathers had told her "that *Tharonhij-
Jagon,* that is, God, once went out walking with his brother, and
a dispute arose between them, and God killed his brother."   I
suppose this fable took its rise from Cain and Abel.   They
have a droll theory of the Creation, for they think that a
pregnant woman fell down from heaven, and that a tortoise,
(tortoises are plenty and large here, in this country, two, three
and four feet long, some with two heads, very mischievous and
addicted to biting) took this pregnant woman on its back,
because every place was covered with water; and that the
woman sat upon the tortoise, groped with her hands in the
water, and scraped together some of the earth, whence it
finally happened that the earth was raised above the water.
They think that there are more worlds than one, and that we
came from another world.

The Mohawk Indians are divided into three tribes, which
are called *Ochkari, Anaware, Oknaho,* that is, the Bear, the
Tortoise and the Wolf.   Of these, the Tortoise is the greatest
and most prominent; and they boast that they are the
oldest descendants of the woman before mentioned.   These
have made a fort of palisades, and they call their castle

Asserué.[1] Those of the Bear are the next to these, and their castle is called by them *Banagiro.*[2] The last are a progeny of these, and their castle is called *Thenondiogo.*[3] These Indian tribes each carry the beast after which they are named (as the arms in their banner) when they go to war against their enemies, and this is done as well for the terror of their enemies, as for a sign of their own bravery. Lately one of their chiefs came to me and presented me with a beaver, an otter, and some cloth he had stolen from the French, which I must accept as a token of good fellowship. When he opened his budget he had in it a dried head of a bear, with grinning teeth. I asked him what that meant? He answered me that he fastened it upon his left shoulder by the side of his head, and that then he was the devil, who cared for nothing, and did not fear any thing.

The government among them consists of the oldest, the most intelligent, the most eloquent and most warlike men. These commonly resolve, and then the young and warlike men execute. But if the common people do not approve of the resolution, it is left entirely to the judgment of the mob. The chiefs are generally the poorest among them, for instead of their receiving from the common people as among Christians, they are obliged to give to the mob; especially when any one is killed in war, they give great presents to the next of kin of the deceased; and if they take any prisoners they present them to that family of which one has been killed, and the prisoner is then adopted by the family into the place of the deceased person. There is no punishment here for murder and other villainies, but every one is his own avenger. The friends of the deceased revenge themselves upon the murderer until peace is made by presents to the next of kin. But although they are so cruel, and live without laws or any punishments for evil doers, yet there are not half so many villainies or murders committed amongst them as amongst Christians; so that I oftentimes think with astonishment upon all the murders committed in the Fatherland, notwithstanding their severe laws and heavy penalties. These Indians, though they live without laws, or fear of punishment, do not (at least, they very seldom) kill

[1] Assereawe appears on Van der Donck's map on the north side of the Mohawk River, not far up.

[2] Kanagiro; see p. 142, *supra.*

[3] See p. 145, *supra.*

people, unless it may be in a great passion, or a hand-to-hand fight. Wherefore we go wholly unconcerned along with the Indians and meet each other an hour's walk off in the woods, without doing any harm to one another.

JOHANNES MEGAPOLENSIS.

FROM THE "KORTE HISTORIAEL ENDE JOUR-
NAELS AENTEYCKENINGE", BY DAVID
PIETERSZ. DE VRIES, 1633-1643 (1655)

INTRODUCTION

THE author from whom the following extracts are taken was a voyager who, after retiring from active life to his native city in Holland, occupied his leisure by writing and printing an account of his adventures. This very curious and rare little book, which was published at Alkmaar in 1655, is entitled: *Korte Historiael, ende Journaels Aenteyckeninge van verscheyden Voyagiens in de vier deelen des Wereldts-Ronde, als Europa, Africa, Asia, ende Amerika gedaen, Door D. David Pietersz. de Vries, Artillerij-Meester vande Ed: M: Heeren Gecommitteerde Raden van Staten van West-Vrieslandt ende 't Noorden-quartier. Waer in verhaelt werd wat Batailjes hy te Water gedaen heeft: Yder Landtschap zijn Gedierte, Gevogelt, wat soorte van Vissen, ende wat wilde Menschen naer 't leven geconterfaeyt, ende van de Bosschen ende Ravieren met haer Vruchten. t'Hoorn. Voor David Pietersz. de Vries, Artillerij-Meester van 't Noorder-quartier. Tot Alckmaer, by Symon Cornelisz. Brekegeest, Anno 1655.*

This title may be translated: "Short Historical and Journal-Notes of various Voyages performed in the Four Quarters of the Globe, viz., Europe, Africa, Asia and America, by David Pieterszoon de Vries, Artillery-Master to the Noble and Mighty Lords the Council of West Friesland and the Northern Quarter [of the Province of Holland], wherein is set forth what Battles he delivered on the Water, Each Country, its Animals, its Birds, its Kinds of Fishes, and its Wild Men counterfeited to the Life, and its Woods and Rivers with their Products."

The book is a small black-letter quarto of 192 pages, embellished with a portrait of the author and 18 other plates, apparently etchings on copper, fairly well executed. Several of these relate to America, but being borrowed from Champlain they have no independent value. The portrait is marked "Æta. 60 Anno MDCLIII.", so that the author was born in 1593 or 1594.

David de Vries was born in Rochelle, France. His father sprang from an old family in Hoorn, North Holland, but had been settled in Rochelle since 1584; his mother was of Amsterdam origin, and had been in Rochelle but three months. From his fourth year De Vries lived mostly in Holland, but he assures us that he was "experienced from my youth in merchandising, both here and in France."

The voyages which the quaint little book chronicles, and in which the author's part was usually that of a supercargo, began in 1618, with a voyage to the Mediterranean. In 1620 he went to Newfoundland, then to the Mediterranean, where he won a notable fight against privateers off Cartagena, and at Toulon was invited by the Duke of Guise, admiral of France, to take service under him. An attempt to go to Canada for furs, in 1624, was frustrated by the new Dutch West India Company. From 1627 to 1630 he was occupied with an East India voyage, of which he gives a long account.

The fourth, fifth and sixth voyages were made to America. In 1630, when De Vries had been at home but two months, an old acquaintance, Samuel Godyn, a director in the West India Company, engaged his interest in a patroonship on the South or Delaware River, which was to be possessed in partnership by Godyn, Kiliaen van Rensselaer, Samuel Blommaert, Johan de Laet and David de Vries. In 1631 an expedition sent out by them founded a small settlement which they called Swanendael, on the west side of Delaware Bay, near the present town of Lewes—the first settlement in Delaware; but it was soon destroyed by the Indians. In 1632 De Vries went out as patroon and commander of a ship and yacht, which, proceeding by way of the West Indies, arrived in Delaware Bay December 5. His party inspected the ruins of Swanendael, got from the Indians the story of its destruction, and remained in the river, warily trading with them, till March. Then De Vries sailed away to Virginia for corn, and in April, 1633, came up along the coast of Manhattan. At this point our extracts begin, and the story of De Vries, and of New Netherland as he saw it, can thenceforward be followed in our text and notes till October, 1636, and again from September, 1638, to June, 1644, the last period being occupied with attempts to plant settlements on Staten Island and at Tappaan (Vriesendael), both frustrated by the outbreak of Kieft's war.

Of De Vries's later life nothing seems to be known. The date of the portrait, and the slip of the pen by which he writes one of his dates 1654 (see p. 227), may be taken as evidence that he wrote his book in that year. But no doubt he wrote it, in its later or American parts, from contemporary notes, of the nature of a journal. It is true that in certain spots he borrows somewhat unconscionably; and his bias is that of a patroon, critical of the Company's management. But in the main the narrative is of original value, the observations those of a capable and energetic trader and a good manager, expressing himself in a homely style but vividly. We owe to him many interesting pictures of life in the young colony, and especially of the ill-advised and exceedingly disastrous warfare waged by Kieft against the Indians.

All the parts of De Vries's book relating to Newfoundland, New Netherland and Virginia are presented, in translation by Henry C. Murphy, in the *Collections of the New York Historical Society*, second series, III. 1–129, and were separately printed in 1853 by James Lenox. The present issue is confined to the portions relating to New Netherland. Mr. Murphy's translation has been carefully revised by comparison with the original, the first pages by Professor A. Clinton Crowell, of Brown University, the greater part by the editor.

FROM THE "KORTE HISTORIAEL ENDE JOUR-NAELS AENTEYCKENINGE," BY DAVID PIETERSZ. DE VRIES, 1633-1643 (1655)

THE fifteenth[1] in the morning it was so foggy that we did not see our large ship. We heard the ground-swell and surf; threw the lead, and found it eight fathoms deep. Let the anchor fall. It was shelly ground. Fished with a drop-line, and caught in a couple of hours eighty-four codfish, very good-flavored sweet fish, better than those in Newfoundland. It began to blow from the southwest, and to be bright and clear again. So we weighed anchor and made sail. Found ourselves before Barende-gat,[2] where the coast began to stretch to the northeast by north, and southwest by south. Towards evening we saw the high mountains, which make a high point running along the sea, for the most part east-southeast, and west-southwest. This is the first mountainous land which you meet when you come from the south. We sailed that evening around Sandy Hook, which forms a large bay close by the point, and is also called Godyn's Point, where we anchored that evening in the bay in seven-fathom water.

The 16th, weighed anchor, and ran over to Staten Island, all along the shore of which runs a great sand-bank, entirely flat. It is necessary to sound the southeast side, but it will not do to come nearer than from three to four and a half fathoms with a large ship. Arrived about noon before Fort Amsterdam, and found a Company's ship there, called the *Soutbergh*, with a prize taken on the way, laden with sugar. She had brought a new governor, Wouter van Twiller of Nieuw-Kercke.[3] He had been a clerk in the West India House at Amsterdam. They had left Holland after us. I

---

[1] Of April, 1633.   [2] Barnegat.

[3] Wouter van Twiller, Director General of New Netherland from April, 1633, to the end of 1637, was the son of a sister of Kiliaen van Rensselaer. His administration was marked by much incompetence. He maintained strictly the rights of

186

went ashore to the fort, out of which he came to welcome me,
and inquired of me also, how the whale-fishery succeeded.
I answered him that we had a sample; but that they were
foolish who undertook the whale-fishery here at such great
expense, when they could have readily ascertained with one,
two, or three sloops in New Netherland, whether it was good
fishing or not.   Godyn had been a manager of the Company
as long as the Company had been in existence, and also of the
Greenland Company at Amsterdam, and ought to have known
how it at first ought to have been undertaken with little
expense. While we stood thus discoursing, our sloop came
from the large ship to the shore, from which we learned that
they had come to anchor at Sandy Hook, and would remain
there until I gave other orders.   In the mean time, I intended
to despatch my yacht to New England and New France, to
explore the bay.

The 18th, arrived here an Englishman,[1] who came from
New England to trade in the river, having on board a trader
named Jacob Eelkes,[2] who had, during the time of the private
association, navigated and commanded on the river, but
whom the Company would not employ, seeking out unfit
persons like this governor, whom they had made out of a clerk
into a governor, who was the sport of the people. This Englishman invited the governor to come and see him. I went with him,
in company with a number of people, who became intoxicated,
and got into such high words, that the Englishman could not
understand how it was that there should be such unruliness
among the officers of the Company, and that a governor should
have no more control over them; he was not accustomed to
it among his countrymen. The Englishman remained six or
seven days lying before the fort, and then said he wished to

the Company as over against settlers and patroons, and quarrelled with the minister, Reverend Everardus Bogardus, who came out with him in the *Soutberg*, and
with many others.

[1] *I. e.*, an English ship (the *William*, of London).

[2] The same whom Wassenaer mentions, p. 86, *supra*, as commander at Fort
Nassau before the days of the West India Company, whom the Company dis-
charged for misconduct. Depositions by him and the English sailors of the
William, giving their side of the transactions which follow, are printed in *N. Y.
Col. Doc.*, I. 72–81. Van Twiller finally sent a force up the river, which broke
up the Englishmen's trade with the Indians, and escorted them out to sea.

go up the river, and that the land was theirs.   This we denied, declaring that they had never made any settlement there. He said that David Hutson first discovered this river, and he was an Englishman.   We answered that he had indeed discovered the river in the year Nine, but he was fitted out at Amsterdam, at the expense of the East India Company; and that the river was now called Mauritius River, after our Prince of Orange.

The 24th, the Englishman weighed anchor and sailed up the river to Fort Orange, where this Jacob Eelkes had formerly resided as commander for the private company; when Commander Wouter van Twiller assembled all his forces before his door, had a cask of wine brought out, filled a bumper, and cried out for those who loved the Prince of Orange and him, to do the same as he did, and protect him from the outrage of the Englishman, who was already out of sight sailing up the river.   The people all began to laugh at him; for they understood well how to drink dry the cask of wine, as it was just the thing that suited them, even if there had been six casks, and did not wish to trouble the Englishman, saying they were friends.   As I sat at the table with him at noon, I told him that he had committed great folly, as the Englishman had no commission to navigate there, but a paper of the custom-house that he had paid so much duty, and might sail with so many passengers to New England, but not to New Netherland. I said, if it were my matter, I would have helped him away from the fort with *beans* from the eight-pounders, and not permitted him to sail up the river—would rather have cut off his tail, as he said he was a man from England.[1]   I told him if the English committed any excesses against us in the East Indies, we should strike back at them; that otherwise one cannot control that nation, for they were of so proud a nature, that they thought everything belonged to them; were it an affair of mine, I would send the ship *Soutberg* after him, and have him hauled down the river, and drive him from it until he brought another commission than a custom-house license; that they were only making sport of him.

The 20th of May, I wished to send my yacht to the north by the way of Hell-gate, as I began to make preparations to return

[1] An allusion to the ancient legend that Englishmen had tails.

with the large ship to Holland, when this governor commenced his pranks of the head, and began again to act foolishly as if he were drunk.   He did not want the yacht to go to the north, and sent alongside of it a *schapan*—a flat lighter-boat, in which the whole yacht could easily have been contained—and wanted to unload the yacht, in which were five or six lasts of brick ballast.   Then I protested to him, pointing to the privileges granted by the College of Nineteen, and approved by the States General, and that I did not wish him to unload the yacht.   If he desired to inspect the yacht, the same as was customary by all princes and potentates, he might do that, and see whether there was anything in it that concerned the Company.   He then ordered the guns at the angles of the fort to be so trained as to shoot at the yacht, when I ran to where he stood at the angle with the secretary and one or two of his council, and asked them whether the land was full of fools; if they wished to shoot anything, they should have shot at the Englishman, who was violating their river in spite of them. Upon this expostulation they desisted from shooting, and set about preparing a yacht to sail along with our yacht.   So they both sailed to the north after I had despatched my yacht.

When we had made everything ready, and were about to take our leave of the governor, he then came to annoy me anew. He did not want me to go with my boat to embark until his boat had first boarded our ship, in order to search her.   I told him that there was nothing to be searched.   I was bound home, and if he wished to make his letters ready, he could do so, and send them afterwards; meanwhile I would go to my boat.   He immediately sent twelve musketeers after me, in order that we should not depart.   My boat's crew asked whether they should row away in the boat.   I said, if I were in the boat I should have them do so, and had they my courage they would.   They immediately did so, and the musketeers were ridiculed with shouts and jeers by all the bystanders, who cried out that they should have stopped the Englishman with shot and muskets, from sailing past the fort up the river, and not our own patroons of the country, who sought to promote its interests.   After a little while I passed over to Long Island, where, behind Nut Island, I had commanded my boat to row. Before I crossed over, I went once more to the fort, and took

my leave of the commander. I told him I wished that he had
omitted the folly of attempting to prevent my departure by
his soldiers, as he had only made himself a subject of sport
among his people; if he desired to write any letters to his masters, the Managers, he might send them after me in the bay, but
I would go my own way. I crossed over the bay to my boat at
Long Island. Night coming on, and the flood-tide making, I
thought it most prudent to let my people row over to Pavonia
and there wait the ebb. Reaching Pavonia, we were immediately well entertained by the agent of Michael Poulusz,[1] who
prepared letters to send to his master. Meanwhile we waited
for the tide. But our people overslept a little their time, as I
had ordered them to be on hand as soon as the ebb began to run.
We passed the fort again early in the morning before break of
day, and before the *reveillé* was beaten in the fort.

We arrived about noon again at our ship which was lying
at Sandy Hook. Saw our ship's boat lying on the point, where
our people were catching fish with a seine, and went there to
tell them to come aboard as soon as they had made a haul or
two. The sail-boat from the fort was also alongside, having
sailed before us in order to bring their letters to us. They
tacked away, and were crossing to see what we were doing on
the point with our boat. I went towards them immediately,
and, coming by them, they inquired of me what I was doing
with my boat when I passed by the ship. I answered that it
did not concern them, so they returned again alongside. In this
boat were the *schout*, Notelman, and the secretary, Remunt.[2]
Coming aboard, I bid them welcome to the ship; and I had
my goods taken from my boat into the ship, among which
were a dozen beaver-skins. These, the secretary said, were
confiscated, because they had not been entered at the fort.
I told him to take them then; but the *schout* said I might let
them lie, we were not now at the fort, and might let him try our
wine, as he was a good bibber, as all of them were. I answered that water was good enough for them, for they might
otherwise fall overboard. At length, the *schout* asked why we
were quarrelling here; he was very thirsty, and would go to

---

[1] Michiel Pauw.

[2] Conrad Notelman and Jan van Remund, the successor of Rasieres. De
Vries, in defending himself, appealed to art. XV. of the Privileges and Exemptions.

the cabin; if there was anything wrong, the patroon might answer for it in Holland. Because the *schout* spoke so well, I told him he might come to the cabin, and I would let him fill a glass from the best cask; if the other one wished to make trouble, they might leave; I was now in my own ship, not under their jurisdiction. The secretary then said they could send the ship *Soutberg* after us to board us. I told him they might do so, for the *Soutberg* had sugar in her, and our crew would be right glad to eat sugar in their groats, as we would have a chance to do. I said to the secretary, that we were surprised that the West India Company would send such fools into this country, who knew nothing, except to drink; that they could not come to be assistants in the East Indies; and that the Company, by such management, must come to naught. In the East Indies, no one was appointed governor, unless he had first had long service, and was found to be fit for it; first, by serving as an assistant, under-koopman, and afterwards as koopman and finally chief-koopman,[1] and promoted then according to their merits; but the West India Company sent, in the first instance, as superior officers, persons who never had command in their lives, for which reason it must come to naught. Upon this, they again returned, with their boat, to the fort, which is five leagues from Sandy Hook. The bay inside of Sandy Hook is a large one, where fifty to sixty ships can lie, well protected from the winds of the sea. Sandy Hook stretches a full half league from the hills, forming a flat sandy beach, about eight or nine paces wide, and is covered with small blue-plum trees, which there grow wild.

The 15th June, we weighed anchor, and made sail for Fatherland. When we were under sail, an Englishman came sailing towards us, who would have run straight upon the bar, and lost his ship, if I, perceiving this, had not fired a shot to warn him, and I sent my boat to him, and he immediately sailed towards me, and perceived that he was not in the right channel. Coming by us, he proved to be an acquaintance—Captain Stoons [Stone],[2] of whom I have before spoken—whose boat

---

[1] *Koopman*=commercial agent.

[2] Captain Stone figures in Bradford, pp. 310, 311 of the edition in this series, as having made Van Twiller drunk and then, obtaining his consent, having seized a bark with a valuable cargo of furs belonging to the Plymouth men. Bradford

had suffered such distress in the West Indies, and whom I had
also met in the English Virginias. His ship was laden with
cows and young cattle, bound to New England. As he was in
want of water, he wished to put in here to take in some. He
sought of me, for the sake of our acquaintance, whether I
would furnish him a man to pilot him in. I asked our crew
whether there was any one of them who wished to make a
longer voyage, and who would be transferred to this Englishman; when one was found who wished to make a long voyage,
whom I gave over to him, and I laid my course southeasterly
to sea, as Long Island lies east and west. The compass here falls
off seventeen degrees northwest, or more than a point and a half.

The 17th, changed our course to east by south, at the forti-
eth degree of latitude, and then ran east, so as to pass in sight
of Korves.[1] . . .

[Second Voyage to America.][2]

The 16th,[3] came in sight of the mainland, and sounded
fourteen fathoms on sandy bottom. Saw the sand-hills of
Virginia, and were near Cape Engano,[4] in latitude 34° and 35°.

The 17th, came before the harbor of the English Virginias,
and as there was no one in the ship except myself who had been
there, the helmsman and boatswain came into the cabin, and
carried me on deck, in order to sail the ship in. We arrived
about four o'clock in the afternoon before the fort called Point
Comfort, where we found a ship from London, in which was
Sir John Haway,[5] governor on behalf of the King of England.
He was sent to London by his council and the people, who had
made a new governor, which later turned out badly for them.
I landed here all the English whom I had rescued,[6] and endeav-

wrongly inserts the episode under 1634. Stone soon came to Boston, and was
prosecuted there. His murder in Connecticut River was one of the immediate
causes of the Pequot War. See Winthrop, I. 102, 108, 118, 139. Winthrop's
date, June 2 (June 12 N. S.), for Stone's arrival at Boston hardly accords with that
here given by De Vries.

    [1] Corvo (Azores).

    [2] De Vries arrived in Amsterdam July 24, 1633. He sailed July 10, 1634, to
the Wild Coast (Guiana) and to the West Indies, whence he sailed up the coast
of the mainland to Virginia.

    [3] May 16, 1635.   [4] Hatteras.   [5] Harvey.

    [6] Refugees from the Tortugas, where the Spaniards had broken up an English
settlement.

ored to obtain some provisions, in order to sail to New Netherland, to make my ship tight, as it was extremely leaky, which
I could not do in the English Virginias. As it was out of
season to trade for tobacco, I let all of my cargo lie here, and
gave directions to trade when the crop of tobacco should be
ripe, and I would return again when the unhealthy season
should be over, that is towards September—for June, July, and
half of August are very unhealthy there for those who have
not lived there a year. The English die there at this season
very fast, but one who has been there over a year, they say is
seasoned; that is, he is accustomed to the land. They attribute the mortality in this land, which lies in latitude thirty-six
to thirty-seven degrees, to the variableness of the climate; one
hour it is so hot, at this season, that a man cannot endure the
heat, the next hour the wind shifts to the northwest with such
freshness, that he has to put on an overcoat, and that causes
the great unhealthiness, as one may expect in unseasonable
weather.

The 28th, after I had provided myself again with everything, we weighed anchor, and sailed for New Netherland,
where we arrived safe behind the point towards the evening
of the 30th.

The 1st of June I went ashore with a boat to Fort Amsterdam, where I found Wouter van Twiller governor, as
before. Asked him if he would let me hire some carpenters,
in order to repair my ship, which was very leaky; if not, I
would sail to New Netherland [New England]. He promised
me assistance. I then sent my boat back, in order to let my
ship come in, which was five leagues from there, and sent also
a young man aboard who might pilot her in, who had formerly, when I went to the East Indies, been in my service.
When my boat was about half an hour from the ship, there
arose a thunder-storm, which they could not well weather, and
the boat got full of water, and drove for two nights and three
days at sea. I wondered very much why my ship delayed so,
with a good wind, with which she could sail in in three hours.
I sent to the ship one of the Company's pleasure boats, which,
the next day but one, came sailing in with the ship; and there
came an Indian from the island [1] to the fort, bringing news that

[1] Long Island.

my boat had come ashore, and that the young man, Flips[1] Jansz. of Haerlem, was in it, and that they had found him lying a fathom or two from the breakers, and had brought him to their savage huts, as he was entirely exhausted, and that the other five men from the ship were lost. The boat the Indians had hauled up on the land.

The 5th, the young man, who had been so wonderfully saved, came to the fort and told us, that when he encountered the travado,[2] there were two Frenchmen in the boat, who betook themselves to the sea, when the boat became full of water, intending to swim to the ship, but they were never seen again. The first night, as they were all seated in the water in the boat, two more of them betook themselves to the water, intending to swim to the land, but they were not seen again. Flips Jansz. and my boatswain, who was with him, remained in the boat the second night; and the third day in the afternoon, the boatswain told this young man Flips Jansz., who was to pilot the ship in, that he also would abandon the boat; but Flips Jansz. answered that he would remain in the boat, and wait the providence of God. In about a quarter of an hour after the boatswain was out of the boat, and had taken his leave of him, he was thrown with the boat on land by the sea and breakers, and he ran through the breakers five or six paces from the water, and was so weak and hungry that he could not go further, and there the Indian found him. He said, that while they were seated in the boat, and driven about with it full of water, there were spooks about them, and one came who offered him food and drink; and, at length, one appeared like a fine lady; so I suppose that these apparitions were only their light-headedness from the hunger and hardships which they suffered.[3] We prepared to empty the ship, in order to get at the leak, and unloaded her, and hauled her upon the strand, as the water rises and falls here seven feet with every daily tide and at spring-tides nine to ten feet, according to the force of the wind. We spent here the unhealthy season of the English Virginias—June, July, and August.

The 1st of September, we were lying ready to go to the English Virginias, to see whether we could obtain our dues

[1] Philip.   [2] A coastwise storm, with lightning and rain.
[3] See Winthrop, I. 158, in this series, and Mather's *Magnalia*, bk. VI., ch. I.

from the rescued English, whom I had brought from the Tortugas, and for the goods left there. While I was taking my leave of the governor, the bark of the Company arrived, bringing fourteen or fifteen English with them, who had taken Fort Nassau from our people, as our people had no one in it, and intended to guard it with sloops; but they found that they must take possession of it again, or else it would be lost to the English.[1] This arrival of the Englishmen delayed me six days longer, as Governor Wouter van Twiller desired that I should take them to the English Virginias, where the English were expected to assist them. They therefore took their leave of Wouter van Twiller, who was governor, and came, bag and baggage, on board my vessel.

The 8th, we again got under sail with these Englishmen. Their commander was named Mr. Joris Hooms.[2] We sailed with a strong northwest wind, along the weather-shore.

The 10th we arrived at Point Comfort, before the English fort, landed the Englishmen whom we had brought with us at Cieketan,[3] where we found a bark lying with twenty men, bound for the Suytravie[4] to aid them, but our arrival with their people prostrated their design. We sailed up the river eight leagues, to Blank Point, and found there thirty-six large ships—all of them English ships of twenty to twenty-four guns —for the purpose of loading with tobacco. Fifteen of the captains were dead, in consequence of their coming too early in the unhealthy season, and not having been before in the country.

The 1st of October, I began to sail up and down the river to my customers, in order to collect my debts; but found that little tobacco had been made, and that there had been this year great mortality among the people, and large quantities of goods brought into the country by the English; and that there were great frauds among the English, who had not paid each other for the tobacco, and that half the ships of their own

[1] This party under Holmes had been sent out by West, provisional governor of Virginia, and had taken Fort Nassau, on the Delaware. Van Twiller had sent thither a bark belonging to the Company, which had dislodged them.

[2] George Holmes.

[3] Kecoughtan stood on the present site of the Soldiers' Home near Hampton, Virginia.   [4] South River.

nation were not laden; so that I consider, in regard to this trade, that he who wishes to trade here, must keep a house here, and continue all the year, that he may be prepared, when the tobacco comes from the field, to seize it, if he would obtain any of his debts. It is thus the English do among themselves; so that there is no trade for us, unless there be an overplus of tobacco, or few English ships.

After I had spent the winter here, I was compelled to return, as did almost all the ships, without tobacco, and to let my debts stand. I determined to go off again, and sold some beaver to the English.

ANNO 1636. The 28th April, I came with my ship again to the fort before Ciketan, where I learnt that my colony, which I had established on the Wild Coast,[1] was broken up by the disorders of some English and seamen who were among them. Those who want to plant a colony must not let any sailors among them, unless the place be so situated that they carry on some trade with vessels. The cause of abandoning the place was: there came a Spaniard with slaves to seek for water, when our people induced the Indians to show them the water. In the mean time our people ran off the bark and killed the Spaniards. And then the English, who were among our people, went to them and told them that if they would go to the Islands with the bark, they (the English) must be the captains; for they would be going to their own nation, and would there share the booty, but our people must acknowledge that they were their servants; and thus they left our fine colony, which, if they had remained there for two months, would have yielded an hundred and fifty thousand guilders' worth of cotton, oranges, and tobacco. But these scoundrels got their reward for abandoning this colony so well begun. When they reached the Islands, the English, who had the title of captains, sold the prize, and the sailors as servants. The English are a villainous people, and would sell their own fathers for servants in the Islands.

The 6th of May, weighed anchor to sail to New Netherland. The English Virginias are an unfit place for our nation to trade, unless they continue the trade from year to year.

The 7th, we saw the South River north by west of us,

[1] Guiana.

about three leagues. Sounded upon the bar which runs along the coast in four fathoms, and veered off because of its being so shallow.

The 8th, arrived towards evening at Sandy Hook, and stood in immediately, so that about two o'clock at night we anchored under the fort, without their being aware of our arrival. At break of day I fired three guns, which caused the people to spring out of their beds all at once, for they were not accustomed for any one to come upon them by such surprise. I went ashore immediately to speak to the commander, Wouter van Twiller, as my ship was very leaky. When I came to the said commander, I was welcomed by him, and I requested assistance to repair my ship.

The 6th,[1] hauled the ship into the Smith's Flats,[2] where we unloaded all our goods and careened the ship.

The 25th, we hauled into the stream again, and found her still leaky, and then resolved that we would let the ship lie, and put the goods aboard the East [West] India Company's ship; but as that was not large, and would not be able to carry our goods, we determined to consult the carpenters whether there was any means of making our own ship answer, and for that purpose sought thoroughly after the leak, and found, what we had not supposed, that it was in the keel, which was entirely eaten by the worms. We then resolved to go into the woods, and cut a good oak tree; where we procured a new keel, sixty feet long, and made the ship tight again, and hauled her up the stream.

The 25th of June, I went with the commander and minister,[3] to Pavonia, over from the fort, in the colony of Michael Pauw, where the person who was in command there for Michael Pauw, was named Cornelis van Vorst. He had arrived, with a small English bark, from the Northern English, bringing with him from thence good Bordeaux wines; and as the commander was fond of tasting good wines, he went over there. Whilst we were there, it so happened that there were some words between the commander and minister and Cornelis van

---

[1] This is evidently a misprint for 16th.

[2] Smits Vly, a tract of low land extending along the shore of the East River from the site of Wall Street to that of Beekman Street.

[3] Reverend Everardus Bogardus.

Vorst, in relation to a murder that had been committed there; but they separated afterwards good friends, when Cornelis van Vorst, wishing to give the commander a parting salute, fired a pederero which stood upon a palisade before his house, when a spark flew upon the house, which was thatched with rushes, and in half an hour it was entirely consumed. We returned to the fort, and I went to the ship and set to work to haul everything aboard again. Whilst we were engaged in shipping our goods, two prizes, taken by the English, arrived. They had first, with a sloop and eighteen men of them, taken near Carthagena a fine new and fast-sailing frigate of about thirty lasts,[1] laden with tobacco and hides, and then with it took a small bark, having hides aboard. They brought them to New Netherland, and ran into the South River, where they found one of our trading sloops, which brought them to Fort Amsterdam. These fellows were fitted out by my Lord Warwick, in order to begin a settlement at the Island of Nombre de Dios;[2] but through want of assistance and provisions were compelled to abandon it, and had obtained a copy of a commission from one of our privateers, with which they had performed this feat. They sold their prizes here at our fort, and shipped their goods in the West India Company's ship and put ten of the Englishmen in mine. As to which the captain maintained that he was ill-treated, as he wished to have his men with his goods; and wanted to have his goods in my ship, as I would have taken all his men with me also; but Commander Wouter van Twiller compelled him to ship all his goods in the Company's ship, and compelled me to carry over ten of the Englishmen, all which dealing by force was very unreasonable.

The 8th of August, the gunner of the fort gave a parting feast, and had a tent erected on one bastion of the fort, where a table and benches were set and many people bidden. When the banquet was at its highest, the trumpeter began to blow, as to which some words were passed; when the keeper of the store, Heyndrick Hudden, and the keeper of the merchandise,

---

[1] About sixty tons.

[2] There seems to be no island of Nombre de Dios; but as the town of that name, on the Isthmus of Panama, was not far from Providence Island, where the Earl of Warwick and his associates were at this time planting, it may be presumed that this island is meant.

Corelaer, railed at the trumpeter, who gave each of them a
sánter quanter,[1] whereupon they ran home, and brought out a
sword, and wished to have revenge upon the trumpeter. They
went to the house of the commander and used much foolish
language, one calling out, "I am the same man who took the
life of Count Floris." But when they had slept upon it, their
soldiership was all over, and they rather feared the trumpeter
than sought him; and thus the matter passed over.

The 9th, let my ship sail up the river to the Great Fall,
which is a league beyond Menates Island, in order to take in
water and wood.

The 13th, I requested Wouter van Twilliger to register
Staten Island for me, as I wished to return and plant a colony
upon it, which he consented to do. I took my leave of him
and went aboard. Weighed anchor, and by evening came to
anchor at Sandy Hook, in company with the Company's
ship, *The Seven Stars.*

The 15th, weighed anchor, as did also the Company's ship,
and set sail for Fatherland, to which may Almighty God
conduct us. . . .

*Here I make my Third Voyage to America and New Netherland,
in order to plant a Colony upon Staten Island for myself
and Frederick de Vries, Secretary of the City of Amsterdam, and a Manager of the West India Company: undertaken at his Request.*

ANNO 1638. The 25th of September I joined a Company's
ship,[2] freighted by them, and in which were some persons in
my service. On the same day, weighed anchor and set sail in
company with some ships bound to the Straits,[3] and two to
Spain.

The 28th, near the Kiscassen,[4] a Dunkirk frigate came into
our fleet, and began to shoot at some of our ships, but received

---

[1] A box on the ear.
[2] *De Liefde* (*Love* or *Charity*). The company had just thrown New Netherland open to free trade and had offered better inducements to emigrants than
hitherto.
[3] Of Gibraltar.   [4] The Caskets, seven miles west of Alderney.

so prompt an answer, that he thanked God that he got away from us.

The 9th of October, we saw the island of Madeira east of us; the wind northwest, and so remained with us to the sixteenth degree of latitude, before we obtained the trade wind from the northeast.

The 28th, we had a west wind with gusts. We were about two hundred leagues from the Cribes[1] Islands—the Island de Seada[2] west of us—and were much surprised to have, in the track of the trade, such a contrary wind, which continued with us five days with much violence.

The 8th November, came in sight of Ladeada, the first island which Franciscus Colombe saw when he discovered the West Indies.

The 10th, we arrived at the Island of Neeres,[3] and anchored in a fine sandy bay, and went ashore to the governor, who treated me well, and would have me spend the evening with him; but imprisoned the master of the ship for refusing the anchorage duty, who was a clownish boor, and was not accustomed to this navigation; so I settled with the governor what was to be paid, and he was set at liberty again.

The 13th, weighed anchor, and went to St. Christophers, where we lay at the sandy point for three days, and then left.

The 16th, having weighed anchor in order to proceed on our voyage to New Netherland, sailed at noon along by St. Martin and Anguilies,[4] and by evening saw Sombareren.[5] When we sailed by Aguillies, the helmsman tried to make me believe it was Sombareren; so well do pilots sometimes remember where they daily go, that they hardly know whether they see one island or another.

The 18th December, sounded in thirty fathoms in the thirty-seventh degree of latitude, and ran into twenty-three fathoms, and tacked again from the shore, as evening approached. Thus they converted a good wind into a bad one. I told the pilot, who was ignorant of this navigation, that he must run into fourteen fathoms, to approach the land, for if we turned at night towards the sea from twenty-three fathoms, we could not during the day get into fourteen fathoms again, as in this latitude a strong current set out from the bay of the English

---

[1] Caribbee.   [2] Deseada.   [3] Nevis.   [4] Anguilla.   [5] Sombrero.

Virginias. I could not make him understand what I told him, till finally, in consequence of the time that was lost, he was compelled to give heed to me. Early in the morning of the 24th, we came opposite Barnde-gat, the wind northeast, blowing so hard that we ran out to sea; afterwards it blew a storm straight on the shore from the southeast, so that we sailed the whole night and also all the day of the 25th under one mainsail. It seems that we felt the same tempest here, as that in which so many ships and men were lost in the Texel.

The 26th, moderate weather again, the wind southwest. Sought land again from on board, and about noon came in sight of the highlands of Sandy Hook, and at four o'clock reached the point, where the pilot wanted to cast anchor and fire a gun, in order that some one might come off and pilot the ship in. I told him that his cannon were not heavy enough for them to hear the report at the fort, as it was fully five leagues distant. Then the skipper said he would return to the West Indies, as he saw the island covered with snow, and wait there till summer. I answered him that, if we could not get in here, I would take him to the South River. But I could not make this mate and skipper understand that there was any South River, inasmuch as they had old false charts by which they wanted to sail. As there were some passengers who had dwelt several years in New Netherland, they urged him to ask me to take him in, as I had formerly come in safely with my own ship at night, as before related. The skipper then came to me, and asked me if I would sail the ship in, as I was well acquainted here. I answered him that I would do so for the sake of the passengers who were on board; and that he, at another time, if he took freight, should employ pilots who were acquainted with the places. So I brought the ship that same evening before Staten Island, which belonged to me, where I intended to settle my people, and in the dark let our anchor fall in eight fathoms.

The 27th, in the morning, the weather was very foggy, so that one could hardly see from the stem to the stern of the ship. The skipper then asked me whether we should lie there, as there was nothing in sight. I told him to weigh anchor, and, although it were even darker, I would, with that breeze, bring him before the fort in an hour. The anchor being raised,

we quickly sailed to the fort, where there was great rejoicing,
inasmuch as they were not expecting any ship at that time of
year. Found there a commander, named Willem Kieft,[1] who
had left France in a hurry, and had come in the spring, having
wintered in the Bermudas, because they did not dare to venture
upon the coast of New Netherland, in consequence of the ignorance of their pilots. Going ashore, I was made welcome by the
commander, who invited me to his house.

ANNO 1639. The 5th January I sent my people to Staten
Island to begin to plant a colony there and build.

The 4th of June I started north in a yacht to the Fresh
River,[2] where the West India Company have a small fort
called the House of Hope, and towards evening came to anchor
in Oyster Bay, which is a large bay which lies on the north side
of the great island, which is about thirty leagues long. This
bay runs up into the island, and is about two leagues wide from
the mainland. There are fine oysters here, whence our nation
has given it the name of Oyster Bay or Harbor.

The 6th had good weather at break of day, and got under
sail, and towards evening arrived at the Roode-berghs,[3] which
is a fine haven. Found that the English had there begun to
build a town on the mainland, where there were about three
hundred houses and a fine church built.

The 7th, having weighed anchor in the morning, arrived at
the Fresh River about two o'clock in the afternoon, where at
the mouth of the river the English have made a strong fort.
There was a governor in it, who had a Netherland wife from
Woerden, and he himself had formerly been an engineer and
workbase[4] in Holland. They cannot sail with large ships into
this river; and vessels must not draw more than six feet water
to navigate up to our little fort, which lies fifteen leagues from
the mouth of the river. Besides, there are many shallow places,
or stone reefs, over which the Indians go with canoes. Re-

---

[1] Kieft was Director General from September, 1637 (date of appointment), to
July, 1646. He had been a bankrupt merchant at Rochelle, and proved to be an
active but injudicious and quarrelsome governor.

[2] Connecticut.   [3] Red Hills, i. e., New Haven, settled in 1638.

[4] Military engineer. This was Lion Gardiner, who had served under the
Prince of Orange, and in 1636 had built this fort for the English patentees of Connecticut, Lord Saye and Lord Brooke and their associates. In 1640 he removed
to Gardiner's Island, which he had purchased from Lord Stirling.

mained at night at this English fort, where we were well entertained by the governor.

The 8th took our leave and went up the river; and, having proceeded about a league up the river, we met, between two high steep points, some Indians in canoes, who had on English garments, and among them was one who had on a red scarlet mantle. I inquired how he came by the mantle. He had some time ago killed one Captain Soon,[1] with his people, in a bark, from whom he had obtained these clothes. This was the captain of whom I have before spoken in my first voyage to America, whose boat met with a misfortune so that his men ate each other; and he had now lost his own life by the Indians.

The 9th arrived with the yacht at the House of Hope,[2] where one Gysbert van Dyck commanded with fourteen or fifteen soldiers. This redoubt stands upon the plain on the margin of the river; and alongside it runs a creek toward a high woodland, out of which comes a water-fall, which makes this creek, and where the English, in spite of us, have begun to build up a small town, and have built a fine church and over a hundred houses. The commander had given me orders to make a protest against them, as they were using our own land, which we had bought of the savages. Some of our soldiers had forbidden them to put the plough into it; but they had opposed them, and had cudgelled some of the Company's soldiers. Going there, I was invited by the English governor[3] to dine. When sitting at the table, I told him that it was wrong to take by force the Company's land, which it had bought and paid for. He answered that the lands were lying idle; that, though we had been there many years, we had done scarcely anything; that it was a sin to let such rich land, which produced such fine corn, lie uncultivated; and that they had already built three towns upon this river, in a fine country. There are many salmon up this river. These English live soberly, drink only three times at a meal, and whoever drinks

[1] Misprint for Stoon=Stone.

[2] The House of Hope, or Fort Good Hope, had been built by Jacob van Curler in 1633. Its site was at "Dutch Point," at the mouth of Little River, within the present limits of Hartford. The English settlement of Hartford was begun in 1635.

[3] John Haynes.

himself drunk they tie to a post and whip him, as they do thieves in Holland.

The 12th. Among the incidents which happened while I was here was that of an English ketch arriving here from the north, with thirty pipes of Canary wine. There was a supercargo on it, who was from the same city, in England, as the servant of the minister of this town, and was well acquainted with him. Now this supercargo invited the minister's servant on board the vessel to drink with him; and it seems that the man became fuddled with wine, or drank pretty freely, and was observed by the minister. So they were going to bring the servant to the church, where the post stood, in order to whip him. The supercargo then came to me, and requested me to speak to the minister, as it was my fault that he had given wine to his countryman. I accordingly went with the commander of our little fort, or redoubt, and invited the minister and the mayor and other leading men, with their wives, who were very fond of eating cherries, as there were from forty to fifty cherry-trees standing about the redoubt, full of cherries. We feasted the minister and the governor and their wives, who came to us; and, as we were seated at the meal in the redoubt, I, together with the supercargo, requested the minister to pardon his servant, saying that he probably had not partaken of any wine for a year, and that such sweet Canary wine would intoxicate any man. We were a long while before we could persuade him; but their wives spoke favorably, whereby the servant got free. While I was here another comical incident occurred. There was a young man who had been married two months. His brother accused him to the church because he had had intercourse with the woman before they were married; whereupon they both were called to account and whipped, and compelled to separate from each other for six weeks. These people give out that they are Israelites, and that we at our colony are Egyptians, and that the English in the Virginias are also Egyptians. I frequently told the governor that it would be impossible for them to keep the people so strict, seeing they had come from so luxurious a country as England.

The 14th took leave of the House of Hope. This river is a fine pleasant stream, where many thousand Christians could live by farming.

The 15th, early in the morning, we arrived again at the mouth of the river, and ran out of it. Sailed this day four leagues past Roode-bergh, and came into a river where the English had begun to make a village, and where over fifty houses were in process of erection, and a portion finished.[1]

The 16th weighed anchor, and sailed by two places which the English were building up, and about noon arrived where two Englishmen had built houses. One of the Englishmen was named Captain Patrick, whose wife was a Holland woman from the Hague. After we had been there two or three hours, proceeded on our voyage, and towards evening reached the Minates, before Fort Amsterdam, where we found two ships had arrived from our Fatherland. One was a ship of the Company, the *Herring*, the other was a private ship, the *Burning of Troy*, from Hoorn, laden with cattle on account of Jochem Pietersz., who had formerly been a commander in the East Indies, for the King of Denmark.[2] It was to be wished that one hundred to three hundred such families, with farm-laborers, had come, as this would very soon become a good country.

The 10th February. I began to make a plantation, a league and a half or two leagues above the fort, as there was there a fine location, and full thirty-one morgens of maize-land, where there were no trees to remove; and hay-land lying all together, sufficient for two hundred cattle, which is a great commodity there. I went there to live, half on account of the pleasure of it, as it was all situated along the river. I leased out the plantation of Staten Island, as no people had been sent me from Holland, as was promised me in the contract which I had made with Frederick de Vries, a director of the West India Company.

The 15th of April, I went with my sloop to Fort Orange, where I wanted to examine the land which is on the river. We arrived at Tapaen [3] in the evening, where a large flat of

---

[1] Stratford, Connecticut. The three places next mentioned are Norwalk, Stamford and Greenwich.

[2] Jochem Pietersen Kuyter played an important part in the subsequent history of the province, serving as one of the Eight Men, leading with Melyn in the struggle against Kieft, punished with him by Stuyvesant.

[3] Orangetown township.

about two or three hundred morgens of clay soil lies under the mountains, three or four feet above the water. A creek, which comes from the highland, runs through it, on which fine water-mills could be erected. I bought this flat from the Indians, as it was only three leagues above my plantation and five leagues from the fort. There was also much maize-land, but too stony to be ploughed.

The 25th. Opposite Tapaen lies a place called Wickquaes-geck,[1] where there is maize-land, but all stony or sandy, and where many pine trees grow. We generally haul pine masts from there. The land is also mountainous.

The 26th, went further up the river. Passed the Averstro,[2] where a kill runs out, formed from a large fall, the noise of which can be heard in the river. The land is also very high. About noon passed the highlands, which are prodigiously high stony mountains; and it is about a league going through them. Here the river, at its narrowest, is about five or six hundred paces wide, as well as I could guess. Towards evening came by the *Dance-chamber*,[3] where there was a party of Indians, who were very riotous, seeking only mischief, so that we were on our guard.

The 27th, we came to Esoopes,[4] where a creek runs in; and there the savages had much maize-land, but all somewhat stony. Arrived about evening, as it blew hard, before the Kats-kil. Found the river up to this point stony and moun-tainous, unfit for habitations. But there was some lowland along the Kats-kil, and here the savages sowed maize.

The 28th, arrived at Beeren [5] Island, where were many savages fishing. Here the land begins to be low along the margin of the river, and at the foot of the mountains are slopes, good for cultivation. At evening we reached Brand-pylen's Island,[6] which lies a little below Fort Orange, and belongs to the patroons, Godyn, Ronselaer, Jan de Laet, and Bloemaert, who had also three more farms, which they had put in good condi-tion at the Company's cost, as the Company had sent the cattle from Fatherland at great expense; and these individuals, being the commissioners of New Netherland, had made a good dis-

---

[1] Greenburg township.   [2] Haverstraw.
[3] This was at a cove in the north part of the town of Newburgh.
[4] Esopus.   [5] Bears'.   [6] The island of Brant Peelen, Castle Island.

tribution among themselves, and, while the Company had nothing but the bare fort, they had the farms and trade around it, and every boor was a merchant. . . .[1]

The 30th of April, while I lay here at Fort Orange, there came such a flood upon the island [2] on which Brand Pijlen dwelt (my host for the time being) that we had to abandon the island, and to use boats in going to the house, for the water stood about four feet deep on the island, whereas the latter lies seven or eight feet above ordinary water. This high water lasted three days before we could use the houses again. The water came into the fort. We had to resort to the woods, where we set up tents and kept great fires going.

The 14th May, took my leave of the commander at Fort Orange, and the same day reached Esopers, where a creek runs in, and where there is some maize-land upon which some savages live.

The 15th, got under sail at break of day, with the ebb-tide, and in the afternoon came by the Dance-chamber, where there were many savages fishing; passed the Highlands, and at evening anchored at Tapaen, and remained there all night, near the savages, who were fishing.

---

[1] The succeeding pages are omitted because the description of the Fort Orange region which De Vries gives is almost wholly "conveyed" from the *Kort Ontwerp* of Megapolensis, already printed in this volume, though De Vries makes occasional attempts to conceal the borrowing by little alterations. *E. g.*, when Megapolensis describes the hills near Cohoes Falls as being "as high as Schoorler Duyn," a dune near his Dutch home, De Vries alters this into "as high as the dunes at Huysduynen," which were near where *he* lived.

He speaks of Curler's telling him at Fort Orange of the Indians' capture of the French Jesuit (Jogues), "whose release our people were hoping that they might yet effect"—but Jogues was not captured till more than two years after De Vries visited the region and had this supposed conversation! Where Megapolensis says that the colony had a dugout canoe big enough to hold 200 schepels (p. 176, above), De Vries declares (p. 158 of original) that *he himself* had possessed one that would hold 225! No doubt the skipper made good use of his eyes during his two weeks at Fort Orange, but when it came to writing, fourteen or fifteen years later, it was easier to borrow from Domine Megapolensis's account, printed four years before. The one original passage in this part of De Vries is printed next above.

[2] Castle Island or West Island, a little below Fort Orange. The fort of 1614 had been built upon it, but had been ruined by floods three years later and abandoned.

The 16th, weighed anchor, and sailed, with the ebb and a strong breeze from the northwest, in three hours to the Fort. The above-named river has nothing but mountains on both sides, little capable of sustaining a population, as there are only cliffs and stones along the river, as I have related before. There is here and there some maize-land, from which the savages remove the stones and cultivate it. The tide flows up the entire river to Fort Orange by the pressure of the sea.

The 16th July, Cornelis van Thienhoven, secretary of New Netherland,[1] departed with a commission from the head men and council of New Netherland, with a hundred armed men, to the Raritanghe, a nation of savages who live where a little stream runs up about five leagues behind Staten Island, for the purpose of obtaining satisfaction from the Indians for the hostilities committed by them upon Staten Island, in killing my swine and those of the Company, which a negro watched—whom I had been solicited to place there—in robbing the swineherds, and in attempting (unsuccessfully) to run off with the yacht *Peace*, of which Cornelis Pietersz. was master, and for other acts of insolence. Van Thienhoven having arrived there with the said troop, demanded satisfaction according to his orders. The troop wished to kill and plunder, which could not be permitted, as Van Thienhoven said he had no orders to do so. Finally, on account of the pertinacity of the troop, the said Van Thienhoven went away, protesting against any injury which should happen by reason of their disobedience and violation of orders; and, when he had gone about a quarter of a league, the troop killed several of the savages, and brought the brother of the chief a prisoner, for whom Van Thienhoven had been surety before in eighty fathoms of *zeewan*, otherwise he, too, must have been put to death. Whereupon the Indians, as will hereafter be related, killed four of my men, burned my house, and the house of David Pietersz. de Vries,[2] in revenge. I learned also from Thienhoven that one Loockmans, standing at the mast, had tortured the chief's brother in his private parts with a piece of split wood, and that such acts of tyranny were

---

[1] He had been the Company's book-keeper throughout Van Twiller's time, and had become secretary under Kieft. A later piece in this volume is by him; see the introduction to it.

[2] This is probably a mistake for Frederick de Vries.

perpetrated by the servants of the Company as were far from making friends with the inhabitants.

The 20th of October, I went with my sloop to Tapaen in order to trade for maize or Indian corn. I found the Company's sloop there for the purpose of levying a contribution from the Indian Christians, of a quantity of corn. The Indians called to me and inquired what I wanted. I answered that I desired to exchange cloth for corn. They said they could not help me. I must go somewhat up the river, and, should the Company's sloop in the mean time get away, they would then trade with me; that they were very much surprised that the Sachem, who was now at the Fort, dare exact it; and he must be a very mean fellow to come to live in this country without being invited by them, and now wish to compel them to give him their corn for nothing; that they had not raised it in great abundance, as one chief had generally but two women who planted corn, and that they had calculated only for their own necessities, and to barter some with us for cloth. So this affair began to cause much dissatisfaction among the savages.

The 1st of December. I began to take hold of Vriessendael,[1] as it was a fine place, situated along the river, under a mountain. There is a flat there, an hour and a half's journey in extent, where hay can be raised for two hundred head of cattle, and where there is thirty morgens of corn-land, where I have sown wheat which grew higher than the tallest man in the country. Here were also two fine falls from the mountains, where two good mills could be erected for grinding corn and sawing plank. It was a beautiful and pleasant place for hunting deer, wild turkeys, and pigeons; but the evil of it was that, though I earnestly took hold of the place, I was not seconded by my partner, according to our agreement, who was Frederick de Vries, a director of the Company, and who thought that colonies could be built up without men or means, as his idea was

---

[1] His plantation previously mentioned. The company had in the previous July issued a new charter of "Privileges and Exemptions," which made provision for patroonships of reduced size, and also for a system of grants of two hundred acres each to lesser colonists. Commercial privileges, under some restrictions, were extended to all free colonists and to all stockholders in the Company. These arrangements, with better provisions for local government, led to a considerable increase of immigration.

that Godyn, Gilliame [1] van Rensselaer, Bloemaert, and Jan de Laet had established their colonies with the means of the Company, which had brought there all the cattle and the farmers. When the work began to progress, these persons were directors of the Company and commissioners of New Netherland, and helped themselves by the cunning tricks of merchants; and the Company, having about that time come into possession of Pieter Heyn's booty,[2] bestowed not a thought upon their best trading-post, at Fort Orange, whether people were making farms there or not; but these fellows, especially Rensselaer, who was accustomed to refine pearls and diamonds, succeeded in taking it from the other managers—their partners. Then Michael Pauw, discovering that they had appropriated the land at Fort Orange to themselves, immediately had the land below, opposite Fort Amsterdam, where the Indians are compelled to cross to the fort with their beavers, registered for himself, and called it Pavonia. The Company seeing afterwards that they were affected, much contention and jealousy arose among them, because they who undertook to plant colonies with their own money should have taken the property of the Company. Thus was the country kept down by these disputes, so that it was not settled; for at that time there were friends enough who would have peopled the country by patroonships, but they were always prevented by the contention of the managers, who were not willing to do anything themselves, for they would rather see booty arrive than to speak of their colonies; but, had the land been peopled, the fruit thereof would have been long continued, while their booty has vanished like smoke. There may be some managers and book-keepers who are well off by it, but it does no good to the community, like the cultivation of the soil whereby everyone is well off, and there is a steady income, which is better than all the booty which we see consumed in bawdy-houses; for where is now all the booty of which the Dunkirkers have robbed us, and also all the booty of Flushing, which was taken from the Portuguese?

[1] Kiliaen.

[2] The chief warlike success of the Dutch West India Company was Admiral Pieter Heyn's capture of the entire Spanish silver-fleet, in the bay of Matanzas, in December, 1628. The booty was valued at twelve millions of guilders. The patroonships mentioned in the ensuing sentences were established in 1630.

It has all gone to smoke, and those privateers who have taken it have gone to naught. They have drunk it up to no purpose.

ANNO 1641. The 20th August, the ship *Oak Tree* [1] arrived here, in which came a person named Malyn, who said that Staten Island belonged to him, that it was given by the directors to him and to Heer vander Horst, which I could not believe, as I had sailed in the year thirty-eight to take possession of said island, and had settled my men upon it. I thought better things of the directors than this, as the sixth article of the Privileges mentions that the first occupant shall not be prejudiced in his right of possession.

The 1st of September, my men on Staten Island were killed by the Indians and the Raritans; and they told an Indian, who worked for our people, that we would now come to fight them on account of our men; that we had before come and treated them badly on account of the swine, that there had been laid to their charge what they were not guilty of, and what had been done by the Company's men when they were on their way to the South River, who came ashore on Staten Island to cut wood and haul water, and then at the same time stole the hogs, and charged the act upon the innocent Indians, who, although they are bad enough, will do you no harm if you do them none. Thus I lost the beginning of my colony on Staten Island, through the conduct of Commander Kieft, who wished to charge upon the savages what his own people had done.

The 2d of November, there came a chief of the savages of Tankitekes, named Pacham, who was great with the governor of the fort. He came in great triumph, bringing a dead hand hanging on a stick, and saying that it was the hand of the chief who had killed or shot with arrows our men on Staten Island, and that he had taken revenge for our sake, because he loved the Swannekens (as they call the Dutch), who were his best friends.

The same day Commander Kieft asked me whether I would permit Mallyn to go upon the point of Staten Island, where the maize-land lay, saying that he wished to let him plant it, and that he would place soldiers there, who would make a signal by displaying a flag, to make known at the fort whenever ships

[1] *Eyckenboom.* Cornelis Melyn, next spoken of, afterward led the opposition to Kieft, and was persecuted and banished by Stuyvesant.

were in the bay, to which I consented—but did not wish to be prejudiced thereby—and to let him have twelve to fourteen or fifteen morgens of land, without abridging my right, as he intended only to distil some brandy there and make goat's leather.

ANNO 1642. As I was daily with Commander Kieft, generally dining with him when I went to the fort, he told me that he had now had a fine inn built and of stone, in order to accommodate the English who daily passed with their vessels from New England to Virginia, from whom he suffered great annoyance, and who might now lodge in the tavern. I replied that it happened well for the travellers, but there was great want of a church, and that it was a scandal to us when the English passed there, and saw only a mean barn in which we preached;[1] that the first thing which the English in New England built, after their dwellings, was a fine church, and we ought to do so, too, as the West India Company was deemed to be a principal means of upholding the Reformed Religion against the tyranny of Spain, and had excellent material therefor—namely, fine oak-wood, good mountain stone, and good lime burnt of oyster shells, much better than our lime in Holland. He then inquired who would undertake the work. I answered, the lovers of the Reformed Religion of whom there were enough. He then said that I must be one of them, as I proposed it, and must give an hundred guilders. I told him that I was satisfied, and that he must be the first to give, as he was commander, and then we chose Jochem Pietersz. Kuyter, a devout person of the Reformed Religion, who had good workmen who would quickly provide a good lot of timber, and also chose Damen,[2] because he lived close by the fort. And so we four, as churchwardens, were the ones to undertake the work of building the church. The commander was to give several thousand guilders on behalf of the Company, and we should see whether the rest would be subscribed by the community. The church should be built in the fort, to guard against any

---

[1] The first church, built early in Van Twiller's administration, stood near the East River, where now stands no. 39 Pearl Street.

[2] Jan Jansen Dam or Damen, a prominent colonist. As to Kieft's collecting of ample subscriptions by taking advantage of a convivial occasion, see post, p. 326. The result was a stone church in the old fort, 72 feet by 50, erected at an expense of 2,500 guilders—equivalent in specie to $1,000.

surprise by the savages. Thus were the walls of the church speedily begun to be laid up with quarry-stone, and to be covered by the English carpenters with overlapping shingles cleft from oak, which, by exposure to the wind and rain, turn blue, and look as if they were slate.

About the same time a harmless Dutchman, named Claes Rademaker,[1] was murdered by a savage. He lived a short league from the fort by the Densel-bay,[2] where he had built a small house, and had set up the trade of wheelwright. It was on the Wickquasgeck road over which the Indians passed daily. It happened that a savage came to this Claes Rademaker for the purpose of trading beavers with him for duffels cloth, which goods were in a chest. This chest he had locked up, and had stooped down in order to take his goods out, when this murderer, the savage, seeing that the man had his head bent over into the chest, and observing an axe standing behind him, seized the axe, and struck Claes Rademaker on the neck therewith, so that he fell down dead by the chest. The murderer then stole all the goods and ran off. The Commander sent to them and made inquiry in Wickquasgeck why this Dutchman had been so shamefully murdered. The murderer answered that, while the fort was being built, he came with his uncle and another savage to the freshwater, bringing beavers, in order to trade with the Dutchmen, that some Swannekes (as they call the Netherlanders) came there, took away from his uncle his beavers, and then killed him. He was then a small boy, and resolved that, when he should grow up, he would revenge that deed upon the Dutch, and since then he had seen no better chance to do so than with this Claes Rademaker. Thus these savages resemble the Italians, being very revengeful. Commander Kieft afterwards tried to attack, sending some soldiers there, of whom Van Dyck, the ensign-bearer, had the command, but in consequence of the darkness of the night the guides missed the way, and arrived there too late in the day, so that the attempt failed, and they returned again without effecting anything.[3] Another expedition against these

---

[1] Claes Smits, *rademaker*, *i. e.*, Claes Smits, wheelwright.

[2] A misprint for Deutels Bay, now called Turtle Bay, in the East River.

[3] De Vries is in error in placing this episode before the election of the Twelve Men. It happened in March, 1642; the latter, on August 29, 1641.

savages was subsequently sent, which also miscarried. When Commander Kieft saw that these attempts against the savages miscarried, and that trouble would follow, and found that the people began to reproach him with being himself protected in a good fort, out of which he had not slept a single night during all the years he had been there, and with seeking the war in order to make a bad reckoning with the Company, and began to feel that the war would be laid to his charge, he called the people together to choose twelve men to aid him in the direction of the affairs of the country,[1] of which number I was, as a patroon, chosen one. Commander Kieft then submitted the proposition whether or not we should avenge the murder of Claes Rademaker and make war upon the savages. We answered that time and opportunity must be taken, as our cattle were running at pasture in the woods, and we were living far and wide, east, west, south, and north of each other; that it was not expedient to carry on a war with the savages until we had more people, like the English, who make towns and villages. I told Commander Kieft that no profit was to be derived from a war with the savages; that he was the means of my people being murdered at the colony which I had commenced on Staten Island in the year forty; and that I well knew that the directors did not desire a war waged against the savages, for when we made our colony in the year 1630, in the South River at Swanendael, otherwise called Hoere-kil, and our people were all murdered through some trifling acts of the commander whom we had stationed there, named Gilles Oset,[2] as I have already mentioned in the beginning of my journal, it was then proposed to the Company to make war upon the savages, but the Company would not permit it, and replied that we must keep at peace with the savages. This I related to Commander Kieft, but he would not listen to it, so it becomes the managers to take care what persons they appoint as Directors, for thereon depends the welfare of the country. Were it the case that the East India Company had gone to work

---

[1] Stated too broadly. They were only to advise as to the Indian war; their advice may be seen in *Collections of the New York Historical Society*, second series, I. 277, 278. But they proceeded further, demanding many reforms in the provincial system, tending in the direction of popular government.

[2] Giles Houset.

in the East Indies, as the West India Company here, they would soon have to leave there like the West India Company; but in the East Indies they make no person commander of a fort, if he be not well acquainted with the country, and [they] have knowledge of the person's competence. But commanders are sent here whether they be fit or not.

About this time also I walked to Ackingh-sack,[1] taking a gun with me, in order to see how far the colony of Heer vander Horst had advanced, as it was only a short hour's journey behind my house. On approaching Ackinsack, about five or six hundred paces from where the colony was started, a savage met me who was very drunk. He came up to me and stroked my arms, which is a token of friendship among them, and said that I was a good chief; that when they came to my house, I let them have milk and everything for nothing; that he had just come from this house, where they had sold him brandy, into which they had put half water; that he could scoop up the water himself from the river, and had no need of buying it; that they had also stolen his beaver-coat, and he would go home and get his bow and arrows, and would kill some one of the villainous Swannekens who had stolen his goods. I told him he must not do so. I then proceeded on to the house of Heer vander Horst, and I told some soldiers and others who were there, that they must not treat the savages in that manner, as they were a very revengeful people, and resembled the Italians in that particular. I then returned home, and on my way, shot a wild turkey weighing over thirty pounds, and brought it along with me. I was not long home, when there came some chiefs from Ackinsack, and from Reckawanck, which was close by me, and informed me that one of their Indians, who was drunk, had shot a Dutchman dead, who was sitting on a barn thatching it. They asked me what they should do; they said they durst not go to the fort; that they would give one or two hundred fathom of *zeewan* to the widow if thereby they would be at peace. I told them that they must go with me to the fort, and speak to the commander; but they

---

[1] Hackensack. In the valley of the Hackensack River, which lay southwest from Vriesendael, a small colony had been established in 1641 on a grant of land which had been made to the lord of Nederhorst and Meyndert Meyndertsen van Keren and others.

were afraid that, on going to the fort, he would not permit them to return home. I made them of good heart, by telling them that I would deliver them safe home. They went with me, at length, to the fort; and, going to Commander Willem Kieft, told him the misfortune which had happened to them. He answered the chief of the savages that he wanted the savage who had done the act to be brought to him. They said they could not do so, as he had run away a two day's journey to Tanditekes;[1] but if the commander would listen to them, they desired in a friendly way to make the widow contented, and to pay for the man's death with *zeewan*, which is their money; it being a custom with them, if any misfortune befel them, to reconcile the parties with money. They laid the blame upon our people, saying that it was because we sold the young Indians brandy or wine, making them crazy, as they were unaccustomed to drink; that they had even seen our people, who were habituated to strong drink, frequently intoxicated, and fight with knives. They therefore desired that no liquor should be sold to the Indians, in order to prevent all accident for the future. It seemed as if they had some fear that the governor would detain them, so they answered him, that they would do their best to get the savage, and bring him to the fort. They then took their departure; but on the way they told me that they could not deliver up the savage to him, as he was a *sackemaker's* son—that is to say, as above, a chief's son. And thus the matter passed off.

Of what Sort and Condition of Men this Nation consists, how they are clothed, and what Magistrates they have.

As I have related the manner of living, and the appearance, of the savages at Fort Orange,[2] I will state something of the nations about Fort Amsterdam; as the Hackinsack, Tapaen, and Wicquas-geck Indians; and these are located at

---

[1] Near Sing Sing.

[2] Omitted in this volume, being a mere reproduction of the description by Megapolensis. The Hackensacks dwelt in the valley of Hackensack River, the Tappaans in the Orangetown region, the Wickquaasgeeks in that extending east from the river at Irvington and Tarrytown.

some two, three, or four leagues from the entrance of the river. Their manner of living is for the most part like that of those at Fort Orange; who, however, are a stronger, and a more martial nation of Indians—especially the Maquas, as before mentioned, who hold most of the others along the river to Fort Amsterdam under tribute. The Indians below here are also tolerably stout, have black hair, with a long lock, which they braid and let hang on one side of the head. The hair is shorn on the top of the head like a cock's-comb, as is shown in the plate.[1] Their disposition is bad. They are very revengeful; resembling the Italians. Their clothing is a coat of beaver-skins over the body, with the fur inside in winter, and outside in summer; they have, also, sometimes a bear's hide, or a coat of the skins of wild cats, or *hesspanen*,[2] which is an animal almost as hairy as a wild cat, and is also very good to eat. I have frequently eaten it, and found it very tender. They also wear coats of turkey's feathers, which they know how to plait together; but since our Netherland nation has traded here, they trade their beavers for duffels cloth, which we give for them, and which they find more suitable than the beavers, as they consider it better for the rain; and take two and a half in length of duffels, which is nine and a half quarters wide. Their pride is to paint their faces strangely with red or black lead, so that they look like fiends. They are then valiant; yea, they say they are *Mannette*, the Devil himself. Some of the women are very well-featured, and of tall stature. Their hair hangs loose from their head; they are very foul and dirty; they sometimes paint their faces, and sometimes draw a black ring around their eyes. When they wish to cleanse themselves of their foulness, they go in the autumn, when it begins to grow cold, and make, away off, near a running brook, a small oven, large enough for three or four men to lie in it. In making it they first take twigs of trees, and then cover them tight with clay, so that smoke cannot escape. This being done, they take a parcel of stones, which they heat in a fire, and then put in the oven, and when they think that

---

[1] None of the copper-plates in the original shows this arrangement particularly well. De Vries's plates, mentioned here and in various places below, are not reproduced in this volume; see the introduction to this piece.

[2] Raccoon.

it is sufficiently hot, they take the stones out again, and go
and lie in it, men and women, boys and girls, and come out
so perspiring, that every hair has a drop of sweat on it. In
this state they plunge into the cold water; saying that it is
healthy, but I let its healthfulness pass; they then become
entirely clean, and are more attractive than before. The girls
consider themselves to have arrived at womanhood when they
begin to have their monthly terms, and as soon as they have
them, they go and disguise themselves with a garment, which
they throw over their body drawing it over the head so that
one can barely see their eyes, and run off for two or three
months, lamenting that they must lose their virginity; but for
all that they do not omit their diversions at night, or other
unseasonable time. This period being over, they throw away
their disguise, and deck themselves with a quantity of *zeewan*
upon the body, head and neck; they then go and sit in some
place, in company with some squaws, showing that they are up
for a bargain. Whoever courts best and gives the most *zeewan*
takes her home with him, and remains with her sometimes
three or four months, and then goes with another; sometimes
a single month, according as they are inclined to each other.
The men are not jealous, and even lend their wives to a friend.
They are fond of meetings, frolic and dance much; but the
women are compelled to work like asses, and when they travel,
to carry the baggage on their backs, together with their infants,
if they have any, bound to a board.

*We will now speak of the Food Products of the Country and other
things which serve for the Support of the Life of Man.*

The food supplies are various. The principal one is maize,
which is their corn, and which is called by us Turkish wheat.
They pound it in a hollow tree, as may be seen in the plate.
When they travel, they take a flat stone, and pound it with
another stone placed upon the first, and when it is pounded,
they have little baskets, which they call *notassen*, and which
are made of a kind of hemp, the same as fig-baskets—which
they make so neatly that they serve them as sieves—and thus
make their meal. They make flat cakes of the meal mixed with

water, as large again as a farthing cake in this country, and bake
them in the ashes, first wrapping a vine-leaf or maize-leaf
around them. When they are sufficiently baked in the ashes,
they make good palatable bread. The Indians also make use
of French beans of different colors, which they plant among
their maize, or, as we call it, Turkish wheat. When the maize
(which is sown three or four feet apart, in order to have room
to weed it thoroughly) is grown two or three feet high, they
stick the beans in the ground alongside of the maize-stalks,
which serve instead of the poles which we use in our Fatherland, for beans to grow on. In New Netherland, the beans
are raised on the maize-stalks, which grow as high as a man
can reach, and higher, according to the fertility of the soil.
There are also pumpkins, water-melons, and melons. They [1]
dry the nuts of trees, and use them for food. There are also
ground-nuts as in this country; and white ground-nuts, but
these are poisonous to eat—a mason of the Company having
died in consequence of eating one of them. There also grow
here hazel-nuts, large nuts in great quantities, chestnuts, which
they dry to eat, and wild grapes in great abundance, which
they also use. Our Netherlanders raise good wheat, rye, barley, oats, and peas, and can brew as good beer here as in our
Fatherland, for good hops grow in the woods; and they who
make it their business can produce enough of those things, as
everything can be grown which grows in Holland, England, or
France, and they are in want of nothing but men to do the
work. It is a pleasant and charming country, if only it were
well peopled by our nation. Medlars grow wild and reversely
from what they do in our country, as they grow in Holland
open and broad above, but here they grow up sharp, the
reverse of those in Holland. Mulberry trees there are too, so
that silkworms could be raised, and good silk made; and good
hemp and flax, and the savages use a kind of hemp, which
they understand making up, much stronger than ours is, and
for every necessary purpose, such as *notassen*, (which are their
sacks, and in which they carry everything); they also make
linen of it. They gather their maize and French beans the last
of September and October, and when they have gathered and
shelled the corn, they bury it in holes, which they have pre-

[1] The Indians.

viously lined with mats, and so keep as much as they want for the winter and while hunting. They sow the maize in April and May.

Of the Animals and Cattle, and how they hunt and catch them.

There are great quantities of harts and hinds, which the savages shoot with their bows and arrows, or make a general hunt of, a hundred more or less joining in the hunt. They stand a hundred paces more or less from each other, and holding flat thigh-bones in the hand, beat them with a stick, and so drive the creatures before them to the river. As they approach the river, they close nearer to each other, and whatever is between any two of them, is at the mercy of their bows and arrows, or must take to the river. When the animals swim into the river, the savages lie in their canoes with lassos, which they throw around their necks, and tighten, whereupon the deer lie down and float with the rump upwards, as they cannot draw breath. At the north, they drive them into a *fuyk*,[1] which they make of palisades split out of trees, and eight or nine feet high, and set close to each other, for a distance of fourteen or fifteen hundred paces on both sides, coming together like a *fuyk*, as is shown in the plates; the opening is one or two thousand paces wide. When the animal is within the palisades, the savages begin to come nearer to each other, and pursue it with great ardor, as they regard deer-hunting the noblest hunting. At the end of the *fuyk* it is so narrow that it is only five feet wide, like a large door, and it is there covered with the boughs of trees, into which the deer or animal runs, closely pursued by the savages, who make a noise as if they were wolves, by which many deer are devoured, and of which they are in great fear. This causes them to run into the mouth of the *fuyk* with great force, whither the Indians pursue them furiously with bows and arrows, and from whence they cannot escape; they are then easily caught. They also catch them with snares, as may be seen in the plate. There are elks, chiefly in the mountains; also hares, but they are not larger than the rabbits in Holland; foxes in abundance, multitudes of wolves, wild cats, squirrels—black as pitch, and gray, also

[1] A peculiar form of net, large at the entrance, and terminating in a snare.

flying squirrels—beavers in great numbers, minks, otters, pole-
cats, bears, and many kinds of fur-bearing animals, which I
cannot name or think of. The savages understand the preparing of deer-skins, of which they make shoes and stockings,
after their fashion, for the winter.

Of the Fowl which are in the Entrance of the River and the Achter Col.[1]

There are great numbers of two kinds of geese, which stay
here through the winter, by thousands, and which afford fine
sport with the gun. One kind is the gray geese, which weigh
fifteen or sixteen pounds each; the other they call white-
heads, weighing six or seven pounds, very numerous, flying
by thousands, and of good flavor. There are large quantities of bernicles, which keep along the saltwater shore, and of
gulls, small star-birds,[2] snipes, curlews, and many other shore-
birds, which I cannot give the names of. The geese and
bernicles come here in September and leave in April. Many of
the savages say that they go to the river of Canada, where
they breed their young; for the fishermen who sail to Newfoundland find them there in great numbers in the summer
time, when they are fishing there. On the fresh water are
many swans. Land birds are also very numerous, such as wild
turkeys, which weigh from thirty to thirty-six and forty pounds,
and which fly wild, for they can fly one or two thousand paces,
and then fall down, tired with flying, when they are taken by
the savages with their hands, who also shoot them with bows
and arrows. Partridges are numerous, but they are small.
There are meadow-hens, as large as a year-old hen, and with
feathers like those of a partridge; and white and gray herons
in great numbers. Nothing is wanted but good marksmen
with powder and shot. Turtle-doves, at the time of year when
they migrate, are so numerous, that the light can hardly be
discerned where they fly. There are white and gray cranes,
and a species of black bird, as large as what is called in our
country the starling or thrush, and which makes its appearance
at harvest, when the corn named maize is ripe. These birds

---

[1] "The Back Bay," i. e., Newark Bay.　　　　　[2] *Ster-vogeltjes.*

are called maize-thieves, because they fall upon the corn by thousands, and do great damage. I have seen one of our Netherlanders kill, in the commander's orchard at Fort Amsterdam, eighty-four of these birds at one shot. They are of good taste, and similar to the thrushes in Fatherland. I have also seen, at different times, thirty to thirty-four pigeons killed at one shot, but they are not larger than turtle-doves, and their bodies are exactly like those of the turtle-doves in Fatherland, except they have longer tails.

Of the kinds of Fish which frequent the Sea and River as far up as the Brackish and Fresh Water.

There are different kinds of fine fish on the seacoast for the wants of man, similar to those in Holland, as the codfish (in winter), haddock, plaice, flounders, herring, sole, and many more kinds of which I cannot give the names. There is a species of fish which by our people is called the *twelve*, and which has scales like a salmon, and on each side six black streaks, which I suppose is the reason they call it twelve.[1] It is the size of a codfish, very delicate, and of good taste for eating; the head is the best, as it is full of brains like a lamb's head. The fish comes from the sea into the river in the spring, about the last of March and April, and continues until the last of May. It is caught in large quantities and dried by the savages, for at this time the squaws are engaged in sowing their maize, and cultivating the land, and the men go a-fishing in order to assist their wives a little by their draughts of fish. Sometimes they catch them with seines from seventy to eighty fathoms in length, which they braid themselves, and on which, in place of lead, they hang stones, and instead of the corks which we put on them to float them, they fasten small sticks of an ell in length, round and sharp at the end. Over the purse, they have a figure made of wood, resembling the Devil, and when the fish swim into the net and come to the purse, so that

---

[1] Striped bass. More likely it was called *twaalf* to match *elft*, the shad, though the latter word really has nothing to do with *eleven*, for *elft*=Fr. *alose* or Eng. *allice*. See Van der Donck in *Collections of the New York Historical Society*, second series, I. 169, 170.

the figure begins to move, they then begin to cry out and call upon the *Mannetoe*, that is, the Devil, to give them many fish. They catch great quantities of this fish; which they also catch in little set-nets, six or seven fathoms long, knit single like a herring-net. They set them on sticks into the river, one, and one and a half fathoms deep. With these they catch many of this fish. There is also another kind of fish on the seacoast, which is called *thirteen* [1] by us, because it is larger than the twelve. The scales of the thirteen are yellow like those of the carp, to which it is not unlike in shape. It is of the size of a codfish. Herring also come into the river. There is a species of fish caught on the shore, called by us stone-bream, and by the English *schip-heet*, that is to say, *sheep's-head*, for the reason that its mouth is full of teeth, above and below, like a sheep's head. Sturgeon are numerous in the brackish water, and as high up in the fresh water as Fort Orange. There are many kinds of fish which we have not in our Fatherland, so that I cannot name them all. In the fresh waters, are pike, perch, roach, and trout. There are fine oysters, large and small, in great abundance. In the summer-time crabs come on the flat shores, of very good taste. Their claws are of the color of the flag of our Prince, orange, white and blue,[2] so that the crabs show sufficiently that we ought to people the country, and that it belongs to us.

In what Manner they bury their Dead.

They make a large grave, and line it inside with boughs of trees, in which they lay the corpse, so that no earth can touch it. They then cover this with clay, and form the grave, seven or eight feet high, in the shape of a sugar-loaf, and place palisades around it. I have frequently seen the wife of the deceased come daily to the grave, weeping and crying, creeping around it with extended body, and grieving for the death of her husband. The oldest wife by whom he has had children does this; if he has also had a young wife, she does not make much ado about it, but looks out for another husband. They give a party when any one is dead in the house.

[1] Drum-fish. See the preceding note.
[2] No doubt the common edible blue crab.

I have seen at the North, great multitudes of savages assembled, who had collected together the bones of their ancestors, cleaned them, and bound them up in small bundles. They dig a square grave, the size and length of the person, and over it erect four pillars, which they cover with the bark of trees, as may be seen in the plate; they set a time when they will bury the body, when all the friends will have a great gathering, and bring ample supplies of provisions, accordingly as is prescribed by their village, that a great festival is to be held, with frolic and dancing. This festival continues some ten days, during which time their friends come from other nations on all sides, in order to see it held, and the accompanying ceremonies, which are attended with great expense. Under cover of these ceremonies, dances, feasts, and meetings, they contract new alliances of friendship with their neighbors; saying, that as the bones of their ancestors and friends are together in the little bundles (using this as a figure), so may their bones be together in the same place, and that as long as their lives shall last, they ought to be united in friendship and concord, as were their ancestors and friends, without being able to be separated from each other, like as the bones of the ancestors and friends of each other are mingled together. One of them—their chief or their devil-hunter—delivers much speech over the bones (saying), "that if they remain thus united, their enemies can have no power over them." They then bury the bones in the grave, with a parcel of *zeewan*, and with arrows, kettles, knives, paper, wicks, and other knick-knacks, which are held in great esteem by them, and cover them with earth, and place palisades around them as before related. Such is the custom on the coast in regard to the dead. The chief doctrine held among them is the belief in the immortality of the soul by some. Others are in doubt of this, but not far from it, saying, when they die they go to a place where they sing like the ravens; but this singing is entirely different from the singing of the angels.

How the Indians at the North arm themselves when they go to War.

When I was at the North, I saw savages who were going to war. They were armed as the figures show; their weapons were bows and arrows in the manner shown, which they carry daily, and each one had in his hand a shield of leather as thick as buffalo-skin. I took it to be elk's-hide, as these animals are numerous there. If they wish to take a journey in winter, when there is snow on the ground, they bind two things under their feet, like the racket with which we strike the balls at tennis, which prevent them from sinking in the snow, as may be seen on the figure (of the man), who is walking with his wife.

This [1] *is a Representation of them when they Dance and have a Feast.*

When they dance they stand two and two beside each other, which I have seen at the north. They dance in two, three, and four pairs. The first pair carry a tortoise in their hands, as this nation say that they have descended from a tortoise-father, at which I laughed. They then asked me where our first father came from. I said he was called Adam, and was made of earth. They said I was a fool to say that he was made of a thing that had no life. I replied that it was full of life, for it produced all the fruits upon which they lived. They answered that the sun, which they looked upon as a God, produced it, for in summer he drew the leaves from the trees, and all the fruits from the ground.

ANNO 1643. The 22d February, there broke out a war among the Mayekander savages, who came from Fort Orange and wanted to levy a contribution upon the savages of Wickquas-geck and Tapaen, and of the adjacent villages. There were eighty to ninety of those from Fort Orange, each with a gun on his shoulder. There came flying to my house, four to five hundred savages, desiring that I would protect them. I answered them that I could not do it, as the Indians from Fort Orange were also our friends, and that we did not interfere in their wars; that I now saw that they were children, that they were flying on all sides from eighty or ninety men, when they were themselves so many hundred strong, and had been wont to boast to me that they were *such* soldiers, yea, Mannetoe himself—that is to say, the Devil; but that I saw now that they were only children. As my house was so full of savages,

---

[1] Referring to a plate in the original.

and I had only five men with me, I thought best to go to the fort to obtain some soldiers for the purpose of having more force in my house. So I took a canoe, as my boat was frozen up in the kill, and went in the canoe, or hollow tree, which is their boat, as before related, between the cakes of ice, down the river to Fort Amsterdam, where I requested Governor Willem Kieft to assist me with some soldiers, as I was not master of my own house, because it was so full of savages, although I was not afraid that they would do any harm; but it was proper that I should be master of my own house. The Governor said he had no soldiers; that I must see how it would be in the morning, and stop at night with him, which I did. The next day the Indians came in troops on foot from my house to Pavonia, by the Oysterbank, where the great body of them encamped, and some of them came over the river from Pavonia to the fort. I spoke to some of them, and they said that they had all left my house. These Indians went to Correlaer's bouwery, where there were some Indians from Reckeweck,[1] opposite the fort, on Long Island, who were under a chief, named Nummerus, whom I well knew.

The 24th of February, sitting at a table with the Governor, he began to state his intentions, that he had a mind to *wipe the mouths* of the savages; that he had been dining at the house of Jan Claesz.[2] Damen, where Maryn Adriaensz. and Jan Claesz. Damen, together with Jacob Planck, had presented a petition to him to begin this work. I answered him that they were not wise to request this; that such work could not be done without the approbation of the *Twelve Men*; that it could not take place without my assent, who was one of the Twelve Men; that moreover I was the first patroon, and no one else hitherto had risked there so many thousands, and also his person, as I was the first to come from Holland or Zeeland to plant a colony; and that he should consider what profit he could derive from this business, as he well knew that on account of trifling with the Indians we had lost our colony in the South River at Swanendael, in the Hoere-kil, with thirty-two men, who

---

[1] Rockaway.

[2] Jansen. Maryn Adriaensen had been one of the Twelve Men. So had Abram Planck, who is probably the person meant by De Vries. Jacob Planck was his father.

were murdered in the year 1630; and that in the year 1640, the cause of my people being murdered on Staten Island was a difficulty which he had brought on with the Raritaen Indians, where his soldiers had for some trifling thing killed some savages, and brought the brother of the chief a prisoner to the Mannates, who was ransomed there, as I have before more particularly related. But it appeared that my speaking was of no avail. He had, with his co-murderers, determined to commit the murder, deeming it a Roman deed, and to do it without warning the inhabitants in the open lands, that each one might take care of himself against the retaliation of the savages, for he could not kill all the Indians. When I had expressed all these things in full, sitting at the table, and the meal was over, he told me he wished me to go to the large hall, which he had been lately adding to his house. Coming to it, there stood all his soldiers ready to cross the river to Pavonia to commit the murder. Then spoke I again to Governor Willem Kieft: "Let this work alone; you wish to break the mouths of the Indians, but you will also murder our own nation, for there are none of the settlers in the open country who are aware of it. My own dwelling, my people, cattle, corn, and tobacco will be lost." He answered me, assuring me that there would be no danger; that some soldiers should go to my house to protect it. But that was not done. So was this business begun between the 25th and 26th of February in the year 1643.[1] I remained that night at the Governor's, sitting up. I went and sat by the kitchen fire, when about midnight I heard a great shrieking, and I ran to the ramparts of the fort, and looked over to Pavonia. Saw nothing but firing, and heard the shrieks of the savages murdered in their sleep. I returned again to the house by the fire. Having sat there awhile, there came an Indian with his squaw, whom I knew well, and who lived about an hour's walk from my house, and told me that they two had fled in a small skiff, which they had taken from the shore at Pavonia; that the Indians from Fort Orange had surprised them; and that they had come to conceal themselves in the fort. I told them that they must go away immediately; that this was no time for them to come to the fort to conceal themselves; that they who had killed their

---

[1] The text has 1654. The errata correct it to 1643. See the introduction.

people at Pavonia were not Indians, but the Swannekens, as they call the Dutch, had done it. They then asked me how they should get out of the fort. I took them to the door, and there was no sentry there, and so they betook themselves to the woods. When it was day the soldiers returned to the fort, having massacred or murdered eighty Indians, and considering they had done a deed of Roman valor, in murdering so many in their sleep;[1] where infants were torn from their mother's breasts, and hacked to pieces in the presence of the parents, and the pieces thrown into the fire and in the water, and other sucklings, being bound to small boards, were cut, stuck, and pierced, and miserably massacred in a manner to move a heart of stone. Some were thrown into the river, and when the fathers and mothers endeavored to save them, the soldiers would not let them come on land but made both parents and children drown—children from five to six years of age, and also some old and decrepit persons. Those who fled from this onslaught, and concealed themselves in the neighboring sedge, and when it was morning, came out to beg a piece of bread, and to be permitted to warm themselves, were murdered in cold blood and tossed into the fire or the water. Some came to our people in the country with their hands, some with their legs cut off, and some holding their entrails in their arms, and others had such horrible cuts and gashes, that worse than they were could never happen. And these poor simple creatures, as also many of our own people, did not know any better than that they had been attacked by a party of other Indians—the Maquas. After this exploit, the soldiers were rewarded for their services, and Director Kieft thanked them by taking them by the hand and congratulating them. At another place, on the same night, on Corler's Hook near Corler's plantation, forty Indians were in the same manner attacked in their sleep, and massacred there in the same manner. Did the Duke of Alva in the Netherlands ever

---

[1] From this point to where De Vries begins to speak of the destruction of his own property, all is borrowed from the *Breeden Raedt* ("Grand Council"), an anti-Kieft, anti-Stuyvesant pamphlet, scurrilous but interesting, and of a certain importance, which was printed at Antwerp in 1649. Its authorship is unknown. There is a translation in the *Collections of the New York Historical Society*, second series, III. 237–284.

do anything more cruel? This is indeed a disgrace to our
nation, who have so generous a governor in our Fatherland as
the Prince of Orange, who has always endeavored in his wars to
spill as little blood as possible.[1] As soon as the savages understood that the Swannekens had so treated them, all the men
whom they could surprise on the farm-lands, they killed; but
we have never heard that they have ever permitted women or
children to be killed. They burned all the houses, farms, barns,
grain, haystacks, and destroyed everything they could get hold
of. So there was an open destructive war begun. They also
burnt my farm, cattle, corn, barn, tobacco-house, and all the
tobacco. My people saved themselves in the house where I
alone lived, which was made with embrasures, through which
they defended themselves. Whilst my people were in alarm
the savage whom I had aided to escape from the fort in the night
came there, and told the other Indians that I was a good chief,
that I had helped him out of the fort, and that the killing of the
Indians took place contrary to my wish. Then they all cried
out together to my people that they would not shoot them;
that if they had not destroyed my cattle they would not do it,
nor burn my house; that they would let my little brewery
stand, though they wished to get the copper kettle, in order to
make darts for their arrows; but hearing now that it[2] had
been done contrary to my wish, they all went away, and left
my house unbesieged. When now the Indians had destroyed
so many farms and men in revenge for their people, I went to
Governor Willem Kieft, and asked him if it was not as I had
said it would be, that he would only effect the spilling of Christian blood. Who would now compensate us for our losses?
But he gave me no answer. He said he wondered that no
Indians came to the fort. I told him that I did not wonder
at it; "why should the Indians come here where you have so
treated them?"

The 4th of March, there came three savages upon Long
Island, with a small white flag, and called out to the fort.
Then Governor Willem Kieft asked who would go over to
them. There was no one who was willing to do so, among
all of them, except Jacob Olfersz. and I, David Pietersz. de

[1] A reference to Prince Frederick Henry, and therefore probably written
before 1650.   [2] The massacre.

Vries. We went to the three savages. They told us that they came from their chief, who had sent them to know the cause why some of his Indians had been killed, who had never laid a straw in our way, and who had done us nothing but favors? We answered them that we did not know that any of their Indians were among them. They then said we must go and speak with their chief, who had fled seven leagues from there on the seacoast. We resolved to go with the Indians, for we believed that they were well disposed towards us two.

At evening we arrived at Rechqua Akie [1] where we found the chief, who had only one eye, with two or three hundred Indians, and about thirty houses. They led us into his house, and treated us to what they had, as oysters, and fish, which they catch there; told us we were tired, and must rest a little; they would early in the morning speak to us about the business upon which we had come there. During the night, I went out of the house, when there came an Indian to me, as the moon was shining, and told me I must come into his hut. I then went into his hut, and by the light saw he was an Indian, who lived half a league from my farm-house at Vriessendael, with his squaws, who lived there with him, at which I was alarmed. But he assured me, saying, that I was a good chief, and that I came to make *Rancontyn Marinit*; that is, in their language, to make a peace. I asked them how they came so far from their dwelling. They answered that they were out a hunting with these Indians, and had friends among them. I then returned to my comrade in the house of the chief. When the day began to dawn, we were awakened, and taken by a savage, who led us into the woods about four hundred paces from the houses, and when we came there, sixteen chiefs were there of this Long Island, which is thirty leagues long. They placed us two by ourselves, and seated themselves around us, so that we sat within a ring. There was one among them who had a small bundle of sticks, and was the best speaker, who began his oration in Indian. He told how we first came upon their coast; that we sometimes had no victuals; they gave us their Turkish beans and Turkish wheat, they helped us with oysters and fish to eat, and now for a reward we had killed their people.

[1] Rockaway.

Then he laid down one of the sticks, which was one point.   He
related also that at the beginning of our voyaging there, we
left our people behind with the goods to trade, until the ships
should come back;[1] they had preserved these people like the
apple of their eye; yea, they had given them their daughters to
sleep with, by whom they had begotten children, and there
roved many an Indian who was begotten by a Swanneken, but
our people had become so villainous as to kill their own blood.
He then laid down another stick.   This laying down of sticks
began to be tedious to me, as I saw that he had many still in
his hand.   I told him that I knew all these things which he said
had happened to the savages of Long Island; they had been
done unwittingly; if any of them had been with the other
savages, they should go with us to the fort, where the Governor
would give them presents for a peace.   The speaking now
ceased and they gave to each of us ten fathoms of *zeewan*—
which is their money, each fathom being worth four guilders.
Then they all rose up and said that they would go with us to the
fort, and speak with our governor Willem Kieft.   We went to
the canoes to go by water, and to make the journey shorter
than when we came, for it made full three hours difference.
When we reached the canoes, we found that the tide had not
yet begun to make, and that we must wait some time before
it would be flood.   In the mean time, an Indian came running
up with a bow and arrow, who had come on a run six leagues
on behalf of a chief who had not been with us, and asked the
chiefs who were going with us to the fort if they were so foolish
as to go to the fort where there was such a villain, who had
caused their friends to be so foully murdered; and who, when
so many of the chiefs were together at the fort, would keep them
there, and thus all the Indians would be in distress, being
without heads or chiefs, and said the chief from whom he came
thought it entirely inadvisable.   They asked us two if we
understood what he said.   We answered that this was a crazy
Indian, that they would find it otherwise, and would return
home with good presents.   Then one of the chiefs who knew

---

[1] The allusion is probably to Cornelis Hendricksen and his men, who spent
the winters of 1614–1615 and 1615–1616 in New Netherland, presumably in the
region of Manhattan or Long Island, before there was any permanent settlement
of the Dutch in it.

me well said, "we will go on the faith of your word, for the Indians have never found you to lie as they have the other Swannekens." Finally, twenty of us went sitting in a canoe or hollow-tree, which is their boat, and the edge was not more than a hand's-breadth above the water. Arrived at the fort about three o'clock in the afternoon, and went to Willem Kieft, who made peace with the Indians, and gave them some presents. He requested them to bring those chiefs to the fort who had lost so many Indians, as he wished also to make a peace with them, and to give them presents. Then some of them went and brought the Indians of Ackin-sack and Tapaen and the vicinity, and the chiefs came with them, to whom he made presents; but they were not well content with them. They told me that he could have made it, by his presents, that as long as he lived the massacre would never again be spoken of; but now it might fall out that the infant upon the small board would remember it. They then went away grumbling with their presents.

The 20th of July, a chief of the savages came to me, and told me that he was very sad. I asked him wherefor. He said that there were many of the Indian youths, who were constantly wishing for a war against us, as one had lost his father, another his mother, a third his uncle, and also their friends, and that the presents or recompense were not worth taking up; and that he would much rather have made presents out of his own purse to quiet them; but he could no longer keep them still, and that I must be careful in going alone in the woods; that those who knew me would do me no harm, but I might meet Indians who did not know me, who would shoot me. I told him that he ought to go to Commander Kieft at the fort, and tell the same things to him. We went to the fort, and coming to the commander, the chief of these Indians told the same things to him. Commander Kieft told this savage he was a chief of the Indians and must kill these young madcaps who wished to engage in a war with the Swannekens, and he would give him two hundred fathoms of *zeewan*. I then laughed within myself, that the Indian should kill his friends for two hundred fathoms of *zeewan*—that is eight hundred guilders—to gratify us. It is true that they do so towards each other, when they are at enmity with each other, but not at the will of foreigners. Then the Indian said this could not be done by him; that there were many malcontents. Had he (the Governor) paid richly for the murder, it would have been entirely forgotten. He himself would do his best to keep them quiet, but he was afraid he could not, for they were continually calling for vengeance.[1]

The 28th of September, arrived a herring buss from Rotterdam; the master was named Jacob Blenck. He was laden with a hundred pipes of Madeira wine, and had come by the way of the West Indies, wishing to go to the Virginias, but could not find them, and had sailed quite to New England. He could not sell his wine there, because the English there live soberly. He was compelled to return, and came along the coast inside of Long Island, through Hellgate to Fort Amsterdam; and coming here he could not dispose of his wines here either, because here was a prize laden with wines which the Company had captured. He sold his wines to an Englishman to be taken to the Virginias. As he could find no one who could pilot him to the Virginias, he asked me if I would take him there, as he understood that I wished to go there in order to take a well-mounted ship for the Fatherland, because my farms, where I had begun my colonies, were lying in ashes; and the Indians were discontented and desired to go to war again, or to have satisfaction. I promised the skipper that I would take him there out of friendship, and told him that he must provide himself with bread here if needed, for it was difficult to obtain it in the Virginias, because every one there only produced for himself.

The 1st of October, nine savages came to Pavonia opposite the fort, where there were three or four soldiers stationed to protect the farmer who lived there, named Jacob Stoffelsz., towards whom they were so well disposed that they did not wish to kill him. So they made a pretended errand, and persuaded him to go over to the fort (Amsterdam), and he came over accordingly; then they went under the guise of friendship, when the soldiers had no arms in their hands, and killed them all, except the young son of his wife by a former marriage,

---

[1] In September Mrs. Anne Hutchinson and other English settlers in the Dutch province were murdered by the Indians. The warfare nearly brought New Netherland to utter ruin.

whom they took with them captive to Tapaen. They set fire to the farm-house and all the other houses at Pavonia; and thus began a new war. The next day the Governor came to me with the step-father of the little boy that was made prisoner by the Indians. He was the son of Cornelis van Vorst.[1] The Governor asked me if I would go to the savages to obtain the release of the boy, as nobody dared go to the Indians except me. I said I would send them one or two Indians; but if I brought them to the fort, they must not be misused, for they would come with me upon my word. So I went over to Long Island and brought with me two Indians to go to Tapaen to obtain the release of the boy. When I brought the Indians over, every one wanted to kill them, and I had enough to do to save them. I took them to a privateer which was lying there, which carried them away, and they released the boy.

The 8th of the same month I took my leave of Commander Kieft, and left in the Rotterdammer buss for the English Virginias; and, in taking leave of Willem Kieft, I told him that this murder which he had committed on so much innocent blood would yet be avenged upon him, and thus I left him. Sailed past Staten Island through the Narrows to Sandy Hook, where we were detained two days by contrary winds. Picked each day some blue-plums, which are abundant there, and grow there naturally wild.

The 11th, weighed anchor to sail from Sandy Hook to the Virginias, with a northwest wind and a weather shore.[2]

[1] Formerly Michiel Pauw's factor at Pavonia.

[2] After a brief visit to the Swedes on the Delaware, De Vries reached Virginia October 21. There he remained through the winter, part of the time as the guest of Governor Berkeley. In April, 1644, he sailed for home, and on June 21, "by the mercy of Almighty God, arrived here within my paternal city of Hoorn, where I have an ancestry of two hundred years on the father's side, and at Amsterdam on my mother's side, and came to my house at three o'clock, for which our God must be eternally praised, that he should have brought me again to my Fatherland, after such long and tedious voyages, and through so many perils of savage heathens."

LETTER AND NARRATIVE OF FATHER ISAAC JOGUES, 1643, 1645

INTRODUCTION

FOR a century and a half after the definite establishment of Protestantism in northern Europe, the missionary activity of the Christian Church, it is not too much to say, was almost confined to its Catholic branch. The missionary efforts and achievements of the Protestant or national churches, mainly perhaps because they were national, were insignificant in comparison with those of the Catholics. While in the latter the older orders did their part, none equalled in ardor and energy the new-born forces of the Society of Jesus. There are no more moving pages in the annals of Christian heroism than those which describe the sacrifices and sufferings of the Jesuit missionaries in the East Indies and Japan, in Africa and America, their holy zeal and their unselfish devotion. In Canada their labors took on especial vigor after the province was restored to the French by the treaty of 1632. Their mission to the Hurons was particularly successful, till the Huron nation and their missionaries were alike overwhelmed by the terrible Iroquois in 1649.

The missionary activity of the Jesuits among the heathen of the American wilderness is mainly chronicled in the series of exceedingly rare little books called the *Relations des Jésuites*, annual bulletins from the missionary field, published for purposes of edification at Paris from 1632 to 1672, and republished in our time in Dr. Reuben G. Thwaites's noble series, *The Jesuit Relations and Allied Documents* (Cleveland, 1896–1901, in 73 volumes). A capital general survey and estimate of this whole body of literature may be found in an article by Professor Charles W. Colby in the *American Historical Review*, VII.

36–55. The relations with which we are particularly concerned, because of the visit of Father Isaac Jogues to New Netherland in 1643, are that of 1642–1643, written early in the autumn of the latter year by Father Vimont, superior of the Jesuits in Canada, and that of 1647 by Father Jerome Lalemant. Only the portions strictly relating to New Netherland are here reprinted. For the full story of Father Jogues's capture by the Iroquois, of the dreadful tortures and sufferings to which he was subjected by them, and of his year of captivity in their villages, the reader is referred to Dr. Thwaites's pages. As he reads, the student should bear ever in mind that the man on whom all these sufferings were inflicted was not a rough, hardened *coureur de bois*, but a refined scholar, a delicate priest.

Isaac Jogues, a Frenchman, born at Orleans in 1607, studied in the Jesuit college in that city, and entered the Company of Jesus at Paris in 1624. For four years, 1629–1633, he was a professor at Rouen; then for three years he studied theology in Paris. Throughout his years of study he was noted for his burning love of souls and his longing for the missionary life. In 1636 he was sent out to New France, where he entered with the greatest ardor into the work of the Huron mission. In August, 1642, while he was making his way up the St. Lawrence with two French coadjutors (*donnés*), René Goupil and Guillaume Couture, and a number of Huron converts, the whole party fell into an ambush of Iroquois, deadly enemies of the Hurons. Refusing the chance of escape, he chose to remain with his French and Indian associates, to share their fate, and to supply to these precious souls the ministrations of a priest. The three Frenchmen were subjected to terrible tortures. Goupil was murdered at the feet of the father. The latter, dragged from village to village of the Mohawks, spent the whole year in miserable captivity and suffering, with the constant prospect of most painful death, happy if he could furtively administer baptism or absolution or comfort to any of his Huron dependents, or make the slightest impression favorable to Christianity upon the hard heart of any Mohawk. The story of his escape, by way of Fort Orange and Manhattan, is related in the following pages.

The sincerity of Father Jogues in professing willingness to be laid upon the altar is attested by his subsequent conduct. After a brief stay in France, early in 1644 he returned again to Canada. In July, 1645, peace was concluded at Three Rivers between the Mohawks and the governor of New France. In May, 1646, when the governor wished to send an embassy to that tribe, Father Jogues undertook the dangerous mission, was well received by his former captors, and returned in safety. Hoping that the way was now open for missionary success, he determined to go back among them. To a friend in France he wrote, "My heart tells me that if I have the good fortune to be employed in this mission, *ibo et non redibo*, I shall go and I shall not return; but I should be happy if it should be the will of Our Lord to finish the sacrifice there where he began it." He set out on September 24, 1646. But the temper of the Mohawks had changed. An influential portion of them now wished to renew war with the French, and public opinion attributed a pestilence from which the tribe had suffered to the evil influence of a box which the missionary had left in a Mohawk village in the spring. The father was seized as he was making his way from Lake George to the Mohawk country. There was much deliberation. It was decided to spare him. But a hostile Indian suddenly slew him with one blow of his hatchet. He died October 18, 1646, at the village of Osseruenon, near the present Auriesville, New York. On the supposed site of his martyrdom a Catholic chapel was erected in 1884 as a memorial to him and to René Goupil, and in the same year the third plenary council of Baltimore requested of the Pope his beatification.

The original documents for the history of Father Jogues's first captivity among the Mohawks have mostly been printed by Dr. Thwaites, and also by the late Dr. John Gilmary Shea in the *Collections of the New York Historical Society*, second series, III. 173–219. They are the following: First, we find the letter of warning which he wrote to the governor of New France, June 30, 1643, along with an account of his captivity by a Huron who had escaped, in the *Relation* of 1642–1643, chapter XII. (Thwaites, XXIV. 295–297; Shea, 206–207). Secondly, there is a long letter which he wrote in Latin from Rensselaerswyck, August 5, 1643, to the Provincial of the Jesuits in Paris, and of which the Latin manuscript is still preserved in the archives of the College of Saint Mary at Montreal. This describes in detail his terrible sufferings among the Iroquois, but says little of New Netherland. It was printed in the original Latin in Alegambe's Jesuit martyrology, *Mortes Illustres* (Rome, 1657), and in Tanner's *Societas Militans* (Prague, 1675), pp. 511–525. A translation by Dr. Shea, from the manuscript at Montreal, is printed in the New York *Collections*, second series, III. 173–206. An Italian version which appeared in Father Bressani's *Breve Relatione* (Macerata, 1653) is reprinted in Thwaites, XXXIX. 175–225, with an English translation. Thirdly, there is the letter written from Rensselaerswyck August 30, 1643, to Father Charles Lalemant, superior of the Jesuits in Canada, covering the journey from the Iroquois village to the Dutch settlement, which is reproduced in the present volume. Its French text is to be found in chapter XIV. of the *Relation* of 1642–1643 (Thwaites, XXV. 43–63; Shea, 207–214). Our English text is, by Dr. Thwaites's kind permission, borrowed from his. Fourthly, there is a brief account of Father Jogues's escape in two letters, one to Lalemant, the other to another friend, dated Rennes, January 5 and 6, 1644, which immediately follow in the *Relation* of 1642–1643. Fifthly, there is the much fuller account of the stay at Rensselaerswyck and the escape which, two or three years afterward, at the time of Father Jogues's second stay in Canada, he wrote out for Father Buteux, then superior of the Jesuits in New France. This is reproduced, partly in the first person, partly in the third, in chapter VII. of the *Relation* of 1647. That relation takes occasion, before narrating Father Jogues's martyrdom, to introduce the story of his early experiences among the Iroquois. To a large extent Father Jogues's story repeats the letter of August 5, 1643, mentioned first in this paragraph. But the portion relating to events after that date is new, and adds to our knowledge of New Netherland beyond what is contained in the letter of August 30. This part, accordingly, has been reprinted from Dr. Thwaites's collection (XXXI. 93–99). Finally, there is the *Novum Belgium,* separately treated in subsequent pages of this book.

I

LETTER OF FATHER ISAAC JOGUES TO HIS SUPERIOR IN CANADA, 1643

I STARTED the very day of the Feast of Our Blessed Father Saint Ignatius [1] from the village where I was captive, in order to follow and accompany some Iroquois who were going away, first for trade, then for fishing. Having accomplished their little traffic, they stopped at a place seven or eight leagues below a settlement of the Dutch, which is located on a river [2] where we carried on our fishing. While we were setting snares for the fish, there came a rumor that a squad of Iroquois, returned from pursuit of the Hurons, had killed five or six on the spot, and taken four prisoners, two of whom had been already burned in our village, with cruelties extraordinary. At this news, my heart was pierced through with a most bitter and sharp pain, because I had not seen, or consoled, or baptized those poor victims. Consequently, fearing lest some other like thing should happen in my absence, I said to a good old woman—who, by reason of her age, and the care that she had for me, and the compassion that she felt toward me, called me her nephew, and I called her my aunt—I then said to her: "My aunt, I would much like to return to our cabin; I grow very weary here." It was not that I expected more ease and less pain in our village, where I suffered a continual martyrdom, being constrained to see with my eyes the horrible cruelties which are practised there; but my heart could not endure the death of any man without my procuring him holy baptism. That good woman said to me: "Go then, my nephew, since thou art weary here; take something to eat on the way." I embarked in the first canoe that was going up to the village, always conducted and always accompanied by the Iroquois.

[1] July 31. [2] Hudson River.

Having arrived, as we did, in the settlement of the Dutch, through which it was necessary for us to pass, I learn that our whole village is excited against the French, and that only my return is awaited, for them to burn us. Now for the cause of such news. Among several bands of Iroquois, who had gone to war against the French, the Algonquins and the Hurons, there was one which took the resolution to go round about Richelieu, in order to spy on the French and the savages, their allies. A certain Huron of this band, taken by the Hiroquois, and settled among them, came to ask me for letters, in order to carry them to the French, hoping, perhaps, to surprise some one of them by this bait; but, as I doubted not that our French would be on their guard, and as I saw, moreover, that it was important that I should give them some warning of the designs, the arms and the treachery of our enemies, I found means to secure a bit of paper in order to write to them, the Dutch according me this charity.[1] I knew very well the dangers to which I was exposing myself; I was not ignorant that, if any misfortune happened to those warriors, they would make me responsible therefor, and would blame my letters for it. I anticipated my death; but it seemed to me pleasant and agreeable, employed for the public good, and for the consolation of our French and of the poor savages who listen to the word of Our Lord. My heart was seized with no dread at the sight of all that might happen therefrom, since it was a matter of the glory of God; I accordingly gave my letter to that young warrior, who did not return. The story which his comrades have brought back says that he carried it to the fort of Richelieu,[2] and that, as soon as the French had seen it, they fired the cannon upon them. This frightened them so that the greater part fled, all naked, abandoning one of their canoes, in which there were three arquebuses, powder and lead, and some other baggage. These tidings being brought into the village, they clamor aloud that my letters have caused them to be treated like that; the rumor of it spreads everywhere; it comes even to my ears. They reproach me that I have done this evil

---

[1] The text of this letter, dated June 30, 1643, is given in an earlier chapter (ch. XII.) of the *Relation of* 1642–1643, and may be seen, with a translation, in Thwaites's *Jesuit Relations*, XXIV. 294–297.

[2] At the mouth of the Richelieu River, where now stands Sorel, P. Q.

deed; they speak only of burning me; and, if I had chanced to be in the village at the return of those warriors, fire, rage and cruelty would have taken my life. For climax of misfortune, another troop—coming back from Mont-real, where they had set ambushes for the French—said that one of their men had been killed, and two others wounded. Each one held me guilty of these adverse encounters; they were fairly mad with rage, awaiting me with impatience. I listened to all these rumors, offering myself without reserve to our Lord, and committing myself in all and through all to His most holy will. The captain of the Dutch settlement where we were,[1] not being ignorant of the evil design of those barbarians, and knowing, moreover, that Monsieur the Chevalier de Montmagny [2] had prevented the savages of New France from coming to kill some Dutch, disclosed to me means for escape. "Yonder," said he to me, "is a vessel at anchor, which will sail in a few days; enter into it secretly. It is going first to Virginia, and thence it will carry you to Bordeaux or to La Rochelle, where it is to land." Having thanked him, with much regard for his courtesy, I tell him that the Iroquois, probably suspecting that some one had favored my retreat, might cause some damages to his people. "No, no," he answers, "fear nothing; this opportunity is favorable; embark; you will never find a more certain way to escape." My heart remained perplexed at these words, wondering if it were not expedient for the greater glory of our Lord that I expose myself to the danger of the fire and to the fury of those barbarians, in order to aid in the salvation of some soul. I said to him then: "Monsieur, the affair seems to me of such importance that I cannot answer you at once; give me, if you please, the night to think of it. I will commend it to our Lord; I will examine the arguments on both sides; and to-morrow morning I will tell you my final resolution." He granted me my request with astonishment; I spent the night in prayers, greatly beseeching our Lord that he should

---

[1] Arent van Curler (1619–1667), chief factor of Rensselaerswyck at this time, and a man of great influence with the Indians. In the preceding September (1642), on hearing of the capture of the Frenchmen, he had gone to the castles of the Mohawks to obtain their release, but in vain. His account of his journey, in a letter to the patroon, June 16, is reprinted in O'Callaghan's *History of New Netherland*, I. 463, 464.   [2] Governor of Quebec.

not allow me to reach a conclusion by myself; that he should give me light, in order to know His most holy will; that in all and through all I wished to follow it, even to the extent of being burned at a slow fire. The reasons which might keep me in the country were consideration for the French and for the Savages; I felt love for them, and a great desire to assist them, insomuch that I had resolved to spend the remainder of my days in that captivity, for their salvation; but I saw the face of affairs quite changed.

In the first place, as regarded our three Frenchmen, led captive into the country as well as I: one of them, named René Goupil, had already been murdered at my feet; this young man had the purity of an angel. Henry, whom they had taken at Mont-Real, had fled into the woods. While he was looking at the cruelties which were practised upon two poor Hurons, roasted at a slow fire, some Iroquois told him that he would receive the same treatment, and I, too, when I should return; these threats made him resolve rather to plunge into the danger of dying from hunger in the woods, or of being de- voured by some wild beast, than to endure the torments which these half-demons inflicted. It was already seven days since he had disappeared. As for Guillaume Cousture, I saw scarcely any further way of aiding him, for they had placed him in a village far from the one where I was; and the savages so occu- pied it on the hither side of that place, that I could no longer meet him. Add that he himself had addressed me in these words: "My Father, try to escape; as soon as I shall see you no more, I shall find the means to get away. You well know that I stay in this captivity only for the love of you; make, then, your efforts to escape, for I cannot think of my liberty and of my life unless I see you in safety." Furthermore, this good youth had been given to an old man, who assured me that he would allow him to go in peace, if I could obtain my deliver- ance; consequently I saw no further reason which obliged me to remain on account of the French.

As for the savages, I was without power and beyond hope of being able to instruct them; for the whole country was so irritated against me that I found no more any opening to speak to them, or to win them; and the Algonquins and the Hurons were constrained to withdraw from me, as from a victim des-

tined to the fire, for fear of sharing in the hatred and rage
which the Iroquois felt against me. I realized, moreover, that
I had some acquaintance with their language; that I knew their
country and their strength; that I could perhaps better procure their salvation by other ways than by remaining among
them. It came to my mind that all this knowledge would die
with me, if I did not escape. These wretches had so little
inclination to deliver us, that they committed a treachery
against the law and the custom of all these nations. A savage
from the country of the Sokokiois,[1] allies of the Iroquois,
having been seized by the upper Algonquins and taken a
prisoner to the Three Rivers, or to Kebec, was delivered and
set at liberty by the mediation of Monsieur the Governor of
New France, at the solicitation of our Fathers. This good
savage, seeing that the French had saved his life, sent in the
month of April, some fine presents, to the end that they should
deliver at least one of the French. The Iroquois retained the
presents, without setting one of them at liberty, which treachery is perhaps unexampled among these peoples, for they in-
violably observe this law, that whoever touches or accepts the
present which is made to him, is bound to fulfil what is asked
of him through that present. This is why, when they are unwilling to grant what is desired, they send back the presents
or make others in place of them. But to return to my subject:
having weighed before God, with all the impartiality in my
power, the reasons which inclined me to remain among those
barbarians or to leave them, I believed that our Lord would
be better pleased if I should take the opportunity to escape.
Daylight having come, I went to greet Monsieur the Dutch
Governor, and declared to him the opinions that I had adopted
before God. He summons the chief men of the ship, signifies
to them his intentions, and exhorts them to receive me, and
to keep me concealed—in a word, to convey me back to Europe.
They answer that, if I can once set foot in their vessel, I am
in safety; that I shall not leave it until I reach Bordeaux or
La Rochelle. "Well, then," the Governor said to me, "return
with the savages, and toward the evening, or in the night, steal
away softly and move toward the river; you will find there a
little boat which I will have kept all ready to carry you secretly

---

[1] An Abnaki tribe, dwelling in Maine.

to the ship." After very humbly returning thanks to all those
gentlemen, I withdrew from the Dutch, in order better to conceal my design. Toward evening, I retired with ten or twelve
Iroquois into a barn, where we passed the night. Before lying
down, I went out of that place, to see in what quarter I might
most easily escape. The dogs of the Dutch, being then untied,
run up to me; one of them, large and powerful, flings himself
upon my leg, which is bare, and seriously injures it. I return
immediately to the barn; the Iroquois close it securely and,
the better to guard me, come to lie down beside me, especially
a certain man who had been charged to watch me. Seeing
myself beset with those evil creatures, and the barn well closed,
and surrounded with dogs, which would betray me if I essayed
to go out, I almost believed that I could not escape. I complained quietly to my God, because, having given me the idea
of escaping, *Concluserat vias meas lapidibus quadris, et in loco
spatioso pedes meos.*[1] He was stopping up the ways and paths
of it. I spent also that second night without sleeping; the
day approaching, I heard the cocks crow. Soon afterward, a
servant of the Dutch farmer who had lodged us in his barn,
having entered it by some door or other, I accosted him softly,
and made signs to him (for I did not understand his Flemish),
that he should prevent the dogs from yelping. He goes out at
once, and I after him, having previously taken all my belong-
ings, which consisted of a little Office of the Virgin, of a little
Gerson,[2] and a wooden Cross that I had made for myself, in
order to preserve the memory of the sufferings of my Savior.
Being outside of the barn, without having made any noise or
awakened my guards, I cross over a fence which confined the
enclosure about the house; I run straight to the river where the
ship was—this is all the service that my leg, much wounded,
could render me; for there was surely a good quarter of a
league of road to make. I found the boat as they had told
me, but, the water having subsided, it was aground. I push it,
in order to set it afloat; not being able to effect this, on account
of its weight, I call to the ship, that they bring the skiff to

[1] Lamentations iii. 9, "He hath inclosed my ways with hewn stone," and
Psalm xxxi. 8, "Thou hast set my foot in a large room."

[2] Probably a small edition of the *Imitatio Christi*, then often attributed to
Johannes Gerson rather than to Thomas a Kempis.

ferry me, but no news.   I know not whether they heard me;
at all events no one appeared.   The daylight meanwhile was
beginning to discover to the Iroquois the theft that I was
making of myself; I feared that they might surprise me in this
innocent misdemeanor.   Weary of shouting, I return to the
boat; I pray God to increase my strength; I do so well, turning
it end for end, and push it so hard that I get it to the water.
Having made it float, I jump into it, and go all alone to the
ship, where I go on board without being discovered by any
Iroquois.   They lodge me forthwith down in the hold; and in
order to conceal me they put a great chest over the hatchway.
I was two days and two nights in the belly of that vessel,
with such discomfort that I thought I would suffocate and die
with the stench.   I remembered then poor Jonas, and I
prayed our Lord, *Ne fugerem a facie Domini*,[1] that I might not
hide myself before his face, and that I might not withdraw far
from his wishes; but on the contrary, *infatuaret omnia consilia
quae non essent ad suam gloriam*, I prayed him to overthrow
all the counsels which should not tend to his glory, and to
detain me in the country of those infidels, if he did not approve my retreat and my flight.   The second night of my
voluntary prison, the minister of the Dutch[2] came to tell me
that the Iroquois had indeed made some disturbance, and that
the Dutch inhabitants of the country were afraid that they
would set fire to their houses or kill their cattle; they have
reason to fear them, since they have armed them with good
arquebuses.   To that I answer: *Si propter me orta est tem-
pestas, projicite me in mare:*[3] "If the storm has risen on my
account, I am ready to appease it by losing my life;" I had
never the wish to escape to the prejudice of the least man of
their settlement.   Finally, it was necessary to leave my cavern;
all the mariners were offended at this, saying that the promise
of security had been given me in case I could set foot in the
ship, and that I was being withdrawn at the moment when it
would be requisite to bring me thither if I were not there;
that I had put myself in peril of life by escaping upon their

---

[1] "Let me not flee from the face of the Lord."

[2] Domine Megapolensis.

[3] "If the storm has risen on my account, throw me into the sea," an allusion
to Jonah, i. 12.

words; that it must needs be kept, whatever the cost. I begged that I be allowed to go forth, since the captain who had disclosed to me the way of my flight was asking for me. I went to find him in his house, where he kept me concealed; these goings and these comings having occurred by night, I was not yet discovered. I might indeed have alleged some reasons in all these encounters; but it was not for me to speak in my own cause, but rather to follow the orders of others, to which I submitted with good heart. Finally, the captain told me that it was necessary to yield quietly to the storm, and wait until the minds of the savages should be pacified; and that every one was of this opinion. So there I was, a voluntary prisoner in his house, from which I am writing back to you the present letter. And if you ask my thoughts in all these adventures, I will tell you.

First, that that ship which had wished to save my life, sailed without me.

Secondly, if our Lord do not protect me in a manner wellnigh miraculous, the savages, who go and come here at every moment, will discover me; and if ever they convince themselves that I have not gone away, it will be necessary to return into their hands. Now if they had such a rage against me before my flight, what treatment will they inflict on me, seeing me fallen back into their power? I shall not die a common death; the fire, their rage, and the cruelties which they invent, will tear away my life. God be blessed forever. We are incessantly in the bosom of His divine and always adorable providence. *Vestri capilli capitis numerati sunt; nolite timere; multis passeribus meliores estis vos quorum unus non cadet super terram sine patre vestro;* [1] he who has care for the little birds of the air does not cast us into oblivion. It is already twelve days that I have been concealed; it is quite improbable that misfortune will reach me.

In the third place, you see the great need that we have of your prayers and of the holy Sacrifices of all our Fathers; procure us this alms everywhere, *Ut reddat me Dominus idoneum ad se amandum, fortem ad patiendum, constantem ad perse-*

---

[1] "The very hairs of your head are all numbered. Fear ye not therefore; ye are of more value than many sparrows. And one of them shall not fall on the ground without your Father."—Matth. x. 30, 31, 29.

verandum in suo amore, et servitio, to the end that God may
render me fit and well disposed to love him; that he may
render me strong and courageous to suffer and to endure; and
that he may give me a noble constancy to persevere in his love
and in his service—this is what I would desire above all,
together with a little New Testament from Europe.   Pray for
these poor nations which burn and devour one another, that
at last they may come to the knowledge of their Creator, in
order to render to Him the tribute of their love.   *Memor sum
vestri in vinculis meis;*[1] I do not forget you; my captivity cannot fetter my memory.   I am, heartily and with affection, etc.

From Renselaerivich, this 30th of August, 1643.

[1] "I am mindful of you in my bonds."

II

NARRATIVE OF FATHER JOGUES, REPORTED BY FATHER BUTEUX, 1645

UPON the return from this journey, they command the Father to go and accompany some fishermen, who conducted him seven or eight leagues below a Dutch settlement. While he was engaged in that exercise, he learned from the lips of some Hiroquois who came to that quarter that they were awaiting him in the village to burn him. This news was the occasion of his deliverance, of which—having sufficiently mentioned it in the *Relation* for the year 1642 and 1643, chapter 14 [1]—I will relate here only some particulars of which there has been but little if any mention. The Dutch having given him the opportunity to enter a ship, the Hiroquois complained of it; he was withdrawn thence and conducted to the house of the captain, who gave him in custody to an old man, until they should have appeased those barbarians. In a word, if they had persevered in their demand, and rejected some presents that were made to them, the Father would have been given up into their hands, to be the object of their fury and food for their fires. Now, while they were awaiting the opportunity to send him back to Europe, he remained six weeks under the guard of that old man, who was very miserly, and lodged him in an old garret, where hunger, and thirst, and heat, and the fear at every moment of falling back into the hands of the Hiroquois, gave him excellent reason to cast and submerge himself within the providence of Him who had so often caused him to realize His presence. This man was the sutler of that settlement; he made lye every fortnight, then carried back his tub to the garret, in which he put water which served the Father for drink until the next lye-making. This

[1] See the preceding pages.

251

water, which soon spoiled in the summer heat, caused him a
severe pain in the stomach. They gave him to eat as much as
was necessary, not to live, but not to die. God alone, and His
saints, were his company. The minister visited him sometimes, and bethinking himself one day to ask him how they
treated him, for never would this good Father have mentioned
it, if he had not been spoken to about the matter, he answered
that they brought him very few things. "I suspect as much,"
the minister answers, "for that old man is a great miser, who
no doubt retains most of the provisions that are sent to you."
The Father assured him that he was content, and that his
sufferings had long since been acceptable to him. In this
garret where the Father was, there was a recess to which his
guard continually led Hiroquois savages, in order to sell some
produce which he locked up there: this recess was made of
planks so slightly joined that one might easily have passed his
fingers into the openings. "I am astonished," says the
Father, "that those barbarians did not hundreds of times discover me; I saw them without difficulty; and unless God had
turned away their eyes, they would have perceived me a thousand times. I concealed myself behind casks, bending myself
into a constrained posture which gave me gehenna and torture
two, three, or four hours in succession, and that very often.
To go down to the court of the dwelling, or to go to other
places, was casting myself headlong; for every place was
filled with those who were seeking me to death. Besides, to
increase my blessings—that is to say, my crosses—the wound
which a dog had inflicted upon me, the night that I escaped
from the Hiroquois, caused me so great a pain that, if the
surgeon of that settlement [1] had not put his hand to it, I
should have lost not only the leg but life; for gangrene was
already setting in.

"The captain [2] of the principal settlement, called Manate,
distant sixty leagues from the one where I was, having learned
that I was not overmuch at my ease in that vicinity of the
Hiroquois, or Maquois, as the Dutch name them, commanded
that I be taken to his fort. By good fortune, at the same time
when they received his letters a vessel was to go down, in which
they made me embark in company with a minister, who showed

---

[1] Presumably Harmen Meyndertsz van den Bogaert.   [2] Kieft.

me much kindness.   He was supplied with a number of bottles, which he dealt out lavishly, especially on coming to an island, to which he wished that my name should be given with the noise of the cannon and of the bottles; each one manifests his love in his own fashion."

This good Father was received in Manate with great tokens of affection; the captain had a black coat made for him, sufficiently light, and gave him also a good cloak and a hat in their own style.   The inhabitants came to see him, showing, by their looks and their words, that they felt great sympathy for him.   Some asked him what recompense the Gentlemen of New France [1] would give him, imagining that he had suffered those indignities on account of their trade.   But he gave them to understand that worldly thoughts had not caused him to leave his own country; and that the publication of the Gospel was the sole good that he had had in view when casting himself into the dangers into which he had fallen.   A good lad, having met him in a retired place, fell at his feet, taking his hands to kiss them, and exclaiming, "Martyr, Martyr of Jesus Christ!"   He questioned him, and ascertained that he was a Lutheran, whom he could not aid for want of acquaintance with his language; he was a Pole.

Entering a house quite near the fort, he saw two images on the mantelpiece, one of the blessed Virgin, the other of our Blessed Louys de Gonzage.[2]   When he betokened some satisfaction at this, the master of the house told him that his wife was a Catholic.   She was a Portuguese, brought into that country by I know not what chance; she appeared very modest and bashful.   The arrogance of Babel has done much harm to all men; the confusion of tongues has deprived them of great benefits.

An Irish Catholic, arriving at Manate from Virginia, confessed to the Father and told him that there were some of our Fathers in those regions; and that latterly one of them— following the savages into the woods in order to convert them —had been killed by other savages, enemies of those whom

[1] The Hundred Associates, or Company of New France, who controlled Canada from 1627 to 1663.

[2] San Luigi di Gonzaga (Aloysius Gonzaga, 1568–1591), a Jesuit saint, beatified 1621, canonized 1726.

the Father accompanied.[1]   Finally, the Governor of the country, sending a bark of one hundred tons to Holland, sent the Father back, at the beginning of the month of November.

[1] The allusion is doubtless to the Jesuits in Maryland.   The tale of martyrdom is perhaps due to a distorted version of the death of Father Ferdinand Poulton *alias* Brooke, who was shot, but, according to the uniform tradition of the mission, by accident.

NOVUM BELGIUM, BY FATHER ISAAC JOGUES, 1646

INTRODUCTION

AT some time before his death in 1800, Father Jean Joseph Casot, the last of the old race of Jesuits in Canada, seeing his order about to expire under the restrictions then imposed by the British government, and determined that all the materials for its history should not perish by reason of his death, made a selection from among its papers, and placed the portion thus preserved in the custody of the Augustinian nuns of the Hotel Dieu of Quebec. There they remained safe till in 1843 they were restored to the Society, then revived and under the charge of Father Martin, as superior of the Jesuits in Canada. Among these papers was the following, in which Father Jogues, at the time of his last sojourn in New France, described New Netherland as he had seen it three years before.

Father Martin presented a transcript of the document, accompanied with an English translation, to the regents of the University of the State of New York. The translation was then published, in 1851, in volume IV. of O'Callaghan's *Documentary History of the State of New York* (pp. 21–24 of the octavo edition, pp. 15–17 of the edition in quarto). The French original was printed for the first time in 1852 in an appendix to Father Martin's translation of Bressani's *Breve Relatione*. In 1857, Dr. John Gilmary Shea printed in the *Collections of the New York Historical Society*, second series, III. 215–219, a translation which, after revision by the present editor, is printed in the following pages. Dr. Shea made separate publication of the French text in his Cramoisy series in 1862, and in the same year published another edition of original and translation. Both likewise appear in Thwaites's

Jesuit Relations, XXVIII. 105–115.   Dr. Thwaites also gives a facsimile of the first page of the original manuscript which Father Jogues wrote at Three Rivers, with hands crippled by the cruel usage of the Mohawks.

NOVUM BELGIUM, BY FATHER ISAAC JOGUES, 1646

NEW HOLLAND, which the Dutch call in Latin *Novum Belgium*—in their own language, *Nieuw Nederland*, that is to say, New Low Countries—is situated between Virginia and New England. The mouth of the river, which some people call Nassau, or the Great North River, to distinguish it from another which they call the South River, and which I think is called Maurice River on some maps that I have recently seen, is at 40 deg. 30 min. The channel is deep, fit for the largest ships, which ascend to Manhattes Island, which is seven leagues in circuit, and on which there is a fort to serve as the commencement of a town to be built here, and to be called New Amsterdam.

This fort, which is at the point of the island, about five or six leagues from the [river's] mouth, is called Fort Amsterdam; it has four regular bastions, mounted with several pieces of artillery. All these bastions and the curtains were, in 1643, but mounds, most of which had crumbled away, so that one entered the fort on all sides. There were no ditches. For the garrison of the said fort, and another which they had built still further up against the incursions of the savages, their enemies, there were sixty soldiers. They were beginning to face the gates and bastions with stone. Within the fort there was a pretty large stone church,[1] the house of the Governor, whom they call Director General, quite neatly built of brick, the storehouses and barracks.

On the island of Manhate, and in its environs, there may well be four or five hundred men of different sects and nations: the Director General told me that there were men of eighteen different languages; they are scattered here and there on the

---

[1] See De Vries, p. 212, *supra*, and the *Representation of New Netherland*, p. 326, *post*.

river, above and below, as the beauty and convenience of the spot has invited each to settle: some mechanics however, who ply their trade, are ranged under the fort; all the others are exposed to the incursions of the natives, who in the year 1643, while I was there, actually killed some two score Hollanders, and burnt many houses and barns full of wheat.

The river, which is very straight, and runs due north and south, is at least a league broad before the fort. Ships lie at anchor in a bay which forms the other side of the island, and can be defended by the fort.

Shortly before I arrived there, three large ships of 300 tons each had come to load wheat; two found cargoes, the third could not be loaded, because the savages had burnt a part of the grain. These ships had come from the West Indies, where the West India Company usually keeps up seventeen ships of war.

No religion is publicly exercised but the Calvinist, and orders are to admit none but Calvinists, but this is not observed; for besides the Calvinists there are in the colony Catholics, English Puritans, Lutherans, Anabaptists, here called Mnistes,[1] etc.

When any one comes to settle in the country, they lend him horses, cows, etc.; they give him provisions, all which he returns as soon as he is at ease; and as to the land, after ten years he pays to the West India Company the tenth of the produce which he reaps.

This country is bounded on the New England side by a river which they call the Fresche River,[2] which serves as a boundary between them and the English. The English, however, come very near to them, choosing to hold lands under the Hollanders, who ask nothing, rather than depend on the English Milords, who exact rents, and would fain be absolute. On the other side, southward, towards Virginia, its limits are the river which they call the South River, on which there is also a Dutch settlement,[3] but the Swedes have one at its mouth extremely well supplied with cannons and men.[4]   It

[1] Mennonistes, Mennonites.   [2] Connecticut.
[3] Fort Nassau, at the mouth of Timber Creek.
[4] He probably means Fort Nya Elfsborg, on the Jersey side of Delaware Bay, below Salem.

is believed that these Swedes are maintained by some Amsterdam merchants, who are not satisfied that the West India
Company should alone enjoy all the commerce of these parts.[1]
It is near this river that a gold mine is reported to have been
found.

See in the work of the Sieur de Laet of Antwerp, the table
and chapter on New Belgium, as he sometimes calls it, or the
map "Nova Anglia, Novum Belgium et Virginia." [2]

It is about fifty years since the Hollanders came to these
parts.[3] The fort was begun in the year 1615; they began to
settle about twenty years ago, and there is already some little
commerce with Virginia and New England.

The first comers found lands fit for use, deserted by the
savages, who formerly had fields here. Those who came later
have cleared the woods, which are mostly oak. The soil is
good. Deer hunting is abundant in the fall. There are some
houses built of stone; lime they make of oyster shells, great
heaps of which are found here, made formerly by the savages,
who subsist in part by that fishery.

The climate is very mild. Lying at $40\frac{2}{3}°$ there are many
European fruits, as apples, pears, cherries. I reached there
in October, and found even then a considerable quantity of
peaches.

Ascending the river to the 43d degree, you meet the second
[Dutch] settlement, which the tide reaches but does not pass.
Ships of a hundred and a hundred and twenty tons can come
up to it.

There are two things in this settlement (which is called
Renselaerswick, as if to say, settlement of Renselaers, who
is a rich Amsterdam merchant)—first, a miserable little fort
called Fort Orenge, built of logs, with four or five pieces of

[1] The reference is to the aid rendered by Samuel Blommaert, an Amsterdam
merchant, formerly a director of the Dutch West India Company, in fitting out the
first Swedish expedition in 1637, and in engaging Peter Minuit to command it.
Blommaert's letters to the Swedish chancellor, Count Axel Oxenstjerna, thirty-
eight in number, 1635-1641, letters of great importance to the history of New
Sweden, have just been published in the *Bijdragen en Mededeelingen* of the Utrecht
Historical Society, vol. XXIX.

[2] De Laet, *Histoire du Nouveau Monde*, table of contents, bk. III. ch. XII.
(see pp. 53, 54, *supra*), and map.

[3] An exaggeration. There is no evidence of Dutch visits before Hudson's.

Breteuil cannon, and as many pedereros. This has been reserved and is maintained by the West India Company. This fort was formerly on an island in the river; it is now on the mainland, towards the Hiroquois, a little above the said island.

Secondly, a colony sent here by this Renselaers, who is the patron. This colony is composed of about a hundred persons, who reside in some twenty-five or thirty houses built along the river, as each found most convenient. In the principal house lives the patron's agent; the minister has his apart, in which service is performed. There is also a kind of bailiff here, whom they call the seneschal,[1] who administers justice. All their houses are merely of boards and thatched, with no mason work except the chimneys. The forest furnishing many large pines, they make boards by means of their mills, which they have here for the purpose.

They found some pieces of ground all ready, which the savages had formerly cleared, and in which they sow wheat and oats for beer, and for their horses, of which they have great numbers. There is little land fit for tillage, being hemmed in by hills, which are poor soil. This obliges them to separate, and they already occupy two or three leagues of country.

Trade is free to all; this gives the Indians all things cheap, each of the Hollanders outbidding his neighbor, and being satisfied provided he can gain some little profit.

This settlement is not more than twenty leagues from the Agniehronons,[2] who can be reached by land or water, as the river on which the Iroquois lie,[3] falls into that which passes by the Dutch; but there are many low rapids, and a fall of a short half league, where the canoe must be carried.

There are many nations between the two Dutch settlements, which are about thirty German leagues apart, that is, about fifty or sixty French leagues.[4] The Wolves, whom the Iroquois call Agotsaganens,[5] are the nearest to the settlement of Renselaerswick and to Fort Orange. War breaking out some years ago between the Iroquois and the Wolves, the Dutch joined the latter against the former; but four men having been taken and burnt, they made peace.[6] Since then some nations near

---

[1] The *schout*. [2] The Mohawks. [3] Mohawk River.
[4] One hundred and fifty English miles. [5] The Mohicans.
[6] See pp. 84, 85, *supra*.

the sea having killed some Hollanders of the most distant settlement, the Hollanders killed one hundred and fifty Indians, men, women and children, they having, at divers times, killed forty Hollanders, burnt many houses, and committed ravages, estimated at the time that I was there at 200,000 l. (two hundred thousand livres).[1] Troops were raised in New England. Accordingly, in the beginning of winter, the grass being trampled down and some snow on the ground, they gave them chase with six hundred men, keeping two hundred always on the move and constantly relieving one another; so that the Indians, shut up in a large island, and unable to flee easily, on account of their women and children, were cut to pieces to the number of sixteen hundred, including women and children. This obliged the rest of the Indians to make peace, which still continues.   This occurred in 1643 and 1644.[2]

From Three Rivers in New France, August 3, 1646.

[1] *Livres tournois* or francs, worth two or three times as much as francs of our time.

[2] See the next piece.

JOURNAL OF NEW NETHERLAND, 1647

INTRODUCTION

An account of the great Indian war which so desolated the province of New Netherland, and of some other actions of Kieft's administration, written from his point of view or that of his supporters, must be regarded as an important piece of evidence. It is the more to be welcomed because on the whole our evidences for New Netherland history come mainly from opponents of the provincial administration and of the West India Company. The archives of the company disappeared almost completely many years ago, the bulk of them having apparently been sold for waste paper not many years before Brodhead went to Holland upon his memorable search. Of Kieft's papers, we may suppose that the greater part were lost when the *Princess* was shipwrecked on the Welsh coast in September, 1647, and the deposed director and all his possessions were lost.

The document which follows was found by Brodhead in the Royal Library of the Hague. It is still there and is designated No. 78 H 32. It has an outside cover forming a title-page, with ornamental lettering, but it is not the "book ornamented with water-color drawings" which Kieft is known to have sent home. A photograph of the first page, which the editor has procured, does nothing to show the authorship, for it is written in the hand of a professional scrivener. Mr. van Laer, archivist of the State of New York, assures the editor that it is not in the hand of Kieft or that of Cornelis van Tienhoven, the provincial secretary.[1] But that it was either inspired by Kieft, or emanated from one of his supporters, is plain not only from

[1] Mr. J. H. Innes tells me that it resembles that of Augustin Herrman.

its general tone but from its citations of documents. Of the documents to which its marginal notes refer, some of those that we can still trace are noted in the archives of the Netherlands as "from a copy-book of Director Kieft's." The rest, or the original copy-book, may have perished with him.

The piece was first printed in 1851, in the *Documentary History of the State of New York*, IV. 1–17. It was printed for the second time in 1856, in *Documents relating to the Colonial History of New York*, I. 179–188. For the present issue this early and imperfect translation has been revised with great care by Dr. Johannes de Hullu of the National Archives of the Netherlands, who has used for this purpose the original manuscript in the Royal Library.

JOURNAL OF NEW NETHERLAND, 1647

Journal of New Netherland, 1647, described in the Years 1641, 1642, 1643, 1644, 1645 and 1646.

Brief Description of New Netherland.

NEW NETHERLAND (so called because it was first frequented and peopled by the free Netherlanders) is a province in the most northern part of America lying between New England (which bounds it on the northeast side) and Virginia lying to the southwest of it. The ocean washes its whole length along a clean sandy coast, very similar to that of Flanders or Holland, having except the rivers few bays or harbors for ships; the air is very temperate, inclining to dryness, healthy, little subject to sickness. The four seasons of the year are about as in France, or the Netherlands. The difference is, the spring is shorter because it begins later, the summer is warmer because it comes on more suddenly, the autumn is long and very pleasant, the winter cold and liable to much snow. Two winds ordinarily prevail: the N. W. in winter and the S. W. in summer; the other winds are not common; the N. W. corresponds with our N. E. because it blows across the country from the cold point as our N. E. does. The S. W. is dry and hot like our S. E. because it comes from the warm countries; the N. E. is cold and wet like our S. W. for similar reasons. The character of the country is very like that of France; the land is fairly high and level, especially broken along the coast by small rocky hills unfit for agriculture; farther in the interior are pretty high mountains (generally exhibiting great appearance of minerals) between which flow a great number of small rivers. In some places there are even some lofty ones of extraordinary height, but not many. Its fertility falls behind no province in Europe in excellence of fruits and seeds. There are three principal rivers, to wit: the Fresh, the Mauritius and the South River,[1] all three reasonably wide and deep, adapted for the navigation of large ships twenty-five leagues up and of common barks even to the falls. From the River Mauritius off to beyond the Fresh River stretches a channel that forms an island, forty leagues long, called Long Island, which is the ordinary passage from New England to Virginia, having on both sides many harbors to anchor in, so that people make no difficulty about navigating it in winter. The country is generally covered with trees, except a few valleys and some large flats of seven or eight leagues and less; the trees are as in Europe, viz. oak, hickory, chestnut, vines. The animals are also of the same species as ours, except lions and some other strange beasts, many bears, abundance of wolves which harm nobody but the small cattle, elks and deer in abundance, foxes, beavers, otters, minks and such like. The birds which are natural to the country are turkeys like ours, swans, geese of three sorts, ducks, teals, cranes, herons, bitterns, two sorts of partridges, four sorts of heath fowls, grouse or pheasants. The river fish is like that of Europe, viz. carp, sturgeon, salmon, pike, perch, roach, eel, etc. In the salt waters are found codfish, haddock, herring and so forth, also abundance of oysters and clams.

The Indians are of ordinary stature, strong and broad shouldered; olive color, light and nimble of foot, subtle of mind, of few words which they previously well consider, hypocritical, treacherous, vindictive; brave and obstinate in self-defence, in time of need right resolute to die. They seem to despise all the torments that can be inflicted on them without once uttering a sigh—go almost naked except a lap which hangs before their private parts, and on the shoulders a deer skin or a mantle, a fathom square, of woven Turkey feathers or peltries sewed together. They now make great use of duffel cloths, blue or red, in consequence of the frequent visits of the Christians. In winter they make shoes of deer skins, manufactured after their fashion. Except their chiefs, they have generally but one wife whom they frequently change according to caprice; she must do all the work, as well corn-planting as wood-cutting and whatever else is to be done. They are

---

[1] Connecticut, Hudson and Delaware.

divided into various nations. They differ even in language, which would be altogether too long to be narrated in this short space. They dwell together in tribes, mostly of one consanguinity, over which commands a chief who is general and is generally called *Sackema*, possessing not much authority and little advantage, unless in their dances and other ceremonies. They have no knowledge at all of God, no divine worship, no law, no justice; the strongest does what he pleases and the youths are master. Their weapons are the bow and arrow, in the use of which they are wonderful adepts. They live by hunting and fishing in addition to maize which the women plant.

By Whom and How New Netherland was peopled.

The subjects of the Lords States General had for a considerable time frequented this country solely for the purpose of the fur trade. Then, in the year 1623, the Chartered West India Company caused four forts to be erected in that country—two on the River Mauritius and one on each of the other [rivers]; the biggest stands on the point where the Mauritius River begins, and the other one,[1] mentioned heretofore, which their Honors named New Amsterdam; and six and thirty leagues upwards another called Orange. That on the South River is called Nassauw and that on Fresh River, the Good Hope. The Company has since continually maintained garrisons there. In the beginning their Honors had sent a certain number of settlers thither, and at great expense had three sawmills erected, which never realised any profit of consequence, on account of their great heaviness, and a great deal of money was expended for the advancement of the country, but it never began to be settled until every one had liberty to trade with the Indians, inasmuch as up to this time no one calculated to remain there longer than the expiration of his bounden time, and therefore they did not apply themselves to agriculture. Yea, even the colony of Renselaerwyck was of little consequence; but as soon as it was permitted, many servants, who had some money coming to them from the Company, applied for their discharge, built houses and formed plantations, spread them-

[1] East River, apparently.

selves far and wide, each seeking the best land, and to be nearest the Indians in order thus to trade with them easily, others bought barks with which to trade goods at the North and at the South, and as the Lords Directors gave free passage from Holland thither, that also caused some to come. On the other hand, the English came also from both Virginia and New England. Firstly, many servants, whose time with their masters had expired, on account of the good opportunity to plant tobacco here, afterwards families and finally entire colonies, forced to quit that place both to enjoy freedom of conscience and to escape from the insupportable government of New England and because many more commodities were easier to be obtained here than there, so that in place of seven farms and two or three plantations which were here, one saw thirty farms, as well cultivated and stocked with cattle as in Europe, and a hundred plantations which in two or three [years] would have become well arranged farms. For after the tobacco was out of the ground, corn was thrown in there without ploughing. In winter men were busy preparing new lands. Five English colonies which by contract had [settled] under us on equal terms as the others. Each of these was in appearance not less than a hundred families strong, exclusive of the colony of Rensselaers Wyck which is prospering, with that of Myndert Meyndertsz [1] and Cornelis Melyn,[2] who began first, also the village New Amsterdam around the fort, a hundred families, so that there was appearance of producing supplies in a year for fourteen thousand souls, without straining the country, and had there been no want of laborers or farm servants twice as much could have been raised, considering that fifty *lasts* of rye and fifty *lasts* of peas still remained over around the fort after a large quantity had been burnt and destroyed by the Indians, who in a short time nearly brought this country to nought and had well nigh destroyed this good hope, in manner following—

[1] The colony of Hackensack, belonging to Meyndert Meyndertsen van Keren and others. See p. 215, note 1.

[2] Cornelis Melyn's colony embraced all Staten Island except De Vries's plantation.

The Causes of the New Netherland War and the Sequel thereof.

We have already stated that the cause of the population of New Netherland was the liberty to trade with the Indians. We shall now prove that it also is the cause of its ruin, producing two contrary effects, and that not without reason as shall appear from the following.

This liberty then which in every respect should have been most gratefully received, of which use should have been made as of a precious gift, was very soon perverted to a great abuse. For every one thought that now the time had come to make his fortune, withdrew himself from his comrade, as if holding him suspect and the enemy of his gains, and sought communication with the Indians from whom it appeared his profit was to be derived. That created first a division of power of dangerous consequence, in opposition to Their High Mightinesses' motto [1]—produced altogether too much familiarity with the Indians which in a short time brought forth contempt, usually the father of hate—not being satisfied with merely taking them into their houses in the customary manner, but attracting them by extraordinary attention, such as admitting them to the table, laying napkins before them, presenting wine to them and more of that kind of thing, which they did not receive like Esop's man, but as their due and desert, insomuch that they were not content but began to hate when such civilities were not shewn them. To this familiarity and freedom succeeded another evil. As the cattle usually roamed through the woods without a herdsman, they frequently came into the corn of the Indians which was unfenced on all sides, committing great damage there; this led to frequent complaints on their part and finally to revenge on the cattle without sparing even the horses, which were valuable in this country. Moreover many of ours took the Indians into service, making use of them in their houses and thus, whilst they were being employed, laying open before those Indians our entire circumstances; and sometimes becoming weary of their work, they took leg-bail and stole much more than the amount of their wages. This freedom caused still greater mischief, for the inhabitants

[1] *Eendracht maakt macht*, union makes strength.

of Renselaerswyck who were as many traders as persons, perceiving that the Mohawks were craving for guns, which some of them had already received from the English, paying for each as many as twenty beavers and for a pound of powder as much as ten to twelve guilders, they came down in greater numbers than was their wont where people were well supplied with guns, purchasing these at a fair price, thus realizing great profit; afterwards they obtained some from their Heer Patroon for their self-defence in time of need, as we suppose This extraordinary gain was not kept long a secret, the traders coming from Holland soon got scent of it, and from time to time brought over great quantities, so that the Mohawks in a short time were seen with firelocks, powder and lead in proportion. Four hundred armed men knew how to use their advantage, especially against their enemies dwelling along the river of Canada,[1] against whom they have now achieved many profitable forays where before they derived little advantage; this causes them also to be respected by the surrounding Indians even as far as the sea coast, who must generally pay them tribute, whereas, on the contrary, they were formerly obliged to contribute to these. On this account the Indians endeavored no less to procure guns, and through the familiarity which existed between them and our people, they began to solicit them for guns and powder, but as such was forbidden on pain of death and it could not remain secret in consequence of the general conversation, they could not obtain them. This added to the previous contempt greatly augmented the hatred which stimulated them to conspire against us, beginning first by insults which they everywhere indiscreetly uttered railing at us as *Materiotty* (that is to say) the cowards—that we might indeed be something on water, but of no account on land, and that we had neither a great sachem nor chiefs.

[*Here two pages are wanting.*]

he of Witqueschreek living northeast of the island Manhatans, perpetrated another murderous deed in the house of an old man,[2] a wheelwright, with whom he was acquainted (having

---

[1] Father Jogues speaks more than once of the ill effects of the Dutch practice of selling fire-arms to the Indians.

[2] Claes Smits Rademaker. See p. 213, note 1.

been in his son's service) being well received and supplied with food, pretending a desire to buy something and whilst the old man was taking from the chest the cloth the Indian wanted the latter took up an ax and cut his head off, further plundering the house, and ran away. This outrage obliged the Director to demand satisfaction from the sachem, who refused it, saying that he was sorry that twenty Christians had not been murdered [1] and that this Indian had only avenged the death of his uncle who, it was alleged, had been slain by the Dutch twenty-one years before. Whereupon all the commonalty were called together by the Director to consider this affair, who all appeared and presently twelve men delegated from among them [2] answered the propositions, and resolved at once on war should the murderer be refused; that the attack should be made on [the Indians] in the autumn when they were hunting; meanwhile an effort should be again made by kindness to obtain justice, which was accordingly several times sought for but in vain.

The time being come many difficulties were alleged and operations were postponed until the year 1642, when it was resolved to avenge the perpetrated outrage. Thereupon spies looked up the Indians who lay in their dwelling-place suspecting nothing, and eighty men were detailed under the command of Ensign Hendrick van Dyck and sent thither. The guide being come with the troops in the neighborhood of the Indian wigwams lost his way in consequence of the darkness of the night. The ensign became impatient, and turned back without having accomplished anything. The journey, however, was not without effect, for the Indians who remarked by the trail made by our people in marching that they had narrowly escaped discovery, sought for peace which was granted them on condition that they should either deliver up the murderer or inflict justice themselves; this they promised, but without any result.

[1] "*Note A* [in the original]. Capt. Patricx letter 21 August 1641." I do not find this letter in print. Captain Patrick, formerly a soldier under the Prince of Orange, was one of the early members of the colony of Massachusetts Bay, but had left that colony in 1639 and settled with his Dutch wife at Greenwich. Concerning his death, at the hands of a Dutch trooper, see Winthrop, II. 153–154, in this series.

[2] "*Note B.* Their answer and resolution dated the 29th August, 1641." This document, "from Director Kieft's copy-book," is in *N. Y. Col. Doc.*, I. 415.

Some weeks after this Miantonimo, principal sachem of Sloops Bay,[1] came here with one hundred men, passing through all the Indian villages [2] soliciting them to a general war against both the English and the Dutch,[3] whereupon some of the neighboring Indians attempted to set our powder on fire and to poison the Director or to inchant him by their devilry, as their ill will was afterwards made manifest as well in fact as by report. Those of Hackingsack, otherwise called Achter Col, had with their neighbors killed an Englishman, a servant of one David Pietersen, and a few days after shot dead in an equally treacherous manner a Dutchman, who sat roofing a house in the colony of Meyndert Meyndertz,[4] which was established there against the advice of the Director and will of the Indians, and which by the continual damage which their cattle committed caused no little dissatisfaction to the Indians, and contributed greatly to the war. The commonalty began then to be alarmed, and not without reason, having the Indians daily in their houses. The murderers were frequently demanded, either living or dead, even with a promise of reward; they always returned a scoffing answer laughing at us. Finally, the commonalty, very much displeased with the Director, upbraided him for conniving with the Indians, and [declared] that an attempt was making to sell Christian blood;[5] yea, that the will of the entire commonalty was surrendered to him, and in case he would not avenge blood they should do it themselves, be the consequences what they might. The Director advised Pacham the sachem,[6] who interested himself in this matter, warning him that we should wait no longer inasmuch as no satisfaction had been given.

Meanwhile God wreaked vengeance on those of Witques-

---

[1] *I. e.*, of the Narragansetts.

[2] "*Note C*. The English Manifest, Page 2." This means that now rare pamphlet, *A Declaration of Former Passages and Proceedings betwixt the English and the Narrowgansets* (Cambridge, 1645), published by order of the Commissioners of the United Colonies. See its text, and the particular passage here referred to, in *Records of Plymouth Colony*, IX. 50.

[3] "*Note D*. Capt. Patricx letter dated 2 Jan'y, 1642." I have nowhere seen this letter.

[4] "*Note E*. The order in the Director's letter and in the deposition thereupon." See De Vries, p. 215, *supra*.

[5] "*Note F*. Resolve of the 12 delegates dated 21 Jan'y, 1642." See *N. Y. Col. Doc.*, I. 414–415.   [6] Of the Haverstraw Indians.

check without our knowledge through the Mahicanders dwelling below Fort Orange, who slew seventeen of them, and made prisoners of many women and children. The remainder fled through a deep snow to the Christians' houses on and around the island Manhatens. They were most humanely received being half dead of cold and hunger; they supported them for fourteen days, even corn was sent to them by the Director. A short time after, another panic seized the Indians which caused them to fly to divers places in the vicinity of the Dutch. This opportunity to avenge the innocent blood induced some of the Twelve Men to represent to the Director that it was now time, whereupon they received for answer that they should put their request in writing which was done by three in the name of them all,[1] by a petition to be allowed to attack those of Hackingsack in two divisions—on the Manhatens and on Pavonia. This was granted after a protracted discussion too long to be reported here, so that the design was executed that same night; the burghers slew those who lay a small league from the fort, and the soldiers those at Pavonia, at which two places about eighty Indians were killed and thirty taken prisoners. Next morning before the return of the troops a man and a woman were shot at Pavonia who had come through curiosity either to look at or plunder the dead; the soldiers had rescued a young child which the woman had in her arms.

The Christians residing on Long Island also requested by petition [2] to be allowed to attack and slay the Indians thereabout; which was refused, as these especially had done us no harm, and shewed us every friendship—(yea, had even voluntarily killed some of the Raritans, our enemies, hereinbefore mentioned). Yet notwithstanding [3] some Christians attempted secretly with two waggons to steal maize from these Indians, out of their cabins, which they perceiving endeavored to prevent, thereupon three Indians were shot dead, two houses standing opposite the fort were in return forthwith set on fire. The Director knowing nought of this sent at once some per-

---

[1] "*Note G.* Their Petition dated 24th Feb. 1643." *N. Y. Col. Doc.*, I. 193. Its true date was February 22.

[2] "*Note H.* Their petition and the answer thereto, dated 27 Feb. 1643." Printed in *N. Y. Col. Doc.*, I. 416–417.

[3] "*Note I.* Contains the information thereupon."

sons to enquire the reason of it. The Indians showing themselves afar off, called out—"Be ye our friends? ye are mere corn stealers"—forth with behaving as enemies. This induced one of the proprietors of the burnt houses to upbraid therewith one Maryn Adriaenzen, who at his request had led the freemen in the attack on the Indians, and who being reinforced by an English troop had afterwards undertaken two bootless expeditions in the open field. Imagining that the Director had accused him, he being one of the signers of the petition he determined to revenge himself.[1] With this resolution he proceeded to the Director's house armed with a pistol, loaded and cocked, and a hanger by his side; coming unawares into the Director's room, he presents his pistol at him, saying, "What devilish lies art thou reporting of me?" but by the promptness of one of the bystanders, the shot was prevented, and he himself immediately confined. A short time after, Marine's man and another entered the fort, each carrying a loaded gun and pistol. The first fired at the Director who having had notice withdrew towards his house, the balls passing into the wall alongside the door behind him; the sentinel firing immediately on him who had discharged his gun, brought him down. Shortly afterwards some of the commonalty collected before the Director, riotously demanding the prisoner; they were answered that their request should be presented in order and in writing, which about 25 men did; they therein asked the Director to pardon the criminal. The matters were referred to them to decide conscientiously thereupon, in such wise that they immediately went forth, without hearing parties or seeing any complaints or documents. They condemn him in a fine of five hundred guilders, and to remain three months away from the Manhatens, but on account of the importance of the affair and some considerations, it was resolved to send the criminal with his trial to Holland, which . . .[2]

In this confusion mingled with great terror passed the winter away; the season came for driving out the cattle; this obliged many to desire peace. On the other hand the Indians, seeing also that it was time to plant maize, were not less solicitous for peace, so that after some negotiation, peace was concluded in May A°. 1643 [more] in consequence of the im-

[1] "*Note K.* His trial therefor."   [2] Gap in manuscript.

portunity of some than because it was generally expected that it would be durable.

The Indians kept still after this peace, associating daily with our people; yea, even the greatest chiefs came to visit the Director. Meanwhile Pachem, a crafty man, ran through all the villages urging the Indians to a general massacre. To this was added moreover that certain Indians called Wappingers, dwelling sixteen leagues up the river, with whom we never had any the least trouble, seized on a boat coming from Fort Orange wherein were only two men, and full four hundred beavers. This great booty stimulated [1] others to join them, so that they seized two boats more, intending to overhaul the fourth also, from which they were driven off with the loss of six Indians. Nine Christians including two women were murdered in these captured barks, one woman and two children remaining prisoners. The other Indians, so soon as their maize was ripe, were likewise roused, and through semblance of selling beavers killed an old man and an old woman, leaving another man with five wounds, who however fled to the fort in a boat with a little child on his arm, who in the first outbreak had lost father and mother, and now grandfather and grandmother, being thus twice through God's merciful blessing rescued from the hands of the Indians, before it was two years old. Nothing was now heard but murders, most of which were committed under pretence of coming to put the Christians on their guard.

Finally they took the field and attacked the farms at Pavonia. There were here at the time two ships of war and a privateer who saved considerable cattle and grain. Nevertheless it was not possible to prevent the destruction of four farms on Pavonia, which were burnt, not by open force, but by stealthily creeping through the brush with fire in hand, thus igniting the roofs which are all either of reed or straw; one covered with plank was saved at that time.

The commonalty were called together; they were sore distressed. They chose eight, in the stead of the previous twelve,[2] persons to aid in consulting for the best; but the occupation every one had to take care of his own, prevented anything

[1] "*Note M*. Their acknowledgment made before the English 16 January, 1643, English style."

[2] "*Note N*. Resolve of 13 Sept'r. 1643." *N. Y. Col. Doc.*, I. 194.

beneficial being adopted at that time—nevertheless it was resolved that as many Englishmen as were to be got in the country should be enlisted, who were indeed now proposing to depart; the third part of these were to be paid by the commonalty; this promise was made by the commonalty but was not followed by the pay.

Terror increasing all over the land the Eight Men assembled, drew [1] up a proposal in writing wherein they asked that delegates should be sent to the north, to our English neighbors, to request an auxiliary force of one hundred and fifty men, for whose pay a bill of exchange should be given for twenty-five thousand guilders, and that New Netherland should be so long mortgaged to the English as security for the payment thereof. One of the most influential among the Eight Men had by letter [2] enforced by precedents previously endeavored to persuade the Director to this course, as they had also a few days before resolved [3] that the provisions destined for Curaçao should be unloaded from the vessels and the major portion of the men belonging to them detained, and to send the ships away thus empty. This was not yet agreed to nor considered expedient by the Director.

[Here four pages are wanting.]

[An expedition was despatched consisting of —— regular soldiers] under the command of the sergeant,[4] forty burghers under their Captain Jochem Pietersen,[5] thirty-five Englishmen under Lieutenant Baxter,[6] but to prevent all confusion, Councillor La Montagne [7] was appointed general. Coming to Staten Island, they marched the whole night, finding the houses empty and abandoned by the Indians; they got five or six hundred *skepels* of corn, burning the remainder without accomplishing anything else.

[1] "*Note O.* Dated 6th Octob. 1643."

[2] "*Note P.* Dated 9th March, 1643."

[3] "*Note Q.* In their resolution 30th September, 1643."   [4] Pieter Cock.

[5] Jochem Pietersen Kuyter, one of the Twelve Men and of the Eight Men.

[6] George Baxter, an exile from New England, now English secretary under Kieft. The number of English colonists in New Netherland, especially on Long Island, was rapidly increasing.

[7] Dr. Johannes la Montagne, a Huguenot physician, who with Kieft constituted the council of the province.

Mayane, a sachem, residing eight leagues northeast of us, between Greenwich (that lies within our jurisdiction) and Stantfort,[1] which is English,—a bold Indian who alone dared to attack with bow and arrows three Christians armed with guns, one of whom he shot dead—whilst engaged with the other, was killed by the third Christian and his head brought hither. It was then known and understood for the first time, that he and his Indians had done us much injury, though we never had any difference with him. Understanding further that they lay in their houses very quiet and without suspicion on account of the neighborhood of the English, it was determined to hunt them up and attack them, and one hundred and twenty men were sent thither under the preceding command. The people landed at Greenwich in the evening from three yachts, marched the entire night but could not find the Indians, either because the guide brought this about on purpose, as was believed, or because he had himself gone astray. Retreat was made to the yachts in order to depart as secretly as possible. Passing through Stantfort some Englishmen were encountered who offered to lead ours to the place where some Indians were. Thereupon four scouts were sent in divers directions to discover them, who at their return reported that the Indians had some notice of our people by the salute which the Englishmen gave us, but without any certainty, whereupon five and twenty of the bravest men were at once commanded to proceed thither to the nearest village. With great diligence they made the journey, killing eighteen or twenty Indians, capturing an old man, two women and some children, to exchange for ours. The other troops found the huts empty, and further came hither with the yachts.

The old Indian captured above having promised to lead us to Wetquescheck, which consisted of three castles, sixty-five men were despatched under Baxter and Pieter Cock, who found them empty, though thirty Indians could have stood against two hundred soldiers since the castles were constructed of plank five inches thick, nine feet high, and braced around with thick balk full of port-holes. Our people burnt two, reserving the third for a retreat. Marching eight or nine leagues further, they discovered nothing but some huts, which

[1] Stamford.

they could not surprize as they were discovered. They came back having killed only one or two Indians, taken some women and children prisoners and burnt much corn. Meanwhile we were advised that Pennewitz,[1] one of the oldest and most experienced Indians in the country, and who in the first conspiracy had given the most dangerous advice—to wit, that they should wait and not attack the Dutch until all suspicion had been lulled, and then divide themselves equally through the houses of the Christians and slaughter all these in one night—was secretly waging war against us with his tribe, who killed some of our people and set fire to the houses. It was therefore resolved to send thither a troop of one hundred and twenty men. The burghers under their company, the English under the Sergeant Major Van der Hyl [2] (who within a few days had offered his services and was accepted), the veteran soldiers under Pieter Cock, all under the command of Mr La Montagne, proceed hence in three yachts, land in Scouts Bay on Long Island,[3] and march towards Heemstede [4] (where there is an English colony dependent on us.) Some sent forward in advance dexterously killed an Indian who was out as a spy. Our force was divided into two divisions—Van der Hil with fourteen English towards the smallest, and eighty men towards the largest village named Matsepe,[5] both which were very successful, killing about one hundred and twenty men; of ours one man remained on the field and three were wounded.

Our forces being returned from this expedition, Capt. Van der Hil was despatched to Stantfort,[6] to get some information there of the Indians. He reported that the guide who had formerly served us, and was supposed to have gone astray in

---

[1] Chief of the Canarsee tribe, in western Long Island.

[2] John Underhill, whose unctuous piety and profligate life have an important place in Winthrop and other New England historians. With Captain John Mason he had the leading part in the crushing of the Pequots in 1637. Banished from Massachusetts and restored, this amusing reprobate had gone to the Dutch, "having good offers made him by the Dutch governor (he speaking the Dutch tongue and his wife a Dutch woman)," but had now settled at Stamford. Later he lived at Flushing and at Oyster Bay, where he died in 1672.

[3] Now called Manhasset Bay.

[4] Now Hempstead, Long Island, where early in 1644 Robert Fordham and other English from Stamford had formed a colony under New Netherland jurisdiction.   [5] Mespath, now Newtown, Long Island.   [6] Stamford.

the night, had now been in great danger of his life among the
Indians, of whom there were about five hundred together. He
offered to lead us there, to shew that the former mischance was
not his fault. One hundred and thirty men were accordingly
despatched under the aforesaid Gen¹ Van der Hil and Hendrick
van Dyck, ensign. They embarked in three yachts, and landed
at Greenwich, where they were obliged to pass the night by
reason of the great snow and storm. In the morning they
marched northwest up over stony hills over which some must
creep. In the evening about eight o'clock they came within a
league of the Indians, and inasmuch as they should have arrived
too early and had to cross two rivers, one of two hundred feet
wide and three deep, and that the men could not afterwards
rest in consequence of the cold, it was determined to remain
there until about ten o'clock. The order was given as to the
mode to be observed in attacking the Indians—they marched
forward towards the houses, the latter being set up in three rows,
street fashion, each row eighty paces long, in a low recess protected by the hills, affording much shelter from the northwest
wind. The moon was then at the full, and threw a strong
light against the hills so that many winter days were not
brighter than it then was. On arriving there the Indians were
wide awake, and on their guard, so that ours determined to
charge and surround the houses, sword in hand. They de-
meaned themselves as soldiers and deployed in small bands, so
that we got in a short time one dead and twelve wounded.
They were also so hard pressed that it was impossible for one
to escape. In a brief space of time there were counted one
hundred and eighty dead outside the houses. Presently none
durst come forth, keeping within the houses, discharging arrows
through the holes. The general perceived that nothing else
was to be done, and resolved with Sergeant Major Van der Hil,
to set the huts on fire, whereupon the Indians tried every
means to escape, not succeeding in which they returned back
to the flames preferring to perish by the fire than to die by our
hands. What was most wonderful is, that among this vast
collection of men, women and children not one was heard to
cry or to scream. According to the report of the Indians
themselves the number then destroyed exceeded five hundred.
Some say, full seven hundred, among whom were also twenty-

five Wappingers, our God having collected together there the greater number of our enemies, to celebrate one of their festivals in their manner, from which escaped no more than eight men in all, and three of them were severely wounded.

The fight ended, several fires were built in consequence of the great cold. The wounded, fifteen in number, among whom was the general, were dressed, and the sentinels being posted the troops bivouacked there for the remainder of the night. On the next day, the party set out very early in good order, so as to arrive at Stantfort in the evening. They marched with great courage over that wearisome range of hills, God affording extraordinary strength to the wounded, some of whom were badly hurt; and came in the afternoon to Stantfort after a march of two days and one night and little rest. The English received our people in a very friendly manner, affording them every comfort. In two days they reached here. A thanksgiving was proclaimed on their arrival.

[The remainder is wanting.]

THE REPRESENTATION OF NEW
NETHERLAND, 1650

INTRODUCTION

THE fussy incompetence of Kieft and the disastrous results of the Indian war he had aroused led at last to his removal, and in May, 1647, a new director-general arrived, Petrus Stuyvesant, who had made a good record as governor of Curaçao in the West Indies. Stuyvesant, the last of the Dutch governors, was a man of character, brave, honest, capable and energetic; but he was proud, headstrong and tyrannical, and had such high notions of a governor's prerogative that from the first he conceived a prejudice against the opponents of Kieft, and presently Kuyter and Melyn were condemned to severe punishment for attempting to bring the latter to justice.

The new director-general was bent on pursuing a vigorous policy toward encroaching English and Swedish neighbors, on repressing the high claims of the patroon's officers at Rensselaerswyck, on putting the province in good condition for defence, on suppressing illegal trading, especially the supplying of fire-arms to the Indians, and on regulating with a strong hand all the doings of his small body of subjects. But such a policy costs money, and to obtain it by taxation he found himself compelled in August, 1647, like many another arbitrary ruler, to summon reluctantly the representatives of the people. Carefully as the functions of the Nine Men were limited, they constituted a permanent element in the governmental system, as the Twelve Men and Eight Men had not. It was inevitable that sooner or later they should become the mouthpiece of popular discontent, which was rapidly increasing under the unprosperous condition of the province and the burdensome taxes, customs and other restrictions imposed upon its economic life.

In December, 1648, the board was partly renewed. One of the new members, Adriaen van der Donck, a lawyer from Breda, who from 1641 to 1646 had been *schout* for the patroon at Rensselaerswyck, soon became the leading spirit of the new board. Their sense of popular grievances increasing, they planned to send a deputation to the mother country to remonstrate. Stuyvesant opposed, arrested Van der Donck, seized some of his papers, and expelled him from the board. Nevertheless, a bold memorial to the States General was prepared, and was signed on July 26, 1649, "in the name and on the behalf of the commonalty of New Netherland," by Van der Donck and ten others, present or former members of the board of Nine Men. In this memorial, which is printed in *Documents relating to the Colonial History of New York*, I. 259–261, the representatives request the Dutch government to enact measures for the encouragement of emigration to the province, to grant "suitable municipal [or civil] government, . . . somewhat resembling the laudable government of the Fatherland," to accord greater economic freedom, and to settle with foreign governments those disputes respecting colonial boundaries and jurisdiction the constant agitation of which so unsettled the province and impeded its growth.

The following document accompanied the memorial, bearing date two days later, July 28, 1649, and was signed by the same eleven men. It is considered probable that Adriaen van der Donck was its main author. Its first part, descriptive of the province, reads like a preliminary sketch for his *Beschryvinge van Nieuw-Nederlant* ("Description of New Netherland"), a very interesting work published at Amsterdam six years later (1655, second edition 1656), and of which a translation appears in the *Collections of the New York Historical Society*, second series, I. 125–242.

With respect to the remaining, or political portion of its contents, it is only fair for the reader to remember that it is a body of *ex parte* statements, and should be compared with those made on behalf of the administration by Secretary van Tienhoven in his *Answer*, the document immediately following this. Stuyvesant, whatever his faults of temper—love of autocratic power, lack of sympathy with the life of a community already far from austere, vindictiveness even—conceived of his province as a political community, not solely as a commercial possession, and honestly tried to govern it with an eye to its own best interest. The directors, moreover, could truthfully say that many of their narrowest actions were prescribed by their instructions from the West India Company. While the States General were often capable of taking a statesmanlike view of New Netherland and its needs, the Company was chiefly intent on profit, was interested far more in Brazil than in New Netherland, and as it lost control of the former found itself involved in greater and greater financial embarrassments, which made it increasingly difficult to do justice to the latter. We may also set down on the credit side of the account that though the administration was slow to concede representative institutions to the province, it did not a little to organize local self-government, Kieft granting village rights, with magistrates and local courts of justice, to Hampstead in 1644, to Flushing in 1645, to Brooklyn in 1646, while Stuyvesant bestowed such rights on a dozen towns during his seventeen years' rule and gave New Amsterdam a somewhat restricted municipal government in 1653.

Of those whose signatures follow Van der Donck's at the end of the *Representation*, Augustin Herrman was a Bohemian of Prague, who had served in Wallenstein's army, had come out to New Netherland in 1633 as agent of a mercantile house of Amsterdam, and had become an influential merchant. A man of various accomplishments, he probably made the drawing of New Amsterdam which is reproduced at the foot of Van der Donck's map in this volume. Later he made for Lord

Baltimore a fine map of Maryland, and received as his reward the princely estate of Bohemia Manor. Arnoldus van Harden-berg, another merchant, had been a victim of judicial oppression by both Kieft and Stuyvesant. Jacob van Couwenhoven had come out in 1633 and resided at first at Rensselaerswyck; he was afterward of note as speculator and brewer in New Amster-dam. Oloff Stevensz van Cortlant had been store-keeper for the Company and deacon of the church; later he was burgo-master of New Amsterdam. Michiel Jansz and Thomas Hall were farmers, the latter, the first English settler in New York State, having come to Manhattan as a deserter from George Holmes's abortive expedition of 1635 against Fort Nassau on South River. Elbert Elbertsz was a weaver, Hendrick Kip a tailor. Govert Loockermans, on the other hand, brother-in-law to both Couwenhoven and Cortlandt, was the chief mer-chant and Indian trader of the province, often in partnership with Isaac Allerton the former Pilgrim of Plymouth. Lastly, Jan Everts Bout, a farmer, had formerly been superintendent for Pauw at Pavonia. Characterizations of these men, by an unfriendly hand, may be seen at the end of Van Tienhoven's *Answer* to this *Representation*.

Three of the signers, Van der Donck, Couwenhoven and Bout, were deputed to go to the Netherlands and present the *Representation* to the States General, while Stuyvesant sent Secretary van Tienhoven to counteract their efforts. The voluminous papers which both parties presented to their High Mightinesses were referred to a committee, which in April, 1650, submitted a draft of a reformed and more liberal govern-ment for the province. The delegates caused their *Representa-tion* to be printed, in a pamphlet of forty-nine pages, now very rare, under the title, *Vertoogh van Nieu-Neder-Land, Weghens de Ghelegentheydt, Vruchtbaerheydt, en Soberen Staet desselfs* (Hague, 1650), *i. e.,* "Representation of New Netherland, con-cerning its Location, Productiveness and Poor Condition."

Much discussion was aroused. "The name of New Netherland," wrote the Amsterdam chamber of the Company to
Stuyvesant, "was scarcely ever mentioned before, and now it
would seem as if heaven and earth were interested in it."
So effective an exposition of the colony's value and of its misgovernment could not fail to awaken consideration and
sympathy. Nevertheless, the company, aided by the *Answer*
which Van Tienhoven submitted in November, 1650, were
able to ride out the storm, and to temporize until the outbreak
of the war of 1652–1654 with England put a new face on
colonial affairs. A few concessions were made—the export
duty on tobacco was taken off, and a municipal government
allowed to New Amsterdam, now a town of 700 or 800 inhabitants (1653). But no serious alteration in the provincial
government resulted. "Our Grand Duke of Muscovy," wrote
one of Stuyvesant's subordinates to Van der Donck, "keeps on
as of old." Disaffection among the Dutch settlers never
ceased till the English conquest, though on the other hand the
English settlers on Long Island were much better disposed
toward Stuyvesant's government, and were treated by him
with more favor.

Van der Donck's two companions returned to New Netherland before long. He, however, remained in the old country
until the summer of 1653, occupied with the business of his
mission, with legal studies, taking the degree of doctor of laws
at the University of Leyden, and with the preparation of his
Beschryvinge van Nieuw-Nederlant. The States General gave
him a copyright for it in May, 1653, but the first edition was
not published till 1655. In that year the author died, leaving
to his widow his estate, or "colonie," which he called Colen-
donck. The name of Yonkers, where it was situated, perpetu-
ates his title of gentility (Jonkheer van der Donck).

The original manuscript of the *Representation* is still preserved in the archives of the Netherlands, and a translation of

it was printed in 1856 in *Documents relating to the Colonial History of New York*, I. 271–318, and reprinted in *Pennsylvania Archives*, second series, V. 124–170. A translation of the printed tract, the text of which differs but very slightly from that of the manuscript, was made by Hon. Henry C. Murphy and printed in 1849 in the *Collections of the New York Historical Society*, second series, II. 251–329. It exists also in a separate form as a pamphlet, and, combined with the *Breeden Raedt*, in a volume privately printed in an edition of 125 copies by Mr. James Lenox. It is this translation which, revised by Professor A. Clinton Crowell, is printed in the following pages.

THE REPRESENTATION OF NEW NETHERLAND, 1650

The Representation of New Netherland concerning its Location, Productiveness, and Poor Condition.

AMONG all the people in the world, industrious in seeking out foreign lands, navigable waters and trade, those who bear the name of Netherlanders, will very easily hold their place with the first, as is sufficiently known to all those who have in any wise saluted the threshold of history, and as will also be confirmed by the following relation. The country of which we propose to speak, was first discovered in the year of our Lord 1609, by the ship *Half Moon*, of which Hendrik Hutson was master and supercargo—at the expense of the chartered East India Company, though in search of a different object. It was subsequently called New Netherland by our people, and very justly, as it was first discovered and possessed by Netherlanders, and at their cost; so that even at the present day, those natives of the country who are so old as to recollect when the Dutch ships first came here, declare that when they saw them, they did not know what to make of them, and could not comprehend whether they came down from Heaven, or were of the Devil. Some among them, when the first one arrived, even imagined it to be a fish, or some monster of the sea, and accordingly a strange report of it spread over the whole land. We have also heard the savages frequently say, that they knew nothing of any other part of the world, or any other people than their own, before the arrival of the Netherlanders. For these reasons, therefore, and on account of the similarity of climate, situation and fertility, this place is rightly called New Netherland. It is situated on the northerly coast of America, in the latitude of 38, 39, 40, 41 and 42 degrees, or thereabouts, coast-wise. It is bounded on the northeast by

293

New England, and on the southwest by Virginia. The coast
runs nearly southwest and northeast, and is washed by the
ocean. On the north is the river of Canada, a large river running far into the interior. The northwest side is still partially
unknown.

The land is naturally fruitful, and capable of supporting
a large population, if it were judiciously allotted according to
location. The air is pleasant here, and more temperate than
in the Netherlands. The winds are changeable, and blow from
all points, but generally from the southwest and northwest;
the former prevailing in summer, and the latter in winter, at
times very sharply, but constituting, nevertheless, the greatest
blessing to the country as regards the health of the people,
for being very strong and pure, it drives far inland or consumes
all damps and superfluous moisture. The coast is generally
clean and sandy, the beach detached and broken into islands.
Eastward from the North River lies Long Island, about forty
leagues in length, forming a fine wide river, which falls at either
end into the ocean, and affording a very convenient passage
between the shores which is protected from the dangers of
the sea by a great number of good bays and other places of
anchorage, so that vessels even in winter can readily pass east
and west. Towards the south approaching the South River,
there are several inlets, but they are muddy and sandy, though
after proper experiments they could be used. Inside these
again there are large streams and meadows, but the waters are
for the most part shallow. Along the seacoast the land is
generally sandy or gravelly, not very high, but tolerably
fertile, so that for the most part it is covered over with beautiful trees. The country is rolling in many places, with some
high mountains, and very fine flats and maize lands, together
with large meadows, salt and fresh, all making very fine hay
land. It is overgrown with all kinds of trees, standing without
order, as in other wildernesses, except that the maize lands,
plains and meadows have few or no trees, and these with little
pains might be made into good arable land.

The seasons are the same as in the Netherlands, but the
summer is warmer and begins more suddenly. The winter is
cold, and further inland, or towards the most northerly part,
colder than in the Netherlands. It is also subject to much

snow, which remains long on the ground, and in the interior, three, four and five months; but near the seacoast it is quickly dissolved by the southerly winds. Thunder, lightning, rain, showers, hail, snow, frost, dew and the like, are the same as in the Netherlands, except that in the summer sudden gusts of wind are somewhat more frequent.

The land is adapted to the production of all kinds of winter and summer fruits, and with less trouble and tilling than in the Netherlands. It produces different kinds of wood, suitable for building houses and ships, whether large or small, consisting of oaks of various kinds, as post-oak, white smooth bark, white rough bark, gray bark, black bark, and still another kind which they call, from its softness, butter oak, the poorest of all, and not very valuable; the others, if cultivated as in the Netherlands, would be equal to any Flemish or Brabant oaks. It also yields several species of nut wood, such as oil-nuts, large and small; walnut of different sizes, in great abundance, and good for fuel, for which it is much used, and chestnut, the same as in the Netherlands, growing in the woods without order. There are three varieties of beech—water beech, common beech, and hedge beech—also axe-handle wood, two species of canoe wood, ash, birch, pine, fir, juniper or wild cedar, linden, alder, willow, thorn, elder, and many other kinds useful for many purposes, but unknown to us by name, and which we will be glad to submit to the carpenters for further examination.

The indigenous fruits consist principally of acorns, some of which are very sweet; nuts of different kinds, chestnuts, beechnuts, but not many mulberries, plums, medlars, wild cherries, black currants, gooseberries, hazel nuts in great quantities, small apples, abundant strawberries throughout the country, with many other fruits and roots which the savages use. There is also plenty of bilberries or blueberries, together with ground-nuts and artichokes, which grow under ground. Almost the whole land is full of vines, in the wild woods as well as on the maize lands and flats; but they grow principally near to and upon the banks of the brooks, streams and rivers, which are numerous, and run conveniently and pleasantly everywhere, as if they were planted there. The grapes comprise many varieties, some white, some blue, some very fleshy, and only fit to make raisins of, others on the contrary juicy;

some are very large and others small. The juice is pleasant, and some of it as white as French or Rhenish wine; some is a very deep red, like Tent,[1] and some is paler. The vines run much on the trees, and are shaded by their leaves, so that the grapes ripen late and are a little sour; but with the intelligent assistance of man, as fine wines would undoubtedly be made here as in any other country. In regard to other fruits, all those which grow in the Netherlands also grow very well in New Netherland, without requiring as much care to be bestowed upon them as is necessary there. Garden fruits succeed very well, yet are drier, sweeter, and more agreeable than in the Netherlands; for proof of which we may easily instance muskmelons, citrons or watermelons,[2] which in New Netherland grow right in the open fields, if the briars and weeds are kept from them, while in the Netherlands they require the close care of *amateurs*, or those who cultivate them for profit in gardens, and then they are neither so perfect by far, nor so palatable, as they are in New Netherland. In general all kinds of pumpkins and the like are also much drier, sweeter and more delicious, which is caused by the temperateness and amenity of the climate.

The tame cattle are in size and other respects about the same as in the Netherlands, but the English cattle and swine thrive and grow best, appearing to be better suited to the country than those from Holland. They require, too, less trouble, expense and attention; for it is not necessary in winter to look after such as are dry, or the swine, except that in the time of a deep snow they should have some attention. Milch cows also are much less trouble than they are in Holland, as most of the time, if any care be requisite, it is only for the purpose of giving them occasionally a little hay.

The wild animals are principally lions,[3] but they are few; bears, of which there are many, elks and deer in great numbers, some of which are entirely white, and others wholly black. The savages say that the white deer are of very great consequence in the estimation of the other deer, and are exceedingly

---

[1] A deep-red Spanish wine.

[2] The original has *water-limoenen*, water-citrons, for the watermelon, little known in Dutch gardens at this time, was regarded rather as a citron than as a melon.　　　　　　　　　　　　　　　　　　　　　[3] Panthers.

beloved, regarded and honored by the others, but that the reverse is true of the black deer. There are various other large animals in the interior, but they are unknown to the Christians. There are also wolves, dangerous only to small cattle, beavers, otters, weasels, wild cats, foxes, raccoons, minks, hares, musk-rats, about as large as cats, pole-cats and squirrels, some of which can fly. There are also ground-hogs and other small animals, but they are for the most part, as we have said, not known to the Christians.

Of birds this country is by no means without its share. There are great numbers of birds of prey, as eagles of two kinds, —the bald-headed, which has the head, tail and principal wing-feathers white, and the common kind; hawks, buzzards, sparrow-hawks, crows, chicken-hawks, and many others, yet all are birds of prey and capable of being trained and used for hunting, though they differ somewhat in shape from those in the Netherlands. There is also a bird which has its head like a cat, and its body like a large owl, colored white.[1] We know no name for it in the Netherlands, but in France it is called *grand duc*, and is esteemed very highly.

The other birds found in this country are turkies, the same as in the Netherlands, but they are wild, and are plentiest and best in winter; several kinds of partridges, some smaller than in the Netherlands, others larger, curlews, wood and water snipes, pheasants, heath-hens, cranes, herons, bitterns, multi-tudes of pigeons resembling ringdoves, but a little smaller; quails, merlins, thrushes, shore-runners, but in some respects different from those of the Netherlands. There are other small birds, some of which sing, but the names of most of them are unknown to us, and would take too long to enumerate. Water fowl are found here of different kinds, but all very good and fit to eat; such as the swans, similar to those in Netherlands and full as large; three kinds of geese, gray geese, which are the largest and best, bernicles and white-headed geese, ducks of different kinds, widgeons, divers, coots, cormorants and several others, but not so abundant as the foregoing.

The river fish are almost the same as in the Netherlands,

---

[1] The cat-owl or great barred owl, *bubo Virginianus*. It is not white, but neither is the *grand duc*, the European *bubo*. Van der Donck, in his *Beschryvinge*, says, "of a light ash color."

comprising salmon, sturgeon, twelves, thirteens,[1] shad, carp, perch, pike, trout, roach, thickhead, suckers, sunfish, eel, nine-eyes or lampreys, both much more abundant and larger than in the Netherlands, besides many other valuable fish which we are unable to name.

In the salt water are caught codfish, haddock, weakfish, herring, mackerel, thornbacks, flounders, plaice, sheepshead, blackfish, sea-dogs, panyns and many others; also lobsters, crabs, great cockles, from which the Indians make the white and black *zeewant*, oysters and muscles in great quantities with many other kinds of shell-fish very similar to each other, for which we know no names, besides sea and land tortoises.

The venomous animals consist, for the most part, of adders and lizards, though they are harmless or nearly so. There are snakes of different kinds, which are not dangerous and flee before men if they possibly can, else they are usually beaten to death. The rattlesnakes, however, which have a rattle on the tail, with which they rattle very loudly when they are angry or intend to sting, and which grows every year a joint larger, are very malignant and do not readily retreat before a man or any other creature. Whoever is bitten by them runs great danger of his life, unless great care be taken; but fortunately they are not numerous, and there grows spontaneously in the country the true snakeroot, which is very highly esteemed by the Indians as an unfailing cure.

The medicinal plants found in New Netherland up to the present time, by little search, as far as they have come to our knowledge, consist principally of Venus' hair, hart's tongue, lingwort, polypody, white mullein, priest's shoe, garden and sea-beach orach, water germander, tower-mustard, sweet flag, sassafras, crowfoot, plantain, shepherd's purse, mallows, wild marjoram, crane's bill, marsh-mallows, false eglantine, laurel, violet, blue flag, wild indigo, solomon's seal, dragon's blood, comfrey, milfoil, many sorts of fern, wild lilies of different kinds, agrimony, wild leek, blessed thistle, snakeroot, Spanish figs which grow out of the leaves,[2] tarragon and numerous other plants and flowers; but as we are not skilled in those things, we cannot say much of them; yet it is not to be doubted that

---

[1] Striped bass and drum-fish. See p. 222, note 1.
[2] Probably the prickly pear.

experts would be able to find many simples of great and different virtues, in which we have confidence, principally because the Indians know how to cure very dangerous and perilous wounds and sores by roots, leaves and other little things.

It is certain that the *Indigo silvestris* grows here spontaneously without human aid. It could be easily cultivated if there were people who would undertake it; at least, the other species would grow very well and yield a good profit. We have seen proof of this in the colony of Renselaerswyck, though it was all sown too late and upon a barren rock where there was little earth. It came up very well, but in consequence of the drought turned very yellow and withered, and was neglected; nevertheless it was evident that if it were well covered it would succeed. Madder plants also would undoubtedly grow well both in fields and gardens, and better than in Zeeland.

There may be discovered casually or by little search, different minerals, upon some of which tests have been made according to our limited means, and which are found good. We have attempted several times to send specimens of them to the Netherlands, once with Arent van Corenben by way of New Haven and of England, but the ship was wrecked and no tidings of it have ever been received.[1] After that Director William Kieft also had many different specimens with him in the ship the *Princess*, but they were lost in her with him.[2] The mountains and mines nevertheless remain, and are easily to be found again whenever it may be thought proper to go to the labor and expense. In New England they have already progressed so far as to make castings of iron pots, tankards, balls and the like out of their minerals, and we firmly believe all that is wanting here is to have a beginning made; for there are in New Netherland two kinds of marcasite, and mines of white

[1] Arent Corssen. Van der Donck says that he and Kieft saw an Indian painting his face with a shining mineral. They had it assayed, and it proved to contain gold. Arent Corssen, sent to Holland with a bag of it, embarked early in 1646 in the "great ship" of New Haven, Captain George Lamberton, for whose return into the harbor as a phantom ship, months afterward, see Cotton Mather's *Magnalia*, I. 84 (ed. of 1853), and Longfellow's poem, "The Phantom Ship."

[2] In August, 1647, some months after Stuyvesant's arrival, Kieft sailed for Holland. With him sailed his enemy Domine Bogardus, and the chief victims of his and Stuyvesant's persecution, Kuyter and Melyn. The ship was wrecked on the Welsh coast. Kieft was drowned; his opponents escaped.

and yellow quicksilver, of gold, silver, copper, iron, black lead
and hard coal. It is supposed that tin and lead will also be
found; but who will seek after them or who will make use of
them as long as there are not more people?

Fuller's earth is found in abundance, and [Armenian]
bole; also white, red, yellow, blue and black clay very solid and
greasy, and should be suitable for many purposes; earth for
bricks and for tiles, mountain-chrystal, glass like that of
Muscovy,[1] green serpentine stone in great abundance, blue
limestone, slate, red grindstone, flint, paving stone, large
quantities of all varieties of quarry stone suitable for hewing
mill-stones and for building all kinds of walls, asbestos and
very many other kinds applicable to the use of man. There
are different paints, but the Christians are not skilled in them.
They are seen daily on the Indians, who understand their
nature and use them to paint themselves in different colors.
If it were not that explorers are wanting, our people would be
able to find them and provide themselves with them.

*Of the Americans or Natives, their Appearance, Occupations,
and Means of Support.*

The natives are generally well set in their limbs, slender
round the waist, broad across the shoulders, and have black
hair and dark eyes. They are very nimble and fleet, well
adapted to travel on foot and to carry heavy burdens. They
are foul and slovenly in their actions, and make little of all
kinds of hardships; to which indeed they are by nature and
from their youth accustomed. They are like the Brazilians in
color, or as yellow as the people who sometimes pass through
the Netherlands and are called Gypsies. The men generally
have no beard, or very little, which some even pull out. They
use very few words, which they first consider well. Naturally
they are very modest, simple and inexperienced; though in
their actions high-minded enough, vigorous and quick to comprehend or learn, be it right or wrong, whenever they are so
inclined. They are not straightforward as soldiers but perfid-
ious, accomplishing all their enterprises by treachery, using
many stratagems to deceive their enemies, and usually order-

[1] Mica.

ing all their plans, involving any danger, by night.   The desire of revenge appears to be born in them.   They are very obstinate in defending themselves when they cannot run, which however they do when they can; and they make little of death when it is inevitable, and despise all tortures which can be inflicted upon them while dying, manifesting no sorrow, but usually singing until they are dead.   They understand how to cure wounds and hurts, or inveterate sores and injuries, by means of herbs and roots, which grow in the country, and which are known to them.   Their clothing, both for men and women, is a piece of duffels or leather in front, with a deer skin or elk's hide over the body.   Some have bears' hides of which they make doublets; others have coats made of the skins of raccoons, wild-cats, wolves, dogs, otters, squirrels, beavers and the like, and also of turkey's feathers.   At present they use for the most part duffels cloth, which they obtain in barter from the Christians.   They make their stockings and shoes of deer skins or elk's hide, and some have shoes made of corn-husks, of which they also make sacks.   Their money consists of white and black *zeewant*, which they themselves make.   Their measure and valuation is by the hand or by the fathom; but their corn is measured by *denotas*, which are bags they make themselves. Ornamenting themselves consists in cutting their bodies, or painting them with various colors, sometimes even all black, if they are in mourning, yet generally in the face.   They hang *zeewant*, both white and black, about their heads, which they otherwise are not wont to cover, but on which they are now beginning to wear hats and caps bought of the Christians. They also put it in their ears, and around their necks and bodies, wherewith after their manner they appear very fine. They have long deer's hair which is dyed red, and of which they make rings for the head, and other fine hair of the same color, to hang from the neck like tresses, of which they are very proud.   They frequently smear their skin and hair with different kinds of grease.   They can almost all swim.   They themselves make the boats they use, which are of two kinds, some of entire trees, which they hollow out with fire, hatchets and adzes, and which the Christians call canoes; others are made of bark, which they manage very skilfully, and which are also called canoes.

Traces of the institution of marriage can just be perceived among them, and nothing more. A man and woman join themselves together without any particular ceremony other than that the man by previous agreement with the woman gives her some *zeewant* or cloth, which on their separation, if it happens soon, he often takes again. Both men and women are utterly unchaste and shamelessly promiscuous in their intercourse, which is the cause of the men so often changing their wives and the women their husbands. Ordinarily they have but one wife, sometimes two or three, but this is generally among the chiefs. They have also among them different conditions of persons, such as noble and ignoble. The men are generally lazy, and do nothing until they become old and unesteemed, when they make spoons, wooden bowls, bags, nets and other similar articles; beyond this the men do nothing except fish, hunt and go to war. The women are compelled to do the rest of the work, such as planting corn, cutting and drawing fire-wood, cooking, taking care of the children and whatever else there is to be done. Their dwellings consist of hickory saplings, placed upright in the ground and bent arch-wise; the tops are covered with barks of trees, which they cut for this purpose in great quantities. Some even have within them rough carvings of faces and images, but these are generally in the houses of the chiefs. In the fishing and hunting seasons, they lie under the open sky or little better. They do not live long in one place, but move about several times in a year, at such times and to such places as it appears best and easiest for them to obtain subsistence.

They are divided into different tribes and languages, each tribe living generally by itself and having one of its number as a chief, though he has not much power or distinction except in their dances or in time of war. Among some there is not the least knowledge of God, and among others very little, though they relate many strange fables concerning Him.

They are in general much afraid of the Devil, who torments them greatly; and some give themselves up to him, and hold the strangest notions about him. But their devils, they say, will have nothing to do with the Dutch. No haunting of spirits and the like are heard of among them. They make offerings to the Devil sometimes, but with few solemnities.

They believe in the immortality of the soul. They have some knowledge of the sun, moon and stars, of which they are able to name many, and they judge tolerably well about the weather. There is hardly any law or justice among them, except sometimes in war matters, and then very little. The nearest of blood is the avenger. The youngest are the most courageous, and do for the most part what they please. Their weapons formerly were the bow and arrow, which they employ with wonderful skill, and the cudgel, but they now, that is, those who live near the Christians or have many dealings with them, generally use firelocks and hatchets, which they obtain in trade. They are exceedingly fond of guns, sparing no expense for them; and are so skilful in the use of them that they surpass many Christians. Their food is coarse and simple, drinking water as their only beverage, and eating the flesh of all kinds of animals which the country affords, cooked without being cleansed or dressed. They eat even badgers, dogs, eagles and such like trash, upon which Christians place no value. They use all kinds of fish, which they commonly cook without removing the entrails, and snakes, frogs and the like. They know how to preserve fish and meat until winter, and to cook them with corn-meal. They make their bread of maize, but it is very plain, and cook it either whole or broken in a pestle block. The women do this and make of it a pap or porridge, which some of them call *Sapsis*,[1] others *Enimdare*, and which is their daily food. They mix this also sometimes with small beans of different colors, which they plant themselves, but this is held by them as a dainty dish more than as daily food.

By whom New Netherland was first Possessed and what its Boundaries are.

That New Netherland was first found, claimed and possessed by Netherlanders, has already been stated; but inasmuch as a dispute has arisen, not only with the Swedes (which is of little moment) but especially with the English, who have already entered upon and seized a great part thereof, it is necessary to speak of each claim in particular and somewhat

[1] Probably a misprint for *sapaan*. For the next word, the manuscript has *Duundare*.

at large. But because this matter has been treated upon by various ingenious minds in its length and breadth, and as those claims are so absurd as to require only a few reasons in answer to them, we will be as brief as is in any wise practicable.

After Their High Mightinesses, the Lords States General, were pleased, in the year of our Lord 1622,[1] to include this province in their grant to the Honorable West India Company, their Honors deemed it necessary to take into possession so naturally beautiful and noble a province, which was immediately done, as opportunity offered, the same as in all similar beginnings. Since the year of our Lord 1623, four forts have been built there by order of the Lords Directors,[2] one on the south point of the Manhatans Island, where the East and North Rivers unite, called New Amsterdam, where the staple-right[3] of New Netherland was designed to be; another upon the same river, six-and-thirty Dutch miles [leagues] higher up, and three leagues below the great Kochoos[4] fall of the Mohawk River, on the west side of the river, in the colony of Renselaers-wyck, and is called Orange; but about this river there has been as yet no dispute with any foreigners. Upon the South River lies Fort Nassau and upon the Fresh River, the Good Hope. In these four forts there have been always from the beginning to the present time some garrisons, although they are all now in a very bad condition, not only in themselves but also as regards garrisons.

These forts, both to the south and north, are so situated as not only to close and control the said rivers, but also to command the plantations between them, as well as those round about them, and on the other side of the river as far as the ownership by occupation extends. These the Honorable Company declared they owned and would maintain against all foreign or domestic powers who should attempt to seize them against their consent. Yet, especially on the northeast side of New Netherland this has been not at all regarded or observed by the English living to the eastward; for notwithstanding possession was already fully taken by the building and occupa-

---

[1] 1621.   [2] *Heeren Majores*, the managers or directors of the Company.
[3] *Staple-right* is a privilege granted to the inhabitants of a place, whereby the masters of vessels or merchants trading along their coasts are compelled to discharge their cargoes there for sale, or else pay duties.   [4] Cohoes.

tion of Fort Good Hope, and there was no neglect from time to time in warning them, in making known our rights, and in protesting against their usurpation and violence, they have disregarded all these things and have seized and possessed, and still hold, the largest and best part of New Netherland, that is, on the east side of the North River, from Cape Cod, (by our people in 1609 called New Holland, and taken possession of [if we are correctly informed] by the setting up of the arms of their High Mightinesses,) [1] to within six leagues of the North River, where the English have now a village called Stamford, from whence one could travel now in a summer's day to the North River and back again, if one knows the Indian path. The English of New Haven also have a trading house which lies east or southeast of Magdalen Island, and not more than six leagues from the North River, in which this island lies, on the east bank twenty-three and a half leagues above Fort Amsterdam.[2] This trading post was established for no other purpose than to divert the trade of the North River or to destroy it entirely, for the river is now quite free. They have also endeavored several times, during eight or nine years past, to buy of the Indians a large quantity of land, (which would have served more than any other thing to draw off the trade), as we have understood from the Indians; for the post is situated not more than three or four leagues from the eastern bounds of the colony of Renselaerswyck.

This and similar difficulties these people now wish to lay to our charge, all under the pretence of a very clear conscience, notwithstanding King James, of most glorious memory, chartered the Virginia Companies upon condition that they should remain an hundred miles from each other, according to our reckoning.[3] They are willing to avail themselves of this grant, but by no means to comply with the terms stipulated in it.

[1] See De Laet, p. 37, *supra*. The words in square brackets appear in the manuscript, but not in the printed pamphlet.

[2] Magdalen Island is in the Hudson near Annandale. It appears that the nearest post to the lower Hudson possessed hitherto by the New Englanders was that which the New Haven people established in 1646 on the Housatonic near the present Derby, Connecticut; and that their nearest post to the upper Hudson was that which Governor Hopkins, of Connecticut, set up in 1641 at Woronoco, now Westfield, Massachusetts. See, on Van der Donck's map, " Mr. Pinser's handel huys (Mr. Pynchon's trading house).

[3] The hundred miles of the Virginia patent of 1606 were English miles.

All the islands, bays, havens, rivers, kills and places, even to a great distance on the other side of New Holland or Cape Cod, have Dutch names, which our Dutch ship-masters and traders gave to them.[1] These were the first to discover and to trade to them, even before they had names, as the English themselves well know; but as long as they can manage it and matters go as they please, they are willing not to know it. And those of them who are at the Fresh River have desired to enter into an agreement and to make a yearly acknowledgment or an absolute purchase, which indeed is proof positive that our right was well known to them, and that they themselves had nothing against it in conscience, although they now, from time to time, have invented and pretended many things in order to screen themselves, or thereby to cause at least delay.

Moreover the people of Rhode Island, when they were at variance with those of the Bay,[2] sought refuge among the Dutch, and sojourn among them. For all these things, and what we shall relate in the following pages, there are proofs and documents enough, either with the secretary of the Company or with the directors.

In short, it is just this with the English, they are willing to know the Netherlanders, and to use them as a protection in time of need, but when that is past, they no longer regard them, but play the fool with them. This happens so only because we have neglected to populate the land; or, to speak more plainly and truly, because we have, out of regard for our own profit, wished to scrape all the fat into one or more pots, and thus secure the trade and neglect population.

Long Island, which, on account of its convenient bays and havens, and its good well situated lands, is a crown of the province, they have also seized at once, except on the west end two Dutch villages—Breuckelen and Amersvoort,[3] not of much importance—and some English villages, as Gravesande, Greenwich and Mespat, (from which[4] the people were driven off

---

[1] An exaggeration, yet the number of such names is considerable, as may be seen by consulting the appendix to Asher's *Bibliography of New Netherland.*

[2] Massachusetts Bay. The most conspicuous instance is Mrs. Anne Hutchinson.   [3] Brooklyn and Flatlands.

[4] *I. e.*, from Mespath or Newtown. Gravesend had been settled by Lady Deborah Moody, Greenwich in 1639 by Captain Daniel Patrick and Robert

during the war, and which was afterwards confiscated by Director Kieft; but as the owners appealed therefrom, it remains undecided.) There are now a very few people in the place. Also, Vlissengen, which is a pretty village and tolerably rich in cattle. The fourth and last village is Heemstede, which is superior to the rest, for it is very rich in cattle.

As we are now on the subject of Long Island, we will, because the English claim it, speak of it somewhat particularly. The ocean on the south, and the East River on the north side of it, shape this island; and as we have said, it is, on account of its good situation, of its land, and of its convenient harbors, and anchoring places, a crown of New Netherland. The East River separates it from Manathans Island as far as the Hellegat. It is tolerably wide and convenient; and has been inhabited by our freemen from the first, according as opportunities offered. In the year 1640 a Scotchman, with an English commission, came to Director William Kieft. He laid claim to the island, but his pretension was not much regarded; for which reason he departed without accomplishing anything, having influenced only a few simple people. Director Kieft also afterwards sent and broke up the English who wished to begin a settlement at Oyster Bay, and thus it remained for a time.[1]

In the year 1647, a Scotchman came here, who called himself Captain Forester,[2] and claimed this island for the Dowager of Sterling, whose governor he gave himself out to be. He had a commission dated in the eighteenth year of King James's reign, but it was not signed by His Majesty or any body else. Appended to it was an old seal which we could not decipher. His commission embraced the whole of Long Island, together with five leagues round about it, the main land as well as the islands. He had also full authority from Mary, dowager of Sterling, but this was all. Nevertheless the man was very consequential, and said on his first arrival that he came here

Feake, Mespath by Francis Doughty in 1642, Flushing and Hempstead by other English in 1645 and 1644.

[1] James Farrett, as agent for Lord Stirling, made grants at Oyster Bay to a company of men from Lynn, who began a settlement there. Stirling had received a grant of Long Island from the Council of New England in April, 1635.

[2] Andrew Forester, of Dundee.

to see Governor Stuyvesant's commission, and if that was
better than his, he was willing to give way; if not, Governor
Stuyvesant must yield to him. To make the matter short, the
Director took copies of the papers and sent the man across [1]
in the *Falconer*; but as this vessel put into England, the man
did not reach Holland, having escaped there, and never troubling the captain afterwards. The English have since boasted
of this very loudly, and have also given out that he had again
arrived at Bastock,[2] but we have not heard of him. It is to
be apprehended that if he came now, some new act would
be committed, for which reason it would be well to hasten the
redress of New Netherland.

Of the Fresh River.

After Fort Good Hope, begun in the year 1623,[3] on the
Fresh River, was finished, some time had elapsed when an
English bark arrived there. Jacob van Curler, factor of the
Company, by order of Director Wouter van Twiller, protested
against it, but notwithstanding his protest they did, a year
or two afterwards, come there with some families. A protest
was also made against them; but it was very manifest that
these people had little respect for it, for notwithstanding
frequent protests, they have finally seized and possessed the
whole of the Fresh River, and have proceeded so far in their
shameless course as, in the year 1640, to seize the Company's
farms at the fort, paying no regard to the protests which we
made. They have gone even still further, and have belabored
the Company's people with sticks and heavy clubs; and have
forcibly thrown into the river their ploughs and other instru-
ments, while they were on the land for the purpose of working,
and have put their horses in the pound. The same things
happened very frequently afterwards. They also took hogs
and cows belonging to the fort, and several times sold some
of them for the purpose, as they said, of repairing the damage.
Against all these acts, and each one in particular, protests were
repeatedly made, but they were met with ridicule. Several

---

[1] Across the ocean.   [2] Boston.
[3] A misprint for 1633. The narrative below relates to the English settlers at
Hartford, founded in 1635. See De Vries, pp. 203, 204, *supra*.

sharp letters about this were written in Latin to their governors; of which letters and protests, minutes or copies remain with the Company's officers, from which a much fuller account of these transactions could be made. But all opposition was in vain, for having had a smack of the goodness and convenience of this river, and discovered the difference between the land there and that more easterly, they would not go back; nor will they put themselves under the protection of Their High Mightinesses, unless they be sharply summoned thereto, as it is desirable they should be at the first opportunity.

Of the Right of the Netherlanders to the Fresh River.

To speak from the beginning, our people had carefully explored and discovered the most northerly parts of New Netherland and some distance on the other side of Cape Cod, as we find it described, before the English were known here, and had set up our arms upon Cape Cod as an act of possession. In the year 1614 our traders [1] had not only traded at the Fresh River, but had also ascended it before any English had ever dreamed of going there, which they did first in the year 1636, after our fort, the Good Hope, had been a long time *in esse* and almost all the lands on both sides the river had been purchased by our people from the Indians, which purchase took place principally in the year 1632. Kievets-hoeck [2] was also purchased at the same time by one Hans den Sluys,[3] an officer of the company. On this cape the States' arms had been affixed to a tree in token of possession; but the English who now possess the Fresh River have torn them down and carved a ridiculous face in their place. Whether this was done by authority or not, cannot be positively asserted; it is however supposed that it was. It has been so charged upon them in several letters, and no denial has been made. Besides they have, *contra jus gentium, per fas et nefas*,[4] invaded the whole river, for the reason, as they say, that the land was lying idle and waste, which was no business of theirs and not true; for

---

[1] Adriaen Block.

[2] Saybrook Point. *Kievit*, or *kiewit*, is the bird *pewit*.

[3] Hans Eencluys in the manuscript, according to *N. Y. Col. Doc.*, I. 287.

[4] "Contrary to the law of nations, regardless of right or wrong."

there was already built upon the river a fort which continued to be possessed by a garrison. There was also a large farm[1] near the fort, belonging to the Dutch or the Company. Most of the land was bought and appropriated and the arms of their High Mightinesses were set up at Kievets Hoeck, which is situated at the mouth of the river, so that everything was done that could be done except that the country was not all actually occupied. This the English demanded in addition, just as if it were their right, since they were in greater numbers, to establish laws for our nation in its own purchased lands and limits, and direct how and in what manner it should introduce people into the country, and if it did not turn out exactly according to their desire and pleasure, that they have the right to invade and appropriate these waters, lands and jurisdiction to themselves.

Of the Roden-Berch,[2] by the English called New Haven, and other Places of less Importance.

The number of villages established by the English, from New Holland or Cape Cod to Stamford, within the limits of the Netherlanders, is about thirty, and they may contain five thousand men capable of bearing arms. Their cattle, cows and horses are estimated at thirty thousand; their goats and hogs cannot be stated; neither of them can be fully known because there are several places which cannot well pass for villages, but which nevertheless are beginnings of villages. Among all these, Roden-Berch, or New Haven, is the first. It has a governor, contains about three hundred and forty families, and is counted as a province or one of the members of New England, of which there are four in all.[3]

This place was begun eleven years ago, in the year 1638, and since then the people have broken off and formed Milford, Stratford, Stamford and the trading house before spoken of, etc.

Director Kieft has caused several protests to be drawn up, in Latin and in other languages, commanding them by

---

[1] *Brouwerye*, brewery, in the printed pamphlet, but *bouwery* in the manuscript.

[2] Red Hill.

[3] *I. e.*, of the United Colonies of New England, the confederation formed in 1643.

virtue of his commissions from the Lords States General,
His Highness the Prince of Orange and the Most Noble Directors of the Chartered West India Company, to desist from their
proceedings and usurpations, and warning them, in case they
did not, that we would, as soon as a fit opportunity should
present, exact of them satisfaction therefor.   But it was knock-
ing at a deaf man's door, as they did not regard these protests
or even take any notice of them; on the contrary they have
sought many subterfuges, circumstances, false pretences and
sophistical arguments to give color to their doings, to throw
a cloud upon our lawful title and valid rights, and to cheat us
out of them.   General Stuyvesant also has had many questions
with them, growing out of this matter, but it remains as it
was.   The utmost that they have ever been willing to come to,
is to declare that the dispute could not be settled in this country, and that they desired and were satisfied that Their High
Mightinesses should arrange it with their sovereign.   It is
highly necessary that this should be done, inasmuch as the
English have already seized, and are in possession of, almost
half of New Netherland, a matter which may have weighty consequences in the future.   It is therefore heartily to be desired
that Their High Mightinesses will be pleased to take this subject
into serious consideration before it shall go further, and the
breach become irreparable.

We must now pass to the South River, called by the English
Delaware Bay, first speaking of the boundaries; but in passing
we cannot omit to say that there has been here, both in the
time of Director Kieft and in that of General Stuyvesant, a
certain Englishman, who called himself Sir Edward Ploeyden,
with the title of Earl Palatine of New Albion, who claimed
that the land on the west side of the North River to Virginia
was his, by gift of King James of England,[1] but he said he did
not wish to have any strife with the Dutch, though he was
very much piqued at the Swedish governor, John Prins, at
the South River, on account of some affront given him, too

---

[1] Plowden claimed under a patent from the viceroy of Ireland under Charles I.,
June, 1634.   The history of his shadowy principality of New Albion is best re-
counted by Professor Gregory B. Keen in Winsor's *Narrative and Critical History
of America*, III. 457-468.   The best account of the Swedish colony in the South
River is by the same writer, *ibid.*, IV. 443-500.

long to relate. He said also that when an opportunity should
offer he would go there and take possession of the river. In
short, according to the claims of the English, it belongs to them,
and there is nothing left for the subjects of Their High Mightinesses—one must have this far, and another that far, but they
all agree never to fall short.

Of the South River and the Boundaries there.

As we have now come to speak of the South River and the
most southerly portion of New Netherland, we will, although
this is well performed by others, relate everything from the
beginning, and yet as briefly as is practicable. The boundaries,
as we find them, extend as far as Cape Henlopen, many miles
south of Cape Cornelius, to the latitude of thirty-eight degrees.
The coast stretches, one course with another, west-southwest
and west, and although this Cape Henlopen [1] is not much
esteemed, it is nevertheless proper that it should be brought
to our attention, as very important, not only in regard to the
position of the country, but also as relates to the trade with
the Indians at the South River, which the English and Swedes
are striving after very hard, as we will show. If the boundaries of this country were settled, these people would conveniently and without further question be ousted, and both the
enjoyment of the productions of the land and the trade be retained for the subjects of Their High Mightinesses.

Of the South Bay and South River.

The South Bay and South River, by many called the second
great river of New Netherland, is situated at the latitude of
38 degrees 53 minutes. It has two headlands or capes—the
more northerly bearing the name of Cape May, the more southerly that of Cape Cornelius. The bay was called New Port-
May, but at the present time is known as Godyn's Bay. These
names were given to the places about the time of their first
discovery, before any others were given them. The discovery,
moreover, took place at the same time with that of the North
River, and by the same ship and persons, who entered the South

---

[1] On the shifting of the name of Henlopen, see p. 52, note 2, *supra*.

Bay before they came to the North Bay, as all can read at length in the *Nieuwe Werelt* of Johannes de Laet.

At the same time that the forts were laid out on the North and Fresh rivers, since the year 1623, Fort Nassau was erected upon this river, which, in common parlance, is called the South River. It was the first of the four, and was built with the same object and design as all the others, as hereinbefore related. It lies on the east bank,[1] but it would have done as well on the west bank, fifteen leagues up the river. The bay runs for the most part north and south; is called New Port-May or Godyn's Bay; and is nine leagues long before you come to the river, and six leagues wide, so that from one shore you cannot see the other. On account of certain bars it is somewhat dangerous for inexperienced navigators, but not so for those who are acquainted with the channels. This bay and river are compared by its admirers with the river Amazon, that is, by such of them as have seen both; it is by everyone considered one of the most beautiful, and the best and pleasantest rivers in the world of itself and as regards its surroundings. Fourteen streams empty into this river, the least of them navigable for two or three leagues; and on both sides there are tolerably level lands of great extent. Two leagues from Cape Cornelius, where you enter on the west side, lies a certain creek, which might be taken for an ordinary river or stream, being navigable far up, and affording a beautiful roadstead for ships of all burdens. There is no other like it in the whole bay for safety and convenience. The main channel for navigation runs close by it; this place we call the Hoere-kil. From whence this name is derived we do not know;[2] it is certain that this place was taken and colonized by Netherlanders, years before any English or Swedes came there. The States' arms were also set up at this place in copper, but as they were thrown down by some mischievous savages, the commissary there very firmly insisted upon, and demanded, the head of the offender. The Indians not knowing otherwise brought a head, saying it was his; and the affair was supposed to be all settled, but some

---

[1] Fort Nassau stood at the mouth of Timber Creek, opposite the present site of Philadelphia. See Van der Donck's map.

[2] Harlot's creek, from the behavior of the Indian women. The story below is that of the short-lived colony of Swanendael, 1631–1632.

time afterwards, when our people were working unsuspectingly in their fields, the Indians came in the guise of friendship, and distributing themselves among the Dutch in proportionate numbers, surprised and murdered them. By this means the colony was again reduced to nothing; but it was nevertheless sealed with blood and dearly enough bought.

There is another kill on the east side called the Varckens Kil,[1] three leagues up from the mouth of the river. Here some English had settled, but Director Kieft protested against their proceedings, and drove them away, assisted somewhat by the Swedes, who agreed with him to keep out the English. The Swedish governor, considering an opportunity then offered to him, caused a fort to be built at this place, called Elsenborch,[2] and manifests there great boldness towards every one, even as respects the Company's boats or all which go up the South River. They must strike the flag before this fort, none excepted; and two men are sent on board to ascertain from whence the yachts or ships come. It is not much better than exercising the right of search. It will, to all appearance, come to this in the end. What authority these people can have to do this, we know not; nor can we comprehend how officers of other potentates, (at least as they say they are, yet what commission they have we do not yet know,) can make themselves master of, and assume authority over, land and goods belonging to and possessed by other people, and sealed with their blood, even without considering the Charter. The Minquas-kil[3] is the first upon the river, and there the Swedes have built Fort Christina. This place is well situated, as large ships can lie close against the shore to load and unload. There is, among others, a place on the river, (called Schuylkil, a convenient and navigable stream,) heretofore possessed by the Netherlanders, but how is it now? The Swedes have it almost entirely under their dominion. Then there are in the river several beautiful large islands, and other places which were formerly possessed by the Netherlanders, and which still bear the names given by them. Various other facts also constitute sufficient and abun-

---

[1] Hog Creek, now called Salem Creek, where New Haven men settled in 1641, at or near the present site of Salem, New Jersey. See Van der Donck's map.

[2] Fort Nya Elfsborg, 1643–1654, a little further down the Delaware River.

[3] Christina Creek; the fort was in what is now Wilmington, Delaware.

dant proof that the river belongs to the Netherlanders, and not
to the Swedes. Their very beginnings are convincing, for
eleven years ago, in the year 1638, one Minne-wits,[1] who before
that time had had the direction at the Manathans, on behalf
of the West India Company, arrived in the river with the ship
Kalmer-Sleutel [Key of Calmar], and the yacht *Vogel-Gryp*
[Griffin], giving out to the Netherlanders who lived up the river,
under the Company and Heer vander Nederhorst, that he was
on a voyage to the West Indies, and that passing by there, he
wished to arrange some matters and to furnish the ship with
water and wood, and would then leave. Some time afterwards,
some of our people going again, found the Swedes still there
but then they had already made a small garden for raising
salads, pot-herbs and the like. They wondered at this, and
inquired of the Swedes what it meant, and whether they
intended to stay there. They excused themselves by various
reasons and subterfuges, but some notwithstanding supposed
that such was their design. The third time it became apparent,
from their building a fort, what their intentions were. Director
Kieft, when he obtained information of the matter, protested
against it, but in vain. It was plainly and clearly to be seen,
in the progress of the affair, that they did not intend to leave.
It is matter of evidence that above Maghchachansie,[2] near the
Sankikans, the arms of Their High Mightinesses were erected
by order of Director Kieft, as a symbol that the river, with all
the country and the lands around there, were held and owned
under Their High Mightinesses. But what fruits has it produced as yet, other than continued derision and derogation of
dignity? For the Swedes, with intolerable insolence, have
thrown down the arms, and since they are suffered to remain so,
this is looked upon by them, and particularly by their governor,
as a Roman achievement. True, we have made several protests, as well against this as other transactions, but they have
had as much effect as the flying of a crow overhead; and it is
believed that if this governor had a supply of men, there would

---

[1] Peter Minuit.

[2] Apparently within the present bounds of Philadelphia, where Andries
Hudde, acting under orders from Kieft, purchased land and set up the arms of
the States General in September, 1646. The Sankikans occupied northern New
Jersey, with an important village at or near Trenton.

be more madness in him than there has been in the English, or any of their governors. This much only in regard to the Swedes, since the Company's officers will be able to make a more pertinent explanation, as all the documents and papers remain with them; to which, and to their journals we ourselves refer.

The English have sought at different times and places to incorporate this river which they say is annexed to their territory, but this has as yet been prevented by different protests. We have also expelled them by force, well knowing that if they once settled there, we should lose the river or hold it with much difficulty, as they would swarm there in great numbers. There are rumors daily, and it is reported to us that the English will soon repair there with many families. It is certain that if they do come and nestle down there, they will soon possess it so completely, that neither Hollanders nor Swedes, in a short time, will have much to say; at least, we run a chance of losing the whole, or the greatest part of the river, if very shortly remarkable precaution be not used. And this would be the result of populating the country; but the Directors of the Company to this day have had no regard to this worth the while, though the subject has been sufficiently brought before them in several documents. They have rather opposed and hindered this; for it has been with this matter as with the rest, that avarice has blinded wisdom. The report now is that the English intend to build a village and trading house there; and indeed if they begin, there is nobody in this country who, on the Company's behalf, can or apparently will, make much effort to prevent them. Not longer ago than last year, several free persons,[1] some of whom were of our own number and who had or could have good masters in Fatherland, wished to establish a trading house and some farms and plantations, upon condition that certain privileges and exemptions should be extended to them; but this was refused by the General, saying, that he could not do it, not having any order or authority from the noble Lords Directors; but if they were willing to begin there without privileges, it could in some way be done. And when we represented to His

[1] Persons who came to New Netherland, not as colonists under the patroons, or as employees of the West India Company, but on their own account.

Honor that such were offered by our neighbors all around us, if we would only declare ourselves willing to be called members of their government, and that this place ran a thousand dangers from the Swedes and English, His Honor answered that it was well known to be as we said, (as he himself did, in fact, well know,) and that reason was also in our favor, but that the orders which he had from the Directors were such that he could not answer for it to them. Now we are ignorant in these matters, but one thing or the other must be true, either it is the fault of the Director or of the Managers,[1] or of both of them. However it may be, one shifts the blame upon the other, and between them both every thing goes to ruin. Foreigners enjoy the country and fare very well; they laugh at us too if we say anything; they enjoy privileges and exemptions, which, if our Netherlanders had enjoyed as they do, would without doubt, next to the help of God, without which we are powerless, have enabled our people to flourish as well or better than they do; *ergo*, the Company or their officers have hitherto been and are still the cause of its not faring better with the country. On account of their cupidity and bad management there is no hope, so long as the land is under their government, that it will go on any better; but it will grow worse. However, the right time to treat this subject has not yet come.

Of the Situation and Goodness of the Waters.

Having given an account of the situation of the country and its boundaries, and having consequently spoken of the location of the rivers, it will not be foreign to our purpose to add a word as to the goodness and convenience of the waters; which are salt, brackish, or fresh, according to their locality. There are in New Netherland four principal rivers; the most southerly is usually called the South River, and the bay at its entrance, Godyn's Bay. It is so called not because it runs to the south, but because it is the most southerly river in New Netherland. Another which this lies south of or nearest to, and which is the most noted and the best, as regards trade and population, is called Rio Montanjes, from certain mountains,

---

[1] *I. e.*, of the governor (director-general) of New Netherland or of the directors of the company.

and Mauritius River, but generally, the North River, because
it reaches farthest north.   The third is the East River, so called
because it runs east from the Manathans.   This is regarded by
many not as a river but as a bay, because it is extremely wide
in some places and connects at both ends with the sea.   We
however consider it a river and such it is commonly reckoned.
The fourth is called the Fresh River, because the water is for
the most part fresh, more so than the others.   Besides these
rivers, there are many bays, havens and inlets, very convenient
and useful, some of which might well be classed among rivers.
There are numerous bodies of water inland, some large, others
small, besides navigable kills like rivers, and many creeks very
advantageous for the purpose of navigating through the
country, as the map of New Netherland will prove.   There
are also various waterfalls and rapid streams, fit to erect mills
of all kinds upon for the use of man, and innumerable small
rivulets over the whole country, like veins in the body; but
they are all fresh water, except some on the sea shore, (which
are salt and fresh or brackish), very good both for wild and
domestic animals to drink.   The surplus waters are lost in the
rivers or in the sea.   Besides all these there are fountains without number, and springs all through the country, even at
places where water would not be expected; as on cliffs and
rocks whence they issue like spring veins.   Some of them are
worthy of being well guarded, not only because they are all
(except in the thickets) very clear and pure, but because many
have these properties, that in the winter they smoke from
heat, and in summer are so cool that the hands can hardly be
endured in them on account of the cold, not even in the hottest
of the summer; which circumstance makes them pleasant for
the use of man and beast, who can partake of them without
danger; for if any one drink thereof, it does him no harm
although it be very warm weather.   Thus much of the pro-
prietorship, location, goodness and fruitfulness of these provinces, in which particulars, as far as our little experience
extends, it need yield to no province in Europe.   As to what
concerns trade, in which Europe and especially Netherland is
pre-eminent, it not only lies very convenient and proper for it,
but if there were inhabitants, it would be found to have more
commodities of and in itself to export to other countries than it

would have to import from them. These things considered, it will be little labor for intelligent men to estimate and compute exactly of what importance this naturally noble province is to the Netherland nation, what service it could render it in future, and what a retreat it would be for all the needy in the Netherlands, as well of high and middle, as of low degree; for it is much easier for all men of enterprise to obtain a livelihood here than in the Netherlands.

We cannot sufficiently thank the Fountain of all Goodness for His having led us into such a fruitful and healthful land, which we, with our numerous sins, still heaped up here daily, beyond measure, have not deserved. We are also in the highest degree beholden to the Indians, who not only have given up to us this good and fruitful country, and for a trifle yielded us the ownership, but also enrich us with their good and reciprocal trade, so that there is no one in New Netherland or who trades to New Netherland without obligation to them. Great is our disgrace now, and happy should we have been, had we acknowledged these benefits as we ought, and had we striven to impart the Eternal Good to the Indians, as much as was in our power, in return for what they divided with us. It is to be feared that at the Last Day they will stand up against us for this injury. Lord of Hosts! forgive us for not having conducted therein more according to our reason; give us also the means and so direct our hearts that we in future may acquit ourselves as we ought for the salvation of our own souls and of theirs, and for the magnifying of thy Holy Name, for the sake of Christ. Amen.

To speak with deference, it is proper to look beyond the trouble which will be incurred in adjusting the boundaries and the first cost of increasing the population of this country, and to consider that beginnings are difficult and that sowing would be irksome if the sower were not cheered with the hope of reaping. We trust and so assure ourselves that the very great experience of Their High Mightinesses will dictate better remedies than we are able to suggest. But it may be that Their High Mightinesses and some other friends, before whom this may come, may think strange that we speak as highly of this place as we do, and as we know to be true, and yet complain of want and poverty, seek relief, assistance, redress, lessening of charges, population and the like, and show that the country is in a poor and ruinous condition; yea, so much so, as that without special aid and assistance it will utterly fall off and pass under foreign rule.   It will therefore be necessary to point out the true reasons and causes why New Netherland is in so bad a state, which we will do as simply and truly as possible, according to the facts, as we have seen, experienced, and heard them; and as this statement will encounter much opposition and reproach from many persons who may take offence at it, we humbly pray Their High Mightinesses and all well wishers, who may chance to read this, that they do not let the truth yield to any falsehoods, invented and embellished for the purpose, and that they receive no other testimony against this relation than that of such impartial persons as have not had, either directly or indirectly, any hand therein, profited by the loss of New Netherland, or otherwise incurred any obligation to it.   With this remark we proceed to the reasons and sole cause of the evil which we indeed have but too briefly and indistinctly stated in the beginning of our petition to Their High Mightinesses.

Of the Reasons and Causes why and how New Netherland is so Decayed.

As we shall speak of the reasons and causes which have brought New Netherland into the ruinous condition in which it is now found to be, we deem it necessary to state first the difficulties.   We represent it as we see and find it, in our daily experience.   To describe it in one word, (and none better presents itself,) it is *bad government*, with its attendants and consequences, that is, to the best of our knowledge, the true and only foundation stone of the decay and ruin of New Netherland.   This government from which so much abuse proceeds, is twofold, that is; in the Fatherland by the Managers, and in this country. We shall first briefly point out some orders and mistakes issuing from the Fatherland, and afterwards proceed to show how abuses have grown up and obtained strength here.

The Managers of the Company adopted a wrong course at first, and as we think had more regard for their own interest than for the welfare of the country, trusting rather to flattering than true counsels. This is proven by the unnecessary expenses incurred from time to time, the heavy accounts of New Netherland,[1] the registering of colonies—in which business most of the Managers themselves engaged, and in reference to which they have regulated the trade—and finally the not peopling the country. It seems as if from the first, the Company have sought to stock this land with their own employees, which was a great mistake, for when their time was out they returned home, taking nothing with them, except a little in their purses and a bad name for the country, in regard to its lack of sustenance and in other respects. In the meantime there was no profit, but on the contrary heavy monthly salaries, as the accounts of New Netherland will show.

Had the Honorable West India Company, in the beginning, sought population instead of running to great expense for unnecessary things, which under more favorable circumstances might have been suitable and very proper, the account of New Netherland would not have been so large as it now is, caused by building the ship *New Netherland* at an excessive outlay,[2] by erecting three expensive mills, by brick-making, by tar-burning, by ash-burning, by salt-making and like operations, which through bad management and calculation have all gone to nought, or come to little; but which nevertheless have cost much. Had the same money been used in bringing people and importing cattle, the country would now have been of great value.

The land itself is much better and it is more conveniently situated than that which the English possess, and if there were not constant seeking of individual gain and private trade, there would be no danger that misfortunes would press us as far as they do.

Had the first Exemptions been truly observed, according to their intention, and had they not been carried out with particular views, certainly more friends of New Netherland would have exerted themselves to take people there and make

---

[1] In 1644 the Bureau of Accounts of the West India Company reported that since 1626 the company had expended for New Netherland 515,000 guilders, say $250,000. At the time of the report the company was practically bankrupt.

[2] A ship of eight hundred tons, built in the province in 1631.

settlements. The other conditions which were introduced have always discouraged individuals and kept them down, so that those who were acquainted with the business, being informed, dared not attempt it. It is very true that the Company have brought over some persons, but they have not continued to do so, and it therefore has done little good. It was not begun properly; for it was done as if it was not intended.

It is impossible for us to rehearse and to state in detail wherein and how often the Company have acted injuriously to this country. They have not approved of our own country-men settling the land, as is shown in the case of Jacob Walingen and his people at the Fresh River, and quite recently in the cases at the South River; while foreigners were permitted to take land there without other opposition than orders and pro-tests. It could hardly be otherwise, for the garrisons are not kept complete conformably to the Exemptions, and thus the cause of New Netherland's bad condition lurks as well in the Netherlands as here. Yea, the seeds of war, according to the declaration of Director Kieft, were first sown by the Fatherland; for he said he had express orders to exact the contribution from the Indians; which would have been very well if the land had been peopled, but as it was, it was pre-mature.

Trade, without which, when it is legitimate, no country is prosperous, is by their acts so decayed, that it amounts to nothing. It is more suited for slaves than freemen, in conse-quence of the restrictions upon it and the annoyances which accompany the exercise of the right of inspection. We approve of inspection, however, so far as relates to contraband.

This contraband trade has ruined the country, and contra-band goods are now sent to every part of it by orders given by the Managers to their officers. These orders should be executed without partiality, which is not always the case. The Recog-nition [1] runs high, and of inspection and confiscation there is no lack; hence legitimate trade is entirely diverted, except a little, which exists *pro forma*, as a cloak for carrying on illicit trading. In the mean time the Christians are treated almost like Indians, in the purchase of the necessaries with which they cannot dispense. This causes great complaint, distress and

[1] Export duty.

poverty: as, for example, the merchants sell those goods which are liable to little depreciation at a hundred per cent. and more profit, when there is particular demand or scarcity of them. And the traders who come with small cargoes, and others engaged in the business, buy them up from the merchants and sell them again to the common man, who cannot do without them, oftentimes at a hundred per cent. advance, or higher and lower according to the demand. Upon liquors, which are liable to much leakage, they take more, and those who buy from them retail them in the same manner, as we have described in regard to dry wares, and generally even more cunningly, so that the goods are sold through first, second and sometimes third hands, at one and two hundred per cent. advance. We are not able to think of all the practices which are contrived for advancing individual and private gain. Little attention is given to populating the land. The people, moreover, have been driven away by harsh and unreasonable proceedings, for which their Honors gave the orders; for the Managers wrote to Director Kieft to prosecute when there was no offence, and to consider a partial offence an entire one, and so forth. It has also been seen how the letters of the Eight Men were treated, and what followed thereupon;[1] besides there were many ruinous orders and instructions which are not known to us. But leaving this at present, with now and then a word, at a convenient point, let us proceed to examine how their officers and Directors have conducted themselves from time to time, having played with the managers as well as with the people, as a cat does with a mouse. It would be possible to relate their management from the beginning, but as most of us were not here then and therefore not eye-witnesses, and as a long time has passed whereby it has partly escaped recollection, and as in our view it was not so bad then as afterwards when the land was made free and freemen began to increase, we will pass by the beginning and let Mr. Lubbert van Dincklaghen, Vice Director of New Netherland, describe the government of Director Wouter van Twiller of which he is known to have information, and will only speak of the last two sad and dire confusions (we would say govern-

---

[1] Nevertheless, the remonstrance of the Eight Men, October 28, 1644, *N. Y. Col. Doc.*, I. 209, did cause the reform of the system of provincial government and the recall of Kieft.

ments if we could) under Director Kieft, who is now no more,
but the evil of it lives after him; and of that under Director
Stuyvesant which still stands, if indeed that may be called
standing which lies completely under foot.

The Directors here, though far from their masters, were
close by their profit. They have always known how to
manage their own matters very properly and with little loss,
yet under pretext of the public business. They have also conducted themselves just as if they were the sovereigns of the
country. As they desired to have it, so it always had to be;
and as they willed so was it done. "The Managers," they say,
"are masters in Fatherland, but we are masters in this land."
As they understand it it will go, there is no appeal. And it has
not been difficult for them hitherto to maintain this doctrine
in practice; for the people were few and for the most part very
simple and uninformed, and besides, they needed the Directors every day. And if perchance there were some intelligent
men among them, who could go upon their own feet, them it
was sought to oblige. They could not understand at first the
arts of the Directors which were always subtle and dark, so
that these were frequently successful and occasionally remained
effective for a long time. Director Kieft said himself, and let it
be said also by others, that he was sovereign in this country,
or the same as the Prince in the Netherlands. This was
repeated to him several times here and he never made any
particular objection to it. The refusing to allow appeals, and
other similar acts, prove clearly that in our opinion no other
proof is needed. The present Director does the same, and in
the denial of appeal, *he is also at home*. He likes to assert the
maxim "the Prince is above the law," and applies it so boldly
to his own person that it confutes itself. These directors,
having then the power in their own hands, could do and have
done what they chose according to their good will and pleasure; and whatever was, was right, because it was agreeable
to them. It is well known that those who assume power, and
use it to command what they will, frequently command and
will more than they ought, and, whether it appear right or
not, there are always some persons who applaud such conduct, some out of a desire to help on and to see mischief,
others from fear; and so men still complain with Jan Vergas

de clementia ducis, of the clemency of the duke.[1] But in order
that we give nobody cause to suspect that we blow somewhat
too hard, it will be profitable to illustrate by examples the
government of Mr. Director Kieft at its close, and the administration of Mr. Director Stuyvesant just prior to the time
of our departure. We frankly admit, however, that we shall
not be able to speak fully of all the tricks, because they were
conducted so secretly and with such duplicity and craft. We
will nevertheless expose some of their proceedings according
to our ability, and thus let the lion be judged of from his paw.

Casting our eyes upon the government of Director Kieft,
the church first meets us, and we will therefore speak of the
public property ecclesiastical and civil. But as this man is
now dead, and some of his management and doings are freely
represented by one Jochem Pietersz Cuyter and Cornelis
Melyn,[2] we will dispose of this point as briefly as we possibly
can.

Before the time that Director Kieft brought the unnecessary
war upon the country, his principal aim and endeavors were
to provide well for himself and to leave a great name after him,
but without any expense to himself or the Company, for this
never did anything remarkable for the country by which it was
improved. Thus he considered the erection of a church a very
necessary public work, the more so as it was in contemplation
to build one at that time at Renselaers-Wyck. With this view
he communicated with the churchwardens—of which body he
himself was one—and they willingly agreed to and seconded
the project. The place where it should stand was then de-
bated. The Director contended that it should be placed in the
fort, and there it was erected in spite of the others, and, indeed,
as suitably as a fifth wheel to a wagon; for besides that the
fort is small and lies upon a point of land which must be very
valuable in case of an increase of population, the church ought

---

[1] Juan de Vargas, the chief member of the Duke of Alva's "Council of Blood,"
who complained that the duke's methods were too lenient.

[2] Stuyvesant, soon after his arrival, at the instance of Kieft, condemned Kieft's
chief opponents, Kuyter and Melyn, for lese-majesty, and banished them, forbidding them to appeal. On reaching Holland, however, after their dramatic escape
from the shipwreck of the *Princess*, they appealed, and secured a reversal of their
condemnation.

to be owned by the congregation at whose cost it was built.   It
also intercepts and turns off the southeast wind from the grist-
mill which stands close by, for which reason there is frequently
in summer a want of bread from its inability to grind, though
not from this cause alone.   The mill is neglected and, in consequence of having had a leaky roof most of the time, has become considerably rotten, so that it cannot now go with more
than two arms, and it has been so for nearly five years.   But
to return to the church—from which the grist-mill has somewhat diverted us—the Director then resolved to build a church,
and at the place where it suited him; but he was in want of
money and was at a loss how to obtain it.   It happened about
this time that the minister, Everardus Bogardus, gave his step-
daughter in marriage; and the occasion of the wedding the
Director considered a good opportunity for his purpose.   So
after the fourth or fifth round of drinking, he set about the
business, and he himself showing a liberal example let the
wedding-guests subscribe what they were willing to give
towards the church.   All then with light heads subscribed
largely, competing with one another; and although some well
repented it when they recovered their senses, they were nevertheless compelled to pay—nothing could avail to prevent it.
The church was then, contrary to every one's wish, placed in
the fort.   The honor and ownership of that work must be
judged of from the inscription, which is in our opinion ambiguous, thus reading: "1642. *Willem Kieft, Director General,
has caused the congregation to build this church.*" [1]   But whatever be intended by the inscription, the people nevertheless
paid for the church.

We must now speak of the property belonging to the
church, and, to do the truth no violence, we do not know that
there has ever been any, or that the church has any income
except what is given to it.   There has never been any exertion
made either by the Company or by the Director to obtain or
establish any.

[1] The inscription was in existence till 1835. This third church stood near
what is now called the Bowling Green.   The inscription, though susceptible of
misconstruction, is not really ambiguous.   Its proper interpretation is: " 1642,
Willem Kieft being Director [General, the congregation caused this church to
be built."

The bowl has been going round a long time for the purpose of erecting a common school and it has been built with words, but as yet the first stone is not laid. Some materials only are provided. The money nevertheless, given for the purpose, has already found its way out and is mostly spent; or may even fall short, and for this purpose also no fund invested in real estate has ever been built up.

The poor fund, though the largest, contains nothing except the alms collected among the people, and some fines and donations of the inhabitants. A considerable portion of this money is in the possession of the Company, who have borrowed it from time to time, and kept it. They have promised, for years, to pay interest. But in spite of all endeavor neither principal nor interest can be obtained from them.

Flying reports about asylums for orphans, for the sick and aged,[1] and the like have occasionally been heard, but as yet we can not see that any attempt, order or direction has been made in relation to them. From all these facts, then, it sufficiently appears that scarcely any proper care or diligence has been used by the Company or its officers for any ecclesiastical property whatever—at least, nothing as far as is known—from the beginning to this time; but on the contrary great industry and exertion have been used to bind closely to them their minions, or to gain new ones as we shall hereafter at the proper time relate. And now let us proceed to the consideration of what public measures of a civil character had been adopted up to the time of our departure, in order to make manifest the diligence and care of the Directors in this particular.

There was not at first, under the government of Director Kieft, so much opportunity as there has since been, because the recognition of the peltries was then paid in the Fatherland, and the freemen gave nothing for excise; but after that public calamity, the rash war, was brought upon us, the recognition of the peltries began to be collected in this country, and a beer-excise was sought to be established, about which a conference was had with the Eight Men, who were then chosen from the people. They did not approve of it as such, but desired to know under what regulations and upon what footing it would take place, and how long it would continue. Director Kieft

[1] Seventeenth-century Dutch towns abounded in institutions of this sort.

promised that it should not continue longer than until a ship of the Company should arrive with a new Director, or until the war should be at an end. Although it was very much distrusted by all, and therefore was not consented to, yet he introduced it by force. The brewers who would not agree to it had their beer given over to the soldiers. So it was enforced, but it caused great strife and discontent.

From this time forward the Director began to divide the people and to create factions. Those who were on his side could do nothing amiss, however bad it might be; those who were opposed to him were always wrong even if they did perfectly right, and the order to reckon half an offence a whole one was then strictly enforced. The jealousy of the Director was so great that he could not bear without suspicion that impartial persons should visit his partisans.

After the war was, as the Director himself said, finished— though in our opinion it will never be finished until the country is populated—every one hoped that this impost would be removed, but Director Kieft put off the removal until the arrival of a new Director, which was longed for very much. When finally he did appear,[1] it was like the crowning of Rehoboam, for, instead of abolishing the beer-excise, his first business was to impose a wine-excise and other intolerable burdens, so that some of the commonalty, as they had no spokesman, were themselves constrained to remonstrate against it. Instead however of obtaining the relief which they expected, they received abuse from the Director. Subsequently a written answer was given them, which the Director had, as usual, drawn up at such length and with such fulness that plain and simple people, such as are here, must be confused, and unable to make anything out of it. . Further attempts have accordingly been made from time to time to introduce new taxes and burdens. In fine it was so managed in Director Kieft's time, that a large yearly sum was received from the recognition and other sources, calculated to amount annually to 16,000 guilders,[2] besides the recognition which was paid in the Fatherland and which had to be contributed by the poor commonalty; for the goods were sold accordingly, and the prices are now

---

[1] Stuyvesant arrived from Holland by way of the West Indies in May, 1647.
[2] Equivalent to $6,400.

unbearably high. In Director Stuyvesant's administration the revenue has reached a much higher sum, and it is estimated that about 30,000 guilders [1] are now derived yearly from the people by recognitions, confiscations, excise and other taxes, and yet it is not enough; the more one has the more one wants. It would be tolerable to give as much as possible, if it was used for the public weal. And whereas in all the proclamations it is promised and declared that the money shall be employed for laudable and necessary public works, let us now look for a moment and see what laudable public works there are in this country, and what fruits all the donations and contributions have hitherto borne. But not to confuse matters, one must understand us not to refer to goods and effects that belong to the Honorable Company as its own, for what belongs to it particularly was never public. The Company's effects in this country may, perhaps, with forts, cannon, ammunition, warehouses, dwelling-houses, workshops, horses, cattle, boats, and whatever else there may be, safely be said to amount to from 60,000 to 70,000 guilders,[2] and it is very probable that the debts against it are considerably more. But passing these by, let us turn our attention to the public property, and see where the money from time to time has been used. According to the proclamations during the administration of Director Kieft, if we rightly consider, estimate and examine them all, we cannot learn or discover that anything—we say *anything* large or small—worth relating, was done, built or made, which concerned or belonged to the commonalty, the church excepted, whereof we have heretofore spoken. Yea, he went on so badly and negligently that nothing has ever been designed, understood or done that gave appearance of design to content the people, even externally, but on the contrary what came from the commonalty has even been mixed up with the effects of the Company, and even the Company's property and means have been everywhere neglected, in order to make friends, to secure witnesses and to avoid accusers about the management of the war. The negroes, also, who came from Tamandare [3] were sold for pork and peas, from the proceeds of which something

---

[1] $12,000.   [2] From $24,000 to $28,000.
[3] A bay on the coast of Brazil, where the Dutch admiral Lichthart defeated the Portuguese in a naval engagement, in September, 1645.

wonderful was to be performed, but they just dripped through
the fingers. There are also various other negroes in this
country, some of whom have been made free for their long
service, but their children have remained slaves, though it is
contrary to the laws of every people that any one born of a free
Christian mother should be a slave and be compelled to remain
in servitude. It is impossible to relate everything that has
happened. Whoever did not give his assent and approval was
watched and, when occasion served, was punished for it. We
submit to all intelligent persons to consider what fruit this has
borne, and what a way this was to obtain good testimony.
Men are by nature covetous, especially those who are needy,
and of this we will hereafter adduce some few proofs, when we
come to speak of Director Kieft's government particularly.
But we shall now proceed to the administration of Director
Stuyvesant, and to see how affairs have been conducted up to
the time of our departure.

Mr. Stuyvesant has almost all the time from his first arrival
up to our leaving been busy building, laying masonry, making,
breaking, repairing and the like, but generally in matters of
the Company and with little profit to it; for upon some things
more was spent than they were worth; and though at the first
he put in order the church which came into his hands very
much out of repair, and shortly afterwards made a wooden
wharf, both acts very serviceable and opportune, yet after
this time we do not know that anything has been done or made
that is entitled to the name of a public work, though there has
been income enough, as is to be seen in the statement of the
yearly revenue. They have all the time been trying for more,
like dropsical people. Thus in a short time very great discontent has sprung up on all sides, not only among the burghers,
who had little to say, but also among the Company's officers
themselves, so that various protests were made by them on
account of the expense and waste consequent upon unnecessary councillors, officers, servants and the like who are not
known by the Managers, and also on account of the monies
and means which were given in common, being privately
appropriated and used. But it was all in vain, there was
very little or no amendment; and the greater the endeavors to
help, restore and raise up everything, the worse has it been;

for pride has ruled when justice dictated otherwise, just as if
it were disgraceful to follow advice, and as if everything should
come from one head.   The fruits of this conduct can speak and
bear testimony of themselves.   It has been so now so long, that
every day serves the more to condemn it.   Previously to the
23d of July 1649, nothing had been done concerning weights
and measures or the like; but at that time they notified the
people that in August then next ensuing the matter would be
regulated.   The *fiscaal* would then attend to it, which was as
much as to say, *would give the pigeons to drink*.   There is frequently much discontent and discord among the people on
account of weights and measures, and as they are never inspected, they cannot be right.   It is also believed that some
of easy consciences have two sets of them, but we cannot
affirm the fact.   As to the corn measure, the Company itself
has always been suspected, but who dare lisp it?   The payment in *zeewant*, which is the currency here, has never been
placed upon a good footing, although the commonalty requested
it, and showed how it should be regulated, assigning numerous
reasons therefor.   But there is always misunderstanding and
discontent, and if anything is said before the Director of
these matters more than pleases him, very wicked and spiteful
words are returned.   Those moreover whose office requires
them to speak to him of such things are, if he is in no good fit,
very freely berated as clowns, bear-skinners, and the like.

The fort under which we are to shelter ourselves, and from
which as it seems all authority proceeds, lies like a molehill or a
tottering wall, on which there is not one gun-carriage or one
piece of cannon in a suitable frame or on a good platform.   From
the first it has been declared that it should be repaired, laid
in five angles, and put in royal condition.   The commonalty's
men have been addressed for money for the purpose, but they
excused themselves on the ground that the people were poor.
Every one, too, was discontented and feared that if the Director once had his fort to rely upon, he would be more cruel
and severe.   Between the two, nothing is done.   He will doubtless know how to lay the blame with much circumstance upon
the commonalty who are innocent, although the Director
wished to have the money from them, and for that purpose
pretended to have an order from Their High Mightinesses.

Had the Director laid out for that purpose the fourth part of
the money which was collected from the commonalty during
his time, it certainly would not have fallen short, as the wine-
excise was expressly laid for that object. But it was sought
in a thousand ways to shear the sheep though the wool was not
yet grown. In regard, then, to public works, there is little
difference between Director Kieft and Director Stuyvesant,
for after the church was built the former was negligent, and
took personal action against those who looked him in the eye.
The latter has had much more opportunity to keep public
works in repair than his predecessor had, for he has had no
war on his hands. He has also been far more diligent and bitter in looking up causes of prosecution against his innocent
opponents than his predecessor ever was.

The Administration of Director Kieft in Particular.

Sufficient has been said of what Director Kieft did in
regard to the church and its affairs, and in regard to the state,
such as buildings and taxes or revenue. It remains for us to
proceed to the council-house and produce thence some examples, as we promised. We will, in doing so, endeavor to be
brief.

The Council then consisted of Director Kieft and Monsieur
la Montagne. The Director had two votes, and Monsieur la
Montagne one; and it was a high crime to appeal from their
judgments. Cornelis vander Hoykens sat with them as *fiscaal*,[1]
and Cornelis van Tienhoven as secretary,[2] and whenever any
thing extraordinary occurred, the Director allowed some, whom
it pleased him—officers of the company for the most part—to
be summoned in addition, but that seldom happened. Never-

---

[1] Cornelis van der Huygens was *schout-fiscaal* (sheriff and public prosecutor)
of New Netherland from 1639 to 1645. He was drowned in the wreck of the
Princess in 1647, along with Kieft.

[2] Cornelis van Tienhoven was a figure of much importance in New Netherland
history. An Utrecht man, he came out as book-keeper in 1633, and served in that
capacity under Van Twiller. In 1638, at the beginning of Kieft's administration,
he was made provincial secretary, and continued in that office under Stuyvesant,
supporting with much shrewdness and industry the measures of the administration.
His endeavors to counteract this *Representation* of the commonalty of New Netherland are described in the introduction, and are exhibited in the piece which follows.

theless it gave discontent. The Twelve Men, and afterwards the Eight,[1] had in court matters neither vote nor advice; but were chosen in view of the war and some other occurrences, to serve as cloaks and cats-paws. Otherwise they received no consideration and were little respected if they opposed at all the views of the Director, who himself imagined, or certainly wished to make others believe, that he was sovereign, and that it was absolutely in his power to do or refuse to do anything. He little regarded the safety of the people as the supreme law, as clearly appeared in the war, although when the spit was turned in the ashes, it was sought by cunning and numerous certificates and petitions to shift the blame upon others. But that happened so because the war was carried too far, and because every one laid the damage and the blood which was shed to his account. La Montagne said that he had protested against it, but that it was begun against his will and to his great regret, and that afterwards, when it was entered upon, he had helped to excuse it to the best of his ability. The secretary, Cornelius van Tienhoven, also said that he had no hand in the matter, and nothing had been done by him in regard to it except by the express orders of the Director. But this was not believed, for there are those who have heard La Montagne say that if the secretary had not brought false reports the affair would never have happened.[2] There are others also who know this, and every one believes it to be so; and indeed it has plausibility. Fiscal van der Hoytgens was not trusted on account of his drinking, wherein all his science consists. He had also no experience here, and in the beginning frequently denounced the war as being against his will. So that the blame rests, and

---

[1] The Twelve Men were representatives chosen at the request of Kieft, to advise respecting war against the Weckquaesgeeks, by an assembly of heads of families convened in August, 1641. They counselled delay, but finally, in January, 1642, consented to war. When they proceeded to demand reforms, especially popular representation in the Council, Kieft dissolved them. After the Indian outbreak of August, 1643, the Eight Men were elected, also at the instance of Kieft, and did their part in the management of the ensuing warfare; but they also, in the autumns of 1643 and 1644, protested to the West India Company and the States General against Kieft's misgovernment, and demanded his recall.

[2] This is intended to connect Kieft's massacre of the refugee Tappaans at Pavonia, February 25–26, 1643, with a previous reconnaissance of their position by Van Tienhoven.

must rest only upon the Director and Secretary Tienhoven.
The Director was entrusted with the highest authority, and if
any body advised him to the land's ruin, he was not bound to
follow the advice and afterwards endeavor to shift the burden
from his own neck upon the people, who however excuse themselves although in our judgment they are not all entirely innocent. The cause of this war we conceive to have been the
exacting of the contribution, (for which the Director said he
had the order of the Managers,)[1] and his own ungovernable
passions, which showed themselves principally in private.
But there are friends whom this business intimately concerns,
and as they have already undertaken it, we will leave the matter with them and proceed to cite one or two instances dis-
closing the aspiration after sovereignty. Passing by many
cases for the sake of brevity, we have that of one Francis
Doughty, an English minister, and of Arnoldus van Herdenberch, a free merchant. But as both these cases appear likely
to come before Their High Mightinesses at full length, we will
merely give a summary of them. This minister, Francis
Doughty, during the first troubles in England, in order to
escape them, came to New England.[2] But he found that he
had got from the pan into the fire. Wherefore in order that he
might, in conformity with the Dutch reformation, have freedom of conscience, which, contrary to his expectation, he missed
in New England, he betook himself to the protection of the
Dutch. An absolute ground-brief [3] with the privileges allowed
to a colony was granted to him by the Director. He had
strengthened his settlement in the course of one year by the
addition of several families, but the war coming on, they were
driven from their lands with the loss of some men and many
cattle, besides almost all their houses and what other property
they had. They afterwards returned and remained a while,

---

[1] Demand of tribute which Kieft made of the river Indians in 1639 and 1640.

[2] Reverend Francis Doughty, Adriaen van der Donck's father-in-law, came to
Massachusetts in 1637, but was forced to depart on account of heresies respecting
baptism. He is reputed one of the first, if not the first, Presbyterian ministers in
America. Further details regarding him, from an unfriendly pen, may be seen in
Van Tienhoven's reply, *post*. The conditions on which he and his associates
settled at Mespath (Newtown) may be seen in *N. Y. Col. Doc.*, XIII. 8; the
patent, in O'Callaghan's *History of New Netherland*, I. 425.

[3] Conveyance.

but consuming more than they were able to raise, they came
to the Manathans where all the fugitives sojourned at that
time, and there Master Doughty officiated as a minister.
After the flame of war was out and the peace was concluded—
but in such a manner that no one much relied upon it—some
of the people again returned to their lands. The Director
would have been glad, in order that all things should be completely restored, if it had pleased this man likewise to go
back upon his land; but inasmuch as the peace was doubtful, and he had not wherewith to begin, Master Doughty was
in no haste. He went however, some time afterwards, and
dwelt there half a year, but again left it. As peace was made,
and in hope that some others would make a village there, a
suit was brought against the minister, and carried on so far
that his land was confiscated. Master Doughty, feeling himself aggrieved, appealed from the sentence. The Director
answered, his sentence could not be appealed from, but must
prevail absolutely; and caused the minister for that remark to
be imprisoned twenty-four hours and then to pay 25 guilders.
We have always considered this an act of tyranny and regarded
it as a token of sovereignty. The matter of Arnoldus van
Herdenberch was very like it in its termination. After Zeger
Theunisz was murdered by the Indians in the Beregat,[1] and
the yacht had returned to the Manathans, Arnoldus van
Hardenbergh was with two others appointed by the Director
and Council curators over the estate, and the yacht was
searched. Some goods were found in it which were not entered, whereupon the *fiscaal* went to law with the curators,
and claimed that the goods were confiscable to the Company.
The curators resisted and gave Herdenberch charge of the
matter. After some proceedings the goods were condemned.
As he found himself now aggrieved in behalf of the common
owners, he appealed to such judges as they should choose for
the purpose. The same game was then played over again.
It was a high crime. The *fiscaal* made great pretensions and a
sentence was passed, whereof the contents read thus: "Having seen the written complaint of the Fiscaal vander Hoytgens
against Arnoldus van Hardenberch in relation to appealing
from our sentence dated the 28th April last past, as appears

[1] Shrewsbury Inlet.

by the signature of the before-named Sr. A. van Hardenberch, from which sentence no appeal can be had, as is proven to him by the commission of Their High Mightinesses the Lords States General and His Highness of Orange: Therefore the Director General and Council of New Netherland, regarding the dangerous consequences tending to injure the supreme authority of this land's magistracy, condemn the before-named Arnold van Herdenberch to pay forthwith a fine of 25 guilders, or to be imprisoned until the penalty be paid; as an example to others." Now, if one know the lion from his paw, he can see that these people do not spare the name of Their High Mightinesses, His Highness of Orange, the honor of the magistrates, nor the words, "dangerous consequences," "an example to others," and other such words, to play their own parts therewith. We have therefore placed this act by the side of that which was committed against the minister Doughty. Many more similar cases would be found in the record, if other things were always rightly inserted in it, which is very doubtful, the contrary sometimes being observed. It appears then sufficiently that everything has gone on rather strangely. And with this we will leave the subject and pass on to the government of Director Stuyvesant, with a single word first, however, touching the sinister proviso incorporated in the ground-briefs, as the consequences may thence be very well understood. Absolute grants were made to the people by the ground-briefs, and when they thought that everything was right, and that they were masters of their own possessions, the ground-briefs were demanded from them again upon pretence that there was something forgotten in them; but that was not it. They thought they had incommoded themselves in giving them, and therefore a proviso was added at the end of the ground-brief, and it was signed anew; which proviso directly conflicts with the ground-brief, so that in one and the same ground-brief is a contradiction without chance of agreement, for it reads thus in the old briefs: "and take in possession the land and the valleys appertaining of old thereto," and the proviso says, "no valley to be used before the Company," all which could well enough be used, and the Company have a competency. In the ground-briefs is contained also another provision, which is usually inserted and *sticks in the bosom* of every one: to wit, that they must submit themselves to all taxes which the council has made or shall make.[1] These impositions can be continued *in infinitum*, and have already been enforced against several inhabitants. Others also are discouraged from undertaking anything on such terms.

The Administration of Director Stuyvesant in Particular.

We wish much we were already through with this administration, for it has grieved us, and we know ourselves powerless; nevertheless we will begin, and as we have already spoken of the public property, ecclesiastical and civil, we will consider how it is in regard to the administration of justice, and giving decisions between man and man. And first, to point as with a finger at the manners of the Director and Council. As regards the Director, from his first arrival to this time, his manner in court has been to treat with violence, dispute with or harass one of the two parties, not as becomes a judge, but as a zealous advocate, which has given great discontent to every one, and with some it has gone so far and has effected so much, that many of them dare bring no matter before the court, if they do not stand well or tolerably so with the Director. For whoever has him opposed, has as much as the sun and moon against him. Though he has himself appointed many of the councillors, and placed them under obligation to him, and some pretend that he can overpower the rest by plurality of votes, he frequently puts his opinion in writing, and that so fully that it covers several pages, and then he adds verbally, "Monsieur, this is my advice, if any one has aught to say against it, let him speak." If then any one rises to make objection, which is not easily done, though it be well grounded, His Honor bursts out immediately in fury and makes such gestures, that it is frightful; yea, he rails out frequently at the

---

[1] Mr. Murphy cites the clause, from a ground-brief or patent issued in 1639. After describing the land conveyed, it is declared to be "upon the express condition and stipulation that the said A. B. and his assigns shall acknowledge the Noble Lords Managers aforesaid as their masters and patroons under the sovereignty of the High and Mighty Lord States General, and shall be obedient to the Director and Council here, as all good citizens are bound to be, submitting themselves to all such taxes and imposts as have been or may be, hereafter, imposed by the Noble Lords."

Councillors for this thing and the other, with ugly words which would better suit the fish-market than the council chamber; and if this be all endured, His Honor will not rest yet unless he has his will. To demonstrate this by examples and proof, though easily done, would nevertheless detain us too long; but we all say and affirm that this has been his common practice from the first and still daily continues. And this is the condition and nature of things in the council on the part of the Director, who is its head and president. Let us now briefly speak of the councillors individually. The Vice Director, Lubbert van Dincklagen,[1] has for a long time on various occasions shown great dissatisfaction about many different matters, and has protested against the Director and his appointed councillors, but only lately, and after some others made resistance. He was, before this, so influenced by fear, that he durst venture to take no chances against the Director, but had to let many things pass by and to submit to them. He declared afterwards that he had great objections to them, because they were not just, but he saw no other way to have peace, as the Director said even in the council, that he would treat him worse than Wouter van Twiller had ever done, if he were not willing to conform to his wishes. This man then is overruled. Let us proceed farther. Monsieur la Montagne had been in the council in Kieft's time, and was then very much suspected by many. He had no commission from the Fatherland, was driven by the war from his farm, is also very much indebted to the Company, and therefore is compelled to dissemble. But it is sufficiently known from himself that he is not pleased, and is opposed to the administration. Brian Newton,[2] lieutenant of the soldiers, is the next. This man is afraid of the Director, and regards him as his benefactor. Besides being very simple and inexperienced in law, he

---

[1] Lubbertus van Dincklagen, doctor of laws, was sent out as *schout-fiscaal* of New Netherland in 1634, quarrelled with Van Twiller, and was sent back by him in 1636. In 1644 he was provisionally appointed as Kieft's successor, but Stuyvesant was finally made Director, and Van Dincklagen went out with him as vice-director and second member of the Council. He opposed some of Stuyvesant's arbitrary acts, supplied the three bearers of this *Representation* with letters of credence to the States General, was expelled from the Council by Stuyvesant in 1651, and died in 1657 or 1658.

[2] An Englishman who had served under the company several years at Curaçao.

does not understand our Dutch language, so that he is scarcely capable of refuting the long written opinions, but must and will say *yes*. Sometimes the commissary, Adrian Keyser, is admitted into the council, who came here as secretary. This man has not forgotten much law, but says that he *lets God's water run over God's field*. He cannot and dares not say anything, for so much can be said against him that it is best that he should be silent. The captains of the ships, when they are ashore, have a vote in the Council; as Ielmer Thomassen, and Paulus Lenaertson,[1] who was made equipment-master upon his first arrival, and who has always had a seat in the council, but is still a free man. What knowledge these people, who all their lives sail on the sea, and are brought up to ship-work, have of law matters and of farmers' disputes any intelligent man can imagine. Besides, the Director himself considers them so guilty that they dare not accuse others, as will appear from this passage at Curaçao, before the Director ever saw New Netherland. As they were discoursing about the price of carracks, the Director said to the minister and others, "Domine Johannes,[2] I thought that I had brought honest ship-masters with me, but I find that I have brought a set of thieves"; and this was repeated to these councillors, especially to the equipment-master, for Captain Ielmer was most of the time at sea. They have let it pass unnoticed—a proof that they were guilty. But they have not fared badly; for though Paulus Lenaertssen has small wages, he has built a better dwelling-house here than anybody else. How this has happened is mysterious to us; for though the Director has knowledge of these matters, he nevertheless keeps quiet when Paulus Len-

---

[1] Ielmer (said to =Ethelmar) Tomassen was skipper of the *Great Gerrit* in 1647, when Stuyvesant made him company's storekeeper and second in military command; in 1649 and 1650, of the *Falcon*. Paulus Leendertsen van der Grift was a captain in the West India Company's service from at least 1644. In 1647 Stuyvesant made him superintendent of naval equipment. In the first municipal government of New Amsterdam, 1653, he was made a *schepen* (magistrate and councillor), later a bnrgomaster.

[2] Reverend Johannes Backerus, minister for the Company at Curaçao from 1642 to 1647, was transferred to Amsterdam when Stuyvesant came out, in order to fill the vacancy left by Reverend Everardus Bogardus, minister at Manhattan from 1633 to 1647, who, after long quarrelling with Kieft, had gone home in the same ship with him, the ill-fated *Princess*.

aertssen begins to make objections, which he does not easily
do for any one else, which causes suspicion in the minds of
many. There remains to complete this court-bench, the
secretary and the *fiscaal*, Hendrick van Dyck,[1] who had previously been an ensign-bearer. Director Stuyvesant has kept
him twenty-nine months out of the meetings of the council,
for the reason among others which His Honor assigned, that
he cannot keep secret but will make public, what is there
resolved. He also frequently declared that he was a villain,
a scoundrel, a thief and the like. All this is well known to
the *fiscaal*, who dares not against him take the right course,
and in our judgment it is not advisable for him to do so; for
the Director is utterly insufferable in word and deed. What
shall we say of a man whose head is troubled, and has a screw
loose, especially when, as often happens, he has been drinking.
To conclude, there is the secretary, Cornelius van Tienhoven.[2] Of this man very much could be said, and more than
we are able, but we shall select here and there a little for
the sake of brevity. He is cautious, subtle, intelligent and
sharp-witted—good gifts when they are well used. He is one
of those who have been longest in the country, and every circumstance is well known to him, in regard both to the Christians
and the Indians. With the Indians, moreover, he has run
about the same as an Indian, with a little covering and a small
patch in front, from lust after the prostitutes to whom he has
always been mightily inclined, and with whom he has had so
much to do that no punishment or threats of the Director can
drive him from them. He is extremely expert in dissimulation.
He pretends himself that he bites when asleep, and that he
shows externally the most friendship towards those whom he
most hates. He gives every one who has any business with
him—which scarcely any one can avoid—good answers and
promises of assistance, yet rarely helps anybody but his
friends; but twists continually and shuffles from one side to
the other. In his words and conduct he is shrewd, false, deceit-
ful and given to lying, promising every one, and when it comes

---

[1] Ensign Hendrick van Dyck came out in 1640 as commander of the militia;
again with Stuyvesant in 1647 as *schout-fiscaal*. In 1652 Stuyvesant removed
him from that office. His defence of his official career, a valuable document, may
be seen in *N. Y. Col. Doc.*, I. 491–513.   [2] See pp. 332, note 2, and 357.

to perform, at home to no one. The origin of the war was ascribed principally to him, together with some of his friends. In consequence of his false reports and lies the Director was led into it, as is believed and declared both by the honest Indians and Christians. Now, if the voice of the people, according to the maxim, be the voice of God, one can with truth say scarcely anything good of this man or omit anything bad. The whole country, save the Director and his party, cries out against him bitterly, as a villain, murderer and traitor, and that he must leave the country or there will be no peace with the Indians. Director Stuyvesant was, at first and afterwards, well admonished of this; but he has nevertheless kept him in office, and allowed him to do so much, that all things go according to his wishes, more than if he were President. Yea, he also says that he is well contented to have him in his service, but that stone does not yet rest. We firmly believe that he misleads him in many things, so that he does many bad things which he otherwise would not do; in a word, that he is an indirect cause of his ruin and dislike in the country. But it seems that the Director can or will not see it; for when it was represented to him by some persons he gave it no consideration. It has been contrived to disguise and manage matters so, that in the Fatherland, where the truth can be freely spoken, nobody would be able to molest him in order to discover the truth. We do not attempt to. Having established the powers of the Council, it is easy to understand that the right people clung by each other, in order to maintain the imaginary sovereignty and to give a gloss to the whole business. Nine men were chosen to represent the whole commonalty, and commissions and instructions were given that whatever these men should do, should be the act of the whole commonalty.[1] And so in fact it was, as long as it corresponded with the wishes and views of the Director. In such cases they represented the whole commonalty; but when it did not so correspond, they were then clowns, usurers, rebels and the like. But to understand this properly it will be best briefly to state all things chronologically, as they have happened during his administration, and in what manner those who have sought the good of the country have been treated with injustice.

[1] See the introduction.

His first arrival—for what passed on the voyage is not for us to speak of—was like a peacock, with great state and pomp. The declaration of His Honor, that he wished to stay here only three years, with other haughty expressions, caused some to think that he would not be a father. The appellation of Lord General,[1] and similar titles, were never before known here. Almost every day he caused proclamations of various import to be published, which were for the most part never observed, and have long since been a dead letter, except the wine excise, as that yielded a profit. The proceedings of the Eight Men, especially against Jochem Pietersz Cuyffer and Cornelis Molyn, happened in the beginning of his administration. The Director showed himself so one-sided in them, that he gave reason to many to judge of his character, yet little to his advantage. Every one clearly saw that Director Kieft had more favor, aid and counsel in his suit than his adversary, and that the one Director was the advocate of the other as the language of Director Stuyvesant imported and signified when he said, "These churls may hereafter endeavor to knock me down also, but I will manage it so now, that they will have their bellies full for the future." How it was managed, the result of the lawsuit can bear witness. They were compelled to pay fines, and were cruelly banished. In order that nothing should be wanting, Cornelis Molyn, when he asked for mercy, till it should be seen how his matters would turn out in the Fatherland, was threatened in language like this, as Molyn, who is still living, himself declares, "If I knew, Molyn, that you would divulge our sentence, or bring it before Their High Mightinesses, I would cause you to be hung immediately on the highest tree in New-Netherland." Now this took place in private, and may be denied—and ought not to be true, but what does it matter, it is so confirmed by similar cases that it cannot be doubted. For, some time after their departure, in the house of the minister, where the consistory[2] had been sitting and had risen, it happened that one Arnoldus van Herdenbergh related the proceedings relative to the estate of Zeger Teunisz,

---

[1] *Myn Heer Generael* is hardly what would be meant in English by "Lord General"; it is most like Fr. *Monsieur le Général*.

[2] The church session, in the Reformed Church, consisting of minister, elders and deacons.

and how he himself as curator had appealed from the sentence; whereupon the Director, who had been sitting there with them as an elder, interrupted him and replied, "It may during my administration be contemplated to appeal, but if any one should do it, I will make him a foot shorter, and send the pieces to Holland, and let him appeal in that way." Oh cruel words! what more could even a sovereign do? And yet this is all firmly established; for after Jochem Pieterz Cuyffer and Cornelis Molyn went to the Fatherland to prosecute their appeal, and letters came back here from them, and the report was that their appeal was granted, or would be granted, the Director declared openly at various times and on many occasions, as well before inhabitants as strangers, when speaking of Jochem Pietersz Cuyter and Cornelis Molyn, "Even if they should come back cleared and bring an order of the States, no matter what its contents, unless their High Mightinesses summon me, I should immediately send them back." His Honor has also always denied that any appeal was or could be taken in this country, and declared that he was able to show this conclusively. And as some were not willing to believe it, especially in matters against the Company or their chief officers, a great deal which had been sought out in every direction was cited, and really not much to the purpose. At the first, while Director Kieft was still here, the English minister,[1] as he had long continued to serve without proper support and as his land was now confiscated, prayed that he might be permitted to proceed to the Islands,[2] or to the Netherlands; but an unfavorable answer was always given him, and he was threatened with this and that; finally it resulted in permission to leave, provided he gave a promise under his hand, that he would not in any place in which he should come, speak or complain of what had befallen him here in New Netherland under Director Kieft or Stuyvesant. This the man himself declares. Mr. Dincklagen and Captain Loper,[3] who then had seats in the council, also say that this is true. One wonders, if the Directors act rightly according to their own consciences, what they wished to do with such certificates, and

---

[1] Francis Doughty.   [2] The West Indies.
[3] Jacob Loper, a Swedish naval captain in the Dutch service, who had married the eldest daughter of Cornelis Molyn.

others like them, which were secretly obtained. The Honorable Director began also at the first to argue very stoutly against the contraband trade, as was indeed very laudable, provided the object was to regulate the matter and to keep the law enforced; yet this trade, forbidden to others, he himself wished to carry on; but to this the people were not willing to consent. His Honor said, and openly asserted, that he was allowed, on behalf of the Company, to sell powder, lead and guns to the Indians, but no one else could do so, and that he wished to carry their resolution into execution. What the resolution of the Company amounts to, is unknown to us,[1] but what relates to the act is notorious to every inhabitant; as the Director has by his servants openly carried on the trade with the Indians, and has taken guns from free men who had brought with them one or two for their own use and amusement, paying for them according to his own pleasure, and selling them to the Indians. But this way of proceeding could amount to nothing, and made little progress. Another plan was necessary, and therefore a merchant, Gerrit Vastrick, received orders to bring with him one case of guns which is known of, for the purpose, as it was said, of supplying the Indians sparingly. They set about with this case of guns so openly, that there was not a man on the Manathans but knew it; and it was work enough to quiet the people. Everybody made his own comment; and, as it was observed that the ship was not inspected as others had been before, it was presumed that there were many more guns, besides powder and lead, in it for the Governor; but as the first did not succeed, silence was therefore observed in regard to the rest; and it might have passed unnoticed, had not every one perceived what a great door for abuse and opportunity the Director so opened to all others, and to the captain and merchant, who were celebrated for this of old, and who were now said to have brought with them a great number of guns,

---

[1] Mr. Murphy quotes an apposite passage from a letter which the company had written to Stuyvesant on April 7, 1648: "As they [the Indians] urge it with such earnestness, that they would rather renew the war with us than be without these articles, and as a war with them, in our present situation, would be very unwelcome, we think the best policy is to furnish them with powder and ball, but with a sparing hand."

which was the more believed, because they went to the right place, and on their return were dumb as to what they did. This begat so much discontent among the common people, and even among other officers, that it is not to be expressed; and had the people not been persuaded and held back, something extraordinary would have happened. It was further declared that the Director is everything, and does the business of the whole country, having several shops himself; that he is a brewer and has breweries, is a part owner of ships, a merchant and a trader, as well in lawful as contraband articles. But he does not mind; he exhibits the orders of the Managers that he might do so, and says moreover that he should receive a supply of powder and lead by the *Falconer* for the purpose. In a word, the same person who interdicts the trade to others upon pain of death, carries it on both secretly and openly, and desires, contrary to good rules, that his example be not followed, and if others do follow it—which indeed too often happens secretly—that they be taken to the gallows. This we have seen in the case of Jacob Reyntgen and Jacob van Schermerhoren, against whom the penalty of death was asked, which the Director was with great difficulty persuaded to withdraw, and who were then banished as felons and their goods confiscated.[1] The banishment was, by the intervention of many good men, afterwards revoked, but their goods, which amounted to much (as they were Scotch merchants [2]), remained confiscated. We cannot pass by relating here what happened to one Joost Theunisz Backer, as he has complained to us of being greatly maltreated, as he in fact was. For the man being a reputable burgher, of good life and moderate means, was put in prison upon the declaration of an officer of the Company, who, according to the General and Council, had himself thrice well deserved the gallows, and for whom a new one even had been made, from which, out of mercy, he escaped. Charges were sought out on every side, and finally, when nothing could be established against him having the semblance of crime, he was released again, after thirteen days confinement, upon satisfactory bail for his appearance in case the *fiscaal* should find anything against him. Nothing has as yet been done about it. After the year and a day had passed by, we have, as representatives of the commonalty,

[1] These sentences were imposed in July, 1648.   [2] Peddlers.

and upon his request, legally solicited, as his sureties were troubling him, that the suit should be tried, so that he might be punished according to his deserts if he were guilty, and if not, that he might be discharged. But there was nothing gained by our interposition, as we were answered with reproachful language, and the *fiscaal* was permitted to rattle out anything that came in his mouth, and the man was rendered odious beyond all precedent, and abused before all as a foul monster. Asked he anything, even if it were all right, he received angry and abusive language, his request was not complied with, and justice was denied him. These things produce great dissatisfaction, and lead some to meditate leaving the country. It happened better with one Pieter vander Linden, as he was not imprisoned. There are many others, for the most of them are disturbed and would speak if they durst. Now the Company itself carries on the forbidden trade, the people think that they too can do so without guilt, if they can do so without damage; and this causes smuggling and frauds to an incredible extent, though not so great this year as heretofore. The publishing of a placard that those who were guilty, whether civilly or criminally, in New England, might have passport and protection here, has very much embittered the minds of the English, and has been considered by every one fraught with bad consequences. Great distrust has also been created among the inhabitants on account of Heer Stuyvesant being so ready to confiscate. There scarcely comes a ship in or near here, which, if it do not belong to friends, is not regarded as a prize by him. Though little comes of it, great claims are made to come from these matters, about which we will not dispute; but confiscating has come to such repute in New Netherland, that nobody anywise conspicuous considers his property to be really safe. It were well if the report of this thing were confined to this country; but it has spread among the neighboring English—north and south—and in the West Indies and Caribbee Islands. Everywhere there, the report is so bad, that not a ship dare come hither from those places; and good credible people who come from thence, by the way of Boston, and others here trading at Boston, assure us that more than twenty-five ships would come here from those islands every year if the owners were not fearful of confiscation. It is true of these places only and the report of it flies everywhere, and produces like fear, so that this vulture is destroying the prosperity of New Netherland, diverting its trade, and making the people discouraged, for other places not so well situated as this, have more shipping. All the permanent inhabitants, the merchant, the burgher and peasant, the planter, the laboring man, and also the man in service, suffer great injury in consequence; for if the shipping were abundant, everything would be sold cheaper, and necessaries be more easily obtained than they are now, whether they be such as the people themselves, by God's blessing, get out of the earth, or those they otherwise procure, and be sold better and with more profit; and people and freedom would bring trade. New England is a clear example that this policy succeeds well, and so especially is Virginia. All the debts and claims which were left uncollected by Director Kieft—due for the most part from poor and indigent people who had nothing, and whose property was destroyed by the war, by which they were compelled to abandon their houses, lands, cattle and other means—were now demanded; and when the people declared that they were not able to pay—that they had lost their property by the war, and asked My Lord to please have patience, they were repulsed. A resolution was adopted and actually put into execution, requiring those who did not satisfy the Company's debts, to pay interest; but the debts in question were made in and by the war, and the people are not able to pay either principal or interest. Again, the just debts which Director Kieft left behind, due from the Company, whether they consisted of monthly wages, or were for grain delivered, or were otherwise lawfully contracted, these the Director will not pay. If we oppose this as an unusual course, we are rebuked and it has to be so. We have by petition and proper remonstrance effected, however, so much, that the collection of the debts is put off for a time.

Besides this, the country of the Company is so taxed, and is burdened and kept down in such a manner, that the inhabitants are not able to appear beside their neighbors of Virginia or New England, or to undertake any enterprise. It seems— and so far as is known by us all the inhabitants of New Netherland declare—that the Managers have scarce any care or regard for New Netherland, except when there is something to receive, for which reason, however, they receive less. The great extremity of war in which we have been, clearly demonstrates that the Managers have not cared whether New Netherland sank or swam; for when in that emergency aid and assistance were sought from them—which they indeed were bound by honor and by promises to grant, unsolicited, pursuant to the Exemptions—they have never made any attempt to furnish them at their own expense. We let the expense go; they have never established any good order or regulation concerning it, although (after all) such a thing had been decreed and commanded by Their High Mightinesses. Neither have they ever allowed the true causes and reasons of the war to be investigated, nor have they attempted to punish those who had rashly begun it. Hence no little suspicion that it was undertaken by their orders; at least it is certain that their officers were chosen more from favor and friendship than merit, which did not make their matters go on better. But this is the loss and damage for the most part of the stockholders. Many of the others doubtless knew well their objects. In a word, they come far short in affording that protection which they owe the country, for there is nothing of the kind. They understand how to impose taxes, for while they promised in the Exemptions not to go above five per cent., they now take sixteen. It is a common saying that a half difference is a great difference, but that is nothing in comparison with this. The evasions and objections which are used by them, as regards merchants' goods, smuggling and many other things, and which the times have taught them, in order to give color to their acts, are of no force or consideration. They however are not now to be refuted, as it would take too long; though we stand ready to do so if there be any necessity for it. These and innumerable other difficulties, which we have not time to express, exist, tending to the damage, injury and ruin of the country. If the inhabitants or we ourselves go to the Director or other officers of the Company, and speak of the flourishing condition of our neighbors, and complain of our own desolate and ruinous state, we get no other answer from them than that they see and observe it, but cannot remedy it, as they follow the Company's orders, which they are compelled to do, and that if we have any thing to say, we must petition their masters, the Managers, or Their High Mightinesses, which in truth we have judged to be necessary. It is now more than a year since the commons-men deemed it expedient, and proposed, to send a deputation to Their High Mightinesses. The Director commended the project and not only assented to it but urged it strongly. It was put well in the mill, so that we had already spoken of a person to go, but it fell through for these reasons: When it was proposed, the Director desired that we should consult him and act according to his wishes; which some who perceived the object would not consent to, and the matter therefore fell asleep. Besides, the English, who had been depended upon and who were associated in the affair, withdrew till the necessity of action became greater, and the Nine Men were changed the next year,[1] when Herr Stuyvesant again urged the matter strongly, and declared that he had already written to the Company that such persons would come. After the election of the Nine Men, and before the new incumbents were sworn in, it was determined and resolved verbally, that they would proceed with the deputation, whatever should be the consequences; but it remained some time before the oath was renewed, on account of some amplification of the commission being necessary, which was finally given and recorded and signed; but we have never been able to obtain an authentic copy of it, although the Director has frequently promised and we have frequently applied for it.

As the Company had now been waited upon a long while in vain, promising amendment from time to time but going on worse, a determined resolution was taken by the commons-men to send some person. They made their intention known to the Director, and requested that they might confer with the commonalty; but their proposition was not well received, and they obtained in reply to their written petition a very long apostil, to the effect, that consultation must be had with the Director, and his instructions followed, with many other things which did not agree with our object, and were impracticable, as we think. For various reasons which we set down in writing, we thought it was not advisable to consult with him, but we represented to his Honor that he should proceed; we would not send anything to the Fatherland without his

[1] December, 1648.

having a copy of it. If he could then justify himself, we should be glad he should; but to be expected to follow his directions in this matter was not, we thought, founded in reason, but directly antagonistic to the welfare of the country. We had also never promised or agreed to do so; and were bound by an oath to seek the prosperity of the country, as, according to our best knowledge, we are always inclined to do.

In the above mentioned apostil it says, if we read rightly, that we should inquire what approbation the commonalty were willing to give to this business, and how the expense should be defrayed; but the Director explained it differently from what we understood it. Now as his Honor was not willing to convene the people however urgent our request, or that we should do it, we went round from house to house and spoke to the commonalty. The General has, from that time, burned with rage, and, if we can judge, has never been effectually appeased since, although we did not know but that we had followed his order herein. Nevertheless it was perceived that the Nine Men would not communicate with him or follow his directions in anything pertaining to the matter. This excited in him a bitter and unconquerable hatred against them all, but principally against those whom he supposed to be the chief authors of it; and although these persons had been good and dear friends with him always, and he, shortly before, had regarded them as the most honorable, able, intelligent and pious men of the country, yet as soon as they did not follow the General's wishes they were this and that, some of them rascals, liars, rebels, usurers and spendthrifts, in a word, hanging was almost too good for them. It had been previously strongly urged that the deputation should be expedited, but then [he said] there was still six months time, and that all that was proper and necessary could be put upon a sheet of paper. Many reports also were spread among the people, and it was sought principally by means of the English to prevent the college of the Nine Men from doing anything; but as these intrigues were discovered, and it was therefore manifest that this could not be effected, so in order to make a diversion, many suits were brought against those who were considered the ringleaders. They were accused and then prosecuted by the fiscaal and other suborned officers, who made them out to be the greatest

villains in the country, where shortly before they had been
known as the best people and dearest children. At this time
an opportunity presented itself, which the Director was as
glad to have, at least as he himself said, as his own life. At
the beginning of the year 1649, clearly perceiving that we
would not only have much to do about the deputation but
would hardly be able to accomplish it, we deemed it necessary
to make regular memoranda for the purpose of furnishing a
journal from them at the proper time. This duty was committed to one Adriaen vander Donck, who by a resolution
adopted at the same time was lodged in a chamber at the house
of one Michael Jansz. The General on a certain occasion
when Vander Donck was out of the chamber, seized this
rough draft with his own hands, put Vander Donck the day
after in jail, called together the great Council, accused him of
having committed *crimen læsæ majestatis*, and took up the
matter so warmly, that there was no help for it but either the
remonstrance must be drawn up in concert with him (and it
was yet to be written,) or else the journal—as Mine Heer
styled the rough draft from which the journal was to be
prepared—was of itself sufficient excuse for action; for Mine
Heer said there were great calumnies in it against Their High
Mightinesses, and when we wished to explain it and asked
for it, to correct the errors, (as the writer did not wish to
insist upon it and said he knew well that there were mistakes
in it, arising from haste and other similar causes, in consequence of his having had much to do and not having read
over again the most of it,) our request was called a libel
which was worthy of no answer, and the writer of which it
was intended to punish as an example to others. In fine we
could not make it right in any way. He forbade Vander
Donck the council and also our meetings, and gave us formal
notice to that effect, and yet would not release him from his
oath. Then to avoid the proper mode of proof, he issued a
proclamation declaring that no testimony or other act should
be valid unless it were written by the secretary, who is of service to nobody, but on the contrary causes every one to complain that nothing can be done. Director Kieft had done the
same thing when he was apprehensive that an attestation
would be executed against him. And so it is their practice

generally to do everything they can think of in order to uphold
their conduct. Those whose offices required them to concern
themselves with the affairs of the country, and did so, did well,
if they went according to the General's will and pleasure; if
they did not, they were prosecuted and thrown into prison,
guarded by soldiers so that they could not speak with any
body, angrily abused as vile monsters, threatened to be
taught this and that, and everything done against them that
he could contrive or invent. We cannot enter into details,
but refer to the record kept of these things, and the documents
which the Director himself is to furnish. From the foregoing
relation Their High Mightinesses, and others interested who
may see it, can well imagine what labor and burdens we have
had upon our shoulders from which we would very willingly
have escaped, but for love of the country and of truth, which,
as far as we know, has long lain buried. The trouble and difficulty which do or will affect us, although wanting no addition,
do not grieve us so much as the sorrowful condition of New
Netherland, now lying at its last gasp; but we hope and trust
that our afflictions and the sufferings of the inhabitants and
people of the country will awaken in Their High Mightinesses a
compassion which will be a cause of rejoicing to New Netherland.

In what Manner New Netherland should be Redressed.

Although we are well assured and know, in regard to the
mode of redress of the country, we are only children, and Their
High Mightinesses are entirely competent, we nevertheless
pray that they overlook our presumption and pardon us if we
make some suggestions according to our slight understanding
thereof, in addition to what we have considered necessary in
our petition to Their High Mightinesses.

In our opinion this country will never flourish under the
government of the Honorable Company, but will pass away
and come to an end of itself without benefiting thereby the
Honorable Company, so that it would be better and more
profitable for them, and better for the country, that they
should divest themselves of it and transfer their interests.

To speak specifically. Provision ought to be made for public buildings, as well ecclesiastical as civil, which, in begin-

nings, can be ill dispensed with.   It is doubtful whether divine
worship will not have to cease altogether in consequence of
the departure of the minister, and the inability of the Company.
There should be a public school, provided with at least two
good masters, so that first of all in so wild a country, where there
are many loose people, the youth be well taught and brought
up, not only in reading and writing, but also in the knowledge
and fear of the Lord.   As it is now, the school is kept very
irregularly, one and 'another keeping it according to his
pleasure and as long as he thinks proper.   There ought also to
be an almshouse and an orphan asylum, and other similar
institutions.   The minister who now goes home,[1] should be able
to give a much fuller explanation thereof.   The country must
also be provided with godly, honorable and intelligent rulers
who are not too indigent, or indeed are not too covetous.   A
covetous chief makes poor subjects.   The manner the country
is now governed falls severely upon it, and is intolerable, for
nobody is unmolested or secure in his property longer than the
Director pleases, who is generally strongly inclined to confiscating; and although one does well, and gives the Heer what is due
to him, one must still study always to please him if he would
have quiet.   A large population would be the consequence of a
good government, as we have shown according to our knowledge in our petition; and although to give free passage and
equip ships, if it be necessary, would be expensive at first, yet if
the result be considered, it would be an exceedingly wise measure, if by that means farmers and laborers together with other
needy people were brought into the country, with the little
property which they have; as also the Fatherland has enough
of such people to spare.   We hope it would then prosper, especially as good privileges and exemptions, which we regard as
the mother of population, would encourage the inhabitants to
carry on commerce and lawful trade.   Every one would be
allured hither by the pleasantness, situation, salubrity and
fruitfulness of the country, if protection were secured within
the already established boundaries.   It would all, with God's
assistance, then, according to human judgment, go well, and
New Netherland would in a few years be a worthy place and

---

[1] Reverend Johannes Backerus.

be able to do service to the Netherland nation, to repay richly the cost, and to thank its benefactors.

High Mighty Lords! We have had the boldness to write this remonstrance, and to represent matters as we have done from love of the truth, and because we felt ourselves obliged to do so by our oath and conscience. It is true that we have not all of us at one time or together seen, heard and met with every detail of its entire contents. Nevertheless there is nothing in it but what is well known by some of us to be true and certain;—the most is known by all of us to be true. We hope Their High Mightinesses will pardon our presumption and be charitable with our plainness of style, composition and method. In conclusion we commit Their High Mightinesses, their persons, deliberations and measures and their people, at home and abroad, together with all the friends of New Netherland, to the merciful guidance and protection of the Most High, whom we supplicate for Their High Mightinesses' present and eternal welfare. Amen.

Done this 28th of July in New Netherland, subscribed, "ADRIAEN VANDER DONCK, AUGUSTIJN HERMANSZ, ARNOLDUS VAN HARDENBERGH, JACOB VAN COUWENHOVEN, OLOFF STEVENSZ" (by whose name was written "Under protest— obliged to sign about the government of the Heer Kieft"), "MICHIEL JANSZ, THOMAS HAL, ELBERT ELBERTSZ, GOVERT LOKERMANS, HENDRICK HENDRICKSZ KIP and JAN EVERTS- BOUT." Below was written, "After collation with the original remonstrance, dated and subscribed as above, with which these are found to correspond, at the Hague, the 13th October, 1649, by me;" and was subscribed,

"D. V. SCHELLUYNEN, Notary Public."

ANSWER TO THE REPRESENTATION OF NEW NETHERLAND, BY CORNELIS VAN TIENHOVEN, 1650

INTRODUCTION

THE origin and value of the following document have been sufficiently described in the introduction to that which precedes. Cornelis van Tienhoven, secretary of the province under Kieft and Stuyvesant, had been sent by the latter to Holland to counteract the efforts of the three emissaries whom the commonalty had sent thither to denounce the existing system of government. Working in close co-operation with the Amsterdam Chamber of the West India Company, he played a skilful game, and succeeded in delaying and in part averting hostile action on the part of the States General. The piece which follows is his chief defensive recital of the acts of the administration, and as such has much value.

Van Tienhoven had the reputation of a libertine, and conducted himself as such while in Holland, finally escaping to New Netherland in 1651 with a girl whom he had deceived, though he had a wife in the province. Yet Stuyvesant retained him in his favor, promoted him in 1652 to be *schout-fiscaal* of New Netherland, and used him as his chief assistant. After a disastrous outbreak, however, understood to have been caused by his advice, the Company ordered Stuyvesant to exclude him from office; and presently Van Tienhoven and his brother, a fraudulent receiver-general, absconded from the province.

The manuscript of Van Tienhoven's *Answer* was found by Brodhead in the archives of the Netherlands, and is still there. Two translations of it, differing but slightly, have been printed, the first in 1849 by Henry C. Murphy, in the *Collections of the New York Historical Society*, second series, II. 329–338, the other in 1856 in the *Documents relating to the Colonial History of New York*, I. 422–432. The former, revised by comparison with the original manuscript at the Hague by Professor William I. Hull, of Swarthmore College, appears in the following pages.

ANSWER TO THE REPRESENTATION OF NEW NETHERLAND, BY CORNELIS VAN TIENHOVEN, 1650

A Brief Statement or Answer to some Points embraced in the Written Deduction of Adrian van der Donk and his Associates, presented to the High and Mighty Lords States General. Prepared by Cornelis van Tienhoven, Secretary of the Director and Council of New Netherland.

IN order to present the aforesaid answer succinctly, he, Van Tienhoven, will allege not only that it ill becomes the aforesaid Van der Donk and other private persons to assail and abuse the administration of the Managers in this country, and that of their Governors there,[1] in such harsh and general terms, but that they would much better discharge their duty if they were first to bring to the notice of their lords and patrons what they had to complain of. But passing by this point, and leaving the consideration thereof to the discretion of your High Mightinesses, he observes preliminarily and generally, that these persons say much and prove nothing, so that it could as easily and with more truth be denied, than by them it is odiously affirmed.

Coming then to the matter, I will only touch upon those points as to which either the Managers or the Directors are arraigned. In regard to point No. 1, I deny, and it never will appear, that the Company have refused to permit our people to make settlements in the country, and allow foreigners to take up the land.

The policy of the Company to act on the defensive, since they had not the power to resist their pretended friends, and could only protect their rights by protest, was better and more prudent than to come to hostilities.

[1] In New Netherland. Van Tienhoven prepared this answer in Holland.

Trade has long been free to every one, and as profitable as ever. Nobody's goods were confiscated, except those who had violated their contract, or the order by which they were bound; and if anybody thinks that injustice has been done him by confiscation, he can speak for himself. At all events it does not concern these people.

As for their complaining that the Christians are treated like the Indians in the sale of goods, this is admitted; but this was not done by the Company, nor by the Directors, because (God help them) they have not had anything there to sell for many years. Most of the remonstrants, being merchants or factors, are themselves the cause of this, since they are the persons who, for those articles which cost here one hundred guilders, charge there, over and above the first cost, including insurance, duties, laborer's wages, freight, etc., one and two hundred per cent. or more profit. Here can be seen at once how these people lay to the charge of the Managers and their officers the very fault which they themselves commit. They can never show, even at the time the Company had their shop and magazines there well supplied, that the goods were sold at more than fifty per cent. profit, in conformity with the Exemptions. The forestalling of the goods by one and another, and their trying to get this profit, cannot be prevented by the Director, the more so as the trade was thrown open to both those of small and those of large means.

It is a pure calumny, that the Company had ordered half a fault to be reckoned for a whole one.

And, as it does not concern the inhabitants what instructions or orders the patroon gives to his chief agent, the charge is made for the purpose of making trouble. For these people would like to live without being subject to any one's censure or discipline, which, however, they stand doubly in need of.

Again it is said in general terms, but wherein, should be specified and proven, that the Director exercises and has usurped sovereign power.

That the inhabitants have had need of the Directors appears by the books of accounts, in which it can be seen that the Company has assisted all the freemen (some few excepted) with clothing, provisions and other things, and in the erection of houses, and this at the rate of fifty per cent. advance above the actual cost in the Fatherland, which is not yet paid. And they would gladly, by means of complaints, drive the Company from the land, and pay nothing.

It is ridiculous to suppose Director Kieft should have said that he was sovereign, like the Prince in the Fatherland; but as relates to the denial of appeal to the Fatherland, it arose from this, that, in the Exemptions, the Island of the Manhatans was reserved as the capital of New Netherland, and all the adjacent colonies were to have their appeal to it as the Supreme Court of that region.[1]

Besides, it is to be remarked, that the patroon of the colony of Renselaerswyck notified all the inhabitants not to appeal to the Manhatans, which was contrary to the Exemptions, by which the colonies are bound to make a yearly report of the state of the colony, and of the administration of justice, to the Director and Council on the Manhatans.[2]

The Directors have never had any management of, or meddled with, church property. And it is not known, nor can it be proven, that any one of the inhabitants of New Netherland has contributed or given, either voluntarily or upon solicitation, anything for the erection of an orphan asylum or an almshouse. It is true that the church standing in the fort was built in the time of William Kieft, and 1,800 guilders were subscribed for the purpose, for which most of the subscribers have been charged in their accounts, which have not yet been paid. The Company in the meantime has disbursed the money, so that the commonalty (with a few exceptions) has not, but the Company has, paid the workmen. If the commonalty desire such works as the aforesaid, they must contribute towards them as is done in this country, and, if there were an orphan asylum and almshouse, there should be rents not only to keep up the house, but also to maintain the orphans and old people.

If any one could show that by will, or by donation of a living person, any money, or moveable or immoveable property, has been bestowed for such or any other public work, the remonstrants would have done it; but there is in New Netherland no instance of the kind, and the charge is spoken or written in anger. When the church which is in the fort was to be built, the churchwardens were content it should be put there.

[1] Art. xx. [2] Art. xxviii.

These persons complain because they considered the Company's fort not worthy of a church. Before the church was built, the grist-mill could not grind with a southeast wind, because the wind was shut off by the walls of the fort.

Although the new school, towards which the commonalty has contributed something, is not yet built, the Director has no management of the money, but the churchwardens have, and the Director is busy in providing materials. In the mean time a place has been selected for a school, where the school is kept by Jan Cornelissen. The other schoolmasters keep school in hired houses, so that the youth, considering the circumstances of the country, are not in want of schools. It is true there is no Latin school or academy, but if the commonalty desire it, they can furnish the means and attempt it.

As to what concerns the deacons' or poor fund, the deacons are accountable, and are the persons to be inquired of, as to where the money is invested, which they have from time to time put out at interest; and as the Director has never had the management of it, (as against common usage), the deacons are responsible for it, and not the director. It is true Director Kieft being distressed for money, had a box hung in his house, of which the deacons had one key, and in which all the small fines and penalties which were incurred on court days were dropped. With the consent of the deacons he opened it, and took on interest the money, which amounted to a pretty sum.

It is admitted, that the beer excise was imposed by William Kieft, and the wine excise by Peter Stuyvesant, and that they continued to be collected up to the time of my leaving there; but it is to be observed here, that the memorialists have no reason to complain about it, for the merchant, burgher, farmer and all others (tapsters only excepted), can lay in as much beer and wine as they please without paying any excise, being only bound to give an account of it in order that the quantity may be ascertained. The tapsters pay three guilders for each tun of beer and one stiver for each can of wine,[1] which they get back again from their daily visitors and the travellers from New England, Virginia and elsewhere.

[1] The stiver was the twentieth part of a *gulden* or guilder, and equivalent to two cents, the guilder being equivalent to forty cents.

The commonalty up to that time were burdened with no other local taxes than the before mentioned excise, unless the voluntary gift which was employed two years since for the continuation of the building of the church, be considered a tax, of which Jacob Couwenhoven,[1] who is one of the church-wardens, will be able to give an account.

In New England there are no taxes or duties imposed upon goods exported or imported; but every person's wealth is there appraised by the government, and he must pay for the following, according to his wealth and the assessment by the magistrates: for the building and repairing of churches, and the support of the ministers; for the building of schoolhouses, and the support of schoolmasters; for all city and village improvements, and the making and keeping in repair all public roads and paths, which are there made many miles into the country, so that they can be used by horses and carriages, and journeys made from one place to another; for constructing and keeping up all bridges over the rivers at the crossings; for the building of inns for travellers, and for the maintenance of governors, magistrates, marshals and officers of justice, and of majors, captains and other officers of the militia.

In every province of New England there is quarterly a general assembly of all the magistrates of such province;[2] and there is yearly a general convention of all the provinces, each of which sends one deputy with his suite, which convention lasts a long time. All their travelling expenses, board and compensation are there raised from the people. The poor-rates are an additional charge.

The accounts will show what was the amount of recognitions collected annually in Kieft's time; but it will not appear

---

[1] Couwenhoven, it will be remembered, was one of the delegates from the commonalty then in Holland.

[2] A loose statement, only so far correct, that each New England colony had several sessions of its magistrates each year, sometimes monthly sessions, while their legislative assemblies ("general courts") were commonly held more than once a year. Van Tienhoven's general contention is correct, that government in New England was far more elaborate and expensive than in New Netherland; but New England had in 1650 a population of about 30,000, New Netherland hardly more than 3,000. The annual meeting mentioned in the next sentence is that of the Commissioners of the United Colonies, in which, however, each colony was represented by two deputies, not one.

that it was as large by far as they say the people were compelled to pay. This is not the Company's fault, nor the
Directors', but of those who charge one, two and three hundred
per cent. profit, which the people are compelled to pay because
there are few tradesmen.

It will not appear, either now or in the future, that 30,000
guilders were collected from the commonalty in Stuyvesant's
time; for nothing is received besides the beer and wine excise,
which amounts to about 4,000 guilders a year on the Manhatans.
From the other villages situated around it there is little or
nothing collected, because there are no tapsters, except one at
the Ferry,[1] and one at Flushing.

If anything has been confiscated, it did not belong to the
commonalty, but was contraband goods imported from
abroad; and nobody's goods are confiscated without good
cause.

The question is whether the Honorable Company or the
Directors are bound to construct any works for the commonalty
out of the recognition which the trader pays in New Netherland
for goods exported, especially as those duties were allowed to
the Company by Their High Mightinesses for the establishment
of garrisons, and the expenses which they must thereby incur,
and not for the construction of poor-houses, orphan asylums, or
even churches and school-houses, for the commonalty.

The charge that the property of the Company is neglected
in order to procure assistance from friends, cannot be sustained
by proof.

The provisions obtained for the negroes from Tamandare
were sent to Curaçao, except a portion consumed on the Manhatans, as the accounts will show; but all these are matters
which do not concern these persons, especially as they are not
accountable for them.

As to the freemen's contracts which the Director graciously
granted the negroes who were the Company's slaves, in consequence of their long service: freedom was given to them on
condition that their children should remain slaves, who are not
treated otherwise than as Christians. At present there are
only three of these children who do any service. One of them

---

[1] The hamlet on the East River opposite Manhattan; the village of Breukelen
stood a mile east of the river.

is at the House of Hope,[1] one at the Company's bouwery, and one with Martin Crigier, who has brought the girl up well, as everybody knows.

That the Heer Stuyvesant should build up, alter and repair the Company's property was his duty. For the consequent loss or profit he will answer to the Company.

The burghers upon the island of Manhatans and thereabouts must know that nobody comes or is admitted to New Netherland (being a conquest) except upon this condition, that he shall have nothing to say, and shall acknowledge himself under the sovereignty of Their High Mightinesses the States General and the Lords Managers, as his lords and patrons, and shall be obedient to the Director and Council for the time being, as good subjects are bound to be.

Who are they who have complained about the haughtiness of Stuyvesant? I think they are such as seek to live without law or rule.

Their complaint that no regulation was made in relation to *sewan* is untrue. During the time of Director Kieft good *sewan* passed at four for a stiver, and the loose bits were fixed at six pieces for a stiver.[2] The reason why the loose *sewan* was not prohibited, was because there is no coin in circulation, and the laborers, farmers, and other common people having no other money, would be great losers; and had it been done, the remonstrants would, without doubt, have included it among their grievances.

Nobody can prove that Director Stuyvesant has used foul language to, or railed at as clowns, any persons of respectability who have treated him decently. It may be that some profligate has given the Director, if he has used any bad words to him, cause to do so.

That the fort is not properly repaired does not concern the inhabitants. It is not their domain, but the Company's. They

---

[1] Near Hartford, Connecticut. The company's bouwery, or farm, next mentioned, was the tract extending between the lines of Fulton and Chambers Streets, Broadway and the North River. Martin Cregier was captain of the militia company.

[2] Kieft's regulation was adopted April 16, 1641. In Connecticut and Massachusetts, in 1640 and 1641, the legal valuations varied from four beads to the penny (or stiver) to six beads.

are willing to be protected by good forts and garrisons belonging to the Company without furnishing any aid or assistance by labor or money for the purpose; but it appears they are not willing to see a fort well fortified and properly garrisoned, from the apprehension that malevolent and seditious persons will be better punished, which they call cruelty.

Had the Director not been compelled to provide the garrisons of New Netherland and Curaçao with provisions, clothing and pay, the fort would, doubtless, have been completed already.

Against whom has Director Stuyvesant personally made a question without reason or cause?

A present of maize or Indian corn they call a contribution, because a present is never received from the Indians without its being doubly paid for, as these people, being very covetous, throw out a herring for a codfish, as everybody who knows the Indians can bear witness.

Francis Doughty, father-in-law of Adrian van der Donk, and an English minister, was allowed a colony at Mestpacht, not for himself alone as patroon, but for him and his associates, dwelling in Rhode Island, at Cohanock and other places, from whom he had a power of attorney, and of whom a Mr. Smith [1] was one of the principal; for the said minister had scarcely any means of himself to build even a hovel, let alone to people a colony at his own expense; but was to be employed as minister by his associates, who were to establish him on a farm in the said colony, for which he would discharge ministerial duties among them, and live upon the profits of the farm.

Coming to the Manhatans to live during the war, he was permitted to act as minister for the English dwelling about there; and they were bound to maintain him without either the Director or the Company being liable to any charge therefor. The English not giving him wherewith to live on, two

---

[1] Richard Smith, a Gloucestershire man, settled early in Plymouth Colony (Taunton). Removing thence on account of religious differences, he settled in what is now Rhode Island, where he became a close friend of Roger Williams. Between 1640 and 1643 he made the first permanent settlement in the Narragansett country, at Cawcamsqussick (Wickford), where he had for many years his chief residence and where his house still stands. His extensive trading interests brought him to Manhattan, where for some years he had a house.

collections were made among the Dutch and English by means of which he lived at the Manhatans.

The said colony of Mespacht was never confiscated, as is shown by the owners, still living there, who were interested in the colony with Doughty; but as Doughty wished to hinder population, and to permit no one to build in the colony unless he were willing to pay him a certain amount of money down for every morgen of land, and a certain yearly sum in addition in the nature of ground-rent, and in this way sought to establish a domain therein, the others interested in the colony (Mr. Smith especially) having complained, the Director and Council finally determined that the associates might enter upon their property—the farm and lands which Doughty possessed being reserved to him; so that he has suffered no loss or damage thereby. This I could prove also, were it not that the documents are in New Netherland and not here.

There are no clauses inserted in the ground-briefs, contrary to the Exemptions, but the words *nog te beramen* (hereafter to be imposed) can be left out of the ground-briefs, if they be deemed offensive.

Stuyvesant has never contested anything in court, but as president has put proper interrogatories to the parties and with the court's advice has rendered decisions about which the malevolent complain; but it must be proven that anyone has been wronged by Stuyvesant in court.

As to what relates to the second [Vice Director] Dinclagen, let him settle his own matters.

It can be shown that Brian Newton not only understands the Dutch tongue, but also speaks it, so that their charge, that Newton does not understand the Dutch language, is untrue. All the other slanders and calumnies uttered against the remaining officers should be required to be proven.

It is true that in New Netherland it was commonly stated in conversation that there was no appeal from a judgment in New Netherland pronounced on the island of Manhatans, founded on the Exemptions by which on the island of Manhatans was established the supreme court for all the surrounding colonies, and also that there had never been a case in which an appeal from New Netherland had been entertained by Their High Mightinesses, although it had been petitioned for when Hendrick Jansen Snyder, Laurens Cornelissen and others, many years ago, were banished from New Netherland.[1] It would be a very strange thing indeed if the officers of the Company could banish nobody from the country, while the officers of the colony of Renselaerswyck, who are merely subordinates of the Company, can banish absolutely from the colony whomever they may deem advisable for the good of the colony, and permit no one to dwell there unless with their approbation and upon certain conditions, some of which are as follows: in the first place, no one down to the present time can possess a foot of land of his own in the colony, but is obliged to take upon rent all the land which he cultivates. When a house is erected an annual ground-rent in beavers must be paid; and all the farmers must do the same, which they call obtaining the right to trade. Where is there an inhabitant under the jurisdiction of the Company of whom anything was asked or exacted for trade or land? All the farms are conveyed in fee, subject to the clause *beraemt ofte nog te beramen*, (taxes imposed or to be imposed.)

The English minister Francis Doughty has never been in the service of the company, wherefore it was not indebted to him; but his English congregation are bound to pay him, as may be proven in New Netherland.

The Company has advanced the said minister, from time to time, goods and necessaries of life amounting to about 1100 guilders, as the Colony-Book can show, which he has not yet paid, and he is making complaints now, so that he may avoid paying it. Whether or not the Director has desired a compromise with Doughty, I do not know.

Director Stuyvesant, when he came to New Netherland, endeavored according to his orders to stop in a proper manner the contraband trade in guns, powder and lead. The people of the colony of Renselaerwyck understanding this, sent a letter and petition to the Director, requesting moderation, especially as they said if that trade were entirely abolished all the Christians in the colony would run great danger of being murdered, as may more at large be seen by the contents of their petition.

---

[1] Hendrick Jansen the tailor was throughout Kieft's administration one of his bitterest and most abusive opponents, and was several times prosecuted for slander. In 1647 he sailed on the *Princess* with Kieft and was lost. Lourens Cornelissen van der Wel was a sea-captain, and also prosecuted by Kieft.

The Director and Council taking the request into consideration, and looking further into the consequences, resolved that
guns and powder, to a limited extent, be sparingly furnished
by the factor at Fort Orange, on account of the Company,
taking good care that no supply should be carried by the boats
navigating the river, until in pursuance of a further order. It
is here to be observed that the Director, fearing one of two
[evils] and in order to keep the colony out of danger, has permitted some arms to be furnished at the fort. Nobody can
prove that the Director has sold or permitted to be sold anything contraband, for his own private benefit. That the
Director has permitted some guns to be seized has happened
because they brought with them no license pursuant to the
order of the Company, and they would under such pretences
be able to bring many guns. The Director has paid for every
one that was seized, sixteen guilders, although they do not
cost in this country more than eight or nine guilders.

It is true that a case of guns was brought over by Vastrick,
by order of Director Stuyvesant, in which there were thirty
guns, which the Director, with the knowledge of the Vice
Director and *fiscaal*, permitted to be landed in the full light of
day, which guns were delivered to Commissary Keyser with
orders to sell them to the Netherlanders who had no arms, in
order that in time of need they might defend themselves, which
Keyser has done; and it will appear by his accounts where these
guns are. If there were any more guns in the ship it was unknown to the Director. The *fiscaal*, whose business it was,
should have seen to it and inspected the ship; and these
accusers should have shown that the *fiscaal* had neglected to
make the search as it ought to have been done.

Jacob Reinsen and Jacob Schermerhorn[1] are Scotch
merchants (pedlers) born in Waterland, one of whom, Jacob
Schermerhorn, was at Fort Orange, the other, Jacob Reintjes,
was at Fort Amsterdam, who there bought powder, lead and
guns, and sent them up to Schermerhorn, who traded them to
the Indians. It so happened that the Company's corporal,
Gerit Barent, having in charge such of the arms of the Company
as required to be repaired or cleaned, sold to the before named
Jacob Reintjes, guns, locks, gun-barrels, etc., as can be proven

[1] See p. 345, *supra*.

by Jacob Reintjes' own confession, by letters written to his partner long before this came to light, and by the accusations of the corporal. The corporal, seduced by the solicitation of Jacob Reintjes, sold him the arms as often as desired, though the latter knew that the guns and gun-barrels belonged to the Company, and not to the corporal. There was confiscated also a parcel of peltries (as may be seen in the accounts) coming chiefly from the contraband goods (as appears from the letters). And as the said Jacob Reintjes has been in this country since the confiscation, he would have made complaint if he had not been guilty, especially as he was sufficiently urged to do so by the enemies of the Company and of the Director, but his own letters were witnesses against him.

Joost de Backer being accused also by the above named corporal of having bought gun-locks and gun-barrels from him, and the first information having proved correct, his house was searched according to law, in which was found a gun of the Company which he had procured from the corporal; he was therefore taken into custody until he gave security [to answer] for the claim of the *fiscaal*.

As the English of New England protected among them all fugitives who came to them from the Manhatans without the passport required by the usage of the country, whether persons in the service of the Company or freemen, and took them into their service, it was therefore sought by commissioners to induce the English to restore the fugitives according to an agreement previously made with Governors Eaton and Hopkins, but as Governor Eaton failed to send back the runaways, although earnestly solicited to do so, the Director and Council, according to a previous resolution, issued a proclamation that all persons who should come from the province of New Haven (all the others excepted) to New Netherland should be protected; which was a retaliatory measure. As the Governor permitted some of the fugitives to come back to us, the Director and Council annulled the order, and since then matters have gone on peaceably, the dispute about the boundaries remaining the same as before.[1]

---

[1] Theophilus Eaton, governor of New Haven 1639–1658, and Edward Hopkins, governor of Connecticut seven times in the period 1640–1654. The recriminations and retaliations alluded to took place in the winter of 1647–1648. Two months before the date of this *Answer*, Stuyvesant had arranged with the Commissioners of the United Colonies at Hartford a provisional agreement as to

Nobody's goods have been confiscated in New Netherland without great reason; and if any one feels aggrieved about it, the Director will be prepared to furnish an answer. That ships or shipmasters are afraid of confiscation and therefore do not come to New Netherland is probable, for nobody can come to New Netherland without a license. Whoever has this, and does not violate his agreement, and has properly entered his goods, need not be afraid of confiscation; but all smugglers and persons who sail with two commissions may well be.

All those who were indebted to the Company were warned by the Director and Council to pay the debts left uncollected by the late William Kieft, and as some could, and others could not well pay, no one was compelled to pay; but these debts, amounting to 30,000 guilders, make many who do not wish to pay, angry and insolent, (especially as the Company now has nothing in that country to sell them on credit,) and it seems that some seek to pay after the Brazil fashion.[1]

The memorialists have requested that the people should not be harassed, which however has never been the case, but they would be right glad to see that the Company dunned nobody, nor demanded their own, yet paid their creditors. It will appear by the account-books of the Company that the debts were not contracted during the war, but before it. The Company has assisted the inhabitants, who were poor and burdened with wives and children, with clothing, houses, cattle, land, etc., and from time to time charged them in account, in hopes of their being able at some time to pay for them.

If the taxes of New England, before spoken of, be compared with those of New Netherland, it will be found that those of New England are a greater burden upon that country than the taxes of New Netherland are upon our people.

The wine excise of one stiver per can, was first imposed in the year 1647.

The beer excise of three guilders per tun, was imposed by Kieft in 1644, and is paid by the tapster alone, and not by the burgher.

boundaries between English and Dutch on Long Island and on the mainland; but the treaty was not ratified by the English and Dutch governments.

[1] The recent conquest of the company's province of Brazil by the Portuguese had enabled many debtors there to avoid paying their debts.

The recognition of eight in a hundred upon exported beaver skins does not come out of the inhabitants, but out of the trader, who is bound to pay it according to contract.

The Director has always shown that he was desirous and pleased to see a deputation from the commonalty, who should seek in the Fatherland from the Company as patrons and the Lords States as sovereigns, the following: population, settlement of boundaries, reduction of charges upon New Netherland tobacco and other productions, means of transporting people, permanent and solid privileges, etc.

For which purpose he has always offered to lend a helping hand; but the remonstrants have pursued devious paths and excited some of the commonalty, and by that means obtained a clandestine and secret subscription, as is to be seen by their remonstrance, designed for no other object than to render the Company—their patrons—and the officers in New Netherland odious before Their High Mightinesses, so that the Company might be deprived of the *jus patronatus* and be still further injured.

The remonstrants say that we had relied upon the English, and by means of them sought to divert the college, (as they call it,) which is untrue, as appears by the propositions made to them. But it is here to be observed that the English, living under the protection of the Netherlanders, having taken the oath of allegiance and being domiciliated and settled in New Netherland, are to be considered citizens of the country. These persons have always been opposed to them, since the English, as well as they, had a right to say something in relation to the deputation, and would not consent to all their calumnies and slanders, but looked to the good of the commonalty and of the inhabitants.

It was not written on their petition, in the margin, that they might secretly go and speak to the commonalty. The intention of the Director was to cause them to be called together as opportunity should offer, at which time they might speak to the commonalty publicly about the deputation. The Director was not obliged, as they say, to call the commonalty immediately together. It was to be considered by him at what time each one could conveniently come from home without considerable loss, especially as some lived at a distance in the country, etc.

That they have not been willing to communicate, was because all whom they now paint in such black colors would have
been able to provide themselves with weapons, and make the
contrary appear, and in that case could have produced something [in accusation of] some of them. And since the Director
and those connected with the administration in New Netherland are very much wronged and defamed, I desire time in
order to wait for opposing documents from New Netherland,
if it be necessary.

As to Vander Donk and his associates' report that the
Director instituted suits against some persons: The Director
going to the house of Michael Jansen, (one of the signers of the
remonstrance,) was warned by the said Michael and Thomas
Hall, saying, there was within it a scandalous journal of Adrian
van der Donck; which journal the Director took with him, and
on account of the slanders which were contained in it against
Their High Mightinesses and private individuals, Van der
Donck was arrested at his lodgings and proof of what he had
written demanded, but he was released on the application and
solicitation of others.

During the administration both of Kieft and of Stuyvesant,
it was by a placard published and posted, that no attestations
or other public writings should be valid before a court in New
Netherland, unless they were written by the secretary. This
was not done in order that there should be no testimony
[against the Director] but upon this consideration, that most
of the people living in Netherland are country and seafaring
men, and summon each other frequently for small matters
before the court, while many of them can neither read nor
write, and neither testify intelligibly nor produce written evidence, and if some do produce it, sometimes it is written by
some sailor or farmer, and often wholly indistinct and contrary
to the meaning of those who had it written or who made the
statement; consequently the Director and Council could not
know the truth of matters as was proper and as justice demanded, etc. Nobody has been arrested except Van der Donk
for writing the journal, and Augustyn Heermans, the agent of
Gabri, because he refused to exhibit the writings drawn up by
the Nine Men, which were promised to the Director, who had
been for them many times like a boy.

Upon the first point of redress, as they call it, the remonstrants advise, that the Company should abandon and transfer the country. What frivolous talk this is! The Company have at their own expense conveyed cattle and many persons thither, built forts, protected many people who were poor and needy emigrating from Holland, and provided them with provisions and clothing; and now when some of them have a little more than they can eat up in a day, they wish to be released from the authority of their benefactors, and without paying if they could; a sign of gross ingratitude.

Hitherto the country has been nothing but expense to the Company, and now when it can provide for itself and yield for the future some profit to the Company, these people are not willing to pay the tenth which they are in duty bound to pay after the expiration of the ten years, pursuant to the Exemptions to which they are making an appeal.

Upon the second point they say that provision should be made for ecclesiastical and municipal property, church services, an orphan asylum and an almshouse. If they are such philanthropists as they appear, let them lead the way in generous contributions for such laudable objects, and not complain when the Directors have endeavored to make collections for the building of the church and school. What complaints would have been made if the Director had undertaken to make collections for an almshouse and an orphan asylum! The service of the church will not be suspended, although Domine Johannes Backerus has departed, who was there only twenty-seven months. His place is supplied by a learned and godly minister who has no interpreter when he defends the Reformed Religion against any minister of our neighbors, the English Brownists.[1]

The foregoing are the points which really require any answer. We will only add some description of the persons who have signed the remonstrance and who are the following:

Adrian van der Donk has been about eight years in New Netherland. He went there in the service of the proprietors of the colony of Renselaerswyck as an officer, but did not long continue such, though he lived in that colony till 1646.

---

[1] Referring to Reverend Johannes Megapolensis, who had been persuaded to remain in New Netherland and assume pastoral care of Manhattan; see p. 165, *supra*.

Arnoldus van Hardenburgh accompanied Hay Jansen to New Netherland, in the year 1644, with a cargo for his brother. He has never to our knowledge suffered any loss or damage in New Netherland, but has known how to charge the commonalty well for his goods.

Augustyn Heermans came on board the *Maecht van Enkhuysen*,[1] being then as he still is, the agent of Gabrie[2] in trading business.

Jacob van Couwenhoven came to the country with his father in boyhood, was taken by Wouter van Twiller into the service of the Company as an assistant, and afterwards became a tobacco planter. The Company has aided him with necessaries as it is to be seen by the books, but they have been paid for.

Olof Stevensen, brother-in-law of Govert Loockmans, went out in the year 1637 in the ship *Herring* as a soldier in the service of the Company. He was promoted by Director Kieft and finally made commissary of the shop. He has profited in the service of the Company, and endeavors to give his benefactor the world's pay, that is, to recompense good with evil. He signed under protest, saying that he was obliged to sign, which can be understood two ways, one that he was obliged to subscribe to the truth, the other that he had been constrained by force to do it. If he means the latter, it must be proven.

Michael Jansen came to New Netherland as a farmer's man in the employ of the proprietors of Renselaerswyck. He made his fortune in the colony in a few years, but not being able to agree with the officers, finally came in the year 1646 to live upon the island Manhatans. He would have come here himself, but the accounts between him and the colony not being settled, in which the proprietors did not consider themselves indebted as he claimed, Jan Evertsen came over in his stead.

Thomas Hall came to the South River in 1635, in the employ of an Englishman, named Mr. Homs, being the same who intended to take Fort Nassau at that time and rob us of the South River. This Thomas Hall ran away from his master, came to the Manhatans and hired himself as a farmer's man to Jacob van Curlur. Becoming a freeman he has made a tobacco plantation upon the land of Wouter van Twÿler, and he has

[1] " Maid of Enkhuizen."
[2] Peter Gabry and Sons, a noted firm of Amsterdam.

been also a farm-superintendent; and this W. van Twÿler knows the fellow. Thomas Hall dwells at present upon a small bowery belonging to the Honorable Company.

Elbert Elbertsen came to the country as a farmer's boy at about ten or eleven years of age, in the service of Wouter van Twyler, and has never had any property in the country. About three years ago he married the widow of Gerret Wolphertsen, (brother of the before mentioned Jacob van Couwenhoven,) and from that time to this has been indebted to the Company, and would be very glad to get rid of paying.

Govert Loockmans, brother in law of Jacob van Couwenhoven, came to New Netherland in the yacht *St. Martin* in the year 1633 as a cook's mate, and was taken by Wouter van Twyler into the service of the Company, in which service he profited somewhat. He became a freeman, and finally took charge of the trading business for Gilles Verbruggen and his company in New Netherland. This Loockmans ought to show gratitude to the Company, next to God, for his elevation, and not advise its removal from the country.

Hendrick Kip is a tailor, and has never suffered any injury in New Netherland to our knowledge.

Jan Evertsen-Bout, formerly an officer of the Company, came the last time in the year 1634, with the ship *Eendracht* [Union], in the service of the Honorable Michiel Paauw, and lived in Pavonia until the year 1643, and prospered tolerably. As the Honorable Company purchased the property of the Heer Paauw, the said Jan Evertsen succeeded well in the service of the Company, but as his house and barn at Pavonia were burnt down in the war, he appears to take that as a cause for complaint. It is here to be remarked, that the Honorable Company, having paid 26,000 guilders for the colony of the Heer Paauw, gave to the aforesaid Jan Evertsen, *gratis*, long after his house was burnt, the possession of the land upon which his house and farmstead are located, and which yielded good grain. The land and a poor unfinished house, with a few cattle, Michiel Jansen has bought for eight thousand guilders.

In brief, these people, to give their doings a gloss, say that they are bound by oath and compelled by conscience; but if that were the case they would not assail their benefactors, the Company and others, and endeavor to deprive them of this noble country, by advising their removal, now that it begins to be like something, and now that there is a prospect of the Company getting its own again. And now that many of the inhabitants are themselves in a better condition than ever, this is evidently the cause of the ambition of many, etc.

At the Hague, 29th *November,* 1650.

LETTER OF JOHANNES BOGAERT TO HANS BONTEMANTEL, 1655

INTRODUCTION

THE chief military exploit of Director Stuyvesant was the conquest in 1655 of the Swedish settlements on the Delaware River. New Sweden had been founded in 1638 by a party of settlers under Peter Minuit, sent out by the Swedish South Company, with private help from Dutch merchants. The history of this little colony belongs to another volume of this series, but some account of its absorption in New Netherland should find a place in this.

At first the Dutch and Swedes on the Delaware, the former with their Fort Nassau on the east side, the latter with their three forts, Nya Elfsborg on the east side, Christina and Nya Göteborg (New Gottenburg) on the west, dwelt together in amity. But competition for the Indian trade was keen, conflicting purchases of land from the Indians gave rise to disputes, and from the beginning of Stuyvesant's administration there was friction. This he greatly increased by proceeding to the South River with armed forces, in 1651, and building Fort Casimir on the west side of the river, near the present site of Newcastle, and uncomfortably near to Fort Christina. In 1654 a large reinforcement to the Swedish colony came out under Johan Rising, who seized Fort Casimir. But the serious efforts to strengthen the colony, made by Sweden in the last year of Queen Christina and the first year of King Charles X., were made too late. The Dutch West India Company ordered Director Stuyvesant not only to retake Fort Casimir but to expel the Swedish power from the whole river. He proceeded to organize in August, 1655, the largest military force which had yet been seen in the Atlantic colonies. The best Dutch account of what it achieved is presented in translation in the following pages; the Swedish side is told by Governor Rising in a report printed in the *Collections of the New York Historical Society*, second series, I. 443–448, and in *Pennsylvania Archives*, second series, V. 222–229.[1]

Of Johannes Bogaert, author of the following letter, we know only that he was a "writer," or clerk. Hans Bontemantel, to whom the letter was addressed, was a director in the Amsterdam Chamber of the West India Company, and a *schepen* (magistrate) of Amsterdam from 1655 to 1672, in which last year he took a prominent part in bringing in William III. The letter was first printed in 1858 in *De Navorscher* (the Dutch *Notes and Queries*), VIII. 185–186. A translation by Henry C. Murphy was published the same year in *The Historical Magazine*, II. 258–259, and this, carefully revised by the present editor, appears below. For a history of New Sweden, see Professor Gregory B. Keen's chapter in Winsor's *Narrative and Critical History of America*, IV. 443–488.

[1] Rising's dates are given according to Old Style, Swedish fashion, Bogaert's according to New Style, as customary in the province of Holland.

LETTER OF JOHANNES BOGAERT TO HANS BONTEMANTEL, 1655

Noble and Mighty Sir:
  Mr. Schepen Bontemantel:
  THIS is to advise your Honor of what has occurred since the 5th of September, 1655, when we sailed with our seven ships,[1] composed of two yachts called the *Hollanse Tuijn* (Dutch Frontier), the *Prinses Royael* (Princess Royal), a galiot called the *Hoop* (Hope), mounting four guns, the flyboat *Liefde* (Love), mounting four guns, the yacht *Dolphijn* (Dolphin), vice-admiral, with four guns, the yacht *Abrams Offerhande* (Abraham's Offering), as rear-admiral, mounting four guns; and on the 8th arrived before the first Swedish fort, named Elsener.[2] This south fort had been abandoned. Our force consisted of 317 soldiers, besides a company of sailors.[3] The general's[4] company, of which Lieutenant Nuijtingh was captain, and Jan Hagel ensign-bearer, was ninety strong. The general's second company, of which Dirck Smit was captain, and Don Pouwel ensign-bearer, was sixty strong. Nicolaes de Silla the marshal's company, of which Lieutenant Pieter Ebel was captain, and William van Reijnevelt ensign-bearer, was fifty-five strong. Frederick de Koningh the major's company, of which Pieter de Coningckx was ensign-bearer, was sixty-two strong. The major's second company, which was composed of seamen and pilots, with Dirck Jansz Verstraten of Ossanen

---

[1] Six are named below. The seventh (or first) was the "admiral" or flag-ship *De Waegh* ("The Balance"), on which the writer sailed. The *Hoop* was a French privateer, *L'Espérance*, which had just arrived at New Amsterdam and was engaged for the expedition.   [2] Nya Elfsborg.
  [3] Rising states the total number of the force as 600 or 700.
  [4] *I. e.*, Stuyvesant's. In the military organization of that day, one or two companies were usually given a primary position as the "general's own" or "colonel's own." Of the persons mentioned below, Nicasius de Sille was a member of the Council, and De Koningh was the captain of *De Waegh*.

as their captain, boatswain's-mate Dirck Claesz of Munniken-
dam as ensign-bearer, and the sail-maker Jan Illisz of Honsum
as lieutenant, consisted of fifty men; making altogether 317
men. The 10th, after breakfast, the fleet got under way, and
ran close under the guns of Fort Casemier, and anchored about
a cannon-shot's distance from it. The troops were landed immediately, and General Stuijvesant dispatched Lieutenant
Dirck Smit with a drummer and a white flag to the commandant, named Swen Schoeten,[1] to summon the fort. In the
meantime we occupied a guard-house about half a cannon-shot
distant from the fort; and at night placed a company of soldiers
in it, which had been previously used as a magazine. The 11th,
the commander, Swen Schoeten, sent a flag requesting to speak
with the general, who consented. They came together, and
after a conference the said commander surrendered Fort
Casemier to the general, upon the following conditions:

First, The commander, whenever he pleases and shall have the
opportunity, by the arrival of ships belonging to the crown, or private
ships, shall be permitted to remove from Fort Casemier the guns of
the crown, large and small: consisting, according to the statement of
the commander, of four iron guns and five case-shot guns, of which
four are small and one is large. *Second,* Twelve men shall march out
as the body-guard of the commander, fully accoutred, with the flag
of the crown; the others with their side-arms only. The guns and
muskets which belong to the crown shall be and remain at the disposition of the commandant, to take or cause them to be taken from
the fort whenever the commander shall have an opportunity to do so.
Third, The commander shall have all his private personal effects
uninjured, in order to take them with him or to have them taken away
whenever he pleases, and also the effects of all the officers. *Fourth,*
The commander shall this day restore into the hands of the General
Fort Casemier and all the guns, ammunition, materials, and other
property belonging to the General Chartered West India Company.
Done, concluded and signed by the contracting parties the 11th
September, 1655, on board the ship *De Waegh,* lying at Fort Casemier.
(Signed)   Petrus Stuijvesant, Swen Schuts.[2]

The 13th, was taken prisoner the lieutenant of Fort
Crist[ina], with a drummer, it being supposed that he had

---

[1] Sven Schüte.

[2] This agrees with the official text in *N. Y. Col. Doc.*, XII. 102.

come as a spy upon the army, in consequence of the drummer's having no drum. The 14th, the small fleet was again under sail with the army for Verdrietige Point,[1] where they were landed. The 15th, we arrived at the west of Fort Christina, where we formed ourselves into three divisions; the major's company and his company of sailors were stationed on the south side of the creek, by the yacht *Eendraght* (Union), where the major constructed a battery of three guns, one eight-pounder and two six-pounders; the general's company and the field marshal's were divided into two. The marshal threw up a battery of two twelve-pounders, about northwest of the fort. The general placed a battery about north of the fort, opposite the land entrance, one hundred paces, by calculation, from the fort, and mounting one eighteen-pounder, one eight-pounder, one six-pounder, and one three-pounder.[2]

The 17th, the flyboat *Liefde* returned to the Manathans with the Swedish prisoners. From the 17th to the 23d nothing particular happened. Then, when we had everything ready, the governor of the fort received a letter from our general, to which our general was to have an answer the next day. The same day an Indian, whom we had dispatched on the 13th to Menades, arrived, bringing news and letters to the effect that some Dutch people had been killed at Menades by the Indians;[3] which caused a feeling of horror through the army, so that the general sent a letter immediately to the fort, that he would give them no time the next morning. Then the general agreed with the Swedish governor to come together in the morning and make an arrangement. The general had a tent erected between our quarter and their fort, and there an agreement was made, whereby the governor, Johan Risingh, surrendered the fort on the 24th of September, upon the conditions mentioned in the accompanying capitulation.[4] On the

[1] On Augustin Herrman's excellent map of Maryland and Delaware, "Virdrietige Hoeck" (Tedious Point) appears as the name of a promontory about where Marcus Hook, Pa., now is. Rising, however, reports the Dutch as landing at Tridje Hoeck ("Third Point"), just north of Christina Creek.

[2] For a plan of the siege, derived from that made by the Swedish engineer Lindström, see Winsor, *Narrative and Critical History of America*, IV. 480.

[3] A hundred were killed, a hundred and fifty taken prisoners.

[4] *N. Y. Col. Doc.*, XII. 104–106.

28th of September the general left with the ships and yachts, and we were ordered to remain from eight to fourteen days, and let the men work daily at Fort Casemier, in the construction of ramparts.[1]

The 11th of October, Governor Rijsingh and Factor Elswijck, with some Swedes, came on board, whom we carried with us to Menades. We ran out to sea for the Menades on the 12th, and on the 17th happily arrived within Sandy Hook. On the 21st we sailed for the North River, from Staten Island, by the watering-place, and saw that all the houses there, and about Molyn's house,[2] were burned up by the Indians; and we learned here that Johannes van Beeck, with his wife and some other people, and the captain of a slave-trader which was lying here at anchor with a vessel, having gone on a pleasure excursion, were attacked by the Indians, who murdered Van Beeck and the captain, and took captive his wife and sister. We found Van Beeck dead in a canoe, and buried him. His wife has got back. The general is doing all that lies in his power to redeem the captives and to make peace. Commending your Honor, with hearty salutations, to the protection of the Most High, that he will bless you and keep you in continued health, I remain your Honor's

Obedient servant,

JOHANNES BOGAERT,

Clerk.

Laus Deo, Ship *De Waegh* (The Balance),
    the 31st October, 1655.
Hon. Mr. Schepen Bontemantel,
    Director of the Chartered West India
        Company, at Amsterdam.

---

[1] Fort Casimir was made the seat of Dutch administration on the South River. In 1657 it was named New Amstel, and the colony there was taken over by the city of Amsterdam.

[2] The house of Cornelis Melyn, on Staten Island.

LETTERS OF THE DUTCH MINISTERS TO THE CLASSIS OF AMSTERDAM, 1655-1664

INTRODUCTION

THE Dutch clergy of the Reformed Church, as has already been mentioned in a previous introduction, were men whose observations we must value because of their intelligence and their acquirements; and they also had a point of view which was to a large extent independent of the Director General and other civil officials. Hence the series of their reports to the Classis of Amsterdam is worthy of much attention. In the absence of a continuous narrative of high importance for the years from 1655 to 1664 it has been deemed best to make use for those years of certain of these clerical letters.

Of their authors, Domine Megapolensis has been already treated, in the introduction to his tract on the Mohawks. He remained at New Amsterdam through the period of the English conquest, and died there in 1669. The Reverend Samuel Drisius (Dries) was born about 1602, of Dutch parents, but was throughout his earlier life a pastor in England, until the troubles in that country caused him to return to the Netherlands. Since he was able to preach not only in Dutch but also in English and even in French, it was natural that the Classis should send him out to New Netherland in response to the urgent requests made for assistance to Megapolensis, especially in dealing with the non-Dutch population at New Amsterdam. He began his pastoral service there in 1653, and continued throughout the remainder of the period represented by this book. In 1669 he is reported as incapacitated by failing mental powers, and he died in 1673. Domine Henricus Selyns was examined as a candidate for the ministry in 1657, ordained by the Classis in 1660, called to Breukelen and inducted there in that year. He returned to Holland in 1664, before the surrender, but came back to New York in 1682 as minister of the Collegiate Church, and died there in 1701.

John Romeyn Brodhead, at the time of his remarkable mission to the Netherlands (1841), included in his endeavors a search for Dutch ecclesiastical papers bearing on New Netherland. The letters which follow were among those which he found in Amsterdam, in the archives of the Classis. In 1842 they were lent, in 1846 given, by the Classis to the General Synod of the Reformed Dutch Church in America. To this material large additions were made by a further search carried out in 1897–1898, by the Reverend Dr. Edward T. Corwin, acting as agent of that church, who is responsible for the translations which follow. An account of all this ecclesiastical material, under the title "The Amsterdam Correspondence," was printed by him in 1897 in the eighth volume of the *Papers of the American Society of Church History*. He edited the material for publication in the first volume of the series called *Ecclesiastical Records, State of New York*, published by the state in 1901. The letters which follow are taken, with slight revision, from various pages (from page 334 to page 562) of that volume.

LETTERS OF THE DUTCH MINISTERS TO THE CLASSIS OF AMSTERDAM, 1655–1664

Rev. Johannes Megapolensis to the Classis of Amsterdam
(March 18, 1655).

Reverendissimi Domini, Fratres in Christo, Synergi observandi:[1]
I FEEL it my duty, to answer the letter of your Reverences, dated the 11th of November, [1654].[2]

We have cause to be grateful to the Messrs. Directors[3] and to your Reverences for the care and trouble taken to procure for the Dutch on Long Island a good clergyman, even though it has not yet resulted in anything. Meanwhile, God has led Domine Joannes Polhemius[4] from Brazil, by way of the Caribbean Islands, to this place. He has for the present gone to Long Island, to a village called Midwout, which is somewhat the *meditullium*[5] of the other villages, to wit, Breuckelen, Amersfoort and Gravesande. There he has preached for the accommodation of the inhabitants on Sundays during the winter, and has administered the sacraments, to the satisfaction of all, as Director Stuyvesant has undoubtedly informed the Messrs. Directors.

As to William Vestiens, who has been schoolmaster and sexton here, I could neither do much, nor say much, in his favor,

---

[1] Most Reverend Masters, Brethren in Christ, Venerable Fellow-workers.
[2] *Ecclesiastical Records, State of New York*, I. 331.
[3] Of the West India Company.
[4] Reverend Johannes Theodorus Polhemus or Polhemius, born about 1598, was in early life a minister in the Palatinate. Driven thence by persecutions in 1635, he was sent to Brazil in 1636 by the Dutch West India Company, and remained there, minister at Itamarca, till the waning of the company's fortunes in that country and the loss of Pernambuco compelled his retirement. In 1654 he went thence to New Netherland, and became provisionally minister of Midwout, the first Dutch church on Long Island. From 1656 to 1660 he was minister of Midwout, Breukelen and Amersfoort, from 1660 to 1664 of Midwout and Amersfoort, from 1664 of all three churches again. He died in 1676.
[5] Middle point. Midwout is now Flatbush; Amersfoort is Flatlands.

to the Council, because for some years past they were not satisfied or pleased with his services.[1] Thereupon when he asked
for an increase of salary last year, he received the answer, that
if the service did not suit him, he might ask for his discharge.
Only lately I have been before the Council on his account, and
spoken about it, in consequence of your letter, but they told me
that he had fulfilled his duties only so-so[2] and that he did little
enough for his salary.

Some Jews came from Holland last summer, in order to
trade.   Later some Jews came upon the same ship as D:
Polheymius;[3] they were healthy, but poor. It would have
been proper, that they should have been supported by their
own people, but they have been at our charge, so that we have
had to spend several hundred guilders for their support.   They
came several times to my house, weeping and bemoaning their
misery.   When I directed them to the Jewish merchant,[4] they
said, that he would not lend them a single stiver.   Some more
have come from Holland this spring.   They report that many
more of the same lot would follow, and then they would build
here a synagogue.   This causes among the congregation here
a great deal of complaint and murmuring.   These people have
no other God than the Mammon of unrighteousness, and no
other aim than to get possession of Christian property, and to
overcome all other merchants by drawing all trade towards
themselves.   Therefore we request your Reverences to obtain
from the Messrs. Directors, that these godless rascals, who are of
no benefit to the country, but look at everything for their own
profit, may be sent away from here.   For as we have here
Papists, Mennonites and Lutherans among the Dutch; also
many Puritans or Independents, and many atheists and various
other servants of Baal among the English under this Govern-

---

[1] Willem Vestiens or Vestens, schoolmaster, of Haarlem, "a good, God-
fearing man," was sent out in 1650 as schoolmaster, sexton and "comforter of the
sick."   In 1655 he asked to be transferred to the East Indies, and was replaced at
New Amsterdam by Harmanus van Hoboken.   [2] *Taliter qualiter*.

[3] Refugees from Brazil, who retired after the capture of Pernambuco by the
Portuguese, in January, 1654. The number of Jews who settled in New Amsterdam became considerable. The West India Company in 1655 repressed all attempts of Stuyvesant and his Council to expel or oppress them.

[4] Jacob Barsimson seems to have been the one Jewish merchant then
there.

ment, who conceal themselves under the name of Christians; it would create a still greater confusion, if the obstinate and immovable Jews came to settle here.

In closing I commend your Reverences with your families to the protection of God, who will bless us and all of you in the service of the divine word.

Your obedient

JOHAN. MEGAPOLENSIS.

Amsterdam in New Netherland the 18th of March, 1655.

Addressed to the Reverend, Pious and very Learned Deputies ad res Ecclesiasticas Indicas, in the Classis of Amsterdam.

Revs. J. Megapolensis and S. Drisius to the Classis of Amsterdam (August 5, 1657).

Reverend, Pious and Learned Gentlemen, Fathers and Brethren in Christ Jesus:

The letters of your Reverences, of the 13th of June 1656, and of the 15th of October of the same year have been received. We were rejoiced to learn of the fatherly affection and care which you show for the welfare of this growing congregation. We also learned thereby of the trouble you have taken with the Messrs. Directors, to prevent the evils threatened to our congregation by the creeping in of erroneous spirits; and of your Reverences' desire, to be informed of the condition of the churches in this country.

We answered you in the autumn of the year 1656, and explained all things in detail. To this we have as yet received no reply, and are therefore in doubt, whether our letters reached you. This present letter must therefore serve the same end.

The Lutherans here pretended, last year, that they had obtained the consent of the Messrs. Directors, to call a Lutheran pastor from Holland.[1] They therefore requested the

---

[1] There were Lutherans at Manhattan at the time of Father Jogues's visit (1643), and they are called a congregation in 1649. In 1653 they petitioned to have a minister of their own and freedom of public worship. Stuyvesant and the ministers were disposed to maintain the monopoly of the Reformed (Calvinistic) Church. In 1656 he forbade even Lutheran services in private houses; but the Company would not sustain this, though they upheld him in sending Gutwasser back to Holland in 1659.

Hon. Director and the Council, that they should have permission, meanwhile, to hold their conventicles to prepare the way for their expected and coming pastor. Although they began to urge this rather saucily, we, nevertheless, animated and encouraged by your letters, hoped for the best, yet feared the worst, which has indeed come to pass. For although we could not have believed that such permission had been given by the Directors, there nevertheless arrived here, with the ship *Meulen*[1] in July last, a Lutheran preacher Joannes Ernestus Goetwater,[2] to the great joy of the Lutherans, but to the special displeasure and uneasiness of the congregation in this place; yea, even the whole country, including the English, were displeased.

We addressed ourselves, therefore, to his Honor the Director-General, the Burgomasters and Schepens of this place,[3] and presented the enclosed petition. As a result thereof, the Lutheran pastor was summoned before their Honors and asked with what intentions he had come here, and what commission and credentials he possessed. He answered that he had come to serve here as a Lutheran preacher, but that he had no other commission than a letter from the Lutheran Consistory at Amsterdam to the Lutheran congregation here. He was then informed by the Hon. authorities here, that he must abstain from all church services, and from the holding of any meetings, and not even deliver the letter which he brought from the Lutherans at Amsterdam without further orders; but that he must regulate himself by the edicts of this province against private conventicles. He promised to do this, adding however that with the next ships he expected further orders and his regular commission. In the meantime, however, we had the snake in our bosom. We should have been glad if the authorities here had opened that letter of the Lutheran Consistory, to learn therefrom the secret of his mission, but as yet they have not been willing to do this.

We then demanded that our authorities here should send back the Lutheran preacher, who had come without the consent of the Messrs. Directors, in the same ship in which he had come, in order to put a stop to this work, which they evidently in-

[1] "The Mill."   [2] Johann Ernst Gutwasser.
[3] New Amsterdam had received a municipal constitution, of about the type usual in the Netherlands, though somewhat less liberal, in 1653.

tended to prosecute with a hard Lutheran head, in spite of and against the will of our magistrates; for we suspect that this one has come over to see whether he can pass, and be allowed to remain here, and thus to lay the foundation for further efforts; but we do not yet know what we can accomplish.

Domine Gideon Schaats[1] wrote to you last year about the congregation at Rensselaerswyck or Beverwyck, as he intends to do again. We know nothing otherwise than that the congregation there is in a good condition; that it is growing vigorously, so that it is almost as strong as we are here at the Manhatans. They built last year a handsome parsonage. On the South River, matters relating to religion and the church have hitherto progressed very unsatisfactorily; first because we had there only one little fort, and in it a single commissary, with ten to twenty men, all in the Company's service, merely for trading with the Indians. Secondly: In the year 1651 Fort Nassau was abandoned and razed, and another, called Fort Casemier, was erected, lower down and nearer to the seaboard. This was provided with a stronger garrison, and was reinforced by several freemen, who lived near it.

But the Swedes, increasing there in numbers, troubled and annoyed our people daily. After they had taken Fort Casemier from us, they annoyed our countrymen so exceedingly, that the South River was abandoned by them. However in the year 1655 our people recovered Fort Casemier, and now it is held by a sufficiently strong garrison, including several freemen, who also have dwellings about. One was then appointed, to read to them on Sundays, from the Postilla.[2] This is continued to this day.[3] The Lutheran preacher who was there was returned to Sweden.

Two miles from Fort Casemier, up the river, is another fort, called Christina. This was also taken by our people, at the same time, and the preacher there[4] was sent away, with the Swedish garrison.

But because many Swedes and Finns, at least two hundred, live above Fort Christina, two or three leagues further up the river, the Swedish governor made a condition in his capitula-

---

[1] Minister at Rensselaerswyck since 1652.   [2] Book of Homilies.
[3] Reverend Peter Hjort, pastor at Fort Trinity.
[4] Reverend Matthias Nertunius.

tion, that they might retain one Lutheran preacher,[1] to teach these people in their language. This was granted then the more easily, first, because new troubles had broken out at Manhattan with the Indians, and it was desirable to shorten proceedings here and return to the Manhattans to put things in order there; secondly, because there was no Reformed preacher here, nor any who understood their language, to be located there.

This Lutheran preacher is a man of impious and scandalous habits, a wild, drunken, unmannerly clown, more inclined to look into the wine can than into the Bible. He would prefer drinking brandy two hours to preaching one; and when the sap is in the wood his hands itch and he wants to fight whomsoever he meets. The commandant at Fort Casimir, Jean Paulus Jacquet, brother-in-law of Domine Casparus Carpentier,[2] told us that during last spring this preacher was tippling with a smith, and while yet over their brandy they came to fisticuffs, and beat each other's heads black and blue; yea, that the smith tore all the clothing from the preacher's body, so that this godly minister escaped in primitive nakedness, and although so poorly clothed, yet sought quarrels with others. *Sed hoc parergicos.*[3]

On Long Island there are seven villages belonging to this province, of which three, Breuckelen, Amersfoort and Midwout,[4] are inhabited by Dutch people, who formerly used to come here[5] to communion and other services to their great inconvenience. Some had to travel for three hours to reach this place. Therefore, when Domine Polheymus arrived here from Brazil, they called him as preacher, which the Director-General and Council confirmed.

The four other villages on Long Island, viz., Gravensand, Middelburgh, Vlissingen, and Heemstede[6] are inhabited by Englishmen. The people of Gravensand are considered Mennonites. The majority of them reject the baptism of infants,

---

[1] Reverend Lars Lock or Lokenius, preacher at Tinicum from 1647 to 1688.

[2] Carpentier was a Reformed minister whom the Dutch had established at Fort Casimir. Jacquet was vice-director on the South River, 1655–1657.

[3] But this incidentally.   [4] Brooklyn, Flatlands and Flatbush.

[5] To New Amsterdam.

[6] Gravesend, Newtown, Flushing and Hempstead.

the observance of the Sabbath, the office of preacher, and any teachers of God's word. They say that thereby all sorts of contentions have come into the world. Whenever they meet, one or the other reads something to them. At Vlissingen, they formerly had a Presbyterian minister[1] who was in agreement with our own church. But at present, many of them have become imbued with divers opinions and it is with them *quot homines tot sententiae.*[2] They began to absent themselves from the sermon and would not pay the preacher the salary promised to him. He was therefore obliged to leave the place and go to the English Virginias. They have now been without a preacher for several years. Last year a troublesome fellow, a cobbler from Rhode Island in New England,[3] came there saying, he had a commission from Christ. He began to preach at Vlissingen and then went with the people into the river and baptized them. When this became known here, the *fiscaal* went there, brought him to this place, and he was banished from the province.

At Middelburgh, alias Newtown, they are mostly Independents and have a man called Joannes Moor,[4] of the same way of thinking, who preaches there, but does not serve the sacraments. He says he was licensed in New England to preach, but not authorized to administer the sacraments. He has thus continued for some years. Some of the inhabitants of this village are Presbyterians, but they cannot be supplied by a Presbyterian preacher. Indeed, we do not know that there are any preachers of this denomination to be found among any of the English of New England.

At Heemstede, about seven leagues from here, there live some Independents. There are also many of our own church, and some Presbyterians. They have a Presbyterian preacher, Richard Denton,[5] a pious, godly and learned man, who is in agreement with our church in everything. The Independents

---

[1] Reverend Francis Doughty.   [2] As many opinions as men.

[3] William Wickenden. The *schout* of the village was fined fifty pounds for allowing him to preach in his house.

[4] John Moore, formerly minister at Hempstead; died this year, 1657.

[5] Reverend Richard Denton (1586–1662), one of the pioneers of Presbyterianism in America, was a Cambridge man, who came over with Winthrop in 1630, and was settled successively at Watertown, Wethersfield and Stamford. His differences with the Congregational clergy of New England had led to his withdrawal, and since 1644 he had been at Hempstead.

of the place listen attentively to his sermons; but when he began to baptize the children of parents who are not members of the church, they rushed out of the church.

On the west shore of the East River, about one mile beyond Hellgate, as we call it, and opposite Flushing, is another English village, called Oostdorp, which was begun two years ago. The inhabitants of this place are also Puritans or Independents. Neither have they a preacher, but they hold meetings on Sunday, and read a sermon of some English writer, and have a prayer.[1]

About eighteen leagues up the North River, half way between the Manhattans and Rensselaer or Beverwyck, lies a place, called by the Dutch Esopus or Sypous, and by the Indians Atharhacton. It is an exceedingly fine country there. Thereupon some Dutch families settled there who are doing very well. They hold Sunday meetings and then one or the other of them reads from the Postilla.

Such is the condition of the church in our province. To this we must add that, as far as we know, not one of all these places, Dutch or English, has a schoolmaster, except the Manhattans, Beverwyck, and now also Fort Casimir on the South River.[2] And although some parents try to give their children some instruction, the success is far from satisfactory, and we can expect nothing else than young men of foolish and undisciplined minds. We see at present no way of improving this state of affairs; first, because some of the villages are just starting, and have no means, the people having come half naked and poor from Holland, to pay a preacher and school-

---

[1] Oost-dorp ("East Village") is the present Westchester. "After dinner [Sunday, December 31, 1656] Cornelis van Ruyven went to the house where they assemble on Sundays, to observe their mode of worship, as they have not as yet any clergyman. There I found a gathering of about fifteen men and ten or twelve women. Mr. Baly made a prayer, which being concluded, one Robbert Basset read a sermon from a printed book composed and published by an English minister in England. After the reading Mr. Baly made another prayer and they sang a psalm and separated." (Journal of Brian Newton et als., to Oostdorp, Doc. Hist. N. Y., octavo, III. 923.)

[2] Harmanus van Hoboken at New Amsterdam, Adriaen Jansz at Beverwyck (Albany), and since April of this year Evert Pietersen at Fort Casimir. Two years later (1659) the company sent over Alexander Carolus Curtius, "late professor in Lithuania," to be master of a Latin school in New Amsterdam.

master; secondly, because there are few qualified persons here who can or will teach.

We can say but little of the conversion of the heathens or Indians here, and see no way to accomplish it, until they are subdued by the numbers and power of our people, and reduced to some sort of civilization; and also unless our people set them a better example, than they have done heretofore.

We have had an Indian here with us for about two years. He can read and write Dutch very well. We have instructed him in the fundamental principles cf our religion, and he answers publicly in church, and can repeat the Commandments. We have given him a Bible, hoping he might do some good among the Indians, but it all resulted in nothing. He took to drinking brandy, he pawned the Bible, and turned into a regular beast, doing more harm than good among the Indians.

Closing we commend your Reverences to the gracious protection of the Almighty, whom we pray to bless you in the Sacred Ministry.

Vestri et officio et effectu,[1]

JOHANNES MEGAPOLENSIS.

SAMUEL DRISSIUS.

Amsterdam, in New Netherland,
the 5th of August, 1657.

Revs. Megapolensis and Drisius to the Classis of Amsterdam
(October 25, 1657).

Brethren in Christ:

Since our last letter, which we hope you are receiving about this time, we have sent in a petition in relation to the Lutheran minister, Joannes Ernestus Gutwasser. Having marked this on its margin, we have sent it to the Rev. Brethren of the Classis. We hope that the Classis will take care that, if possible, no other be sent over, as it is easier to send out an enemy than afterward to thrust him out. We have the promise that the magistrates here will compel him to leave with the ship *De Wage.* It is said that there has been collected for him at Fort Orange a hundred beaver skins, which are valued here at

---

[1] Yours both officially and actually.

eight hundred guilders, and which is the surest pay in this
country. What has been collected here, we cannot tell. Our
magistrates have forbidden him to preach, as he has received
no authority from the Directors for that purpose. Yet we
hear that the Hon. Directors at Amsterdam gave him permission to come over. We have stated in a previous letter the
injurious tendency of this with reference to the prosperity of
our church.

Lately we have been troubled by others. Some time since,
a shoemaker,[1] leaving his wife and children, came here and
preached in conventicles. He was fined, and not being able
to pay, was sent away. Again a little while ago there arrived
here a ship with Quakers, as they are called. They went away
to New England, or more particularly, to Rhode Island, a place
of errorists and enthusiasts. It is called by the English themselves the *latrina* [2] of New England. They left several behind
them here, who labored to create excitement and tumult
among the people—particularly two women, the one about
twenty, and the other about twenty-eight.[3] These were quite
outrageous. After being examined and placed in prison, they
were sent away. Subsequently a young man at Hempstead,
an English town under the government, aged about twenty-
three or twenty-four years,[4] was arrested, and brought thence,
seven leagues. He had pursued a similar course and brought
several under his influence. The magistrate, in order to repress
the evil in the beginning, after he had kept him in confinement
for several days, adjudged that he should either pay one hundred guilders or work at the wheelbarrow two years with the

[1] William Wickenden, of Rhode Island; see p. 397.   [2] Sink.
[3] Dorothy Waugh, afterward whipped at Boston, and Mary Wetherhead.
[4] Robert Hodgson, who had come on the same ship with the preceding. A
contemporary Quaker writer attributes his release to the intercession of Stuyvesant's sister, Mrs. Anna Bayard. Persecution of Quakers and other sectaries in
New Netherland was continued by Stuyvesant, and finally culminated in the case
of John Bowne, of Flushing, a Quaker, who has left us an interesting account of his
sufferings, printed in the *American Historical Record*, I. 4–8. Banished from the
province and transported to Holland, Bowne laid his case before the directors of
the West India Company, who reproved Stuyvesant by a letter in which they said
(April 16, 1663): "The consciences of men ought to remain free and unshackled.
. . . This maxim of moderation has always been the guide of the magistrates in
this city; and the consequence has been that people have flocked from every land
to this asylum. Tread thus in their steps, and we doubt not you will be blessed."

negroes. This he obstinately refused to do, though whipped on his back. After two or three days he was whipped in private on his bare back, with threats that the whipping would be repeated again after two or three days, if he should refuse to labor. Upon this a letter was brought by an unknown messenger from a person unknown to the Director-General. The import of this, (written in English), was, Think, my Lord-Director, whether it be not best to send him to Rhode Island, as his labor is hardly worth the cost.

Since the arrival of *De Wage* from the South River [the Director?] has again written to Joannes Ernestus Gutwasser to go away. On this he presented a petition, a copy of which is herewith transmitted, as also a copy signed by several of the Lutheran denomination. We observe that it is signed by the least respectable of that body, and that the most influential among them were unwilling to trouble themselves with it. Some assert that he has brought with him authority from the West India Company to act as minister. Whether dismission and return will take place without trouble remains to be seen.

We are at this time in great want of English ministers. It is more than two years since Mr. Doughty, of Flushing which is a town here, went to Virginia, where he is now a preacher. He left because he was not well supported. On October 13, Mr. Moore, of Middelburg, which is another town here, died of a pestilential disease, which prevailed in several of our English towns and in New England. He left a widow with seven or eight children. A year before, being dissatisfied with the meagre and irregular payments from his hearers, he went to Barbadoes, to seek another place. Mr. Richard Denton, who is sound in faith, of a friendly disposition, and beloved by all, cannot be induced by us to remain, although we have earnestly tried to do this in various ways. He first went to Virginia to seek a situation, complaining of lack of salary, and that he was getting in debt, but he has returned thence. He is now fully resolved to go to old England, because his wife, who is sickly, will not go without him, and there is need of their going there, on account of a legacy of four hundred pounds sterling, lately left by a deceased friend, and which they cannot obtain except by their personal presence. At Gravesend there never has been a minister. Other settlements, yet in their infancy, as Aernem,[1] have no minister. It is therefore to be feared that errorists and fanatics may find opportunity to gain strength. We therefore request you, Rev. Brethren, to solicit the Hon. Directors of the West India Company, to send over one or two English preachers, and that directions may be given to the magistracy that the money paid by the English be paid to the magistrate, and not to the preacher, which gives rise to dissatisfaction, and that at the proper time any existing deficiency may be supplied by the Hon. Directors. Otherwise we do not see how the towns will be able to obtain ministers, or if they obtain them, how they will be able to retain them. Complaints continually reach us about the payment of ministers. Nevertheless in New England there are few places without a preacher, although there are many towns, stretching for more than one hundred leagues along the coast. Hoping that by God's blessing and your care something may be effected in this matter, we remain,

Your friends and fellow laborers,

JOHANNES MEGAPOLENSIS.

Manhattans,   SAMUEL DRISIUS.
Oct. 22, 1657.

Rev. Brethren:

Since the writing of the above letter, and before sealing it, we have learned from the Hon. Directors and the *fiscaal*, that Joannes Ernestus Gutwasser is not to be found, that his bedding and books were two days ago removed, and that he has left our jurisdiction. Still it is our opinion that he remains concealed here, in order to write home, and make his appearance as if out of the Fatherland; and to persevere with the Lutherans in his efforts. We therefore hope and pray that you may, if possible, take measures to prevent this.

Oct. 25, 1657.   SAMUEL DRISIUS.

To the Rev. Learned, etc.,
the Deputies ad res Indicas
of the Classis of Amsterdam.

---

[1] Arnhem was a village begun on Smith's Island in Newtown Creek.

Rev. J. Megapolensis to the Classis of Amsterdam (September 28, 1658).

Rdi. Patres et Fratres in Christo:[1]

In a preceding letter of September 24, 1658,[2] mention was made of a Jesuit who came to this place, Manhattans, overland, from Canada. I shall now explain the matter more fully, for your better understanding of it. It happened in the year 1642, when I was minister in the colony of Rensselaerswyck, that our Indians in the neighborhood, who are generally called Maquaas, but who call themselves Kajingehaga, were at war with the Canadian or French Indians, who are called by our Indians Adyranthaka. Among the prisoners whom our Indians had taken from the French, was this Jesuit,[3] whom they according to their custom had handled severely. When he was brought to us, his left thumb and several fingers on both hands had been cut off, either wholly or in part, and the nails of the remaining fingers had been chewed off. As this Jesuit had been held in captivity by them for some time, they consented that he should go among the Dutch, but only when accompanied by some of them. At last the Indians resolved to burn him. Concerning this he came to me with grievous complaint. We advised him that next time the Indians were asleep, he should run away and come to us, and we would protect and secure him, and send him by ship to France. This was done. After concealing him and entertaining him for six weeks, we sent him to the Manhattans and thence to England and France, as he was a Frenchman, born at Paris.[4]

Afterward this same Jesuit came again from France to Canada. As our Indians had made peace with the French, he again left Canada, and took up his residence among the Mohawks. He indulged in the largest expectations of converting them to popery, but the Mohawks with their hatchets put him to a violent death. They then brought and presented to me his missal and breviary together with his underclothing,

---

[1] Reverend Fathers and Brothers in Christ.
[2] *Ecclesiastical Records, State of New York*, I. 432–434.
[3] Father Jogues; see pp. 235–254, *supra*.
[4] Father Jogues was born in Orleans.

shirts and coat. When I said to them that I would not have thought that they would have killed this Frenchman, they answered, that the Jesuits did not consider the fact, that their people (the French) were always planning to kill the Dutch.

In the year 1644 our Indians again took captive a Jesuit,[1] who had been treated in the same manner as to his hands and fingers as the above mentioned. The Jesuit was brought to us naked, with his maimed and bloody fingers. We clothed him, placed him under the care of our surgeon, and he almost daily fed at my table. This Jesuit, a native of Rouen,[2] was ransomed by us from the Indians, and we sent him by ship to France. He also returned again from France to Canada. He wrote me a letter, as the previously mentioned one had done, thanking me for the benefits I had conferred on him. He stated also that he had not argued, when with me, on the subject of religion, yet he had felt deeply interested in me on account of my favors to him; that he was anxious for the life of my soul, and admonished me to come again into the Papal Church from which I had separated myself. In each case I returned such a reply that a second letter was never sent me.

The French have now for some time been at peace with our Indians. In consequence thereof, it has happened that several Jesuits have again gone among our Indians, who are located about four or five days' journey from Fort Orange. But they did not permanently locate themselves there. All returned to Canada except one, named Simon Le Moyne. He has several times accompanied the Indians out of their own country, and visited Fort Orange. At length he came here to the Manhattans, doubtless at the invitation of Papists living here, especially for the sake of the French privateers, who are Papists, and have arrived here with a good prize.

He represented that he had heard the other Jesuits speak much of me, who had also highly praised me for the favors and benefits I had shown them; that he therefore could not, while present here, neglect personally to pay his respects to me, and thank me for the kindness extended to their Society. 1. He told me that during his residence among our Indians he had discovered a salt spring, situated fully one hundred leagues from the sea; and the water was so salt that he had himself

---

[1] Father Giuseppe Bressani (1612–1672).   [2] Of Rome, in fact.

boiled excellent salt from it.[1] 2. There was also another spring
which furnished oil. Oleaginous matter floated on its surface,
with which the Indians anointed their heads. 3. There was
another spring of hot sulphurous water. If paper and dry
materials were thrown into it, they became ignited. Whether
all this is true, or a mere Jesuit lie, I will not decide. I mention
the whole on the responsibility and authority of the Jesuit.

He told me that he had lived about twenty years among the
Indians. When he was asked what fruit had resulted from his
labors, and whether he had taught the Indians anything more
than to make the sign of the cross, and such like superstitions,
he answered that he was not inclined to debate with me, but
wanted only to chat. He spent eight days here, and examined
everything in our midst. He then liberally dispensed his in-
dulgences, for he said to the Papists (in the hearing of one of
our people who understood French), that they need not go to
Rome; that he had as full power from the Pope to forgive their
sins, as if they were to go to Rome. He then returned and
resided in the country of the Mohawks the whole winter. In
the spring, however, troubles began to arise again between our
Indians and the Canadians. He then packed up his baggage,
and returned to Canada. On his journey, when at Fort
Orange, he did not forget me, but sent me three documents:
the first, on the succession of the Popes; the second, on the
Councils; and the third was about heresies, all written out by
himself. He sent with them also, a letter to me, in which he
exhorted me to peruse carefully these documents, and meditate
on them, and that Christ hanging on the Cross was still ready
to receive me, if penitent. I answered him by the letter herewith forwarded, which was sent by a yacht going from here to
the river St. Lawrence in New France.[2] I know not whether I
shall receive an answer.

Valete, Domini Fratres, Vester ex officio,[3]
1658, Sept. 28. JOANNES MEGAPOLENSIS.

[1] Father Le Moyne made this discovery while sojourning among the Onondagas in 1654.

[2] One of the fruits of Father Le Moyne's visit to New Netherland was that
the Dutch obtained from the governor of Canada permission to carry on trade,
except the fur trade, on the St. Lawrence.

[3] Farewell, brethren; yours officially.

Rev. Henricus Selyns to the Classis of Amsterdam (October 4, 1660).

Reverend, Wise and Pious Teachers :

We cannot be so forgetful as to omit to inform you concerning our churches and services.   While at sea, we did not neglect religious worship, but every morning and evening we besought God's guidance and protection, with prayer and the singing of a psalm.   On Sundays and feast-days the Holy Gospel was read, when possible.   The sacrament was not administered on shipboard, and we had no sick people during the voyage. God's favor brought us all here in safety and health.   Arrived in New Netherland, we were first heard at the Manhattans; but the peace-negotiations at the Esopus,[1] where we also went, and the general business of the government necessarily delayed our installation until now.   We have preached here at the Esopus, also at Fort Orange;   during this time of waiting we were well provided with food and lodging.   Esopus needs more people, but Breuckelen more money;   wherefore I serve on Sundays, in the evenings only, at the General's bouwery,[2] at his expense.   The installation at Brooklyn was made by the Honorable Nicasius de Sille, *fiscaal*,[3] and Martin Kriegers, burgomaster,[4] with an open commission from his Honor the Director-General.[5]   I was cordially received by the magistrates and consistory, and greeted by Domine Polhemius. We do not preach in a church, but in a barn;   next winter we shall by God's favor and the general assistance of the people erect a church.

The audience is passably large, coming from Middelwout, New Amersfort, and often Gravesande increases it;   but most

---

[1] The Indians of Esopus had broken out in hostilities in the autumn of 1659. The next summer Stuyvesant went there, after some defeats of the tribe, and made peace formally, July 15, 1660.   A congregation had lately been formed there, which called Domine Harmanus Blom to be its pastor.

[2] Stuyvesant's Bowery, or farm, acquired by him in 1651, lay in the present region of Third Avenue and Tenth Street.   Near the present site of St. Mark's Church he built a chapel for his family, his negro slaves, some forty in number, and the other inhabitants of the neighborhood.

[3] Of New Netherland.   [4] Of New Amsterdam.

[5] For this letter of induction, see *Ecclesiastical Records*, I. 480.

come from the Manhattans. The Ferry, the Walebacht, and Guyanes,[1] all belong to Breuckelen. The Ferry is about two thousand paces from Breuckelen, and it is about four thousand paces across the river, or to the Manhattans, from the Breuckelen Ferry. I found at Breuckelen one elder, two deacons, twenty four members, thirty one householders, and one hundred and thirty-four people. The consistory will remain for the present as it is. In due time we will have more material and we will know the congregation better. Cathechizing will not be held here before the winter; but we will begin it at the Bouwery at once, either on week days, or when there is no preaching service there. It will be most suitable to administer the Lord's Supper on Christmas, Easter, Whitsuntide and in September. On the day following these festival-days a thanksgiving sermon will be preached. I might have taken up my residence at the Manhattans, because of its convenience; but my people, all of them evincing their love and affection for me, have provided me a dwelling of which I cannot complain. I preach at Breuckelen in the morning; but at the Bouwery at the end of the catechetical sermon. The Bouwery is a place of relaxation and pleasure, whither people go from the Manhattans, for the evening service. There are there forty negroes, from the region of the Negro Coast, besides the household families. There is here as yet no consistory, but the deacons from New Amsterdam provisionally receive the alms; and at least one deacon, if not an elder, ought to be chosen there. Besides myself, there are in New Netherland the Domines Joannes Megapolensis and Samuel Drisius at New Amsterdam; Domine Gideon Schaats at Fort Orange; Domine Joannes Polhemius at Middelwout and New Amersfort; and Domine Hermanus Blom at the Esopus. I have nothing more to add, except to express my sincere gratitude and to make my respectful acknowledgments. I commend your Reverences, wise and pious teachers, to God's protection, and am, Yours humbly,

HENRICUS SELYNS, Minister of the
Holy Gospel at Breuckelen.

From Amsterdam, on
the Manhattans, Oct. 4, 1660.

[1] Wallabout and Gowanus.

Rev. Henricus Selyns to the Classis of Amsterdam (June 9, 1664).

Very Reverend, Pious and Learned Brethren in Christ:

With Christian salutations of grace and peace, this is to inform you, that with proper submission, we take the liberty of reporting to the Very Rev. Classis the condition and welfare of the Church of Jesus Christ, to which your Reverences called me, as well as my request and friendly prayer for an honorable dismission.

As for me, your Rev. Assembly sent me to the congregation at Breuckelen to preach the Gospel there, and administer the sacraments. This we have done to the best of our ability; and according to the size of the place with a considerable increase of members. There were only a few members there on my arrival; but these have with God's help and grace increased fourfold.

Trusting that it would not displease your Reverences, and would also be very profitable to the Church of Christ, we found it easy to do what might seem troublesome; for we have also taken charge of the congregation at the General's Bouwery in the evening, as we have told you before. An exception to this arrangement is made in regard to the administration of the Lord's Supper. As it is not customary with your Reverences to administer it in the evening, we thought, after conference with our Reverend Brethren of the New Amsterdam congregation, and mature deliberation, that it would be more edifying to preach at the Bouwery, on such occasions, in the morning, and then have the communion, after the Christian custom of our Fatherland.

As to baptisms, the negroes occasionally request that we should baptize their children, but we have refused to do so, partly on account of their lack of knowledge and of faith, and partly because of the worldly and perverse aims on the part of said negroes. They wanted nothing else than to deliver their children from bodily slavery, without striving for piety and Christian virtues. Nevertheless when it was seemly to do so, we have, to the best of our ability, taken much trouble in private and public catechizing. This has borne but little fruit among the elder people who have no faculty of comprehension;

but there is some hope for the youth who have improved reasonably well. Not to administer baptism among them for the reasons given, is also the custom among our colleagues.[1] But the most important thing is, that the Father of Grace and God of Peace has blessed our two congregations with quietness and harmony, out of the treasury of his graciousness; so that we have had no reason to complain to the Rev. Classis, which takes such things, however, in good part; or to trouble you, as we might have anticipated.

Meanwhile, the stipulated number of years, pledged to the West India Company, is diminishing; although the obligation we owe to them who recommended us [2] naturally continues. Also, on account of their old age, we would love to see again our parents, and therefore we desire to return home. On revolving the matter in my mind, and not to be lacking in filial duty, I felt it to be proper to refer the subject to God and my greatly beloved parents who call for me, whether I should remain or return home at the expiration of my contract.

As we understand, they are, next to myself, most anxious for my return, and have received my discharge from the Hon. Directors, and have notified the Deputies ad Causas Indicas thereof, which has pleased us. We trust that we shall receive also from your Reverences a favorable reply, relying upon your usual kindness. Yet it is far from us to seem to pass by your Reverences, and give the least cause for dissatisfaction. I have endeavored to deserve the favor of the Rev. Classis by the most arduous services for the welfare of Christ's church, and am always ready to serve your Reverences.

It is my purpose when I return home, when my stipulated time is fulfilled, to give a verbal account of my ministry here,

---

[1] The enslaving of Africans having at first been justified on the ground of their heathenism, the notion that to baptize them would make it unlawful to hold them in bondage was frequent among owners in the seventeenth century, and operated to deter them from permitting the Christianizing of their slaves. "I may not forget a resolution which his Ma^{ty} [James II.] made, and had a little before enter'd upon it at the Council Board, at Windsor or Whitehall, that the Negroes in the Plantations should all be baptiz'd, exceedingly declaiming against that impiety of their masters prohibiting it, out of a mistaken opinion that they would be ipso facto free; but his Ma^{ty} persists in his resolution to have them christen'd, wch piety the Bishop [Ken] blessed him for." Evelyn, *Diary*, II. 479 (1685).

[2] The classis.

and the state of the church, that you may be assured that any omissions in duty have been through ignorance.

Domine Samuel Megapolensis [1] has safely arrived, but Domine Warnerus Hadson,[2] whom you had sent as preacher to the South River, died on the passage over. It is very necessary to supply his place, partly on account of the children who have not been baptized since the death of Domine Wely,[3] and partly on account of the abominable sentiments of various persons there, who speak very disrespectfully of the Holy Scriptures.

In addition there is among the Swedes a certain Lutheran preacher, who does not lead a Christian life.[4] There is also another person, who has exchanged the Lutheran pulpit for a schoolmaster's place. This undoubtedly has done great damage among the sheep, who have so long wandered about without a shepherd except the forementioned pastor, who leads such an unchristian life. God grant that no damage be done to Christ's church, and that your Reverences may provide a blessed instrument for good.

In view of the deplorable condition of New Netherland, for the savages have killed, wounded and captured some of our people, and have burnt several houses at the Esopus, and the English, with flying banners, have declared our village and the whole of Long Island to belong to the King:[5] therefore the first

---

[1] Reverend Samuel Megapolensis, born in 1634, studied three years at Harvard College and three at the University of Utrecht. In 1662 he was called by the classis of Amsterdam to the ministry in New Netherland, and ordained by them. In 1664, having meanwhile studied medicine at Leyden, he went out to New Netherland, and was minister of Breukelen from that time to 1669, when he returned to Holland. He died in 1700 as pastor emeritus of the Scottish church at Dordrecht.   [2] Elsewhere called Hassingh.

[3] Reverend Everardus Welius, minister of New Amstel from 1657 to 1659, died in the latter year, leaving without pastor a church of sixty members.

[4] Lokenius's wife ran away from him, and he too hastily married another before obtaining his divorce. The person next alluded to is probably Abelius Selskoorn, a student, who for a time had conducted divine service at Sandhook (Fort Casimir).

[5] The boundaries between New England and New Netherland had always been in dispute (see the introduction to the next section but one). The English population on Long Island grew, and encroached upon the Dutch towns at the west end; and the towns in that region which were partly English, partly Dutch in population were of doubtful allegiance. The graceless Major John Scott, coming

Wednesday of each month since last July has been observed
as a day of fasting and prayer, in order to ask God for his
fatherly compassion and pity.   The good God, praise be to him,
has brought about everything for the best, by the arrival of the
last ships.   The English are quiet, the savages peaceful; our
lamentations have been turned into songs of praise, and the
monthly day of fasting into a day of thanksgiving.   Thus
we spent last Wednesday, the last of the days of prayer.
Blessed be God who causes wars to cease to the ends of the
earth, and breaks the bow and spear asunder.   Herewith,
Very Reverend, Pious, and Learned Brethren in Christ, be
commended to God for the perfecting of the saints and the
edification of the body of Christ.   *Vale.*

Your Reverences' humble servant in

Breuckelen, in   Christ Jesus,
New Netherland,   HENRICUS SELYNS.
June 9, 1664.

[The following account of the English encroachments upon
Long Island has not been previously translated.   It may serve
as a summary of the events, or at least of the version of them
which came before the Dutch public soon after.   It is derived
from the *Hollantze Mercurius* of 1664 (Haerlem, 1665), being
part 15 of the *Mercurius*, which was an annual of the type of the
modern *Annual Register* or of Wassenaer's *Historisch Verhael*,
which preceded it.   The passage is at page 10.

In New Netherland the English made bold to come out of New
England upon various villages and places belonging under the protection of Their High Mightinesses and the Dutch West India Company even upon Long Island, setting up the banner of Britain and
proclaiming that they knew of no New Netherland but that that land
belonged solely to the English nation.   Finally their wisest conceded,
since thus many troubles had arisen about the boundary, that representatives of both nations should come together upon that subject.

to the island with some royal authority, formed a combination of Hempstead,
Gravesend, Flushing, Newtown, Jamaica and Oyster Bay, with himself as
president, and then proceeded (January, 1664), at the head of 170 men, to reduce
the neighboring Dutch villages.   Some account of the affair, in the shape in which
it reached the Dutch public, may be seen in the extract printed at the end of this
letter.

This was carried out in November last. The Dutch commissioners went to Boston, where they were received by four companies of citizens and a hundred cavalrymen. There they were told that the commissioners on the English side could not arrive to treat of the matter for eight days.[1] Meanwhile the English incited three or four villages to revolt against their government. But all those that were of divided population, like those of Heemstede and Gravesande, refused to accept the English king but said that they had thus far been well ruled by Their High Mightinesses and would so remain, though they were English born. Afterward Heemstede was also subdued but Vlissingen held itself faithful, and some places remained neutral, while the commissioners were detained and finally came again to Amsterdam without having accomplished anything. Meanwhile also the savages of Esopus played their part, having made bold at a place on the river to attack two Dutchmen and cut off their heads.][2]

Rev. Samuel Drisius to the Classis of Amsterdam (August 5, 1664).

The Peace of Christ.

Reverend, Learned and Beloved Brethren in Christ Jesus:
I find a letter from the Rev. Classis, which I have not yet answered; and a good opportunity now offering itself by the departure of our colleague, Domine Henricus Selyns, I cannot omit to write a letter to your Reverences. We could have

---

[1] The journalist here confounds Stuyvesant's visit to Boston in September, 1663, to meet the Commissioners of the United Colonies of New England, with that which his envoys, Van Ruyven, Van Cortlandt and Lawrence, made to Hartford in October, to confer with the General Assembly of Connecticut. His date of November is wrong for both. The attempt to revolutionize the English villages on Long Island had taken place in September; their internal revolt occurred in November. Stuyvesant was obliged to acquiesce. The "Combination" of the English towns under the presidency of Major John Scott, and his attempt to win the Dutch towns from their allegiance, took place in January and February, 1664. Stuyvesant was again unable to make effectual resistance, but made a truce with Scott for twelve months.

[2] After three years of peace at Esopus, the Indians again broke out in hostilities in June, 1663, resulting in the slaughter of twenty-one settlers and the captivity of forty-five others. Three successive expeditions, under Burgomaster Martin Kregier, in July, September and October, destroyed the forts of the Indians, broke down their resistance, and released most of the captives. Captain Kregier's journal of these expeditions is printed in O'Callaghan's *Documentary History*, IV. 45-98.

wished, that Domine Selyns had longer continued with us, both on account of his diligence and success in preaching and catechizing, and of his humble and edifying life. By this he has attracted a great many people, and even some of the negroes, so that many are sorry for his departure. But considering the fact that he owes filial obedience to his aged parents, it is God's will that he should leave us. We must be resigned, therefore, while we commit him to God and the word of His grace.

Concerning the places in which he has preached, especially the village called Breuckelen, and the Bouwerie, nothing has been decided yet; but I think that the son of Domine Megapolensis, who has recently come over, will take charge of them, as he has not been sent by the Directors to any particular place.

The French on Staten Island would also like to have a preacher, but as they number only a few families, are very poor, and cannot contribute much to a preacher's salary, and as our support here is slow and small, there is not much hope, that they will receive the light. In the meantime, that they may not be wholly destitute, Director Stuyvesant has, at their request, allowed me to go over there every two months, to preach and administer the Lord's Supper. This I have now done for about a year. In the winter this is very difficult, for it is a long stretch of water, and it is sometimes windy, with a heavy sea. We have, according to the decision of the Classis, admitted the Mennonist, who is quite unknown to us, to the communion, without rebaptism;[1] but last week he and his wife removed to Curaçao in the West Indies, to live there. The preacher, sent to New Amstel on the South River, died on the way, as we are told. Ziperius left for Virginia long ago.[2] He behaved most shamefully here, drinking, cheating and forging other people's writings, so that he was forbidden not only to preach, but even to keep school. Closing herewith I commend

---

[1] In a letter of October 4, 1660, Drisius had consulted the classis on the question whether a well-behaved young man residing in New Amsterdam, formerly one of the Mennonites and baptized by them, might be admitted to the Lord's Supper without rebaptism. The classis, by letter of December 16, 1661, ruled that according to the practice of the Dutch churches, his Mennonite baptism was to be regarded as sufficient.

[2] Michael Ziperius and his wife came from Curaçao in 1659, hoping to receive a call in New Netherland. The classis warned Drisius against him.

the Rev. Brethren to God's protection and blessing in their work. This is the prayer of

Your Reverences' dutiful friend in Christ,

New Amsterdam,   SAMUEL DRISIUS.
August 5, Anno 1664.

The Rev. Samuel Drisius to the Classis of Amsterdam (September 15, 1664).[1]

To the Reverend, Learned and Pious Brethren of the Rev. Classis of Amsterdam:

I cannot refrain from informing you of our present situation, namely, that we have been brought under the government of the King of England. On the 26th of August there arrived in the Bay of the North River, near Staten Island, four great men-of-war, or frigates, well manned with sailors and soldiers. They were provided with a patent or commission from the King of Great Britain to demand and take possession of this province, in the name of His Majesty. If this could not be done in an amicable way, they were to attack the place, and everything was to be thrown open for the English soldiers to plunder, rob and pillage. We were not a little troubled by the arrival of these frigates.

Our Director-General and Council, with the municipal authorities of the city, took the matter much to heart and zealously sought, by messages between them and General Richard Nicolls, to delay the decision. They asked that the whole business should be referred to His Majesty of England, and the Lords States General of the Netherlands; but every effort was fruitless. They landed their soldiers about two leagues from here, at Gravezandt, and marched them over Long Island to the Ferry opposite this place. The frigates came up under full sail on the 4th of September with guns trained to one side. They had orders, and intended, if any resistance was shown to them, to give a full broadside on this open place, then take it by assault, and make it a scene of pillage and bloodshed.

Our Hon. rulers of the Company, and the municipal authorities of the city, were inclined to defend the place, but

[1] There is another translation of this letter in *N. Y. Col. Doc.*, XIII. 393–394.

found that it was impossible, for the city was not in a defensible condition.[1] And even if fortified, it could not have been defended, because every man posted on the circuit of it would have been four rods distant from his neighbor. Besides, the store of powder in the fort, as well as in the city, was small. No relief or assistance could be expected, while daily great numbers on foot and on horseback, from New England, joined the English, hotly bent upon plundering the place. Savages and privateers also offered their services against us. Six hundred Northern Indians with one hundred and fifty French privateers, had even an English commission. Therefore upon the earnest request of our citizens and other inhabitants, our authorities found themselves compelled to come to terms, for the sake of avoiding bloodshed and pillage. The negotiations were concluded on the 6th of September.[2] The English moved in on the 8th, according to agreement.

After the surrender of the place several Englishmen, who had lived here a long time and were our friends, came to us, and said that God had signally overruled matters, that the affair had been arranged by negotiations; else nothing but pillage, bloodshed and general ruin would have followed. This was confirmed by several soldiers who said that they had come here from England hoping for booty; but that now, since the matter turned out so differently, they desired to return to England.

The Articles of Surrender stipulate that our religious services and doctrines, together with the preachers, shall remain and continue unchanged. Therefore we could not separate ourselves from our congregation and hearers, but consider it our duty to remain with them for some time yet, that they may not scatter and run wild.

The Hon. Company still owes me a considerable sum, which I hope and wish they would pay. Closing herewith I recommend your Honors' persons and work to God's blessing and remain,

Your willing colleague,   SAMUEL DRISIUS.
Manhattan, September 15, 1664.

[1] See the remonstrance which the inhabitants addressed to Stuyvesant, *N. Y. Col. Doc.*, II. 248; and Stuyvesant's defence, the last piece in this volume.

[2] Articles of capitulation, *ibid.*, 250–253, and Brodhead, *History of New York*, I. 762–763.

DESCRIPTION OF THE TOWNE OF MANNADENS, 1661

INTRODUCTION

THE following piece was found by the editor's friend, Miss Frances G. Davenport, in the papers of the Royal Society of London, *Guard Book No.* 7, part 1, and is here printed by permission of the secretaries of that society. How it came into their archives is not known. The manuscript, two pages folio, bears no evidence concerning its origin. A photograph, submitted to friends of the editor who have exceptional familiarity with the handwritings of New-Englanders of the time when the document was penned, has not thus far shown its authorship. It must therefore be taken for what it is. It is topographical rather than narrative, yet as it has never been printed before it has been thought worth while to include it in this volume as giving a picture of New Amsterdam, with a sketch of the rest of New Netherland, as it appeared to the eyes of the English just before they conquered it. As a plain description of this sort, it has value and interest.

It may, indeed, be of much more importance than this. Mr. J. H. Innes, who has been so kind as to examine it, and whose authority stands exceedingly high, thinks that it lends very strong support to the view, that the English seizure of New Netherland did not take place without an interior impulse. He derives from internal evidence the opinion that the document is not the work of a native Englishman, or at any rate of one brought up to the language, but of a foreigner having a good but not a perfect knowledge of English. The editor, feeling more doubtful as to these deductions, contents himself with mentioning them. It is also possible, in view of the intimate connection of the younger Governor John Winthrop with

the Royal Society in its earliest days, that this description of
Manhattan may have come into the archives of the society
through his means. Commissioned as agent in England to procure a charter for Connecticut, in this very year 1661, Winthrop, accompanied by Reverend Samuel Stone, of Hartford,
went to New Amsterdam to take ship, and sailed thence in the
Dutch ship *De Trouw*. It is true that he sailed in July, and
that the heading of the description reads, "as it was in Sept:
1661." But *De Trouw* seems to have reached Holland about
the middle of September, and some member of the governor's
party may have written the description in London, as of the
month in which he wrote; that it was written either by
Winthrop or by Stone is made unlikely, apart from hand-
writing, by the nature of its contents, which betray neither
political nor ecclesiastical interests.

The striking similarity between the title of this piece and
that of the map in the British Museum which is reproduced
on the ensuing page, and the possibility of connection between
the two, have been spoken of in the prefatory note to this
volume. The reader will find it interesting to compare map
and description.

PLAN OF NEW AMSTE

ELAND ·

Hudson

The · MAINE · L

AM, SEPTEMBER, 1661

DESCRIPTION OF THE TOWNE OF MANNADENS, 1661

Description of the Towne of Mannadens in New Netherland, as it was in Sept: 1661.

THE Easter-side of the Towne is from the North-East gate unto the point, whereon the Governors new house [1] stands, and yt contains 490 yards, and lyeth Southwest and North-east, one from the other. Between the gate and point the ground falls a litle out and in. On this side of the towne there is a gutte, whereby at high water boats goe into the towne.[2] Also on this side stands the Stat-house,[3] before wch is built a half moon of stone, where are mounted 3 smal bras guns, tho it be large enough to mount 8 guns on it: they then said they would build 2 halfe moons more between yt and the North-east gate. Between this side and Long iland all ships usually ly at anchor, to lade and unlade goods, secure from hurt of any wind and weather. From the towne right over unto long island it is ¾ of a mile, being an arme of the Sea between them, that embraceth long iland from the maine land, afording a navigable passage each way unto the Sea, for good ships, frequented much by New Engl'd men, Hollanders and others.

[1] The so-called "Whitehall," built at the southernmost point of the island. The north-east gate was the water-gate at the east end of the palisade which defended the town on the north; it stood near the foot of modern Wall Street.

[2] The canal (running north nearly to Beaver Street), which in Dutch fashion the town had in 1657–1659 constructed in Broad Street, and which drained the swamp known as the Vly.

[3] The Stadhuis or town hall. It was a large stone building, erected in 1641 by Kieft as a town tavern (see p. 212, *supra*), and used as such till 1654, when the new municipal government obtained the grant of it for a town hall. Its site is marked by the corner of Coenties Alley and Pearl Street. A picture of it, derived from a drawing made in 1680 by the Labadists Dankers and Sluyter, may be seen in Winsor, *Narrative and Critical History*, III. 419.

The Souther-side or roundhead of the Town [1] is bounded with the arm of the Sea, as it were dividing the bay and arme of the Sea, turning part of the indraught of water by the wester-side of the Towne into Hudson river, and part by the Easter-side of the towne, between the maine and long iland. Nearest the westerside of this head is a plot of ground a litle higher than the other ground, on wch stands a windmill; [2] and a Fort foursquare, 100 yards on each side, at each corner flanked out 26 yards. In the midst of the East and westside is a gate opposit to the other; [3] the walls are built with lime and stone, and within filled up with Earth to a considerable breadth for planting guns, whereon are mounted 16. guns. In this Fort is the Church, the Governors house, and houses for soldiers, ammunition, etc.

The wester-side of the towne is from the windmill unto the Northwest corner [4] 480 yards, and lyeth neer North-north-east and South-southwest, bounded with the Arme of the Sea, that stretches itself into Hudsons river, by the Hollanders calld the North river. From the town unto the other side its 3 miles broad, and a fit road for ship'g to ride. The said river goes far into the land N. E. ward. About 40 leagues up this river on the river side they have a towne calld Forterain, [5] in compas as big as Manados but not so much built nor so populous. This towne afford their chief trade for beaver-skins, otterskins, muskins, [6] Dear-skins, etc. None but their owne people may goe there to trade, except they have purchased the burgership of Manados for 50 gild. [7] Between Fortrain and Manados is a Fort, with soldiers in it, and a smal town of 60. Dutch families, calld Soppase, [8] but is something from the river; there they plant corne etc. and have some trade for beaver and other skins.

---

[1] The region of the Battery.   [2] On the present site of Battery Park.

[3] Mr. J. H. Innes informs the editor that this is an error; the gates were upon the north and south.

[4] I. e., to the point where the palisade erected in 1653, on the line of Wall Street prolonged westward, reached the North River.

[5] A corruption of the Dutch "Fort Oranië," Fort Orange.

[6] Muskrat skins.

[7] Great and small burgher-right were established in 1657, after Amsterdam example. For the former, which alone qualified for office, one paid fifty guilders per annum.   [8] Esopus.

The land side of the towne is from the Northwest corner unto the North E. gate 520 yards and lyeth neer N. W. and S. E. having six flankers[1] at equal distance, in four of wch are mounted 8 guns.

Within the towne, in the midway between the N. W. corner and N. E. gate, the ground hath a smal descent on each side much alike, and so continues through the town unto the arme of the water on the Easter-side of the Towne: by the help of this descent they have made a gut almost through the towne,[2] keyed it on both sides with timber and boards as far in as the 3. small bridges; and near the coming into the gut they have built two firme timber bridges with railes on each side.[3] At low water the gut is dry, at high water boats come into it, passing under the 2. bridges, and go as far as the 3 small bridges. In the contry stand houses in several places.

The bay between Long iland and the maine below the towne and Southwest of Nut iland within the heads [4] is 6. mile broad, and from the towne unto the heads tis 8. mile, and beares one from the other S. S. W. and N. N. E.

The town lyeth about 40. deg. lat. hath good air, and is healthy, inhabited with severall sorts of trades men and marchants and mariners, whereby it has much trade, of beaver, otter, musk, and other skins from the indians and from the other towns in the River and Contry inhabitants thereabouts. For payment give wampen and Peage [5] mony of the indians making, wch they receave of them for linnen cloth and other manufactures brought from Holland.

From Long iland they have beef, pork, wheat, butter, some tobacco, wampen and peage. From New England beef, sheep, wheat, flower, bisket, malt, fish, butter, cider-apples, iron, tar, wampen and peage.

From Virginia, store of tobacco, oxhides, dried, some beef, pork and fruit, and for payment give Holland and other linnen, canvage,[6] tape, thrid, cordage, brasse, Hading cloth, stuffs, stockings, spices, fruit, all sorts of iron work, wine, Brandy, Annis, salt, and all usefull manufactures.

---

[1] *I. e.*, bastions. Five are shown in the map of 1661.

[2] The canal in Broad Street, as above.   [3] At the present Bridge Street.

[4] The *Hoofden* or headlands of Bay Ridge and Staten Island north of the Narrows.   [5] Wampumpeag, wampum.   [6] Canvas, no doubt.

The town is seated between New England and Virginia, commodiously for trades, and that is their chief employment for they plant and sow litle.

From Amsterdam come each year 7. or 8. big ships with passengers and all sorts of goods, and they lade back beaver and other skins, dry oxehides, and Virginia tobacco. Tis said that each year is carried from thence above 20000 sterl. value in beaver skins only.

The Governor of Manados and New Netherland (so called by the Hollanders) is called Peter Stazan;[1] he exerciseth authority from thence southward (towards Virginia) as far as Dillow-bay[2] being about 40 leagues. The Suedes had plantations in Dillow-bay formerly; but of late years the Hollanders went there, dismissed the Suedes, seated themselves there, have trade for beaver, etc. He exercises also authority Eastwards towards New England unto West Chester, wᶜʰ is about 20 miles and inhabited by English, Also on Long iland inhabitants as far as Osterbay,[3] (being further eastward on the iland side than West Chester is on the maine) being about one quarter part of the iland. The said iland is in length 120 miles east and west, between 40 and 41 deg. lat., a good land and healthy. The other part of the said iland Eastward from Osterbay is under the authority of New England Colonies, as it stretches itself on their coast. The Christian inhabitants are most of them English.

[1] Stuyvesant.   [2] Delaware Bay.
[3] In 1662 both West Chester and Oyster Bay were annexed by Connecticut.

THE JOURNAL OF VAN RUYVEN, VAN CORT-
LANT AND LAWRENCE, 1663

INTRODUCTION

THE charter of the Dutch West India Company had granted rights of commerce and settlement throughout the whole coast of America and the west coast of Africa, but had not specifically mentioned New Netherland or any other place for colonization. Therefore the Dutch claim to New Netherland rested rather on prior discovery and occupation than on any specific grant of territory. But prior discovery and occupation were in the seventeenth century deemed the best bases for claims to territory populated by the heathen. England could advance no better claim to the region at the mouth of the Hudson River than such as could be founded on the parchment of 1606, whereby James I. had given the Virginia Companies general rights of settlement anywhere on the Atlantic Coast between the thirty-fourth and the forty-fifth parallels. Yet as early as 1621, when England had no settlement between New Plymouth and Cape Charles, the English court began a series of remonstrances to the Dutch government, continued from time to time throughout the whole history of New Netherland, in which it represented that settlement as an unlawful intrusion on territory which by undoubted right belonged to the King of Great Britain.

Assertions so ill founded might of themselves have had little effect. But, unfortunately for New Netherland, there flowed into New England an abundant population, vigorous, self-confident, and bent on agricultural occupation of territory. New Netherland, on the other hand, grew but slowly. The Dutch West India Company had by its charter, indeed, been permitted to populate its colonial territories. A careful reading of the document shows that it had not been enjoined to do so, as many historical writers have asserted. But its mind was bent on commercial gains rather than on agricultural development, and the same continued to be true of most of the settlers in the province. Under these circumstances New Netherland, whatever its formal rights, was no match for New England. The people of the latter hardly needed the advice which the English ambassador at the Hague gave them, that they should "not forbear to put forward their plantations, and crowd on—crowding the Dutch out of those places where they have occupied." Their ultimate victory was as inevitable as, in later times, the American occupation of Texas.

The whole colony of New Haven, and much of the area of Connecticut colony, lay on soil originally claimed and partly occupied by the Dutch. The directors-general of New Netherland, as we have seen, finally acquiesced in the formation of those colonies, and recognized their existence even as New England governments recognized that of New Netherland. But there were frequent disputes as to boundaries, and all attempts to settle them were made difficult by the fact that on one side of the line lay a population rapidly expanding and eager for new lands, and on the other side one far smaller and more stationary. The difficulty was increased, especially on Long Island, by the fact that many Englishmen, in the first instances impelled by New England persecution, in others by the prospect of economic gain, settled well within the Dutch jurisdiction and even in the Dutch towns. Stuyvesant favored them—perhaps they were more congenial to his severe and puritanical mind than the lax cosmopolitan society by which he was immediately surrounded; but it could never be certain how far one could rely upon them in case of conflict with the English colonies to the eastward, from which they had come.

In 1650 Stuyvesant, proceeding in state to Hartford, concluded, after negotiations with the Commissioners of the

United Colonies of New England, a treaty defining the boundary between his province and the colonies of New Haven and Connecticut. On Long Island the line was to run from the westernmost part of Oyster Bay straight across to the sea. On the mainland it was to begin at the west side of Greenwich Bay, and then to run northward twenty miles up into the country; above this it was undefined. The Dutch were to retain the lands in Hartford which they were still actually occupying. In America both parties observed the treaty for some years as a *modus vivendi*, but it was not ratified by the States General until 1656, and never by England.

From the Restoration of Charles II. in 1660, the English government began to take a new view of its colonial possessions and of the possibility of bringing them under a unified and systematic administration. Now that the Dutch had absorbed New Sweden, it was natural to reflect that the absorption of New Netherland by England would give her an unbroken dominion along the whole Atlantic coast, from Nova Scotia to Florida. In 1662 Connecticut obtained from the King a charter which not only permitted her to swallow up New Haven, but assigned to her, in terms which ignored the very existence of New Netherland, a territory running indefinitely southward from the south bounds of Massachusetts, and extending from Narragansett Bay on the east to the South Sea (Pacific Ocean) on the west. Forthwith Connecticut proclaimed her jurisdiction over Greenwich and West Chester on the mainland, and over Jamaica, Flushing, Gravesend, Hempstead and Middelburg (Newtown) on Long Island. Captain John Talcott was sent with armed men in July, 1663, to enforce her claim to West Chester, an agent of his proceeded on similar errands to the towns on the island, and many of their inhabitants joined in a petition to the general assembly of Connecticut, praying that that colony would cast over them "the skirts of its government and protection."

It was under these circumstances that Stuyvesant, having without success visited Boston in September to confer with the Commissioners of the United Colonies and remonstrate against violations of the Hartford treaty of 1650, appointed, on October 13, 1663, the three commissioners whose narrative is printed in the following pages, and charged them to proceed to Hartford and seek redress or explanations from the offending colony. The General Court (assembly) of Connecticut was to meet on October 8, old style, October 18, new style. Cornelis van Ruyven was the secretary of the province of New Netherland, and had held that office since 1653. He was the son-in-law of Domine Megapolensis, having married Hillegond Megapolensis, his daughter. Oloff Stevensz van Cortlant had been one of the Eight Men in 1645, one of the Nine Men in 1649–1652. Some comments on him, by the unfriendly hand of Van Tienhoven, may be seen on a previous page (p. 375). He was now one of the burgomasters of New Amsterdam, a position which he occupied most of the time from 1655 to 1664; and he became one of the aldermen under the English rule. John Lawrence was an Englishman, one of the founders of Flushing in 1645, and its town-clerk from 1648 to 1657, but in the appointment he is designated as "merchant," of New Amsterdam. He was afterward an alderman, was mayor of the city several times, and at the time of his death, in 1699, was a judge of the Supreme Court of New York.

The journal will show how they fared in their embassy. Its ineffectual conclusion is indicated by the following vote of the General Court of Connecticut: "This Court doth leave the determination of the business respecting entertainm^t of the plantations on Long Island, and the difference between us and the Dutch, with the Councill."[1]

The document which follows is preserved in the archives of the state of New York at Albany, where it is designated as

---

[1] *Colonial Records of Connecticut*, I. 413.

"New York Colonial Manuscripts, vol. 15, p. 69." A translation of it was first printed in 1794, in Ebenezer Hazard's *Historical Collections*, II. 623–633. It is also printed in *Documents relating to the Colonial History of the State of New York*, II. 385–392. By the kindness of Mr. A. J. F. van Laer, archivist of the state, a corrected translation has been supplied for this volume.

THE JOURNAL OF VAN RUYVEN, VAN CORT-
LANT AND LAWRENCE

*Journal kept by the Commissioners Cornelis van Ruyven, Burgo-
master van Cortlant and Mr. John Laurence, Burgher and
Inhabitant of the Town of New Amsterdam, during their
Journey to Hartford.*

Anno 1663, 15th October, being Monday.

WE departed, with the rising of the sun, in Dirck Smith's
sloop. Though the wind was contrary, we arrived with that
tide at Hog's Island, and, as in consequence of the strong ebb
we could not make much progress by rowing, we cast anchor
and went on shore, while the crew took in some ballast. When
the ebb was passed we weighed anchor, passed Hellegat
[Hellgate] at low water, and arrived, by tacking and rowing,
near Minnewits Island,[1] where we stopped.

16*th*. We weighed anchor before day-break; the wind
remaining contrary, stopped during the tide, near Oyster Bay.
In the afternoon, the wind being somewhat more favorable,
we discovered Straetforts [Stratford] point, but the wind shifting again and the tide being gone, we cast anchor.

17*th*. In the morning, before day-break, with a strong tide,
we again set sail, the wind ahead; however, by force of rowing
and tacking, we arrived at Milfort between eight and nine
o'clock. We directly called on Mr. Bryan,[2] a merchant in that
place, requesting him to procure us three horses to ride to
Herfort [Hartford], which he promised to do. He said that he
proposed to go thither himself. Meanwhile, we visited the
magistrates, Mr. Treat and Mr. Fenn,[3] but we did not find

---

[1] Apparently Manussing Island, on the coast of Rye, New York.
[2] Ensign Alexander Bryan, of Milford.
[3] Robert Treat and Benjamin Fenn. Both were magistrates ("assistants")
of the New Haven colony, but the process of absorption of that colony into Con-

either of them at home. Mr. Treat visited us afterwards at
the tavern. After salutation, we communicated to him the
cause of our arrival [there] and [intended] departure for Hartford, and requested him to take charge of our sloop, which we
left in the harbor, till we returned, so that some vagabonds,
who, we were informed, were there roving about, might
not cause us any damage. This he consented to. We recommended the same to young Mr. Bryan. Meanwhile, we were
informed that two horses only could be obtained, unless a
young man who had arrived there from Hartford would hire
his horse. The young man being called, we agreed to hire his
horse at fourteen English shillings, but when he was to give the
horse he hesitated. We inquired why? as we agreed together
unconditionally. He could not at first be persuaded to disclose
his mind; at last he said he apprehended that his folks at
Hartford would find fault with him for assisting us, who were
not their friends. The magistrates present at this conversation
were very much dissatisfied, telling him that he must deliver
his horse, in conformity to the agreement, which he at last,
though reluctantly, did. After dinner, as soon as the horses
were ready, we rode on towards Nieuhaeven [New Haven],
where we arrived about an hour or two before sunset. The
horses being attended, we went to pay our respects to Mr.
Gilbert, the deputy governor,[1] but he was not at home; we
tarried that night at New Haven.

18th. Thursday. Started from New Haven at the rising
of the sun, in company of Mr. Bryan, merchant at Milfort
[Milford], and Mr. Pell;[2] arrived, we suppose about four o'clock,
at Hartford. Understanding that the Governor and Court[3]
were assembled, we resolved, in order not to lose any time, to
inform the Court without delay of our arrival, and solicit at the
same time an audience. This being performed, we received
for answer, that we might appear, if it pleased us, either now

necticut was now actively going on. Connecticut, acting under her new charter, no
longer recognized as magistrates the officials of the New Haven government; but
they were still locally regarded as such.

[1] Matthew Gilbert, the last deputy-governor of the New Haven colony.

[2] Doubtless Thomas Pell, of Fairfield, the proprietor of Pelham Manor.

[3] The general assembly or legislature of Connecticut was called the General
Court.

or to-morrow morning. We requested that we might do it
without further delay, which was consented to. After friendly
welcome we delivered our letters. When these were read, we
added that if the Governor and Court desired any further explanation, we were ready to give it either to the entire Court,
or to a committee, to which proposition no other answer was
made than that they would examine the letters. Having
recommended the matter seriously to their attention, we took
our leave, when we were informed by Major Mason, the deputy
governor,[1] that a room was prepared for us at the house of their
marshal, where we were requested to take our lodgings, which
we gratefully accepted.

19*th*. Early in the morning, before the Court met, we paid
our respects to the Hon. John Wintrop [Winthrop], and requested him to contribute his most strenuous exertions for the
removal of all misunderstandings and the continuance of peace
and harmony, which he promised to do. Whereupon we desired
to be informed what had taken place after we delivered our
letter. He said he did not know exactly, as he left the meeting
a little while after us, being indisposed; but he was confident
that the Court had appointed a committee to enter into
negotiation with us.[2] As we could learn nothing to the purpose from his Honor, and the time of the meeting of the Court
was approaching, we took our leave, and presented the following request to that body:

To the Honorable, the Governor and Court of Hartford Colony.

The purport of these few lines is merely to thank you for our
amicable reception, and the acceptance of the letters which we delivered, soliciting now to be favored with a categorical answer thereto, so that we may know in what manner we ought to regulate our
conduct. In the meanwhile remaining, etc.

---

[1] John Mason, the conqueror of the Pequots, was now deputy-governor, John
Winthrop the younger being governor.

[2] "This Court desires and appoyntes Mr. Mathew Allyn, Capt Talcott, Lnt
Clark, as a Comitty to treat with the Gent[n] come from the Manhatoes about the
matters in controversie between this Corporation and the Dutch at Manhatoes, and
in case Mr Clark comes not down to the Court, the Secretary to supply Mr Clarkes
place." *Colonial Records of Connecticut*, I. 410. Accordingly the committee
consisted of Matthew Allyn, John Talcott and John Allyn the secretary, all members of the council.

Which being carried in, we were told by the marshal that three persons were appointed to speak further with us, who would meet within an hour at the house of Mr. Howart Muller [Howard, the Miller],[1] being about half-way between our lodgings and the town hall, with request that we should also be there at that time, to which we agreed and went there at the hour appointed. After waiting there about an hour in vain, the marshal came and told us, that the committee had been hindered by some other business intervening from waiting on us, and as it was almost noon, that the Governor and Court begged the favor of us to dine with them in the town hall; to which we answered, that it appeared strange to us that the gentlemen of the committee excused themselves as they had appointed the time; that nevertheless we should come where we were invited. In a short time thereafter the deputy governor and secretary came to excuse the committee, as some business had happened wherein their presence was required, which [excuse] we accepted. After some discourse, we went with them to the town hall. After dinner, we desired that our business might be forwarded, upon which the persons who were appointed as a committee promised to follow us immediately to the aforesaid place, as they did. After some discourse little to the purpose, and being seated, we showed our commission, with request that they would do the same, upon which they delivered in an extract, as they said, out of their minutes, in which they, to wit: Allyne, Senior, Captain Talcot, John Allyne, Junior, were qualified to treat with us, adding that the showing a commission was superfluous, as we had been informed, ourselves, by the Court that they were appointed for that purpose, upon which we let that matter drop, and asked whether they would be pleased to make answer to the propositions contained in the letter we had delivered, to which they replied: That they would like to know briefly what the propositions were to which we required an answer. We said, that they were briefly contained in the aforesaid letter (to wit):

First. That we desired to know whether they would be pleased to conform themselves to the advice of the Commis-

[1] "Att a publiqe Towne meeteinge at Hartford December the 4th [16]61 Robt Howard the miller was Admitted inhabitant of the Towne of Hartford." *Hartford Town Votes*, p. 136.

sioners of the other three colonies, containing in substance that
everything with respect to the limits should remain as was
agreed upon in the year 1650, till the next meeting of the
Commissioners, in the year 1664.

Secondly. Or else, that they would be pleased to appoint
some persons to treat farther about the limits now in dispute.

Thirdly. If not, that the matters should then be referred
to our respective superiors in Europe, on condition that everything should meanwhile remain as was agreed to in the year
1650. Many debates, pro and con, arose on the aforesaid
points, so that the whole afternoon was spent without effecting
anything. The result substantially was,

To the first: That they could not conform themselves to
the advice of the aforesaid Commissioners for the following
reasons:

First. That they had already given notice, to the English
on Long Island, of their patent and of the King's grant.

Secondly. That the same, at least the greater part of them,
had voluntarily betaken themselves under their government.

Thirdly. That they neither could nor dared refuse them
(if they would not incur the King's displeasure), as the same
were included in their patent, to which they further added that,
though the fixing of the limits should be deferred to the next
meeting of the Commissioners, in the year 1664, they were not
to regulate themselves by the advice of the Commissioners
nor of the other colonies, but by the King's patent; and, in
case the Commissioners should do anything contrary to it,
that they would much rather separate themselves from the
other colonies, as they would never permit anything to be
done contrary to it, or any change made in it, except by His
Majesty himself, as those who would make any such change or
alteration in it, would put themselves above and lord it over
His Majesty.

What we alleged against this: that His Majesty's meaning
was not to give anything away which had already been so long
possessed by others; also, that it could not be proved out of
the patent, etc., was in vain; they persisted in their groundless
opinion.

To the second point they made no direct answer, only proposed, by way of question, Whether the General had sufficient

qualification from the Prince of Orange and the States General. To which we answered, that the commission of the States General sufficiently qualified the General for that purpose, and dropped that point; and proceeded

To the third. To which they answered, that they were willing that matters should be referred to our mutual superiors, on condition that the English towns on Long Island and Westchester should, provisionally, be under the government of Hartford. This being thus proposed, old Mr. Alyn made a long harangue to this effect: That he was well assured that the English towns would no longer remain under the Dutch government, and in case we should compel them, that they were resolved to band themselves together and to risk life and property in their defense; that he was therefore of opinion that it would be more to our advantage, to prevent farther mischief and bloodshed, that the said towns should remain under the government of Hartford till such time as His Majesty and the States General should agree otherwise (to wit), those who had voluntarily submitted themselves to their government.

To which we answered: That it would not now nor ever be allowed. They replied, that for the present they could then not act any further with us, nor hinder the aforesaid towns from betaking themselves under the obedience of His Majesty. We answered, that they were the cause of it, since they had, by different deputations, encouraged and excited the towns to it. They replied, that they were bound to make the King's grant known to them. We answered, that they might do it to the King's subjects, but not to Their High Mightinesses and the Company's subjects. To which they again replied, that they were subjects of His Majesty, as they dwelt according to the patent upon his Majesty's territories. Upon which proposition we asked them, In what light they looked upon the provisional settlement of the limits in the year 1650? They answered, absolutely as a nullity and of no force, as His Majesty had now settled the limits for them, the other being done only provisionally, etc. Whereupon we again appealed to the advice of the other colonies, to which was answered: That they (to wit, the other colonies) could make no alteration unless they assumed to themselves greater authority than that of the King; saying, that they had, in that respect, nothing to do with the other colonies. The time being spent with many such like propositions and answers without effecting anything, we concluded, from all these circumstances, that the acts of Ritchard Mils [1] [Richard Mills] at Westchester, of Coo [Coe], Pantom and others on Long Island, were committed and executed at their instigation, and that they now only sought to put a spoke in the wheel, and to keep matters in agitation till such time as the towns (whose deputies, namely, of Westchester, Middelborgh and Rustdorp, we daily saw here before our eyes, having free access to the principal men) revolted; as they openly declared that, in case the towns who had freely betaken themselves under their government and protection should ask assistance, they neither could nor might deny it them. All these matters being duly considered by us, and moreover that if we should depart without settling anything the English towns on Long Island would apparently have revolted before our arrival at the Manhatans; to prevent this and the danger which might ensue therefrom, and to show that we would contribute, as much as possible, to prevent bloodshed, we resolved to make the following proposal as the last: To wit,

That if they would firmly and faithfully keep the provisional settlement of the limits made in the year 1650, till such time as His Majesty and the High and Mighty Lords the States-General were agreed about the limits, and would not presume to take any of the English settlements belonging to this government under their protection, nor assume to themselves any jurisdiction over the same, we, on our part, would, in like manner, till that time, assume no jurisdiction over Oostdurp, otherwise called Westchester, to which we added: That if they would not acquiesce in this our proposal (having now contributed all possible means in our power to preserve peace and unity), we declared ourselves and our constituents innocent, before God and man, of all the calamities which should arise from their unjust proceedings. After a few debates, little to the purpose, it being now late in the evening, they said, they would take until to-morrow morning to consider the proposal, and took leave.

---

[1] Richard Mills had been the ringleader of revolt against Dutch authority at West Chester, John Coe at Middelburg, Richard Panton at Rustdorp (Jamaica) and Midwout.

20 *October*. Between nine and ten o'clock, according to appointment, the abovementioned gentlemen of the committee came to our lodgings. We went with them to the aforesaid place at the house of Mr. Houwert [Howard]. After some introductory discourse, we asked them whether they had considered our proposal, and what their answer was to it. After some frivolous exceptions, that the English on Long Island would not stand under us, and that if we should compel them to obedience, it would be the cause of much bloodshed, they expressly said that they could not agree with us unless the English towns, viz., Oostdurp, Middelborch, Rustdorp and Heemsteede were under their government; if we would comply with this, they would defer the matter, and not proceed further till another convention, but that we, in the meantime, should not in the least interfere nor exercise any right or jurisdiction over them, and if we could not, that they also could not hinder the aforesaid towns (being by His Majesty of England included in their patent) from betaking themselves under their protection, and consequently that they should be obliged to defend them, in case they were attacked. We answered hereunto: That we attributed to his Majesty more discretion than to include in their patent the subjects of Their High Mightinesses, and the lands which they had possessed for so many years; that such was an erroneous interpretation; that the patent contained a tract of land lying in America, in New England, and consequently not in New Netherland; that Governor Wintrop had declared, in the hearing of us all, that it must be so understood; and that it must be understood in this case like the Boston patent,[1] in which it is expressly said: *On condition that the lands shall not have been previously possessed by any prince or state.* Long Island being now so many years possessed by the subjects of Their High Mightinesses, the English therefore could not claim any right or title to it. In short, what amicable proposals and inducements soever we made use of, we could not proceed any further with them. In the meantime, it being dinner time, we were again invited to dine at the town hall with the Governor and the gentlemen of the committee, which we did. After dinner, we complained to the Governor and members that we did not advance in our business

[1] That of Massachusetts Bay.

with the committee on account of their unreasonable and un-
justifiable demands; such as giving up the English towns, etc.
We desired therefore that they would be pleased to answer the
letter delivered them and the neighborly and friendly propositions contained in it, which they promised to do, but nothing
was concluded upon this afternoon, as it was Saturday, and
some of the members were obliged, before dusk, to go to
Windsor and Wetherfield [Wethersfield].

21 *ditto. Sunday.* Went to church and supped in the evening with the Governor. After supper, being in discourse
with his Honor, among other things, he frankly declared:
that the intent of the grantor of the patent was by no means to
claim any right to New Netherland, but that it only comprehended a tract of land in New England, etc. We begged the
favor of his Honor to indulge us with such declaration in writing, that we might avail ourselves of it; but he declined, saying
that it was sufficiently plain from the patent itself. We said
that a different construction was put on it by others, and that
such declaration would give much light; but as we observed
that the Governor adhered to his first saying and was not inclined thereto after some more discourse, we took leave.

22 *ditto. Monday.* We desired by the marshal an answer in
writing to the letter we delivered and the propositions contained
in it, which was promised us. We dined with one Mr. Wels,
whose father had been Governor of Hartford.[1] Nothing was
done this day, as we expected the promised answer, but did not
receive it.

23 *ditto. Tuesday morning.* We were told that the aforesaid committee would meet us at Mr. Howard's. We went there.
The aforesaid committee being also come, we demanded an
answer in writing to the propositions contained in the delivered
letter. They said that they were come once more to speak
with us about the aforesaid towns, as they had endeavored to
persuade the deputies of those towns to remain quiet under our
government till farther determination, but that these would
not consent to it. That it would therefore be best for us not
to claim them, in order to prevent farther mischief. We
answered that those of Hartford were the cause of it, as they
had, by frequent deputations, drawn the subjects of Their

---

[1] Thomas Welles had been governor of Connecticut in 1655 and 1658.

High Mightinesses from their oath and allegiance, and had encouraged them to revolt, etc. They did not deny it, but said: It is so now, and we would fain have them remain quiet, but what can we do now that they are included in our patent, and desire to be received and protected by us, which we cannot deny them? Much was said against this; that they were not included in the patent; that the patent mentioned a tract of land in New England and not in New Netherland; that the Governor so understood it himself. They answered, the Governor is but one man. We and more besides us understand it so that our patent not only takes them in, but extends northward to the Boston line and westward to the sea, unless another royal patent intervene. We asked them where New Netherland then lay? They answered without hesitation: They knew of no New Netherland, unless a patent for it from His Majesty could be produced. We said, that we had no need of a patent from His Majesty. They replied, that they were willing to agree with us if we could show a patent from any prince or from Their High Mightinesses, by which such a tract of land was given. We appealed to the charter and to the approval of Their High Mightinesses of the provisional settlement of the limits made with Hartford in the year 1650. They answered, that the charter is only a commercial charter, and the said settlement of the limits was only conditional, etc. If you can't show a special patent for the land, it must fall to us. We said, that the right of Their High Mightinesses was indisputable, as appears by first discovery—purchase from the natives—earliest possession, etc. They answered, that they would let us keep as much as was actually possessed and occupied by our nation, but that we could not hinder them from taking possession of that which was not occupied by our nation. Many objections were made to this, that the possession of part was taken for the possession of the whole, etc., but it availed nothing. They said, we had no right to hinder them from possessing the unoccupied lands, inasmuch as they were comprehended in their patent, and we could show no patent from any prince or state. After many debates pro and con, we asked them, how they would have it for the present, as they had not as yet answered our reasonable proposals. In the mean time, it being noon, they promised to acquaint us after dinner with their meaning; whereupon we went with them to the town hall, but before we got there a few propositions were shown us by young Allyn and one Willits,[1] a magistrate of Hartford, containing in substance that, if we would give up all right and title first to Westchester, with all the lands as far as Stantfort [Stamford] and, further, divest ourselves of all authority and jurisdiction over the English towns on Long Island, they would then agree farther with us.   As these propositions were full of blots (it being the rough draft), we desired that the same might be copied fair, which they undertook to do. In the meantime we dined; after dinner we desired that they would expedite matters, as we had been there so long without effecting anything, upon which they promised to make an end at present.   After some talk the following unreasonable articles were delivered to us:[2]

1st That Westchester and all the People and Lands between that and Stanfort shal belonge to the Colony off Connecticut till it be otherwise Issued.

2d That Connecticut wil forbeare excersiseinge any Authority over the Plantations off Heamstede, Jamecoe etc: until the Case be further Considered, provided the Dutch wil forbeare to exercise any Coercive Power towards any off the english Plantat[ns] upon Longe Island until there be a determination off the Case.

3d It is alsoo agreed that the Issue off these differances shal be by o[r] mutual accord or by a third person or persons mutually Chosen by us, or by o[r] Superiors in Europa, and that the Magestrates now in beinge on Longe Island, in those plan[tions], shal govern those said Plantations, until there be an Issue off these differances as aforesaid.

4th That all and every person on Longe Island shall Be wholly indemnified for all Passages and transactions Respectinge these Affaires to this day.

That wee mutually advice all Persons Conserned, both English and Dutch, to Cary it peaceably, Justly and friendly each to other.

The above propositions being read by us, we answered: That they were wholly unreasonable and we should not be justified in consenting to them.   We desired that they should desist from their pretensions to the towns on Long Island, situate

---

[1] Samuel Wyllys.

[2] These articles, and the proposals put forward to meet them by the three commissioners of New Netherland, are recorded in English.

within our government, when we should express ourselves on
the other points; but to no purpose. They said, as before,
that they could not refuse receiving these towns and defending
them against all persons whatsoever, which they said they
would also do, etc. Seeing that we did not advance, in order
to prevent further encroachments and damages, and being
inclined to fix something certain, of which we had no prospect
unless we made some concessions, we resolved, for the reasons
aforesaid and to obviate further mischief, to make the following
offer:

Weschester, With the Land and People, to Stanfort, shal abide
under this government off Connecticut, til the tyme that the Bounds
and Limits betwixt the abovesaid Colony and the province off the
N Netherlands shall be determined, heere By o^r mutual accord, or by
persons mutual Chosen by his Royal magesty off England and the
high and mighty estates general off the United Provinces. The
Plantations off middleborrow Rustdorp and Heemstede, the which are
s^d to Revolt and to Come under the Colony off Connecticut shall
absolutely abide under the governm^t off N Netherland, till the abovesaid determination, and that the magestrates for the tyme beinge on
Longe Island in those plantations shall govern those said Plantations
under the s^d government, until there be an Issue off these differances
as aforesaid.

That al and every person on Longe Island shall be wholly In-
deminified for al passages and transactions respectinge these affaires
to these day.

That we mutually advyce all persons Conserned both English and
dutch to Carry it Peaceably Just and friendly each to other.

That both Parties in differance, namely Connecticut Collony and
the governour and Counsel off N Netherlands, shal be Ingaged to
use theire utmost endeavours to promote and accomplisse the Issueinge
off the aboves^d differances.

Being, at our request, admitted within, and having delivered the above propositions, which they read, we were
answered by some of them, that whether we proposed it or not
it was all the same; the aforesaid towns would not continue
under us. Others said, that they did not know any Province
of New Netherland, but that there was a Dutch Governor over
the Dutch plantation on the Manhatans; that Long Island
was included in their patent and that they would also possess
and maintain it, and much more such like discourse.

To the first was answered, that we were assured they would continue under our government if Hartford Colony did not claim a right to them. .

To the other, that they had, in the making of the provisional settlement of the limits in the year 1650, acknowledged a Province of New Netherland, etc. But observing we made no progress with them, we desired that the matter might remain as it is at present, till a farther determination of His Majesty and the States General. To which they answered, that His Majesty's patent fixed the limits, and if we could not acquiesce in their propositions nothing could be done, but if we would sign them, they would then treat farther with us. As we deemed a compliance on our part wholly unwarrantable, we desired, if they proposed to make any answer to the letter we delivered, that they would not delay it, as we intended to depart early the next day and acquaint the General and Council of New Netherland how we fared. They answered that they would have a letter ready. After begging of them to take the matter into serious consideration and endeavor all in their power to continue everything in peace and unity till His Majesty and the States General should determine the limits, we took leave. This happening in the afternoon, we went to them again in the evening to know whether the letter was ready. We were answered, that it would be brought to our lodgings, and as we were resolved to depart next day early in the morning, we took leave of the Assembly as we also did that evening of the Governor, to whom we complained that nothing more was done on our reasonable proposals. To which his Honor answered, that it was so concluded upon in the Assembly, and that he wished something had been fixed upon. We answered, that we had done everything in our power to effect it. After some compliments we took our leave. In the evening a letter was delivered to us with this superscription: *These for the Right honnorable Peter Stuyvesant d^r generael at the manados.*[1] We said to the secretary who brought it, that it ought to be, Director-General of New Netherland. He answered, that it was at our option to receive it or not, etc.

[1] "It is ordered by this Court, that the letter drawn up to the Director Gen^{ll} at the Manhattoes be sighned by the Sec^{ry} in the name of the Court, and sent to the said Generall." *Colonial Records of Connecticut*, I. 411.

24th ditto. Wednesday.   As we were obliged to wait some time for one of our horses, we departed between eight and nine o'clock from Hartford and came to New Haven about sunset.

25th ditto. Thursday morning.   We left Newhaven and came, about ten o'clock, to Milford. Towards evening, the tide serving, we went on board our sloop, got out of the creek and cast anchor, it being very dark.

26th ditto.   In the morning, about two hours before day-break, we weighed anchor, with a fair wind, and came, in the evening, between eight and nine o'clock, to the Manhatans.

C: v: Ruÿven,
O. Stevensz v. Cortlant,
John Lawrence.

LETTER OF THE TOWN COUNCIL OF
NEW AMSTERDAM, 1664

INTRODUCTION

THE wars of the seventeenth century between England and the Netherlands grew out of the keen commercial rivalry existing between the two nations. The first occurred in 1652–1654. The second was preceded by a bitter struggle for trade, particularly on the African coast. In March, 1664, King Charles II., having resolved to achieve the annexation without waiting for any formal declaration of war, issued letters patent granting all the region from the Connecticut to the Delaware, without mention of New Netherland or the Dutch and quite as if it were and always had been in the possession of his crown, to his brother James, Duke of York. The actual taking of New Netherland into possession was intrusted to Colonel Richard Nicholls, Sir Robert Carr, Colonel George Cartwright and Mr. Samuel Maverick, four commissioners whom the King appointed to reduce the Puritan colonies of New England, particularly Massachusetts, into due subordination, and whom he provided with a military force of about four hundred men, embarked on four frigates. They arrived at Boston late in July, and appeared at the entrance of New York Bay at the end of August, accompanied by additional forces from New England. Nicholls, as chief commander of the expedition, summoned Stuyvesant to surrender Manhattan. The popular voice was all for compliance. Stuyvesant resisted stoutly as long as he could, protesting that he would rather be carried out dead than surrender; but finally he was forced to yield, and appointed commissioners who agreed upon terms of capitulation. Thus, on September 6, 1664, the history of "New York" began, and that of New Netherland ended,

save for one brief postscript. In August, 1673, in the course
of the third war between England and the United Provinces,
two Dutch naval commanders recaptured the town and province, and they remained in Dutch hands till November, 1674,
when the war had been ended by a treaty restoring these possessions to England.

The following document explains itself. It is found spread
on the minutes of the Court of Burgomasters and Schepens of
New Amsterdam (*i. e.*, the town council). Of those who
signed it, Pieter Tonneman was the schout, or sheriff and prose-
cuting officer of the city. Paulus Leenderzen van der Grift,
whose house is satirically referred to in the *Representation of
New Netherland* (p. 339, supra), and Cornelis Steenwyck, who
was probably the richest merchant of the town, were the
burgomasters. The rest were schepens. The text is taken
from *Records of New Amsterdam from* 1653 *to* 1674, edited by
Berthold Fernow (New York, 1897), V. 114–116. A translation had previously been printed by David T. Valentine in the
Manual of the Common Council of New York for 1860, pp.
592–593.

LETTER OF THE TOWN COUNCIL OF NEW AMSTERDAM, 1664

Right Honorable Prudent Lords, the Lords Directors of the Honorable West India Company, Department of Amsterdam:

Right Honorable Lords:

WE, your Honors' loyal, sorrowful and desolate subjects, cannot neglect nor keep from relating the event, which through God's pleasure thus unexpectedly happened to us in consequence of your Honors' neglect and forgetfulness of your promise—to wit, the arrival here, of late, of four King's frigates from England, sent hither by His Majesty and his brother, the Duke of York, with commission to reduce not only this place, but also the whole New Netherland under His Majesty's authority, whereunto they brought with them a large body of soldiers, provided with considerable ammunition. On board one of the frigates were about four hundred and fifty as well soldiers as seamen, and the others in proportion.

The frigates being come together in front of Najac in the Bay,[1] Richard Nicolls, the admiral, who is ruling here at present as Governor, sent a letter to our Director General, communicating therein the cause of his coming and his wish. On this unexpected letter the General sent for us to determine what was to be done herein. Whereupon it was resolved and decided to send some commissioners thither, to argue the matter with the General and his three commissioners, who were so sent for this purpose twice, but received no answer, than that they were not come here to dispute about it, but to execute their order and commission without fail, either peaceably or by force, and if they had anything to dispute about it, it must be done with His Majesty of England, as we could do nothing

[1] Nyack or Gravesend Bay, just below the Narrows, between New Utrecht and Coney Island.

here in the premises. Three days' delay was demanded for consultation; that was duly allowed. But meanwhile they were not idle; they approached with their four frigates, two of which passed in front of the fort, the other anchored about Nooten Island and with five companies of soldiers encamped themselves at the ferry, opposite this place, together with a newly raised company of horse and a party of new soldiers, both from the North and from Long Island, mostly our deadly enemies, who expected nothing else than pillage, plunder and bloodshed, as men could perceive by their cursing and talking, when mention was made of a capitulation.

Finally, being then surrounded, we saw little means of deliverance; we resolved what ought to be here done, and after we had well enquired into our strength and had found it to be full fifteen hundred souls strong in this place, but of whom not two hundred and fifty men are capable of bearing arms exclusive of the soldiers, who were about one hundred and fifty strong, wholly unprovided with powder both in the city and in the fort; yea, not more than six hundred pounds were found in the fort besides seven hundred pounds unserviceable; also because the farmers, the third man of whom was called out, refused, we with the greater portion of the inhabitants considered it necessary to remonstrate with our Director General and Council, that their Honors might consent to a capitulation, whereunto we labored according to our duty and had much trouble; and laid down and considered all the difficulties, which should arise from our not being able to resist such an enemy, as they besides could receive a much greater force than they had under their command.

The Director General and Council at length consented thereunto, whereto commissioners were sent to the admiral, who notified him that it was resolved to come to terms in order to prevent the shedding of blood, if a good agreement could be concluded.

Six persons were commissioned on each side for this purpose to treat on this matter, as they have done and concluded in manner as appears by the articles annexed.[1] How that will result, time shall tell.

[1] The articles of capitulation are printed in *N. Y. Col. Doc.*, II. 250–253, and in Brodhead's *History of New York*, I. 762–763.

Meanwhile since we have no longer to depend on your Honors' promises of protection, we, with all the poor, sorrowing and abandoned commonalty here, must fly for refuge to Almighty God, not doubting but He will stand by us in this sorely afflicting conjuncture and no more depart from us: And we remain

Your sorrowful and abandoned subjects
PIETER TONNEMAN,
PAULUS LEENDERZEN VAN DER GRIFT,
CORNELIS STEENWYCK,
JACOB BACKER,
TYMOTHEUS GABRY,
ISAACK GREVENRAAT,
NICOLAAS DE MEYER.

Done in Jorck [York] heretofore named Amsterdam in New Netherland Anno 1664 the 16th September.

REPORT ON THE SURRENDER OF NEW NETH-
ERLAND, BY PETER STUYVESANT, 1665

INTRODUCTION

LARGELY as the loss of New Netherland was due to their own supineness and want of attention to its necessities, neither the directors of the West India Company nor the States General were willing to accept the blame for what had happened. Expostulating with England and presently declaring war, the States General summoned Stuyvesant home, to give an account of his stewardship, and particularly to explain the facts of the surrender. Arriving in Holland in October, 1665, the unhappy governor presented to them the following report, accompanied by many affidavits and other justifying documents. The original is in the National Archives at the Hague. The translation, which appeared in *Documents relating to the Colonial History of New York*, II. 365–370, has been carefully corrected for the editor, by comparison with the original manuscript, by Professor William I. Hull of Swarthmore College.

In 1667 the treaty of Breda confirmed the English in possession of New York. Stuyvesant soon returned to the colony, and lived there on his farm called the Great Bouwery till his death in February, 1672.

REPORT ON THE SURRENDER OF NEW NETHERLAND, BY PETER STUYVESANT, 1665

Report of the Honᵇˡᵉ Peter Stuyvesant, late Director-General of New Netherland, on the Causes which led to the Surrender of that Country to the English, 1665.

Illustrious, High and Mighty Lords:

WHILST I, your Illustrious High Mightinesses' humble servant, was still in New Netherland I was informed, verbally and in writing, that the unfortunate loss and reduction of New Netherland were, in consequence of ignorance of the facts, spoken of and judged in this country by many variously, and by most people not consistently with the truth, according to the appetite and leaning of each. Therefore your Illustrious High Mightinesses' servant, sustained by the tranquillity of an upright and loyal heart, was moved to abandon all, even his most beloved wife, to inform you, Illustrious, High and Mighty, of the true state of the case, that you, when so informed, may decide according to your profound wisdom;

Not doubting that you, Illustrious, High and Mighty, will judge therefrom that this loss could not be avoided by human means, nor be imputed to me, your Illustrious High Mightinesses' humble servant.

I dare not interrupt your Illustrious High Mightinesses' most important business by a lengthy narrative of the poor condition in which I found New Netherland on my assuming its government. The open country was stripped of inhabitants to such a degree that, with the exception of the three English villages of Heemstede, New Flushing and Gravesend, there were not fifty bouweries and plantations on it, and the whole province could not muster 250, at most 300 men capable of bearing arms.

Which was caused, first, (in default of a settlement of the boundary so repeatedly requested) by the troublesome neighbors of New England, who numbered full fifty to our one,[1] continually encroaching on lands within established bounds, possessed and cultivated in fact by your Illustrious High Mightinesses' subjects.

Secondly, by the exceedingly detrimental, land-destroying and people-expelling wars with the cruel barbarians, which endured two years before my arrival there, whereby many subjects who possessed means were necessitated to depart, others to retreat under the crumbling fortress of New Amsterdam, which, on my arrival, I found resembling more a molehill than a fortress, without gates, the walls and bastions trodden under foot by men and cattle.

Less dare I, to avoid self-glorification, encumber your weighty occupations, Illustrious, High and Mighty, with the trouble, care, solicitude and continual zeal with which I have endeavored to promote the increase of population, agriculture and commerce; the flourishing condition whereunto they were brought, not through any wisdom of mine, but through God's special blessing, and which might have been more flourishing if your formerly dutiful, but now afflicted, inhabitants of that conquest had been, Illustrious, High and Mighty, protected and remained protected by a suitable garrison, as necessity demanded, against the deplorable and tragical massacres by the barbarians, whereby (in addition to ten private murders) we were plunged three times into perilous wars,[2] through want of sufficient garrisons; especially had they, on the supplicatory remonstrances of the people and our own so iterated entreaties, which must be considered almost innumerable, been helped with the long sought for settlement of the boundary, or in default thereof had they been seconded with the oft besought reinforcement of men and ships against the continual troubles, threats, encroachments and invasions of the English neighbors and government of Hartford Colony, our too powerful enemies.

[1] A great exaggeration. In 1647 New Netherland had probably a population of about 1,500, New England of about 25,000.

[2] Presumably Kieft's war, 1643–1645 (or else the outbreak at New Amsterdam in 1655, while Stuyvesant was conquering New Sweden), and the two wars with the Indians of Esopus, 1659–1660, 1663–1664.

That assistance, nevertheless, appears to have been retarded so long (wherefore and by what unpropitious circumstances the Honble Directors best know) that our abovementioned too powerful neighbors and enemies found themselves reinforced by four royal ships, crammed full with an extraordinary amount of men and warlike stores.   Our ancient enemies throughout the whole of Long Island, both from the east end and from the villages belonging to us united with them, hemmed us by water and by land, and cut off all supplies.   Powder and provisions failing, and no relief nor reinforcement being expected, we were necessitated to come to terms with the enemy, not through neglect of duty or cowardice, as many, more from passion than knowledge of the facts, have decided, but in consequence of an absolute impossibility to defend the fort, much less the city of New Amsterdam, and still less the country. As you, Illustrious, High and Mighty, in your more profound and more discreet wisdom, will be able to judge from the following:

First, in regard to want of powder: The annexed account shows what had been received during the last four years and what was left over, from which it appears that there were not 2000 pounds in store in the city and fort; of that quantity there were not 600 pounds good and fit for muskets; the remainder damaged by age, so that when used for artillery, the cannon required a double charge or weight.

If necessary and you, Illustrious High and Mighty, demand it, the truth hereof can be sought from the gunner, who accompanies me hither, and who will not deny having said in the presence of divers persons and at various times: "What can my lord do? he knows well that there is no powder, and that the most of it is good for nothing; there is powder enough to do harm to the enemy, but 'tis no good; were I to commence firing in the morning, I should have all used up by noon."

What efforts we have employed to receive this and some other reinforcements and assistance may appear from the copies of two letters sent to the colonie of Renselaerswyck and village of Beverwyck, marked N° A.[1]

Whose answers intimate, that we could not be assisted by either the one or the other, because of the difficulties into

[1] See *N. Y. Col. Doc.*, II. 371–372.

which they had just then fallen with the northern Indians owing to the killing of three or four Christians and some cows, whether urged to do so by evil disposed neighbors, I submit to wiser opinions.

In regard to provisions: Although our stores were reasonably well supplied with them the whole fore part of the summer, even more than ever heretofore, the falling off being commonly caused by the want of credit or ready money to lay up an abundant stock of provisions;

Nevertheless our supplies became, from various accidents, so much diminished that on capitulating to the enemy, not 120 *skepels* [1] of breadstuffs, and much less of peas and meat were remaining in store,

This scarcity being caused by the exportation of a large quantity of provisions to the island of Curaçao, in the little craft *De Musch*, dispatched thither three weeks previous to the arrival of the frigates, without any apprehension or suspicion of experiencing a want of provisions, as the good wheat harvest was not only at hand, but between the barn and the field.

In addition to this favorable prospect, we were relieved from all fear of any approaching enemy or imminent danger from Old England, by the last letters from the Honble Directors, dated 21 April, and received one month before the arrival of the frigates; in the words following:

On the other hand, according to the intelligence we receive from England, His Royal Majesty of Great Britain, being disposed to bring all his kingdoms under one form of government, both in church and state, hath taken care that commissioners are ready at present to repair to New England, and there to install the Episcopal government as in Old England; wherefore we are in hopes that as the English at the North have removed mostly from Old England for the causes aforesaid, they will not give us henceforth so much trouble, but prefer to live free under us at peace with their consciences, than to risk getting rid of our authority and then falling again under a government from which they had formerly fled.

Two reasons which will serve you for speculation, in order to make a disposition of our force, and assist considerably the execution of our intentions and maintenance of our conquest by that means without difficulty, until a final agreement shall be concluded.

[1] Equivalent to 90 bushels.

The settlement of the boundary now begins to assume a different aspect from that it formerly wore, partly in consequence of our efforts, partly from other circumstances.

Placed by the aforesaid advices beyond all apprehension, we felt no difficulty in letting the aforesaid little vessel, *De Musch*, go with the loaded provisions; indeed we would have sent off more if we could have procured them anywhere.

The asserted scarcity of provisions is proved by the annexed declaration of the commissary himself, and of Sergeant Harmen Martensen, and moreover by the efforts we employed to obtain a greater quantity of these, were that possible.   No B.[1]

Provisions were likewise so few and scarce in the city, in consequence of the approaching harvest, for the inhabitants are not in the habit of laying up more provisions than they have need of, that about eight days after the surrender of the place, there was not in the city of New Amsterdam enough of provisions, beef, pork and peas, to be obtained for the transportation of the military, about ninety strong, and the new grain had to be thrashed.

In addition to the want of the abovementioned necessaries, and many other minor articles, a general discontent and unwillingness to assist in defending the place became manifest among the people,

Which unwillingness was occasioned and caused in no small degree, first among the people living out of the city, and next among the burghers, by the attempts and encroachments experienced at the hands of the English in the preceding year, 1663.

First, through Captain John Talcot's reducing Eastdorp,[2] situate on the main, not two leagues from New Amsterdam, by order and commission of the government of Hartford.

Next, through Captain Co's later invasion and subjugation of all the English villages and plantations on Long Island, which were under oath and obedience to you, Illustrious, High and Mighty, and the Honble Company, with an armed troop of about 150 to 160 of John Schott's horse and foot.   That this was done also by the order of Hartford's Colony appears

---

[1] See *N. Y. Col. Doc.*, II. 373, 374.
[2] Oostdorp, or West Chester.   This occurred in July, 1663.

from the fact that in the following year, 1664, Governor Winthrop himself came with two commissioners from Hartford, and one from the east end of Long Island, with a considerable number of people on foot and on horseback, to the reduced English towns, in order to get the inhabitants to take the oath of allegiance in the King's name.

Owing to the very serious war with the Esopus Indians and their confederates, in consequence of a third deplorable massacre perpetrated there on the good inhabitants, we could not at the time do anything against such violent attempts and encroachments, except to protest against them verbally and in writing.

All this, recorded fully in the form of a journal, was, on November 10, 1663, and last of February, 1664, transmitted to the Honorable Directors, together with our, and the entire commonalty's grievances, remonstrances and humble petitions for redress, either by means of a settlement of the boundary, or else by an effective reinforcement of men and ships.[1]

I could and should lay the authenticated copies before you, Illustrious, High and Mighty, were it not that I am apprehensive of incumbering thereby your present much more important business. On that account, therefore, in verification of what is set forth, are most humbly submitted to you, Illustrious, High and Mighty, only

No. 1. An humble remonstrance of the country people on Long Island, whereof the original was sent on the last of February to the Honorable Directors, setting forth the threats and importunity made use of towards them by the English troop aforesaid, with a request for redress; otherwise, in default thereof, they shall be under the necessity of abandoning their lands or submitting to another government.

No. 2 is a copy of a letter sent to all the Dutch villages for a reinforcement, whence can be inferred our good inclination to defend the city and fort as long as possible. The answer thereto intimates their refusal, as they, living in the open country unprotected, could not abandon their lands, wives and children.

---

[1] These important documents are to be found in *N. Y. Col. Doc.*, II. 484–488 and 230–234, respectively. The three mentioned next in the text are *ibid.*, 374–376, 248–250.

No. 3. The burghers' petition and protest exhibits their uneasiness; wherein they set forth at length the very urgent necessity to which they were reduced in consequence of the overwhelming power of the enemy; the impossibility, owing to want of provisions and munitions of war, especially powder, of defending the city one, and the fort three, days; and the absence of any relief to be expected or reinforcement to be secured, certainly not within six months; whereas by effective resistance everything would be ruined and plundered, and themselves, with wives and children, more than 1,500 in number, reduced to the direst poverty.

This dissatisfaction and unwillingness on the part of burgher and farmer were called forth by the abovementioned and other frequently bruited threats, by the hostile invasions and encroachments that had been experienced and the inability to oppose them for want of power and reinforcements; but mainly by the sending of proclamations and open letters containing promises, in the King's name, to burgher and farmer, of free and peaceable possession of their property, unobstructed trade and navigation, not only to the King's dominions, but also to the Netherlands with their own ships and people.

Besides the abovementioned reasons for dissatisfaction and unwillingness, the former as well as the ruling burgomasters and schepens, and principal citizens, complained that their iterated remonstrances, letters and petitions, especially the last, of the 10th of November, wherein they had informed the Honble Directors of the dire extremity of the country both in regard to the war with the barbarians and to the hostile attacks of the English, had not been deemed worthy of any answer; publicly declaring, "If the Honble Company give themselves so little concern about the safety of the country and its inhabitants as not to be willing to send a ship of war to its succor in such pressing necessity, nor even a letter of advice as to what we may depend on and what succor we have to expect, we are utterly powerless, and, therefore, not bound to defend the city, to imperil our lives, property, wives and children without hope of any succor or relief, and to lose all after two or three days' resistance."

Your patience would fail you, Illustrious, High and Mighty, if I should continue to relate all the disrespectful speeches and treatment which, Illustrious, High and Mighty, your servants of the Superior Government have been obliged to listen to and patiently to bear, during the approach of the frigates, whenever they sought to encourage the burghers and inhabitants to their duty, as could be verified by credible witnesses.

This further difficulty was made by the burghers that they were not certain of their lives and properties on account of the threats of plundering heard from some of the soldiers, who had their minds fixed more on plunder than on defence; giving utterance, among other things, to the following: We now hope to find an opportunity to pepper the devilish Chinese, who have made us smart so much; we know well where booty is to be got and where the young ladies reside who wear chains of gold.   In verification whereof, it was alleged and proved, that a troop of soldiers had collected in front of one Nicolaus Meyer's house in order to plunder it, which was prevented by the burghers.

In addition to the preceding, many verbal warnings came from divers country people on Long Island, who daily noticed the growing and increasing strength of the English, and gathered from their talk that their business was not only with New Netherland but with the booty and plunder, and for these were they called out and enrolled.   Which was afterwards confirmed not only by the dissolute English soldiery, but even by the most steady officers and by a striking example exhibited to the colonists of New Amstel on the South River,[1] who, notwithstanding they had offered no resistance, but requested good terms, could not obtain them, but were invaded, stripped, utterly plundered and many of them sold as slaves to Virginia.

To prevent these and many other misfortunes, calamities and mischiefs overtaking evidently and assuredly the honest inhabitants, owing to the aforesaid untenableness of the place and fort without assistance from Fatherland, which was not to be expected for six months, we and the Council, on the presentation of so many remonstrances, complaints and warnings, were under the necessity, God and the entire community know without any other object than the welfare of the public and the Company, to come to terms with the enemy and neighbors

---

[1] Sir Robert Carr, one of Nicholls's fellow-commissioners, was sent by him to reduce the settlements on the South River, which he accomplished with little of the moderation and kindness shown by Nicholls at New Amsterdam.

whose previous hostile invasions and encroachments neither we nor our predecessors have been able to oppose or prevent.

And, even if the good God had, for the moment, been pleased to avert the misfortune from us, to delay or prevent the arrival of those frigates, yet had we, through want of the reinforcements of men and ships from Fatherland so repeatedly demanded but not come, shortly after fallen, by this war with England, into a worse state and condition, in consequence of the overpowering might of the neighbors. This is sufficiently evident and plain from their hostile acts and encroachments against the inhabitants in a season of profound peace; being, as already stated, fifty to our one, they would afterwards, *jure belli*, have attacked, overwhelmed, plundered us and the good inhabitants whom they would have utterly expelled out of the country.

Many more reasons and circumstances could be adduced, Illustrious, High and Mighty, for your greater satisfaction and my vindication, if your occupations, Illustrious, High and Mighty, permitted you to cast your eyes over, or allow others to take cognizance of, the continual remonstrances, applications and petitions for a settlement of the boundary or a reinforcement, particularly of the latest of the years 1663 and 1664, and of the daily entries in the minutes bearing thereupon.

But fearing that your patience, Illustrious, High and Mighty, will be exhausted by this too long and unpalatable relation, I shall break off here and submit myself, Illustrious, High and Mighty, to your most wise and discreet opinion, command and order—with this prayer, that you, Illustrious, High and Mighty, would please to dispatch me, your humble servant, as quickly as your more important occupations will possibly allow; meanwhile praying that God will temper this loss with other more notable successes and prosper your government.

Illustrious, High and Mighty,

Your most humble servant,

Exhibited 16th October, 1665.   P. STUYVESANT.

INDEX

INDEX

Abraham's Offering, ship, 383.
Achkokx, 86.
Adriaensen, Maryn, 226, 226 n., 278.
Albany, N. Y., 22, 22 n., 67 n.
Allyn, John, 434 n., 435, 442.
Allyn, Matthew, 434 n., 435, 437.
American Historical Association, Papers, 64; *Annual Report*, 137.
American Historical Record, 400 n.
American Historical Review, 237.
American Society of Church History, Papers of the, 390.
Anchor Bay, *see* Narragansett Bay.
Animals, 71, 169, 220, 270, 296–297.
Answer to the Representation of New Netherland, by Cornelis van Tienhoven, 355–377.
Aquamachuques, 45 n.
Armeomecks, 52 n., 53.
Arms of Amsterdam, ship, 83 n., 87, 88, 102.
Asher, G. M., *Henry Hudson the Navigator*, 5, 14, 35; *Bibliography of New Netherland*, 306 n.
Asserué, 179.
Athens, N. Y., 21 n., 23 n.

Backer, Jacob, 453.
Backer, Joost T., 345–346, 370.
Backerus, Rev. Johannes, 167, 339, 339 n., 353, 353 n., 374.
Balance, ship, 383, 384, 399, 401.
Banagiro, *see* Canagero.
Barentsen, Pieter, 85–86.
Barnegat, 186, 186 n.
Barsimson, Jacob, 392.
Baxter, George, 280, 280 n., 281.
Bayard, Mrs. Anna, 400 n.
Bears' Island, 47, 47 n.
Beauchamp, Dr. William M., *Aboriginal Occupation of New York*, 139 n.; *Aboriginal Place Names of New York*, 139 n.
Bedloe's Island, 45, 45 n.
Beeck, Johannes van, 386.

Berkeley, Gov. William, 234 n.
Birds, 221, 270, 297.
Black Tom Island, 45, 45 n.
Blenck, Jacob, 233.
Block, Adriaen, 34, 39, 41, 42, 44, 47 n., 50, 309, 309 n.
Block Island, 41.
Blom, Rev. Harmanus, 406 n., 407.
Blommaert, Samuel, 96 n., 184, 206, 261 n.; life, 101; letter to, from Isaac de Rasieres, 97–115.
Bogaert, Harmen M. van den, 138, 252, 252 n.
Bogaert, Johannes, 382; *Letter to Hans Bontemantel*, 379–386.
Bogardus, Rev. Everardus, 187 n., 197, 299 n., 326, 339 n.
Bontemantel, Hans, 382; *Letter to*, 379–386.
Boston, Mass., 308, 308 n.
Bout, Jan Evertsen, 290, 354, 375, 376.
Bowne, John, 400 n.
Bradford, Gov. William, 100; *History of Plymouth Plantation*, 109 n., 110 n., 113 n., 191 n.
Bressani, Giuseppe, 404, 404 n.
Brodhead, John R., 99, 167, 267, 357, 390; *History of New York*, 415 n., 452 n. *See also Documents*.
Brooklyn, N. Y., 289, 306.
Brouwer, Jan J., 122 n.
Brownists, 86, 89.
Bruyas, Jacques, 139 n.
Bryan, Alexander, 432, 432 n.
Buchell, Arend van (Arnoldus Buchellius), vi; note on his chart, ix–xiii.
Bulletin de l'Académie Royale de Belgique, 31.
Burning of Troy, ship, 205.
Buteux, Father, 251.
Buzzard's Bay, 41, 41 n.

Canagero, 142, 179.
Canarsus, 282.
Canoes, 48, 57.

ORIGINAL NARRATIVES
OF EARLY AMERICAN HISTORY

REPRODUCED UNDER THE AUSPICES OF THE
AMERICAN HISTORICAL ASSOCIATION

GENERAL EDITOR, J. FRANKLIN JAMESON, PH.D., LL.D.

DIRECTOR OF THE DEPARTMENT OF HISTORICAL RESEARCH IN THE
CARNEGIE INSTITUTION OF WASHINGTON

Each volume octavo, cloth-bound, about 450 *pages*

$3.00 net. Postage extra

VOLUMES ALREADY PUBLISHED

Each with Full Index, Maps and Facsimile Reproductions

The Northmen, Columbus, and Cabot, 985-1503
Edited by JULIUS E. OLSON, Professor of the Scandinavian Languages and Literatures in the University of Wisconsin, and EDWARD GAYLORD BOURNE, Ph.D., Professor of History in Yale University.

The Spanish Explorers in the Southern United States, 1528-1543
Edited by FREDERICK W. HODGE, of the Bureau of American Ethnology, and THEODORE H. LEWIS, of St. Paul.

Early English and French Voyages, Chiefly Out of Hakluyt, 1534-1608
Edited by the REV. DR. HENRY S. BURRAGE, of the Maine Historical Society.

Voyages of Samuel de Champlain, 1604-1618
Edited by W. L. GRANT, M.A. (Oxon.), Beit Lecturer on Colonial History in the University of Oxford.

Narratives of Early Virginia, 1606-1625
Edited by LYON GARDINER TYLER, LL.D., President of the College of William and Mary.

Bradford's History of Plymouth Plantation, 1606-1646
Edited by WILLIAM T. DAVIS, Formerly President of the Pilgrim Society.

Winthrop's Journal (History of New England), 2 vols., 1630-1649
Edited by DR. JAMES K. HOSMER, Corresponding Member of the Massachusetts Historical Society and of the Colonial Society of Massachusetts.

Narratives of New Netherland, 1609-1664
Edited by DR. J. F. JAMESON.

VOLUMES IN PREPARATION

Johnson's Wonder-Working Providence of Sion's Savior in New England
Edited by Dr. J. F. Jameson.

Narratives of Early Delaware, New Jersey and Pennsylvania.
Edited by Dr. Albert Cook Myers.

Narratives of Early Maryland.

Narratives of Early Carolina.

Narratives of the Indian and French Wars.

Narratives of the Witchcraft Persecution.
Edited by Professor George L. Burr, of Cornell University.

The Explorers of the Mississippi Valley.

The Insurrections of 1688.

WHAT EMINENT HISTORICAL SCHOLARS SAY OF THE SERIES

From the Preface of the General Editor, Dr. J. F. Jameson:
"At its annual meeting in December, 1902, the American Historical Association approved and adopted the plan of the present series, and the undersigned was chosen as its general editor. The purpose of the series was to provide individual readers of history, and the libraries of schools and colleges, with a comprehensive and well-rounded collection of those classical narratives on which the early history of the United States is founded, or of those narratives which, if not precisely classical, hold the most important place as sources of American history anterior to 1700.

"The plan contemplates, not a body of extracts, but in general the publication or republication of whole works or distinct parts of works. In the case of narratives originally issued in some other language than English, the best available translations will be used, or fresh versions made. The English texts will be taken from the earliest editions, or those having the highest historical value, and will be reproduced with literal exactness. The maps will be such as will give real help toward understanding the events narrated in the volume. The special editors of the individual works will supply introductions, setting forth briefly the author's career and opportunities, when known, the status of the work in the literature of American history, and its value as a source, and indicating previous editions; and they will furnish such annotations, scholarly but simple, as will enable the intelligent reader to understand and to estimate rightly the statements of the text."

George B. Adams, Ph.D., Litt.D., Professor of History in Yale University and President of the American Historical Association:
"I feel like congratulating you heartily on the impression which I am sure the volumes already published of the 'Original Narratives of Early American History' must make on all who examine them. They seem to me admirably done both from the editorial and the publishing side, and likely to be of constantly increasing usefulness to students, schools, and libraries, as time goes on."

Charles M. Andrews, Ph.D., Professor of History, Johns Hopkins University:

"The series is one of unquestioned importance in that it contains complete texts selected with excellent judgment of narratives valuable to every student and reader of American history. The series for this reason will always stand on a higher level than the ordinary source book, and will appeal to a much wider range of persons interested. Its value grows with each volume issued, not only because the amount of valuable text material is thereby increased, but also because the later volumes contain reprints of rarer and more indispensable narratives. Such reprints will be especially serviceable for class use where valuable originals could not be placed in the hands of students, and will be important additions to the libraries of small colleges which cannot afford generally to purchase rare and expensive texts."

Frank H. Hodder, Ph.M., Professor of American History, University of Kansas:

"Of the set as a whole I may say that it is indispensable to any library of American history, and the smaller the library, the more indispensable it is, as in a very large library the subject-matter may be found in original editions and reprints, but in a small library this is out of the question. Even in the largest library the set will be useful in saving scarce and valuable editions in ordinary student use."

Albert Bushnell Hart, Professor of History in Harvard University and First Vice-President of the American Historical Association:

"I have felt great interest in the series since its inception, and it is likely to be of considerable service to scholars, and particularly to libraries which can no longer find originals at the price within their means."

Max Farrand, Ph.D., Professor of History, Stanford University:

"The narratives chosen, the scholarly editing of those narratives, and the form in which they are presented, combine to render this an unusually good series. You have rendered a genuine service to American scholarship by thus placing within reach of every one, and in a serviceable form, documents which have hitherto been more or less inaccessible or unusable. The series is one which every student of American history must use, and he should have access to it either in his own library or in the library from which he draws his material."

William MacDonald, Ph.D., LL.D., Professor of American History in Brown University:

"For all historical study beyond the most elementary, the systematic and extended use of the sources is of course indispensable. The output of documentary material for the American Colonial Period has been these twenty years past very considerable, although vast quantities of significant documents still exist only in manuscript. In the field of narrative sources, however, republication has been far less frequent, and the scarcity of these originals, together with the high prices which copies command, have made it practically impossible for students who do not have access to the largest libraries to make more than occasional or incidental use of this kind of historical material.

"If the volumes of 'Original Narratives' thus far published are a sufficient indication — as I have no doubt they are — of what the series will be as a whole, a great gap in valuable material for the study of American origins will be worthily filled.

"The editorial work of the volumes shows a commendable union of care and restraint. The introductions both of the general editor and of the editors of the several volumes are sufficient without being too long, while the explanatory foot-notes are kept well within bounds. Mechanically, the volumes are well made, open easily in the hand, and are issued at a price which puts them within the reach of libraries and individuals of modest means.

'A series so well vouched for on the editorial side can need little commendation from other quarters, for the volumes are their own best commendation. As a teacher of American history to college classes, however, I am always glad to find valuable material for student use increase, and the 'Original Narratives' deserve, and I hope will receive, a cordial reception and a generous use."

Worthington C. Ford, Chief of Division of Manuscripts, Library of Congress, Washington, D. C.:
"I look upon it as one of the best series undertaken to encourage the study of American history. Not only is the original plan rarely intelligent, but the individual volumes prove the care and critical capacity of each editor. The volumes are not only our source books of American history, but they are also readable and in such convenient form that they should be in every library, and used as text books in the teaching of history."

Senator Henry Cabot Lodge, in the North American Review:
"In this volume on 'The Northmen, Columbus, and Cabot,' and as the prospectus indicates, in its successors, the selection could not be improved. Judging from this volume alone, it may also be said that nothing could be better than the editing. We have the best texts accompanied by brief but clear introductions, and explained by notes which are sufficient to guide and instruct and not sufficient to puzzle and encumber. In each case a short list of authorities is given which will direct those who wish to pursue their inquiries upon any one of the three subjects in the way in which they should go, to find all the sources and the last works of modern research and antiquarian learning. The selection and editing could not in fact have been better done for the purpose which the editors had in view.

"If any one wishes to wrestle with the endless questions and controversies of the Columbian voyages, it is easy to plunge into the countless books upon the subject. Meantime the general reader, little concerned with dates and identification of places, but profoundly interested in the fact of America's discovery, can find in these letters and journals the man himself, and live over with him the triumph, one of the greatest ever won, and the tragedy, one of the most piteous ever endured.

"After all, there is nothing better than this that history can do for us, and very few histories can do it quite so well as an original narrative with all its errors and imperfections on its head, if we are only fortunate enough to possess one which has both literary quality and real human feeling."

A NECESSITY IN EVERY LIBRARY

The American Library Association Book List says of "Narratives of Early Virginia":
"A careful edition of the most readable original narratives having to do with the early history of Virginia. No better introduction to the use of source material could be given, and the general reader of history will find these accounts more fascinating than the latest historical novel. They should be found in every library that can afford to purchase them."

For Fuller Information, send to the Publishers

CHARLES SCRIBNER'S SONS
153-157 Fifth Avenue, New York